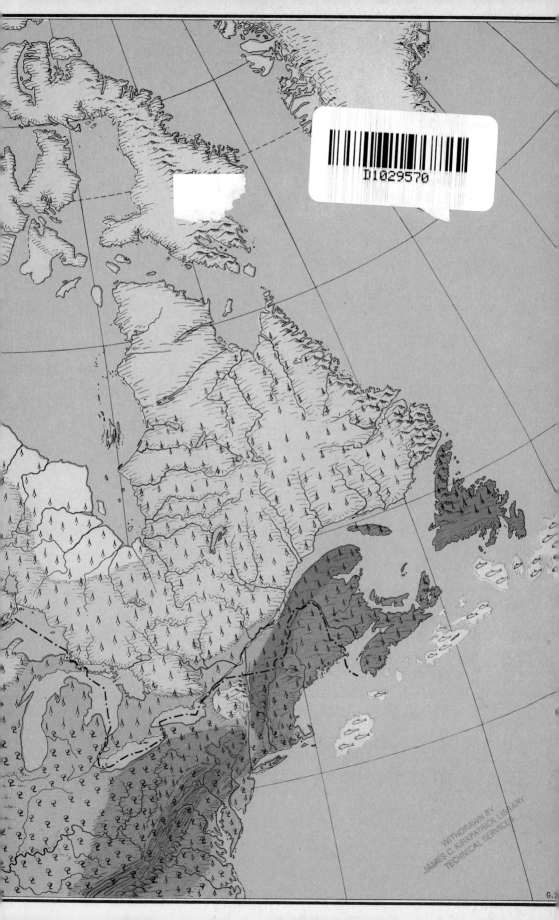

D1029570

G.

CANADIAN-AMERICAN INDUSTRY

A STUDY IN INTERNATIONAL INVESTMENT

THE RELATIONS OF
CANADA AND THE UNITED STATES

———

A SERIES OF STUDIES
PREPARED UNDER THE DIRECTION OF THE
CARNEGIE ENDOWMENT FOR INTERNATIONAL PEACE
DIVISION OF ECONOMICS AND HISTORY

JAMES T. SHOTWELL, *Director*

CANADIAN-AMERICAN INDUSTRY

A STUDY IN
INTERNATIONAL INVESTMENT

BY

HERBERT MARSHALL
DOMINION BUREAU OF STATISTICS

FRANK A. SOUTHARD, JR.
CORNELL UNIVERSITY

KENNETH W. TAYLOR
MCMASTER UNIVERSITY

WITH AN EXCURSUS ON

THE CANADIAN BALANCE OF PAYMENTS

BY FRANK A. KNOX
QUEEN'S UNIVERSITY

NEW HAVEN : YALE UNIVERSITY PRESS
TORONTO : THE RYERSON PRESS
FOR THE CARNEGIE ENDOWMENT FOR INTERNATIONAL
PEACE : DIVISION OF ECONOMICS AND HISTORY
1936

EDITOR'S PREFACE

THIS book is a pioneering enterprise. It is the first attempt to make a detailed survey of that vast movement of industrial capital across the Canadian-American frontier which is one of the outstanding facts in the relations of these two countries. Both in magnitude and in its persistence, this movement is unique in the world today. Its significance lies not merely in the fact that almost four billion dollars of American money is invested in Canada, or that a proportionately larger amount of the industrial capital of Canada is invested outside its frontiers, but that the forces which have produced this movement have been able to maintain it, although at varying rate, through all the political vicissitudes of these years of strain and crisis. Only the most hardy growths in the field of economics could endure throughout such a depression as that which has tested and is still testing the vitality of American and Canadian business. One secret of this strength may perhaps be found in the absence of government action, such as so often instigates or controls foreign investments of European countries. The scene disclosed here is that of democracies at work, democracies of individual interests not only free from political tutelage but even moving against political currents, sometimes apparently with accelerated pace in proportion as the opposing trend of political nationalism grew stronger.

It is obvious that there is much food for thought in the data which this book supplies. But the authors have been conscious of the restraining hand of the scientific technique which has held them to the initial task of those who break ground in any new field. While here and there they pause to point out the larger implications of the facts with which they deal, they have upon the whole confined themselves to the exploration and mapping of an uncharted area, to which by implication they invite the coöperative study of all serious students of the North American economy and the interest of that larger public whose fortunes are so deeply involved in matters like this, of which they may have been only partly aware.

This volume is the first to appear in a series which will deal with many and varied aspects of Canadian-American relations. For the last two years scholars and experts have been at work in both countries not only in economics but also in history, politics, international law, sociology, and education, in the fulfilment of a coöperative program designed to cover all of the more important elements in the past and present relations of the two countries. These investigations were made possible by the interest and support of the Carnegie Corporation and the Carnegie Endowment for International Peace. The former covers within the scope of its trust the British Dominions as well as the United States; the latter has turned aside in this instance from the study of disturbed areas where peace is menaced to a part of the world in which it is most firmly established, to analyze pacific international relationships when working under the most favorable of circumstances. The task, however, would not have been undertaken had it not been for the almost incredible fact that these relationships had been so taken for granted in the past, or so neglected in the ordinary routine of constant intercourse, that there is no comprehensive study of the varied elements which have made and are still making an international neighborhood.

The planning of the Series called for international coöperation in the fullest sense of the word. Editors and editorial committees were appointed in both countries to deal with each of the major subjects. These prepared their outlines after consultation both with their fellow-craftsmen across the line and with their colleagues in the different subjects at home. The editors charged with the planning and oversight of the present volume were Professor Jacob Viner, of the University of Chicago, and Professor Harold A. Innis, of the University of Toronto, to whose mature counsel and helpful coöperation the authors have registered their grateful appreciation below.

It is fortunate that from the first this series of Canadian-American studies was able to draw to it such leaders in the social sciences of both countries. For without their aid it would have been impossible to build up a consistent picture of the whole without distorting the perspective by an overemphasis of any one technique or any one point of view. The project therefore had the difficult task of maintaining scientific objectivity in the presentation of facts or conclusions while serving at the same time the not unethical purpose of a better international understanding. In the pursuit of this aim it soon became evident that various kinds of studies would be called for. First of all, research would have to fill many gaps in our knowledge,

both past and present. Some of this is so highly specialized that it
will be available only for students of the subject in question. But
there will be some thirty volumes of published text, thus furnishing a
body of material which will make possible for the first time consistent
and developed courses on Canadian-American relations in our col-
leges and universities as well as supplying the interested reader with
a new outlook in North American history.

This is not the place to describe in full the enterprise of which this
volume is a part, but this much is perhaps necessary in order to explain its setting in the plan as a whole. It would be wrong, however,
to give the impression that the volumes are to be closely articulated
under a rigid scheme of editorial arrangement. Each monograph
stands by itself, scope as well as treatment being determined by the
nature of the subject with which it deals. The same principle holds
with reference to the order of publication. By a happy chance the
first volume to appear is one that opens up a field of major interest;
but subsequent volumes will be published as they are finished without regard to the subject matter. This necessary adjustment to the
exigencies of research work does not in any way lessen the fundamental unity of the series as a whole, although that fact may not be
so apparent to the general reader as would have been the case with a
closely knit, encyclopedic survey. For those who look beyond the
façade of national organization to the varied and elusive elements
which give it significance, this method of studying and of presenting
the interplay of the political, economic, and social forces of the two
nations with which these studies deal will be justified by the nature
of the problem itself.

J. T. S.

AUTHORS' PREFACE

It is a commonplace of public utterances that the international boundary between Canada and the United States is marked by an absence of fortifications and by a lack of formality almost unique. But even cordial friendship between the two countries has not prevented a divergence in both culture and policies which has made the boundary much more than an invisible and imperceptible line. The unusual degree of similarity in the economy of the two countries has, however, meant that business men and capitalists in either country have always been attracted by economic opportunities in the other, and found few obstacles to investing in and developing them. In consequence there have emerged the many hundreds of enterprises which we have termed "Canadian-American": the mines, factories, stores, banks, insurance companies, railroads, public utilities, which, located in the one country, are controlled by citizens in the other. Inescapably important in Canadian-American economic relations, these companies form the subject matter of this book: why they have been established, their history and importance, their mode of operation, their position in the economy of which they are part.

Completely to isolate and examine the alien-owned industry in a country is virtually impossible. Not only are there in all probability some companies in which the foreign interest is not admitted, but even among the more than a thousand known cases many refuse to respond to any queries. But patient search in newspaper and magazine files and financial handbooks; the generous coöperation of many agencies, both public and private; and the friendly response of several hundred companies have revealed much of the complicated structure of the subsidiary companies in either country which look for guidance to parent companies in the other.

To all the many hundred persons and organizations who answered our questionnaires, gave us interviews, compiled statistics for us, we make grateful acknowledgment. We are particularly conscious of our indebtedness to Professor Jacob Viner, of the University of Chicago, and Professor Harold A. Innis, of the University of Toronto, who read and criticized the entire manuscript; to Mr. Louis Domeratzky, Dr. Amos Taylor, and Dr. Paul Dickens, of the United

States Department of Commerce; to Mr. R. G. Lewis, Mr. W. H. Losee, and Mr. G. S. Wrong, of the Dominion Bureau of Statistics; to Dr. Edward White, of the United States Bureau of Internal Revenue; to Mr. Harry Tipper and Mr. Francis T. Cole, of the American Manufacturers Export Association; to Mr. Frank E. Gannett; to President Robert C. Stanley, of the International Nickel Company of Canada, Ltd.; to Mr. J. E. Macpherson, of the Bell Telephone Company of Canada; to Mr. R. S. Kellogg, of the Newsprint Service Bureau; to Mr. John Langdon, of the *Financial Post;* to Mr. George P. Oslin, of the Western Union Telegraph Company; to Mr. J. A. Walker, of the Dominion Securities Corporation, Ltd.; to Mr. W. H. Hall and Mr. A. A. Nelson, of the Canadian Surety Company and the American Surety Company, respectively; to the officers and staffs of the *Monetary Times* and of the *Financial Post;* and to Mr. W. L. G. Joerg, of the American Geographical Society, who supervised the designing of the railway maps. Professor Frank A. Knox, of Queen's University, was a member of the planning committee and gave much assistance in the early stages of the work. He has permitted the inclusion herein of his study of the Canadian balance of international payments. At every stage of our researches we were able to rely on the encouragement and enthusiasm of Dr. James T. Shotwell. It is fair to add that the authors have not always been able to accept the criticisms and points of view offered by these many persons, and that where experts have disagreed we have necessarily had to assume the responsibility of choosing between them.

H. M.
F. A. S.
December, 1935.   K. W. T.

CONTENTS

TABLES

CHARTS

MAPS

CANADIAN–AMERICAN INDUSTRY

CHAPTER I

HISTORICAL BACKGROUND

GEOGRAPHY and history have made it inevitable that the economic structures of Canada and the United States should become closely intertwined. The common North American setting and atmosphere which makes, or has made, so similar many of their political and economic problems, the large interchange of population, and the to some extent complementary nature of their resources have conspired to produce a growth of interdependence which public policy and private antipathy have been powerless seriously to impede. Indeed, the very attempts on Canada's part to preserve an independent economy, through tariffs, through Imperial preference, through appeals to local patriotism, have not infrequently promoted the "American penetration" which they were designed to repel.

The boundary between Canada and the United States is geographically a natural one. An economy based on the canoe and the flowing rivers dictated boundaries of which the present is a rough approximation.[1] But in an age of railways and gasoline there are no serious physical obstacles to contacts. In both countries the centers of population and the principal industrial areas lie close to the mutual boundary. Contacts between corresponding sections of the two countries are physically easier than between different parts of the same country. The language and idiom of commerce and industry are practically the same in both countries. Movies and magazines, travel and migration have by no means produced an identity of culture, but have given rise to a degree of common culture that is probably unique. The organization of industry is very similar in the two countries, possessing very largely the same virtues and the same vices—vigorous expansion, restless mobility, giant corporations, coast-to-coast organizations, colossal advertising, high pressure salesmanship, chain stores, concentration of financial control. In matters of trade each finds the other its best customer. Given such

1. See H. A. Innis, *The Fur Trade in Canada* (New Haven, 1930), *passim.*

conditions, economic penetration of each country by the other is a most natural and normal result.

This volume is concerned chiefly with economic relationships, and, more narrowly, with the nature and extent of industrial and financial expansion of the nationals of one country into the territory of the other. It is a description of what is often loosely called "the branch-plant movement." There are two points that it is particularly desirable to emphasize at the beginning. The first is that this has been a movement in both directions. The impact of the United States on the Canadian economy is, of course, of almost immeasurably greater consequence to Canada than is the impact of Canada on the United States to the American. But relative to wealth and population Canadians have as large industrial investment in the United States as Americans have in Canada, and much the same forces have established Canadian branch plants in the United States as have drawn American companies into Canada.[2] The second is that this is not a new phenomenon. The first attempt to negotiate reciprocal trading arrangements—and like many of its successors an unsuccessful one—was initiated by New England merchants in 1647–51.[3] Early in the eighteenth century New York merchants had their agents in Montreal, and an active though illegal trade flowed north and south.[4] Neither American investment in Canada, nor even the branch plant movement, is a product of the twentieth century, though there was a rapid and increasing acceleration of this movement between 1900 and 1932. Capital, promotion, and management in the earlier days of each country found themselves with plenty of scope for action at home. But even as early as 1840 American enterprise was spilling over into Canada, and by the 1880's Canadian branch plants began to appear in the United States.

The following chapters are devoted primarily to a description and analysis of the current situation, but there is enough misunderstand-

2. See pp. 175 ff.

3. R. G. Thwaites, ed., *Jesuit Relations and Allied Documents* (Cleveland, 1899), XXXVI, 107 ff. Also in *New York Historical Society Collections* (New York, 1857), 2nd ser., III, 319 ff.

4. See Cadwallader Colden, "Memoir to Burnet on the Fur Trade in New York" (November, 1724), reprinted in *Documents Relative to the Colonial History of New York* (Albany, 1855), V, 728 ff. Many other sources could be cited.

ing and fear of this movement to justify a short sketch of its history. American industrial investments in Canada, and certainly Canadian industrial investments in the United States, are not to be thought of in terms of "economic imperialism" (except in a very few cases), but rather as a normal result of geographical propinquity. That is not to say, however, that these normal tendencies do not create very vital and difficult problems, especially in Canada. The threat to the self-control of the Canadian economy is none the less real because it is the product of natural forces.

While it would be an interesting historical excursion to pursue Canadian-American economic relationships back into the eighteenth and early nineteenth centuries, it is convenient to begin with the coming of the railway. Prior to that time the migration of the United Empire Loyalists to the British colonies, carrying with them economic institutions and techniques shaped in the American states, laid the basis for much of the later technical borrowings and cultural interchange. In spite of official opposition, contacts were maintained and grew. The first sawmills built by the Loyalists were of the same kind and type evolved in the United States. The "Durham boat" was introduced in 1800 from Ohio, and the first builders of these in Canada were specially brought over from that district. American tools and implements were better adapted to Canadian conditions than British tools. American capital began to flow into the Canadian lumber trade before 1840, American capital and technical assistance helped to found an early cotton mill in Sherbrooke in 1844, and Americans had been attracted to the Lake Superior copper and silver mining areas by 1846.[5] Early Canadian banks and banking laws

5. For these and other examples see documents quoted in H. A. Innis and A. R. M. Lower, *Select Documents in Canadian Economic History, 1783–1885* (Toronto, 1933), pp. 20, 21, 138, 243, 253, 301, 308, 517. The following quotation from the *Montreal Gazette,* July 20, 1839, is especially apt. "The iron tools of America have completely superseded Birmingham and Sheffield goods; the excessively bad quality of [British] edged tools, made like Pindar's razors, to sell and not to shave, had brought them into disuse and discredit—even in Upper Canada, States' tools are universally preferred at a great difference in price. The American axe is as different in shape as superior in manufacture; the Pennsylvania sickle is in like manner superior both in shape and material. Scythes also are differently, as well as better made, for mowing among the stumps."

were obviously modeled on American.[6] Small and short-lived banks were organized in Montreal in 1820 and in Upper Canada in 1836 by Americans with American capital. As early as 1823 the Bank of Montreal had an agent in New York.[7]

AMERICAN INDUSTRIES IN CANADA

These were but the hesitant beginnings. The really significant movement set in after 1870. In the following pages we attempt to trace briefly these American direct investments in Canada prior to 1890. No exhaustive study of the available sources of information has been made, because it is not our purpose to do more than emphasize the fact that Canadian-American industry has its roots far back in the nineteenth century.[8]

As has already been observed, American interest in Canadian lumbering goes back a hundred years or more, though in the early years American enterprise was limited by the strict application of the rule restricting ownership of lands to British subjects. The depletion of the better timber reserves in New England resulted in the migration of individuals engaged in the lumber trade to Canada. Several well-known names in the history of Canadian lumbering were such migrants—among them Bronson, Calvin, Eddy, and Rathbun.[9] But the slowness with which natural resources could be de-

6. See Adam Shortt, "The Early History of Canadian Banking," *Journal of the Canadian Bankers' Association*, 1896–97, IV, 1–19.

7. *Op. cit.*, pp. 353–355; R. M. Breckenridge, "The Canadian Banking System, 1817–1890," *Journal of the Canadian Bankers' Association*, 1894, II, 121, 152, 158, 160. Breckenridge quotes a witness before the Select Committee on the Monetary System of Upper Canada in 1837 as calling Upper Canada "a limb of the monetary system of the United States."

8. While a variety of sources have been searched, such as Innis and Lower, *op. cit.*, a number of old city and trade directories, and numerous volumes of the Dominion of Canada Parliamentary *Sessional Papers*, the principal source has been the *Monetary Times* (Toronto), the files of which have been carefully read throughout the period 1867 to 1888. The authors desire to thank the present owner and editor of the *Monetary Times* for their courtesy in providing every facility for the study of the extremely rare first ten volumes of their journal, and the Librarian of the University of Toronto for courtesies in facilitating the examination of some of the later volumes.

9. John R. Booth, while born in Quebec, received his early timber and construction experience in Vermont.

veloped by reliance solely on Canadian capital soon resulted in much impatience with these restrictions, especially in Upper Canada. In 1836 a bill to permit foreigners to hold real estate was introduced into the legislature of Upper Canada, backed by a petition containing many influential names. The purpose was quite frankly to invite American capital and develop the American market. While this particular bill failed,[10] the restrictions complained of were later removed, and American enterprise began to move in. In 1853 an American firm built an extensive steam sawmill on the St. Maurice River.[11] In 1870 the *Monetary Times* in a review of the lumber trade remarked on the eagerness with which United States interests were acquiring Canadian limits "at figures unheard of until the past year or two."[12]

As examples of this American enterprise, the following details may be noted. In 1874 Boston speculators bought the island of Campobello, New Brunswick, with a view to exploiting its timber and later developing it as a summer resort.[13] In 1880 the New Brunswick Land and Lumber Company was organized by wealthy Montreal and New York men, with an original capital of $1,500,-000.[14] In 1885 Messrs. Todd and Company, of Calais, Maine, are reported "to be rebuilding their fine mill at St. Margaret's Cove, Nova Scotia, where they have a large stock of logs."[15] In Quebec we find in 1880 a Boston firm buying 1,400 acres of woodland as a reserve for its butter-tub factory,[16] and in 1881 a Vermont lumber company building a fine subsidiary mill a few miles inside the Quebec border.[17] In Ontario, W. E. and A. M. Dodge, of the Lackawanna Iron and Steel Company, established the Collingwood Lumber Company in 1879 which, within a few years, became one of the prominent firms engaged in the Northern Ontario lumber industry.[18] In

10. The *Montreal Gazette,* August 27, 1836, denounced the bill as a "treasonable scheme that would take the bread from out the mouths of King's subjects, to bestow it upon men who are the King's natural enemies." See Innis and Lower, *op. cit.,* p. 254.

11. Innis and Lower, *op. cit.,* p. 517.

12. *Monetary Times,* December 23, 1870.

13. *Ibid.,* November 27, 1874. 14. *Ibid.,* December 3, 1880.

15. *Ibid.,* July 31, 1885. 16. *Ibid.,* July 2, 1880.

17. *Ibid.,* March 11, 1881.

18. *Ibid.,* February 7, 1879; February 23, 1883.

1882 John Dollar was the manager of the large sawmill of the American Lumber Company at French River, Ontario.[19] In 1885 a Michigan syndicate purchased limits containing 200,000,000 feet of pine on the north shore of Lake Huron.[20] The first reference to Americans acquiring British Columbia limits is in 1887, when the Minneapolis and Ontario Lumber Company bought 1,500,000,000 feet of standing timber in that Province.[21]

In 1886 Canada increased the export duty on logs to two dollars per thousand feet, with a view to forcing American timber companies to establish sawmills in Canada. As a result of this a number of American companies which had recently acquired limits across the Border with easy access to their home mills had to either abandon their limits or erect mills in Canada.[22] In general, it may be said that American enterprise occupied an important though hardly a dominating position in the Canadian lumber industry from 1850 to 1890.

American interest in Canadian mining goes back to the 1840's. The Nova Scotia coal deposits were known in the seventeenth century, but commercial development even on a small scale dates only from the last quarter of the eighteenth century. In 1826 George IV granted all mineral rights in Nova Scotia as a Royal monopoly to his brother, the Duke of York, who in turn leased them to the General Mining Association of London. This organization provided the capital and necessary technical assistance and forged ahead rapidly, though its success was hampered by the uncertainty of its markets (the American tariff to the south, and in the St. Lawrence valley the competition of English coal carried as ballast on their westward voyage by the ships engaged in the timber trade). The monopoly became increasingly unpopular and was rescinded in 1856.[23] Very little, if any, American capital found its way into eastern Canadian coal mining prior to 1900. Iron mining and production in the Maritimes reached appreciable proportions only after 1850. A considerable amount of British capital was invested in this industry, but the only recorded instance of American interest is the purchase in 1880 of the charcoal ironworks at Upper Woodstock, New Bruns-

19. *Monetary Times,* December 1, 1882.
20. *Ibid.,* October 23, 1885.   21. *Ibid.,* February 18, 1887.
22. *Ibid.,* June 10, 1886.   23. Innis and Lower, *op. cit.,* p. 426.

wick, by an American company which built a short railway to connect up with the main line.[24]

Gold, copper, manganese, and antimony attracted much more American interest. Many Americans participated in the Nova Scotia gold rush of 1861. The mining processes used were all rather primitive, and while in a few years some 200,000 ounces of gold were produced, by 1870 many of the claims were no longer being worked.[25] After 1880, however, American companies with adequate backing reëntered the field and for a few years gold mining ran a new lease of life.[26] Copper attracted some attention in the Eighties. Three American-controlled companies with total capitalization of a little less than $1,000,000 have been noted in these years.[27] In 1880 two manganese mining companies were incorporated to develop New Brunswick deposits, one Canadian with substantial American participation, and the other wholly American.[28] Two minor oil discoveries in Cape Breton may be noted, both with Americans dominating the development.[29] Antimony was discovered in New Brunswick also in 1880, a number of companies were incorporated, and New Brunswick antimony shares were for a time very active on the Boston exchange.[30] Minor direct American investments in silver and quarrying are also recorded.[31]

In the Province of Quebec the most important mineral deposits to attract attention in the years we are discussing were gold, copper, nickel, asbestos, iron, and phosphates. Alluvial gold was found in the Eastern Townships in considerable quantities between 1863 and 1882. Several American companies were in the field; one, the Colonial Gold Mining Company, had a paid-up capital of $2,500,000, and diverted the Du Loup River to facilitate its operations. Some of

24. *Monetary Times,* February 4, 1881.

25. Innis and Lower, *op. cit.,* p. 713.

26. *Monetary Times,* February 4, April 29, 1881.

27. *Ibid.,* December 31, 1880; December 28, 1883; February 4, 1887.

28. *Ibid.,* April 16 and 30, 1880. Capitalization $125,000 and $500,000, respectively.

29. *Ibid.,* September 1, 1876; August 20, December 31, 1880.

30. *Ibid.,* April 30, May 14, August 27, 1880.

31. *Ibid.,* September 1, 1876; October 24, 1879; June 18, 1880; December 16, 1881.

these adventures were highly profitable; many, of course, were not.[32] Properties changed from British to American to Canadian hands and vice versa not infrequently. Copper and nickel were important not merely of themselves but for the part that one early Quebec property played in the origins of the International Nickel Company of Canada, Ltd.[33] The Orford Nickel and Copper Company began its career in 1878 and was steadily profitable, though more as a copper than a nickel producer.[34] The copper properties were all controlled by either British or American capital. Of the five producers in 1882, two were under American control and three under British.[35] The early history of asbestos is described later.[36] In 1886 production was about evenly divided among British, American, and Canadian companies.[37] A number of iron prospects attracted American capital, but none were more than very briefly successful.[38] Phosphate mining has had a much longer and more profitable history. American chemical and fertilizer firms as well as a large number of speculative mining companies (originating chiefly in Boston) acquired many parcels of phosphate lands on the Quebec side of the Ottawa River. British, French, and German capitalists also took part in this development.[39] American direct investments in Quebec mining also included oil, mica, and plumbago properties, all of very minor importance.

The first considerable interest of American capitalists in Ontario mining dates from about 1846 in the copper prospects on the bleak north shore of Lake Superior, an interest which was largely a carry-

32. *Monetary Times,* September 5, 1867; June 18, July 23, 1880; April 1, November 25, 1881.

33. See pp. 95 ff.

34. There are frequent references to the Orford Company in the files of the *Monetary Times* from 1879 to 1887. The annual meeting was always held at Capelton, Quebec, and for a time it was the practice to bring the shareholders up from Boston in a special train.

35. *Ibid.,* January 12, 1883.   36. See p. 109.

37. *Monetary Times,* January 7, 1887.

38. *Ibid.,* December 4, 1874; October 29, 1875; July 30, 1880; April 8, 1881.

39. The files of the *Monetary Times* from 1880 to 1886 contain very frequent references to phosphate mining. In 1886, the Quebec Government auctioned 136 parcels of phosphate lands, of which only two were bought in by Canadians. *Ibid.,* July 2, 1886.

over of the discoveries on the American south shore. British and
Canadian companies were, however, more important in the early development of these copper properties.[40] Silver was discovered in the
same region about 1868, and for 15 years much capital and energy
was expended. From the beginning nearly all these silver properties
passed into the hands of Americans, though the original Canadian
owners often sold at very handsome prices. At least five undeveloped
properties were sold by Canadians to Americans at reported prices
of from $100,000 to $250,000, all but one of which eventually
yielded only meagre returns. The exception was Silver Islet, a tiny
low-lying rock 80 feet in diameter, which was sold by the Montreal
Mining Company to a New York syndicate in 1870, and which before it closed up, in 1884, had yielded $3,500,000 of silver. In 1873
its shares were quoted at $2,000 each.[41]

From the files of the *Monetary Times* could be prepared a long
list of American ventures in iron, gold, phosphate, peat, salt, and
mica lands in Ontario prior to 1890. None of these are presently important except those that are among the antecedents of International Nickel. But they serve to reënforce the statement that American enterprise in Canada is no new thing. A few examples only will be
given. At least three railways running north from Lake Ontario
were part of, or related to, American mining ventures.[42] In 1879 a
list of mining leases in Madoc Township (iron lands) shows all to be
owned or controlled by New York, Cleveland, Youngstown, or Detroit companies.[43] In 1880 there was a small gold boom in Hastings
County in which about $250,000 of American money was invested
and practically none recovered.[44] There was much optimism about
the Hastings County iron deposits in the Eighties. Some of the
largest American steel companies took up properties. But the whole
series of projects was spoiled by difficulties of eliminating impurities

40. Innis and Lower, *op. cit.*, p. 308.
41. *Ibid.*, p. 582; *Monetary Times,* October 7, 1870; September 29, 1871;
January 1, May 31, 1872; December 24, 1875; September 6, 1878; November 19, 1886.
42. Cobourg, Peterborough, and Marmora Railway and Mining Company; Belleville and North Hastings Railway; and Central Ontario Railway (Trenton to Coe Hill).
43. *Monetary Times,* January 9, 1880.
44. *Ibid.*, August 6, September 17, October 15, 1880; November 10, 1882.

in the ore.[45] The principal mica properties north of Kingston were all operated by New York firms.[46] In general it has been estimated that in the Eighties more than half of the capital employed in mining in Ontario and Quebec came from the United States.[47]

The early years even of prairie history did not escape a mining boom. Between 1882 and 1885 at least five companies were organized by New York or St. Paul capitalists with nominal capitalization of from $1,000,000 to $2,000,000. The properties to be developed were either gold, iron ore, or mica.[48] In the Rocky Mountains and on the Pacific coast the major mineral developments have been more recent than the period this chapter attempts to cover. The early gold rush of 1858 attracted the usual polyglot mob of prospectors, among them several thousand from California. In 1884 there was a minor rush from Montana and Idaho into the eastern Rockies.[49] But apart from these sporadic occurrences and a few minor American acquisitions of iron and base metal prospects we find no evidence of American mining interest on the Pacific coast prior to 1890.

The early history of American interest in Canadian railways, telegraphs and telephones fits in more naturally in a later chapter.[50] It is sufficient here to remark that that interest was greater than has generally been recognized. To what is said later it may be added that the early steamer service on the Red River between Emerson and Winnipeg was in fact, though not in law, American owned and operated.[51]

We may now turn to a brief résumé of early American enterprise

45. *Monetary Times*, February 11 and June 17, 1881. See also below, pp. 95–96. As typical of a certain modern type of promotion, and interesting because of its early date, there may be cited the New York and Ontario Furnace Company, which offered in 1882 to erect a $500,000 smelter in Belleville provided it was given a free site complete with deep water frontage and railway sidings, tax exemption, and a substantial block of local stock subscriptions. The offer was not accepted. *Ibid.*, March 24, 1882.

46. *Ibid.*, August 20, 1869; September 11, 1885.

47. Innis and Lower, *op. cit.*, p. 586.

48. *Monetary Times*, November 3, 1882; January 5, 1883; July 18, 1884; August 28, 1885.

49. *Ibid.*, April 18, 1884. "Nearly 300 miners and prospectors from Montana and Idaho are in the Rockies near Calgary. As much as $10,000 is being paid for claims."

50. See pp. 113 ff.   51. *Monetary Times*, July 16, 1880.

in Canadian manufacturing. Probably the first form that this took was the migration to Canada of young men who, with experience gained in the United States, organized and operated factories in Canada. These were in no sense branch plants, and at least in the case of those starting in a small way involved no importation of capital. They represent, however, a valuable importation of enterprise and skill. A very few examples will suffice. Wall and Jackson, both Americans, built a paper mill at St. Andrews, Quebec, in 1804.[52] E. W. Hyman came to London, Ontario, from Williamsport, Pennsylvania, in 1835, set up a tannery and later branched out into the manufacture of shoes on a large scale. Edward and Charles Gurney came to Hamilton, Ontario, from Steuben, New York, with their father in 1842 and set up a foundry. Gurney stoves and Gurney scales are today as well known in the United States and abroad as they were in Hamilton 80 years ago. J. M. Williams came to London, Ontario, from Camden, New Jersey, in 1845 and opened a carriage works. Later he became prominent in the oil business. The four last mentioned were founders and directors of the Bank of Hamilton in 1872 (merged with the Canadian Bank of Commerce in 1923).[53] Three Americans founded successful manufacturing companies in Guelph in 1859 and 1860—Cossitt (agricultural implements), Charles Raymond (sewing machines), and Goldie (flour milling).[54] The Goldie family still maintains its long and honorable connection with the industrial and political life of Guelph. Hiram Walker, born in Massachusetts, built his distillery at Walkerville, Ontario, in 1857.

The first actual case of an American "branch plant" we have observed is a file factory at St. Catharines, Ontario, established in 1870, but for its later history our records are blank. In 1876 the American Screw Company of Providence, Rhode Island, which is said to have had a virtual monopoly in its line in the United States, acquired the Dundas Screw Company and reëquipped and enlarged it to 8 times its former capacity. It was further enlarged in 1881.[55]

52. *Ibid.*, August 4, 1882.
53. A. St. L. Trigge, *History of the Canadian Bank of Commerce* (Toronto, 1934), III, 66–67.
54. Innis and Lower, *op. cit.*, pp. 595, 602.
55. *Monetary Times,* March 3, April 21, 1876; December 23, 1881.

TABLE I

American Controlled and Affiliated Manufacturing Establishments in Canada, 1870–1887

Year established	Branch and controlled plants	Companies with one or more American directors	"Contemplated" companies	License arrangements	Total
1870	1	..	..	..	1
1871	..	..	..	..	..
1872	..	1	..	..	1
1873	..	1	..	..	1
1874	..	..	..	..	..
1875	..	1	..	..	1
1876	2	..	2	..	4
1877	3	..	..	..	3
1878	5	1	1	..	7
1879	13	2	6	..	21
1880	4	3	..	..	7
1881	1	..	1	..	2
1882	4	5	..	1	10
1883	5	1	1	..	7
1884	2	2	1	1	6
1885	5	1	1	..	7
1886	2	..	..	..	2
1887	1	..	1	..	2
Total	48	18	14	2	82

The accompanying tables were prepared from careful notes taken from the *Monetary Times*. They show year by year the number of American branch or controlled plants established in Canada, together with a short classification of the type of factory and the geographical distribution. In Table I, the first column includes only those owned outright or clearly controlled in the United States; the second column includes those in which the control is not clear but where there was at least one but not a majority of American directors; the third column, "contemplated," includes those cases where it was definitely stated that a plant was about to be established, but where no evidence that it actually operated was obtained; the fourth column refers to definite arrangements whereby a Canadian firm was licensed to produce a definite branded line—the two cases being Simonds Saws in 1882, and Westinghouse Automatic Engines in 1884.

TABLE II

*American Controlled and Affiliated Manufacturing Establishments
in Canada, 1870–1887, Classified by Industries*

Year established	Metals	Textiles	Wood products	Miscellaneous	Total
1870	1	..	..	..	1
1871	..	..	..	..	..
1872	1	..	..	..	1
1873	..	..	..	1	1
1874	..	..	..	..	..
1875	..	..	..	1	1
1876	2	..	1	1	4
1877	..	1	..	2	3
1878	2	2	1	2	7
1879	12	2	4	3	21
1880	2	1	..	4	7
1881	1	1	..	..	2
1882	6	2	..	2	10
1883	6	..	..	1	7
1884	3	1	..	2	6
1885	2	2	1	2	7
1886	..	..	1	1	2
1887	..	..	1	1	2
Total	38	12	9	23	82

The three tables are largely self-explanatory. Attention may be
called to the great increase in numbers after the change in tariff
policy in 1879. More than half our recorded cases come in the period
1879–1883. The geographical distribution conforms in a general
way to the present-day distribution.[56] For only 13 of these companies was the capital or capitalization given. Their arithmetic average is $326,500 (median $100,000). Only 4 withdrawals were noted
in this period, 2 in 1880 and 2 in 1884.

Only a few actual examples will be given, and these of firms related to presently existing companies. In 1876 the Windsor and
Hamilton Powder Mills were purchased by the American powder
trust, the later Canadian properties of which are now part of
Canadian Industries Ltd.[57] In 1877 Belding Brothers, silk manu-

56. See pp. 221–222.
57. *Monetary Times,* January 19, 1877; see below, p. 83.

81541

TABLE III

American Controlled and Affiliated Manufacturing Establishments in Canada, 1870–1887, According to Geographical Distribution

Year established	Toronto	Hamilton	Windsor	Other Ontario	Total Ontario	Montreal	Other Quebec	Total Quebec	Maritimes	Western Canada	Total
1870	..	..	..	1	1	..	..	..	..	..	1
1871	..	..	..	..	..	..	..	..	..	..	..
1872	..	..	..	1	1	..	..	..	..	..	1
1873	..	1	..	..	1	..	..	..	..	..	1
1874	..	..	..	..	..	..	..	..	..	..	..
1875	..	..	..	1	1	..	..	..	..	..	1
1876	..	1	3	..	4	..	..	..	..	..	4
1877	..	1	1	..	2	1	..	1	..	..	3
1878	..	..	1	3	4	1	1	2	1	..	7
1879	2	2	6	4	14	4	1	5	2	..	21
1880	1	1	..	..	2	3	..	3	2	..	7
1881	..	..	..	..	..	2	..	2	..	..	2
1882	1	1	1	3	6	2	2	4	..	..	10
1883	1	..	1	3	5	1	..	1	..	1	7
1884	2	..	..	1	3	2	1	3	..	..	6
1885	..	1	1	2	4	2	..	2	1	..	7
1886	1	..	..	1	2	..	..	..	..	..	2
1887	..	..	..	..	..	..	2	2	..	..	2
Total	8	8	14	20	50	18	7	25	6	1	82

facturers, opened a plant in Montreal with 90 employees.[58] In 1879 Wyeth and Son, pharmaceutical manufacturers of Philadelphia, opened a Montreal plant; Meriden Britannia Ware of Connecticut (now International Silver Company) established its Hamilton factory; and Cleveland capitalists apparently acquired control of the Ontario Rolling Mills and the Hamilton Nail Works (which after various changes of name and ownership became part of the Steel Company of Canada).[59] In 1882 the Ingersoll Rock-Drill Company (now Canadian Ingersoll-Rand) was incorporated in Montreal.[60]

58. *Monetary Times,* October 5, 1877.
59. *Ibid.,* May 16, August 5, and October 24, 1879.
60. *Ibid.,* December 8, 1882.

In 1883 the North American Agricultural Implement and General Manufacturing Company was formed with a capital of $1,000,000 and was a merger of two London, Ontario, factories and a Winnipeg selling organization. The 2 American directors (out of a total of 7) were Charles Deere, President of the John Deere Plough Company, Moline, Illinois, and M. Rosenfield, President of the Moline Waggon Company.[61] Also in 1883 there were established the Edison Electric Light Company in Hamilton (later one of the constituents of Canadian General Electric),[62] and the Singer Sewing Machine Company in Montreal. In 1884 Chase and Sanborn opened a Montreal factory and warehouse.[63]

The list of articles made in these factories included pins, ribbons, buttons, corsets, vinegar, liquors, barrel hoops and staves, seeds, barbed wire, clocks, rubber, tobacco, canned fruits and vegetables, and an enterprising establishment to produce fertilizer from lobster shells. It is impossible to give any quantitative estimate of the importance of these varied plants in the Canadian industrial development of the time, but undoubtedly they formed a significant fraction of Canadian manufacturing production.

This influx of American plants did not attract much public attention at the time. In 1878 the *Monetary Times* carried an editorial commenting on the fact that Halifax, as a result of the new tariff, had invited American firms to locate branch factories in Nova Scotia and expressing the opinion that the limited size of the Canadian market offered little attraction to such undertakings.[64] In 1885 the *Report Relative to Manufacturing Industries in Existence in Canada* noted with satisfaction that the "National Policy" of 1879 had induced the establishment of several American branch factories in Canada.[65] But so far as journalistic comment or parliamentary debate is an indication of public interest, it is evident that the beginnings of the "American invasion" passed almost unnoticed.

A few illustrations of miscellaneous American undertakings in Canada may be given. Three hotels, in Hamilton, Brantford, and Quebec, were American owned.[66] A New York firm spent $100,000

61. *Ibid.*, August 10, 1883.   62. *Ibid.*, November 30, 1883.
63. *Ibid.*, March 6, 1885.   64. *Ibid.*, October 11, 1878.
65. Dominion of Canada, *Sessional Papers*, 1885 (no. 37).
66. *Monetary Times*, October 8, 1869; July 14, 1871; May 27, 1881.

trying to develop hop plantations in Ontario.[67] American produce firms had branches in Montreal, Brockville, Belleville and Winnipeg.[68] In 1872 the youthful Metropolitan Life began writing insurance in Canada. Americans used to catch bull-frogs on a large scale in Rice Lake for the New York market,[69] and in 1885 the American Clean Towel Company introduced into Montreal the novel idea of supplying a clean towel daily for 20 cents a week.[70]

During the period we are here discussing Canadian security sales in the United States were negligible, with the exception of some of the early Canadian Pacific Railway issues. In 1879 a $3,000,000 Province of Quebec loan was placed in New York; in 1880 a small block of Winnipeg debentures was purchased by a St. Paul group; and in 1882 about $1,000,000 of North West Land Company stock was subscribed for in New York.[71] It is of some interest to note that a few "three-way payment" bonds (payable in Canada, London, or New York) appear even at this early date.[72]

CANADIAN INDUSTRIES IN THE UNITED STATES

Canadian industrial investments in the United States prior to 1890 can be summarized much more briefly.[73] Canadian banks found it necessary almost from the beginning to maintain agents or branches in New York. Particular banks, depending on their field of service and type of customers, had branches in other American cities; for example, the Bank of Nova Scotia in Minneapolis (1885 to 1892), in Chicago (from 1892 on), and in Boston (since 1899); the Bank of British Columbia in San Francisco and Portland (1864), and in Tacoma and Seattle (1889 to 1896); the Canadian Bank of

67. *Monetary Times,* November 14, 1884.
68. *Ibid.,* April 18, 1879; December 15, 1882.
69. *Ibid.,* October 11, 1878.   70. *Ibid.,* July 10, 1885.
71. *Ibid.,* May 2, 1879; April 9, 1880; January 12, 1883.
72. Winnipeg $1,000,000 (*ibid.,* December 8, 1882), Brandon $20,000 (*ibid.,* November 30, 1883), Queen Victoria Niagara Falls Park (Ontario guarantee) $525,000 (*ibid.,* May 20, 1887). It is not clear from the advertisements whether these bonds were to carry the option as to payment throughout their life, or whether the original purchaser merely had the right to elect the currency to be specified in the bond.
73. Canadian railways in the United States are described in Chapter III, pp. 187 ff.

Commerce in Chicago (1875 to 1886) and in New Orleans (1896 to 1900, and through a controlled bank 1900 to 1915).[74] With the exception of the branches of the Bank of British Columbia, which were primarily designed to broaden the basis of its operations and to increase its profits, these branches were established almost entirely to give better service to the banks' Canadian customers. Once established, however, they played an important part in the New York market, especially in the earlier days.[75] It may be added that as early as 1870 the *Monetary Times* carried many advertisements by Toronto and Montreal brokers calling attention to their special facilities for buying and selling New York stocks and produce.

In the 1870's, with the increasing market for lumber in the United States, several Canadian lumber firms found it advantageous to acquire piling yards and other facilities in the United States.[76] In the 1880's two companies with head offices in Toronto, but backed largely by Scottish capital, had their principal timber limits and operations in Michigan.[77]

Half a dozen Canadian branch factories were established in the United States between 1885 and 1890. The Dominion Suspender Corporation of Hamilton built a factory at Niagara Falls, New York. The Morse Soap Company of Toronto had a factory and a large business in Rochester. Heaps Patent Dry Earth Closet opened a branch in Muskegon, but the parent company went in bankruptcy shortly afterwards. Waterous and Company of Brantford, well-known makers of engines and boilers, opened a factory in St. Paul, E. and C. Gurney of Hamilton established a branch of their stove works in Boston, and the Brantford Soap Works organized and controlled the Buffalo Electric Soap Works in Buffalo.[78]

In the following chapters the main emphasis is on the current

74. See p. 197.

75. The *Monetary Times*, December 4, 1874, in an editorial says that the Canadian banks in New York were getting a large share of the sterling exchange business, and that if they continued to show the same rate of progress they would in ten years largely control the exchange business. The same thing was occurring in Chicago and San Francisco.

76. *Ibid.*, May 12, 1876.

77. *Ibid.*, February 1, 1884. Both these companies failed a few years later.

78. *Ibid.*, March 13, October 16, 1885; January 22, August 6, 1886; January 7, May 6, 1887.

situation. This brief survey of the earlier stages of these Canadian-American industrial relationships will have served its purpose if it has helped to make clear the naturalness and the gradual development of this movement, which is so vital to Canada, so important to the United States, and so interesting to the economist and historian.

CHAPTER II

THE EXTENT OF AMERICAN INDUSTRY IN CANADA

INTRODUCTION

THE establishment of American subsidiaries across the Border is not solely a twentieth century development, as the preceding chapter has shown; at the turning of the century probably over a hundred companies in Canada were controlled by or definitely affiliated with American firms. Neither war nor depression was able to halt the movement, and by the end of 1934 the list had grown to somewhat more than 1,350 companies.[1] The accompanying chart gives the record, year by year, of the establishment of those companies, from 1900 to 1934. Five per cent of them began operations before 1900, 11 per cent were established from 1900 to 1909, 22 per cent from 1910 to 1919, 36 per cent from 1920 to 1929, and 26 per cent from 1930 to 1934. It must be observed that there is no allowance made in either chart or percentages for companies which for one reason or another withdrew from Canada.[2] Particularly as to companies organized prior to, say, 1928, the chart is a record by years of establishment of American-owned companies in Canada which proved relatively successful. Consequently there is considerable exaggeration of the rate at which new companies were incorporated in the later as compared with the earlier years, i.e., the curve for the

1. Including manufacturing, mining, lumbering, merchandising, etc. But the subsidiaries of those companies have not been classed as separate establishments, nor have companies been included whose sole affiliation is by way of a license or manufacturing arrangement with an American company. By various methods of computation and elimination, larger or smaller figures may be arrived at of total American-controlled companies in Canada. It is explained below (p. 22) how the Dominion Bureau of Statistics determined on 1,177 as a total at the end of 1932. The above figure of about 1,350 includes all cases up to the end of 1934 which were not only known to be American-owned but concerning which at least some further information is available. This figure, also, was provided by the Dominion Bureau of Statistics.

2. See Chapter VI for a discussion of withdrawal and repatriation.

AMERICAN-OWNED COMPANIES IN CANADA
DISTRIBUTION, 1900-32, ACCORDING TO YEAR WHEN ESTABLISHED OF TOTAL NUMBER IN EXISTENCE DEC. 31, 1932; AND THE NUMBER ESTABLISHED IN 1933 AND IN 1934.

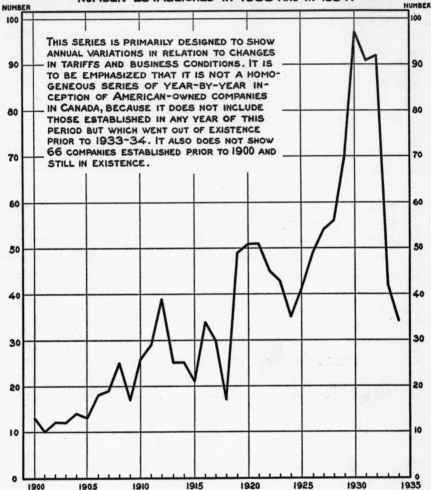

THIS SERIES IS PRIMARILY DESIGNED TO SHOW ANNUAL VARIATIONS IN RELATION TO CHANGES IN TARIFFS AND BUSINESS CONDITIONS. IT IS TO BE EMPHASIZED THAT IT IS NOT A HOMO-GENEOUS SERIES OF YEAR-BY-YEAR IN-CEPTION OF AMERICAN-OWNED COMPANIES IN CANADA, BECAUSE IT DOES NOT INCLUDE THOSE ESTABLISHED IN ANY YEAR OF THIS PERIOD BUT WHICH WENT OUT OF EXISTENCE PRIOR TO 1933-34. IT ALSO DOES NOT SHOW 66 COMPANIES ESTABLISHED PRIOR TO 1900 AND STILL IN EXISTENCE.

earlier years would be at a higher level if we had a complete record of the dates of establishment of all American-owned companies in Canada, whether or not they withdrew or were sold to Canadians subsequently. With those qualifications, however, the chart does reveal very clearly the general trend in the rate at which American-controlled companies have been established in Canada. It reflects the acceleration in the movement under the stimulus of the increases in Canadian tariffs following 1906 and during the years 1920–22 and 1930–32, as well as the relative deceleration in periods either of quiescence in tariff-making or business inactivity.[3]

During recent years efforts have been made by the governments of both countries to find out more exactly the magnitude of these investments. In 1930 the United States Department of Commerce published the results of a questionnaire sent to every company believed to have a subsidiary or affiliate outside of the United States.[4] It revealed total "direct" investments made by Americans in foreign countries of $7,477,735,000, of which $1,960,320,000, or 26 per cent, was in Canada and Newfoundland. The questionnaires returned to the Department indicated that the almost $2,000,000,000 was invested in 1,024 companies.[5]

3. The year-by-year figures from which both chart and percentages were computed follow:

Year	Number	Year	Number	Year	Number	Year	Number
Before 1900	66	1908	25	1917	30	1926	49
1900	13	1909	17	1918	17	1927	54
1901	10	1910	26	1919	49	1928	56
1902	12	1911	30	1920	51	1929	70
1903	12	1912	39	1921	51	1930	97
1904	14	1913	25	1922	45	1931	91
1905	13	1914	25	1923	43	1932	92
1906	18	1915	21	1924	35	1933	42
1907	19	1916	34	1925	41	1934	34

The record for the years 1900–1932 was obtained from a census of American-owned companies known to be in operation as of December 31, 1932, taken by the Dominion Bureau of Statistics (see p. 22). The figures for 1933 and 1934 were obtained by the Dominion Bureau from its current file of new American branch companies.

4. *American Direct Investments in Foreign Countries,* Trade Information Bulletin No. 731 (Washington, 1930).

5. The records of the Dominion Bureau of Statistics show 1,020 American-owned companies in Canada at the end of 1929. That figure does not include Newfoundland.

The Dominion Bureau of Statistics survey of American-controlled or affiliated companies in Canada, which forms the statistical skeleton around which this chapter is written, is based on 1932 data, whereas the Department of Commerce chose December 31, 1929 as its base. In the following table are the summary results of these two surveys.

TABLE IV

American Controlled and Affiliated Companies in Canada; United States Department of Commerce and Dominion Bureau of Statistics Surveys Compared

	U. S. Department of Commerce, 1929		Dominion Bureau of Statistics, 1932	
	Number of firms	Value (thousands)	Number of firms	Capital employed (thousands)
Manufacturing	524	$ 540,593	690	$ 545,692
Paper and Pulp	46	278,875	115	287,600
Mining and Smelting	123	400,000	49	236,599
Public Utilities	76	541,471*	81	707,751
Petroleum	14	55,047	†	....
Selling	117	37,874	257‡	291,725
Agriculture	15	15,000	†	....
Fishing	14	5,749	†	....
Miscellaneous	95	85,711	39§	97,882‖
	1,024	$1,960,320	1,177	$2,167,249

* Includes $107,000,000 for Canadian Pacific Common held by Americans. This is considered a "portfolio" investment by the Dominion Bureau, and is excluded from their figures.

† Included elsewhere.

‡ Of these 54 are counted under other groups.

§ Exclusive of land, timber limits, real estate, etc.

‖ Inclusive of $60,000,000 for land, timber limits, real estate, etc.

The figures cannot be wholly reconciled, because the details of both compilations cannot be compared. However, many of the differences can be satisfactorily explained.

The files of the Dominion Bureau of Statistics contained the names of 1,607 firms when the investigation was started. For one reason or another the number to be included in the tabulation was reduced to 1,177; 276 were unknown or not operating in 1932; 103 were established after 1932; and concerning 51 the information was inadequate.

It will be seen that data could not be secured for a considerable number because they had but recently entered the field. A very important group was eliminated because the concerns were inactive. This fact throws light on the difference in the two estimates for capital invested in mining and smelting. The United States Department of Commerce shows 123 firms and $400,000,000 capital, as against 49 firms and $236,000,000 capital in the Dominion Bureau of Statistics estimate. In the original Bureau list there were 118 firms, but all except 49 were eliminated because they were not operating mines. The Canadian Census of Industry takes account only of operating firms. Part of the difference is also due to classification. Some firms classed as mining and smelting in the Department of Commerce figures appear under other classes such as manufacturing in the Bureau estimate. Ore reserves are not included in the Bureau figures for capital employed, which would probably account for a considerable proportion of the difference between $400,000,000 and $236,000,000. How much capital is actually employed in the 69 mining firms struck from the list is problematical. Most of the firms are merely in the prospecting stage. Some, though former producers, have now ceased to be such.

Making due allowance for the difference in time and for the inclusion of Newfoundland in the Department of Commerce figures, the two surveys are in approximate agreement on the manufacturing and paper investments. The influx of branch plants between 1929 and 1932 justifies the larger total for manufacturing in the Bureau figures. In the latter figures a branch concern with two or more factories under the same name is counted as one, but in the case of a holding company each constituent firm is listed separately. Certain firms which are not at present operating have not been included by the Bureau, even though the shut-down may be temporary. The large difference between the amounts assigned to "selling" in the two surveys is accounted for by the inclusion, by the Bureau, of the sales division of branch plants.

The valuations used by the Department of Commerce, taken at the end of 1929, were virtually at the pre-depression peak. In a number of cases the "capital employed" has been written down during the depression. Reported "capital employed" figures have, in some cases, been cut by more than one half since 1929.

In the light of those explanations, the results of the two surveys appear reasonably harmonious. It might be noted that neither this nor a subsequent survey[6] by the Department of Commerce includes as many cases of Canadian companies owned by individual Americans—rather than by American corporations—as does that of the Dominion Bureau. The Dominion Bureau of Statistics survey is not only more recent and—based on a census rather than on a questionnaire—more complete, but it includes data on minority interests, value of output, and so on. Consequently it has been used as the statistical basis for the present chapter.

It is important clearly to understand the methods of evaluation used in these studies and at certain points in this chapter. The 1929 investigation of the Department of Commerce requested, on its questionnaire, "the present book value or the fair market value" of the investment.[7] Minority interests were included at their market value. As far as is known the same basis was used in the Senate Document referred to. It is not altogether certain how uniform the results are which that method yields. If the book value of a Canadian subsidiary has not been revised since earlier years, despite great growth of the branch plant, a large understatement may result. However, the results obtained, when compared with those of the Dominion Bureau, lend support to the belief that most of the reporting companies carry their foreign subsidiaries at a figure which fairly reflects the investment.

6. Senate Resolution No. 138, January 15, 1932, requested the Department of Commerce to study the operations abroad of companies or individuals engaged in producing in the United States whose foreign investment exceeded $50,000. That report is published as *American Branch Factories Abroad,* Senate Document No. 120, 73rd Congress, 2nd Session (Washington, 1934). For Canada and Newfoundland it cites 806 *factories,* employing 69,374 workers, and representing an investment of $460,989,113. An additional 97 branch companies producing raw materials deemed competitive with the article produced by the parent company (meat, coal, metallic ores, refined aluminum and asbestos, petroleum, tobacco, and wood and paper) had an investment of $373,587,947.

7. Trade Information Bulletin No. 731, pp. 4–5.

The Dominion Bureau of Statistics requested in its survey the "capital employed" directly in the venture at hand. For example, in the case of a mine the Bureau desired to exclude underground ore reserves and asked for a statement of capital actually employed in developing and operating the mine and getting the product to market. In the case of a factory, depreciation reserves, marketable securities, advances to affiliates, etc., were excluded from the "capital employed" by that particular plant in its own operations. In contrast with the two United States surveys, the Dominion Bureau derived its statistics not by a special investigation but from its Census of Industry.

Many times throughout this chapter reference is made to the "assets" of individual companies, in order to provide some sort of measuring rod whereby their relative size may be gauged.[8] While no serious conflict arises, it must be observed that there is a considerable difference in some cases between "capital employed," as above defined, and "assets," as a general balance-sheet concept. A few examples may make this clearer. The balance sheet of the Ford Motor Company of Canada, Ltd., shows assets of approximately $55,000,-000. We do not know what "capital employed" it reports to the Dominion Bureau, but an examination of its balance sheet in relation to the definition of "capital employed" reveals marketable securities, $11,000,000, and advances to affiliated companies, which would not be reported. Such companies as Imperial Oil, Ltd., Aluminium, Ltd., and International Nickel of Canada, Ltd., have large assets in foreign countries which will appear in their balance sheets but, certainly, are not included as "capital employed." From our point of view the use of the "capital employed" concept probably results in an understatement of the investment in some of the larger American companies in Canada. But for the great majority of subsidiaries it gives acceptable results.

Some of the information used in this chapter and in Chapters IV and V was obtained from two questionnaires.[9] One, prepared with the assistance of the American Manufacturers Export Association,

8. We did not, of course, have access to the individual returns in the files of the Dominion Bureau, and consequently could not obtain the "capital employed" figures for the companies we wished to use as illustrations.

9. See Appendix IV for text of questionnaires.

went to 1,100 American companies which have Canadian subsidiaries. The other was dispatched from McMaster University, Hamilton, Ontario, to about 900 of those Canadian subsidiaries. Each of these questionnaires yielded about 170 usable replies. Allowing for duplications, they provide us with the experience of more than 300 companies that are directly a part of the "Canadian-American Industry" which is the *raison d'être* of this book. These two surveys will be referred to throughout as the American questionnaire and the Canadian questionnaire. In some cases—more particularly in Chapter V—there is advantage in keeping separate the results from these two inquiries, inasmuch as the viewpoint of an executive in the parent company may be at variance with that of the manager of the Canadian company. Where no such advantage is apparent the results are treated in combination.

Table V presents in more extended form the results of the survey made by the Dominion Bureau of Statistics to which reference has already been made. To discuss it now is needless, since many times in the following pages the reader will be referred back to it. But particular attention should be directed to the third column. Here is presented for each industry the minority non-American interest in these American-owned companies. Largely in Canadian hands, this minority ownership amounts to between a fourth and a fifth of the total capital employed by American-controlled companies in Canada. It represents a notable offset to the "alien" nature of the American investment with which this book is concerned.

In Table V there is no differentiation between large and small companies. The grand total of 1,177 companies, the 805 factories, the 49 mining companies, and so on, might, so far as this table is concerned, be of equal importance one with another. In Tables VI and VII, however, the companies shown in Table V are reclassified, except for certain small exceptions, according to the amount of capital employed. Table VI gives the frequency distributions, while Table VII gives the percentages calculated therefrom. Attention may be called to several exceedingly important relationships revealed very clearly in Table VII. The most prevalent American-controlled company in Canada is apparently one employing from $50,000 to $199,999 capital. Twenty-nine per cent of all companies, and 31 per cent of the manufacturing companies, are of this size.

TABLE VII

American controlled and affiliated companies in Canada classified according to amount of capital employed, showing percentage of total companies, capital employed, and gross value of products in each size group, 1932

Classification	Capital under $50,000 — Per cent of total			Capital $50,000 to $199,999 — Per cent of total			Capital $200,000 to $499,999 — Per cent of total			Capital $500,000 to $999,999 — Per cent of total			Capital $1,000,000 and over — Per cent of total			Classification
	Com-panies	Capital employed	Value of products	Com-panies	Capital employed	Value of products	Com-panies	Capital employed	Value of products	Com-panies	Capital employed	Value of products	Com-panies	Capital employed	Value of products	Grand total
Grand total	24	*	2	29	2	6	17	3	6	11	5	7	19	90	79	
1 Manufacturing companies	24	1	2	31	3	6	19	6	8	12	8	9	14	82	75	1
2 Vegetable products	21	1	1	29	3	4	16	4	5	9	5	10	25	87	80	2
6 Animal products	26	1	1	19	2	1	23	9	4	16	18	10	16	70	84	6
7 Textiles	19	1	2	36	9	13	19	12	16	15	23	22	11	55	47	7
8 Wood and paper products	23	*	1	26	1	4	21	3	7	10	3	6	20	93	82	8
11 Iron and its products	18	*	1	31	4	6	22	8	9	16	12	10	13	76	74	11
16 Non-ferrous metals	27	1	2	27	3	7	19	7	14	15	12	13	12	77	64	16
19 Non-metallic minerals	22	*	*	20	1	1	28	5	3	8	3	2	22	91	94	19
20 Chemicals and allied products	36	2	4	36	11	20	13	12	15	7	14	15	8	61	46	20
23 Miscellaneous manufactures	29	2	3	40	11	12	17	17	17	12	6	6	7	58	62	23
24 Mining companies	12	*	*	12	*	*	10	1	*	19	3	4	47	96	96	24
27 Utility companies	9	*	*	9	*	*	16	1	1	10	1	1	56	98	98	27
32 Merchandising companies	26	1	3	35	3	7	13	4	6	8	4	6	18	88	78	32
33 Merchandising business of companies classified above	4	*	*	31	1	4	17	1	4	15	3	4	33	95	88	33
34 Other merchandising companies	31	1	8	36	6	12	12	7	9	6	7	7	15	79	64	34
35 Miscellaneous companies	16	1	2	18	2	6	24	8	21	21	14	21	21	75	50	35

* Less than one per cent.

But, as one would expect, very few mining or public utility companies are that small. The next most prevalent size of company is the very smallest: that employing a capital under $50,000. But it must be observed that although these relatively small branch companies—those employing a capital under $200,000—comprised more than half of the grand total and of the total manufacturing in 1932, they employed little more than 2 per cent of the total capital and produced, in value, only about 8 per cent of the products. The reason is fairly obvious: in branch companies, as in industry as a whole, both in Canada and in the United States, the "typical company" in terms of numbers is small, but overwhelmingly the greater proportion of both capital and products are accounted for by a relatively few large enterprises. Thus, as is shown in Table VII, 19 per cent of the grand total of American-owned companies in Canada, and 14 per cent of the manufacturing companies, employ a capital of $1,000,000 and over. Further, companies in that class employ 90 per cent of all capital used by American-owned companies, and 82 per cent of the capital used in manufacturing, and turn out, in value, between 75 and 80 per cent of the products.

But a study of Table VII will indicate that the concentration of companies in one or the other of the size groups is not uniform as between the various industrial classes. Consider first the manufacturing companies. The vegetable products and wood and paper products companies show the greatest concentration in the class employing a capital over $1,000,000. The tire and rubber companies in the former, and the newsprint mills in the latter, group account for the greater number of large companies in proportion to the total in each group. Textiles, non-ferrous metals, chemicals and miscellaneous companies are definitely concentrated in the smaller size groups. The American textile mill in Canada is generally a specialty rather than a yardage-goods producer. Consequently it is unlikely to be a large factory. The non-ferrous metals group is one in which the small electrical goods accessory plant predominates; further, the huge International Nickel Company is classified under mining rather than non-ferrous metals. More factories employing a capital less than $50,000 are to be found in "chemicals and allied products," both in number and relative to the total, than in any other industrial group. This is because here are to be found the several score pharmaceutical and toilet articles plants, which may occupy only a floor or two of a building for the purpose of packaging and compounding. The $1,000,000 class, in this case, accounts for only 8 per cent of the total companies, and while it employs 61 per cent of the capital it accounts for only 46 per cent of the value of products. The mining and utility companies stand alone, in that almost the entire capital is employed by the $1,000,000 companies, virtually all the products are produced by them, and even in terms of number of companies about half are of this size. This is to be expected: neither the small mine nor the small public utility is likely to have attracted migrant capital.

Other relationships may be found on closer examination of the two tables. But the primary conclusion to be drawn is that while the companies employing up to $200,000 capital are most prevalent in numbers, it is the relatively uncommon "big" company in which most of the capital has been invested and which turns out most of the products.

MANUFACTURING

THE tables just preceding include 805 companies controlled in the United States which, employing a capital of $833,293,135, account for about 24 per cent of the gross value of the products of Canadian factories. In some industries only a scattered dozen, or score or so, of American plants are to be found. In others they loom so large that to describe their history and operations is to write the story of that section of Canadian industry.

VEGETABLE PRODUCTS

Some 73 American-owned firms produce nearly 18 per cent of the Canadian factory output of vegetable products. The most important are the 15 tire and rubber factories, manufacturing almost 65 per cent of the rubber goods in Canada. The foodstuffs factories, although embodying more than half the capital in the American-owned vegetable products plants, are relatively less important, having shares of 10 to 15 per cent in this branch of Canadian industry.

Not many of the cereal and other vegetable food factories need be nentioned in detail. Names such as Campbell, Heinz, Libby, Quaker Oats, Baker, Cream of Wheat, Shredded Wheat, Kellogg, and Wrigley are as familiar, probably, in Canada as in the United States. A few, however, justify separate description.

General Foods Corporation has grouped together in Canada 8 or 9 subsidiaries, whose sales are managed by General Foods, Ltd., incorporated in 1930. Separate Canadian companies—branches of the constituents of General Foods—produce Maxwell House Coffee, Baker's Cocoanut, Postum, Grapenuts, Post Toasties, Jell-O, Pectin, and so on. The chief factories are in Windsor, Ontario, with others in Toronto and Cobourg, Ontario, and Montreal. And, although statistically in the animal products group, there is a Halifax, Nova Scotia, subsidiary, Mitchell and McNeil, Ltd., which packs fish and lobster.

The National Biscuit Company bought its way into Canada during the Twenties. In 1927 it purchased the Telfer Biscuit Company, Ltd., which was in financial difficulties, for about $300,000, an amount sufficient only to give the preferred shareholders 45 per cent in settlement. A year later it acquired the well-known biscuit company, Christie, Brown and Company, Ltd., and in 1929 it took over the Shredded Wheat factories in both countries.

In 1906 the Royal Baking Powder Company acquired the E. W. Gillett Company, Ltd., which it owned for over 20 years. In 1929 it offered to distribute to its shareholders 20,000 shares in the Canadian company, explaining that the original purpose of the purchase had been served, and there would be tax savings in divorcing the two companies. It was disposing of American Maize Products Company also. The Canadian company had assets of almost $3,000,000. Soon afterwards Standard Brands, Inc., was formed to acquire The Fleischmann Company, Royal Baking Powder Company, and E. W. Gillett Company, Ltd. In 1929 Standard Brands, Ltd., a new company, took over the various Canadian properties, and by 1933 had four divisions: the former Fleischmann yeast and vinegar plant in Montreal, the old Canadian Diamalt malt plant in Guelph, Ontario, the former Chase and Sanborn coffee and tea packing plant in Montreal, and the Gillett baking powder, dry yeast, and lye plant in Toronto.

There are only 3 American-owned milling companies in Canada.

One is a small concern owned not by a corporation but by individual Americans. The other 2 are subsidiaries of Quaker Oats and the International Milling Company. As long ago as 1910 a group of Minneapolis men bought the New Prague Flouring Mill in Minnesota, and the Saskatchewan Flour Mills, Ltd., at Moose Jaw. Two years later an Alberta mill, the Calgary Milling Company, was added. In 1911 there was an abortive attempt to combine those mills with certain mills in Ontario under a new holding company incorporated in Canada. The Ontario end of the venture, however, had a bad year, 1911–12, and the original Minnesota undertaking regained its independence.[10] It now operates, under the name Robin Hood Mills, Ltd., mills in Saskatoon, Saskatchewan, Moose Jaw, and Calgary, fed by its own elevators. It has 5 American mills. The Quaker Oats Company's Canadian organization is simpler. In 1912 it purchased the Saskatoon Milling Company, in Alberta, to supplement the rolled oats mill it had acquired in Peterborough, Ontario, in 1906. The Ontario mill had previously been owned by the American Cereal Company of Ohio. The Peterborough Hydraulic Power Company, Ltd., also owned by Quaker Oats, generates power for the mill. Quaker Oats' Canadian organization operates two flour mills—and country elevators—and two cereal plants. It claims that its Cedar Rapids, Iowa, Akron, Ohio, and Peterborough cereal mills are the largest in the world.

Another half dozen plants manufacture aerated water, such as Canada Dry Ginger Ale,[11] Coca-Cola (made in 19 Canadian plants now as against 3 in 1919), and Hires.

American-owned factories produce about 65 per cent of all rubber goods in the Dominion. The score or more factories are of two kinds. One group consists of the subsidiaries of the leading American tire companies. The others are the branches of various rubber goods companies producing wringers, heels, battery cases, sanitary goods, and so on. To this latter group no more space will be given. But the tire companies are more important. There are in Canada large plants owned by Firestone, Goodyear, Goodrich, and United States Rubber, as well as several smaller American-owned plants.

10. See *Commercial and Financial Chronicle,* April 22, p. 1113, May 13, p. 1313, August 3, p. 349, 1911; June 22, p. 1700, Sept. 14, p. 682, 1912.

11. See p. 261.

The first of these companies to enter Canada seems to have been the United States Rubber Company. In 1906 three rubber companies in Canada—the Granby, Canadian, and Maple Leaf—were combined in Canadian Consolidated Rubber Company, Ltd., "at which time United States Rubber had a chance to buy much more than a controlling interest on what has proved to be very favorable terms."[12] During the next 10 years a number of companies were added to the consolidation. In 1910 three felt companies were consolidated as Canadian [now Dominion] Consolidated Felt Company, controlled by Canadian Consolidated Rubber. In 1926 the tire company was renamed Dominion Rubber Company, Ltd. All the preferred and over 90 per cent of the common stock is owned by the American company. Its sales reached a peak of $20,000,000 in 1928 and in 1933 its assets were $17,500,000. Its latest acquisition, in 1933, was the Ames-Holden McCready Rubber Company, Ltd.

The Goodyear Tire and Rubber Company of Canada, Ltd., a predecessor of the present company by that name, was founded in 1910 and is now probably the largest tire factory in Canada. In contrast with the Dominion Rubber Company it has not absorbed other rubber companies, although in 1926 it acquired the Canadian Manhasset Cotton Company, renaming it Goodyear Cotton Company of Canada, Ltd. In 1924 the Goodyear Improvement Company, Ltd., was formed to own the Toronto offices and warehouse. The two factories, at Bowmanville and New Toronto, Ontario, and the cotton mill at St. Hyacinthe, Quebec, comprise the bulk of its $23,000,000 assets. The cotton mill, bought at a price which left nothing for its former common shareholders (presumably chiefly American), is guaranteed sales to the tire company sufficient to cover all costs including bond interest. In 1919 the capital of the tire company was increased from $3,000,000 to $30,000,000, equally divided into preferred and common. The outstanding stock, then $850,000 preferred and $880,500 common, was to be increased by the public issue of $5,000,000 preferred, chiefly in Canada. Capacity had been expanded, by the addition of the New Toronto plant in 1917, to 6,000 tires a day. Crude rubber was purchased 6 months ahead for a daily output of 5,000 tires. By July, 1920, the full force

12. In United States Rubber Company's Annual Report, as quoted in *Commercial and Financial Chronicle,* May 13, 1911, p. 1316.

of the post-war depression and price collapse was felt and production was cut from 3,600 to 350 daily. In the reorganization which became necessary the American company took $3,000,000, 6 per cent preferred stock in lieu of debts owned to it. In 1931 there were 3,500 Canadian shareholders, but 80 per cent of the common stock was owned by the Ohio company.

The other two companies are more recent in origin. The Firestone Tire and Rubber Company of Canada, Ltd., incorporated in 1919, opened a tire factory in Hamilton, Ontario, three years later with a daily capacity of 3,500 tires. Its $3,000,000 common and preferred stock is all owned by the American company, and an issue of $517,000 in bonds was floated in the United States. By 1929 factory capacity had been increased to 6,500 tires daily. In 1923 the B. F. Goodrich Company acquired an interest in the Ames-Holden Tire and Rubber Company, Ltd. Two years afterwards it acquired over 99 per cent of the stock and changed the name to Canadian Goodrich Company, Ltd. In the factory at Kitchener, Ontario, it produces Ames-Holden and Goodrich tires and several brands of rubber shoes. The assets are about $5,500,000.

These four companies, capable of producing probably 30,000 tires a day, have not been conspicuously successful. Concerning Firestone's results nothing is known. Dominion and Goodyear have paid preferred dividends regularly; Goodrich has paid no common dividends; Dominion, a single one of $25 since 1914. Goodyear began paying common dividends in 1927 and continued them through 1932.

ANIMAL PRODUCTS

These American-owned companies in Canada, some 40 in number, represent an investment of only $20,000,000, and produce about 10 per cent of the packed fish, the leather goods, and the meat and dairy products turned out by Dominion plants. The Atlantic Coast Fisheries Company, one of New England's two largest, controls Maritime-National Fish, Ltd., which operates the 3 steam trawlers permitted by the Canadian Government. No other steam trawlers are operated off the east coast of Canada. The parent company carries on an extensive business in the cod, haddock, and mackerel fisheries in New England, but Maritime-National sells more than 80 per cent of its Canadian output in Canada.[13] Other American fishing companies have ventured into Canada to supplement a declining supply of this or that kind of sea food in the United States. Here are to be found the 21 lobster packing stations operated by Burnham and Morril Company in Nova Scotia. Frank E. Davis, who long ago developed a mail-order business in fresh mackerel in Gloucester, Massachusetts, now also ships lobsters which he packs in Canada. F. W. Field found, in 1913, that earlier fishing companies on Lake Winnipeg were operated by subsidiaries of A. Booth and Company of Chicago.[14] But at that time the fishing was done by Canadian companies, although most of the catch was sold to Booth's buying agents, Winnipeg Fish Company, Ltd. The present Booth Fisheries Company catches or buys about 10,000,000 pounds of fish in the northern lakes of Manitoba—Winnipeg, Winnipegosis, and Manitoba.[15] It also owns Booth Fisheries Canadian Company, Ltd., organized in 1916 to acquire a sardine plant in New Brunswick.

Bordens, Ltd., is the only other company in this group deserving special description. The Borden Company entered Canada at least as early as 1912, buying dairy companies and beginning the development of its fresh milk and milk products business. Continuously during the next two decades it acquired one company after another—the City Dairy Company, Cairns Creameries, Hamilton Dairies, and so on—until by 1930, when it incorporated Bordens, Ltd., it owned more than 20 dairies, cheese and milk factories. The capitalization had grown to $19,000,000 and sales had reached $28,000,000.

Textiles

This is another industry in which the American-owned companies are scattered and relatively unimportant. The investment—as noted in Table V—is a little larger than in the previous industry, but the half a hundred factories produce less than 7 per cent of Canada's total textile output. Half a dozen of the mills are spinners and weavers, such as the finishing and weaving plant of Associated Tex-

13. *Fortune*, April, 1935, p. 146.
14. F. W. Field, *Capital Investments in Canada* (Toronto, 1914 ed.), pp. 37–38. Field at that time was editor of the *Monetary Times*.
15. *Fortune*, April, 1935, p. 156.

tiles of Canada, Ltd., owned by United Merchants and Manufacturers, Inc., or the pile fabrics plants of La France Industries, and
Collins and Aikman. Eight or 10 more manufacture silks. Another
10 produce hosiery. Such familiar companies as Allen-A, Gotham,
Holeproof, and Kayser have established Canadian mills, which, in
several cases, have been in operation for 15 or 20 years. A still larger
group manufacture various sorts of garments: collars, ties, corsets,
suits, overalls. Others turn out ropes, bags, blankets—even horse
collar pads and parachutes. It was remarked in recent hearings of
the Royal Commission on Price Spreads[16] that 6 of the 10 largest
silk manufacturers in Canada were under American control. In contrast, the Dominion Textile Company, which employs 41 per cent of
the cotton textile workers in Canada, is a Canadian-owned enterprise.

Wood and Paper Products

We have so far been considering American branch plants in
Canada whose main concern has been the Canadian, and in some
cases certain export, markets. Consequently they have been limited
by the size of the market and are merely northward extensions of an
organization initially established in the United States. But when we
turn to the wood and paper industry there is a very different
alinement.

Some American paper and wood products companies, to be sure,
have established Canadian plants mainly to serve Canadian consumers. The branch plants of a few other companies supply Canada
incidentally. But, taking the industry as a whole, American companies, attracted by easily accessible forests, have gone to Canada
to produce pulpwood, woodpulp, newsprint, and lumber chiefly for
the United States market.[17] As a result, the investment is second only
to that in public utilities among the fields in which American companies are operating in Canada. In 1929 and 1932 the United States
Department of Commerce reported American-owned pulp and paper
companies in Canada and Newfoundland with investments of about
$280,000,000.[18] The Canadian statistics from which we have been

16. *New York Times,* December 25, 1934.
17. Also, in some cases, kraft and other industrial paper products.
18. Senate Document No. 120, and Trade Information Bulletin No. 731.

quoting give a total investment in American controlled and affiliated companies in Canada alone of $287,600,990, excluding investment in timber lands. They produce 34 per cent of the pulp, newsprint, and lumber, and about 8 per cent of the other wood and paper products. In the aggregate they account for 21 per cent of the total production of the wood and paper products in Canada.

The industry bulks no less large in Canadian economy as a whole. In 1931 pulp and paper products, valued at $174,000,000, took first place among Canadian manufactures.[19] In both Quebec and New Brunswick pulp and paper ranks first in manufacturing industries; in British Columbia it ranks third; and even in more largely industrialized Ontario it is very important.

Newsprint. Since the United States is the world's largest consumer of newsprint and newsprint is admitted to that market duty-free, in recent years about 85 per cent of all paper produced in Canada has been for newspaper use. In 1929, 84 per cent, in 1930, 80 per cent, and in 1934, 82 per cent of that newsprint was shipped to the United States.

In 1909 Canada was supplying less than 4 per cent of the newsprint used in the United States. By 1916 it was supplying 25 per cent, and in 1934, 62 per cent. There had taken place in those 25 years a northward migration of the production of newsprint. Some American paper companies—newsprint and others—had purchased timber reserves or leased Crown lands in Canada, and were importing part of their pulpwood. But although there was no doubt awareness among American producers of a cost differential in the manufacture of newsprint in favor of Canada, their investments were already made in this country and, sheltered by a tariff, they were in no hurry to move their mills north.

The Province of Ontario began the process of stimulating the erection of pulp and paper mills in 1900 by prohibiting the export of pulpwood from the Crown lands in the Province. Similar legislation was passed by the Dominion Parliament in 1907 with reference to Dominion Crown lands in the Prairie Provinces. In 1910 export of pulpwood from Crown lands within its borders was prohibited

19. C. P. Fell, "The Newsprint Industry," *The Canadian Economy and Its Problems* (Toronto, 1934), p. 40. The dollar values in the last few years have sharply declined, but the relative position is unchanged.

by Quebec, in 1911 by New Brunswick, and in 1913 by British Columbia.[20] In 1911 newsprint for the first time was admitted duty-free by the United States.[21] There has, in the past, been enough privately-owned timber land in Canada to contribute to the pulp-wood piles of paper mills in northeastern United States. Consequently Provincial prohibitions are not to be regarded as completely shutting off pulpwood exports. But for American companies who were planning to supplement decreasing wood supplies in the United States with imports from their own Crown leases in Canada the prohibitions were influential in their decision to migrate. Constant Southworth concluded that ". . . giving free entry to Canadian newsprint only hastened a little a process which was bound to begin in any case."[22] But it *did* hasten the process, and that probably more than "a little."

Conveniently located, inexpensive timber and water power were mainly responsible for the shift of the center of newsprint production to Canada. Costs in the industry were declining in both countries after 1910, but in 1916 they were $30.23 per ton, on the average, in the United States and $25.71 in Canada. In 1922 Southworth found that a 10 per cent differential in favor of Canada was generally admitted, due to the cheap wood and the lower labor cost—as against wage scale—needed to get it to the mill.[23] Also, at that time 60 per cent of Canadian paper machines were over 140 inches in width, as compared with only 27 per cent in the United States.

20. *The Pulp and Paper Industry, 1932–33,* Census of Industry, Dominion Bureau of Statistics (Ottawa, 1935), p. 8; Nathan Reich, *The Pulp and Paper Industry in Canada,* McGill University Economic Studies, No. 7 (Montreal, 1926), pp. 47–50. It was stated in 1935 that Ontario intends to license some pulpwood exports from Crown lands.

21. In accordance with Section II of the Reciprocity Act later rejected by Canada. Newsprint was continued on the free list in the Tariff Act of 1913 and subsequent acts.

22. Constant Southworth, "The American-Canadian Newsprint Paper Industry and the Tariff," *Journal of Political Economy,* October, 1922, p. 683.

23. But it is the opinion of the Industrial Adviser to the N.R.A. that the mills in the United States are not obsolete, and that a 1933 survey reveals little or no Canadian cost advantage. (See quotations from the report in Fell, *op. cit.,* pp. 46–59; and R. S. Kellogg, *Sweden: Newsprint* [a privately printed brief presented by the Association of Newsprint Manufacturers of the United States to Committee on Reciprocity Information in Washington,

These conditions were reflected in statements made by executives of the International Paper Company. In 1913 President Dodge said:

The paper industry is passing through a severe trial, owing to tariff changes, the establishment of competing mills in Canada, the increasing cost of wood, and the refusal of Canada to permit the exportation of its cheap wood for use of the United States manufacturers.[24]

Thirteen years later, with his company in the midst of a huge program of Canadian expansion, President Graustein explained that the

. . . proposed purchase of Canadian paper mills, waterpower and timber lands . . . means . . . the transfer of a large part of the American newsprint industry to Canada. American paper mills which cannot compete with the cheaper wood supply and continuous water power of the Canadian mills will have to be diverted from newsprint production to other kinds of paper.

The new Canadian mills are not direct substitutes for our American mills, but we recognize that gradually . . . some of our mills will have to be withdrawn from manufacture of newsprint and turned to the manufacture of some kind of paper protected by the tariff from competition with lower cost producers such as the Canadian and Scandinavian.[25]

The extent of this migration is the substance of the next dozen pages, so it need not be summarized here. By 1934 Canadian newsprint mills had a daily capacity of 12,455 tons, of which the 12 American-owned mills accounted for 4,798 tons.[26] During the same period, however, Canadians had repurchased several mills—Thunder Bay, St. Maurice, etc.

The forest reserves of these voracious mills dwarf many an Ameri-

1934], pp. 25 ff.) Nevertheless, United States production began declining in 1926; since then there has been a net withdrawal of 241,220 tons per annum capacity from newsprint production in the United States. Many may be obsolete as far as competition with Canadian newsprint mills is concerned, but still are efficient as producers of more expensive types of paper.

24. Annual Report, February 26, 1913.

25. New York Times, March 7, 1925, p. 15.

26. The list is given in Appendix III. In the same year the capacity of mills in the United States was 5,623 tons.

can state in size. Lands owned in fee simple represent heavy investments, but cutting rights on Crown lands involve only small annual
rentals[27] plus stumpage fees as the trees are cut, which reached a low
point of $2.00 in Quebec in 1932, although they were increased later
to $2.35 per thousand feet. Holders of Crown leases also pay a sub-
stantial bonus before being granted cutting rights. In many cases
licensees had to undertake to build pulp and paper mills. The pulpwood resources of Canadian pulp and paper companies are difficult
to ascertain, because enough companies withhold their acreage figures to hinder reaching an accurate total. A very careful unpublished survey made a year or two before the present depression did
include a statement of the forest resources of a number of Canadian
companies. From it have been obtained figures for all but one of the
companies in each of the two groups of newsprint companies listed
in Appendix III. Nine of the 10 American-owned companies either
owned or leased 40,765 square miles,[28] containing an estimated
118,300,000 cords. The 13 independent or semi-independent Canadian companies had similar rights on 57,464 square miles, with 213,-
201,000 cords of wood. On the basis of those statistics and the
ownership distribution in the Appendix,[29] it is evident that the
American-owned mills control 40 per cent of the capacity and 36
per cent of the timber reserves of the Canadian newsprint industry.
They accounted in 1929 for 37½ per cent, in 1933 for 51 per cent,
and in 1934 for 47 per cent of the newsprint produced in Canada.
The largest reserves of any of the American group are those of the
Canadian International Paper Company, which in 1933 owned
5,500 square miles (15,407,000 cords) and had Crown Limits on
31,800 square miles (90,932,000 cords) in Canada and Newfoundland.[30] A smaller company, the Spruce Falls Power and Paper
Company, Ltd., which is partly owned by and supplies the *New*

27. *Fortune,* May, 1930, stated that International Paper and Power Company pays $8 per year per square mile for its Quebec rights.

28. An area as large as Maine and Massachusetts combined, and only a
little smaller than the combined provinces of Nova Scotia and New Brunswick.

29. Which admittedly contains a twilight zone in which it could not be
ascertained which way the balance of ownership lies.

30. About 87 per cent in Canada. See Annual Reports, International
Paper and Power Company, 1932, and International Power and Paper Com-

York Times, has cutting rights on 4,700 square miles, an area as large as Connecticut.

The complicated and rather acrimonious history of newsprint prices belongs somewhere in any account of this section of Canadian-American industry, as do the depression hardships of most of the companies. But that can be postponed until the migration of American companies to Canada has been described. In 1920 newsprint spot market prices reached $270 a ton at New York ($120 on contract f.o.b. mill). The migration speeded up: in the 10 years after 1919 United States newsprint production increased only 40,000 tons, while Canadian output jumped from 807,000 to 2,381,100 tons.[31] In 1929 prices fell to $62—a much lamented low—and drifted down to an average of $41.20 in 1933. During 1934 some of the tonnage in both countries sold under $40 per ton. To anyone familiar with heavy fixed-cost industries the whole story is wrapped up in those few figures of prices and output.

The "Big Three" of the Canadian newsprint industry are Abitibi Power and Paper Company, Ltd., Consolidated Paper Corporation, Ltd., and the International Paper and Power Company, each capable of producing in the neighborhood of 2,000 tons a day. Abitibi and Consolidated have subsidiaries which were once American-owned, and Americans are among their security holders. But Consolidated and Abitibi are Canadian-controlled, although a larger American interest may emerge when Abitibi is reorganized. The International company, on the other hand, has always been American.[32]

On the next page is a diagram showing the Canadian properties of the International Paper and Power Company. The power plants and transmission lines are operated by the Canadian Hydro-Electric Corporation, Ltd., which will be described later in this chapter.[33] It is with the other sections of the chart that we are now concerned.

pany of Newfoundland, Ltd., 1931. "Crown Limits" are cutting rights on state-owned lands.

31. "Paper and Power," *Fortune,* May, 1930, pp. 70 ff.

32. As of March, 1934, Canadians owned 7 per cent of the 7 per cent Preferred, and from 3 to 4 per cent of the A, B, and C Common. It is extremely difficult to trace the ownership of bonds, but approximately 8 per cent of the power bonds and possibly 3 per cent of the pulp and paper bonds are held in Canada.

33. See pp. 146 ff.

INTERNATIONAL PAPER AND POWER COMPANY

CANADIAN SUBSIDIARIES OF INTERNATIONAL PAPER COMPANY

Continental Paper Products, Ltd.
Bag mill, Ottawa

Continental Wood Products, Ltd.
Lumber mill, Elsas, Ont.

International Fibre Board Co., Ltd.
Mills, Gatineau, Que.
Midland, Ont.

Canadian International Paper Company, Ltd.*

PAPER MILLS
Three Rivers, Que.
Gatineau, Que.

New Brunswick International Paper Co., Ltd.
Mill: Dalhousie, N.B.
Coal mine: Minto, N.B.

Bathurst Power and Paper Co., Ltd.
Mill: Bathurst, N.B.
(minority interest)

PULP MILLS
Kipawa, Timiskaming, Que. (rayon)
Hawkesbury, Ont. (bleached sulphite)
Nipigon, Ont. (groundwood)

LUMBER MILLS†
Calumet, Que.
Cap-de-la-Magdelaine, Que.

CANADIAN SUBSIDIARIES OF INTERNATIONAL HYDRO-ELECTRIC SYSTEM

Canadian Hydro-Electric Corporation, Ltd.

E. B. Eddy, Ltd.
49%
Hull, Que.

Gatineau Power Company

DISTRIBUTING COMPANIES
Gatineau Electric Light Co.
Gatineau Transmission Co.

HYDRO-ELECTRIC PLANTS
Bell Falls, Que.
Bryson, Que.
Chaudière Falls, Ont. (2 plants)
Chelsea, Que.
Corbeau Rapids, Que.
Farmers Falls, Que.
Grand Falls, N.B.
High Falls, Que.
Kipawa, Que.
Paugan, Que.
Rawdon, Que.
Ripon, Que.
St. Adele, Que.
St. Jerome, Que.
Table Falls, Que.
Thurso, Que.
Wilson Chute, Que.

STORAGE DAMS
Cabonga, Que.
Mercier, Que.
Temiscouata, Que.

* Also owns Newfoundland Power and Paper Company, Ltd., with a large mill at Corner Brook, Newfoundland.

† There are also 9 other sawmills and drum barkers devoted chiefly to preparing pulpwood, notably at Gaspé, Pentecost, Batiscan, Three Rivers, Hull, Que.; Rockland, Ont.

The International Paper Company,[34] predecessor of the present enterprise, was incorporated in New York in 1898 as a merger of 19 companies in New York and New England. Few of the mills had perpetual timber reserves in the United States. They were becoming dependent on imported pulpwood. Seven years previously the St. Maurice Lumber Company (New York) had begun operations in Three Rivers, Quebec—evidently the first entrance of this group into Canada. In 1916 it was reincorporated in Quebec and, to anticipate, in 1925 its name was changed to Candian International Paper Company. For the first 15 years of its life the new International Company added much Canadian timber to its reserves.

In 1914 President Dodge called the stockholders' attention to the increasing newsprint imports. The Company began to convert some of its mills to other paper and by 1916 one third of its capacity was devoted to the production of non-newsprint paper. Out of increased profits of the war period the first of the company's Canadian mills— at Three Rivers, Quebec—was built and opened in 1921.

The administration of Archibald Graustein began in 1924. He was confronted by a company with inadequate timber reserves near its mills,[35] by increasingly obsolete equipment and by growing Canadian competition. He decided upon a program to meet those conditions which involved (1) building new newsprint and pulp mills at Canadian points where perpetual reserves could be acquired; (2) abandoning higher-cost American mills and converting the more efficient ones to other grades of paper; (3) developing water power, both to reduce power costs and to diversify the company's income. In that program, carried out between 1925 and 1930, can be found the explanation of the Canadian organization shown on the chart.

The Three Rivers mill was doubled in capacity in 1926, making it the largest in the world. In 1925 the properties of the bankrupt Riordon Company, Ltd., were bought at auction, properties which included the Kipawa and Hawkesbury pulp mills, several sawmills,

---

34. The following account has been gathered from many sources, but the most important are: *International Paper and Power Company,* copyrighted manuscript, Harvard School of Business Administration; Annual Reports, International Paper and Power Company and subsidiaries; "Paper and Power," *Fortune,* May, 1930, pp. 65–72; and *Historical Summaries of Consolidations in Canadian Industries,* MS, Dominion Bureau of Statistics, 1934.

35. Pulpwood costs had almost doubled between 1912 and 1923.

10,000 square miles of timber, and water power sites on the Gatineau and Nation rivers. The Kipawa mill, at Timiskaming, Quebec, enlarged to an annual capacity of 100,000 tons, produces almost half of the world's supply of rayon cellulose. At Gatineau a new newsprint mill was built which, with its 600 tons daily capacity, is not much smaller than the one at Three Rivers.

These properties were added to those already owned by Canadian International Paper Company which, in turn, was placed under the jurisdiction of still another company, Canadian International Paper, Ltd., created in 1925. By 1932 Canadian International Paper Company and its subsidiaries owned, as the chart shows, newsprint,[36] sulphite, and ground-wood pulp mills and sawmills in Canada, and the Newfoundland mill, acquired in 1928. The mills at Three Rivers, Gatineau, Dalhousie and Corner Brook; the Bathurst mill, which Canadian International operates and partly owns; and the Eddy mill, in which the Canadian Hydro-Electric Corporation, Ltd., has a 49 per cent interest, have a combined daily capacity of more than 2,500 tons of newsprint, as compared with the 1,262 tons of the International's mills in the United States.

The newsprint mills are almost entirely dependent on the American market for their existence. But the pulp and the lumber, the latter due at least partly to the United States tariff, are sold largely in Canada and abroad. As the chart indicates, there are, outside the Canadian International Paper organization, two fibre-board mills[37] and a bag mill. Those three plants also are solely concerned with Canadian and other foreign markets.

At the end of 1933 the consolidated balance sheet of the International Paper and Power Company showed total assets of $881,-000,000. Of those assets about $270,000,000 were in the Canadian properties.[38]

The remaining American newsprint companies in Canada can be more briefly described. Two of them are owned by American newspapers; two are owned by companies which do not produce news-

36. The New Brunswick mill was opened in 1930.

37. The International Company does not produce or sell fibre board in the United States.

38. Computed by combining the assets of Canadian International Paper Company, Ltd., and Canadian Hydro-Electric Corporation, Ltd., adding $2,000,000, arbitrarily, for other Canadian assets, and deducting the assets

print in the United States; the others are subsidiaries of the Backus-Brooks and the Crown Zellerbach companies, both newsprint producers.

The Backus-Brooks Company was formed in 1882 by four persons—three of them the Backus brothers. Even before the war they had turned to Canada for pulpwood. In 1911 the Minnesota and Ontario Power Company (which became the Minnesota and Ontario Paper Company in 1918) issued in London $1,000,000 in bonds, guaranteed by Backus-Brooks. It was then stated that the company, located close to the Border, was completing a dam on the Canadian side and had power plants on both sides.[39] The Canadian power plant was (and still is) selling its excess power to the cities of International Falls, Minnesota, and Fort Frances, Ontario. The parent company was then planning to supplement its American newsprint mill with a Canadian woodpulp mill.

The diagram below outlines the organization resulting from the Canadian expansion of the Backus interests between 1911 and 1932. In 1934 their 3 Canadian newsprint mills had a daily capacity of 850 tons, while their only American mill—in Minneapolis—had a daily capacity of 262 tons.

This chart shows Backus-Brooks Company as the owner of the Canadian mills. Strictly speaking, that is the case, inasmuch as a majority of the common stock of both Great Lakes and Minnesota and Ontario, and the Great Lakes preferred stock are still owned by that holding company. But business adversity has almost wiped out the shareholders' equity. In 1931 the Minnesota and Ontario Paper Company—with its subsidiaries as described—was put into receivership, and continued to have heavy deficits in both 1932 and 1933.

of the Newfoundland company. The International Company segregates its *property* accounts, after deducting reserves, as follows (1933):

	Canada and Newfoundland	United States	Total
Power and Utility	$106,329,842	$423,861,797	$530,191,639
Pulp and Miscellaneous	105,495,832	98,399,135	203,894,967
Woodland	26,808,377	7,385,679	34,194,056
Totals	$238,634,051	$529,646,611	$768,280,662
Less Newfoundland, about	40,000,000		
Total Canada	$198,634,051		

39. *Commercial and Financial Chronicle*, March 4, 1911, p. 600.

BACKUS–BROOKS COMPANY

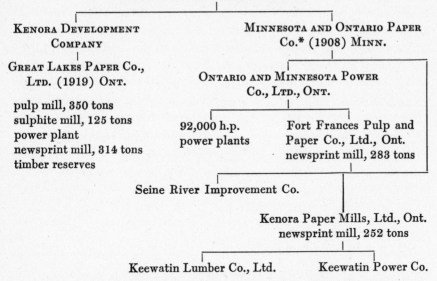

KENORA DEVELOPMENT COMPANY

GREAT LAKES PAPER CO., LTD. (1919) ONT.

pulp mill, 350 tons
sulphite mill, 125 tons
power plant
newsprint mill, 314 tons
timber reserves

MINNESOTA AND ONTARIO PAPER Co.* (1908) MINN.

ONTARIO AND MINNESOTA POWER Co., LTD., ONT.

92,000 h.p. power plants

Fort Frances Pulp and Paper Co., Ltd., Ont. newsprint mill, 283 tons

Seine River Improvement Co.

Kenora Paper Mills, Ltd., Ont. newsprint mill, 252 tons

Keewatin Lumber Co., Ltd.   Keewatin Power Co.

* The Canadian companies produce kraft liner board and insulating material, but it is not clear just which mills handle those products.

Later in 1931 E. W. Backus was removed as receiver.[40] The Great Lakes Company also was put into receivership in 1931, under the management of the National Trust Company, Ltd., of Toronto, trustee for the bondholders. Consequently, the bondholders and other creditors of the companies formerly clearly under Backus-Brooks' control are now virtually owners of the property.[41] A close observer, long associated with the newsprint industry, says: "I am somewhat uncertain as to Great Lakes. It is under separate receivership of the National Trust Company, Toronto, and will eventually pass, no doubt, into the hands of its bondholders, of which, I presume, there is a good deal of American interest. The other Backus mills are continuing in their receivership, which is an American interest."

The *Chicago Tribune*, in 1912, built and still owns the mill of the Ontario Paper Company, Ltd., at Thorold, Ontario, which sells to

40. He died in October, 1934, still trying to regain the properties.
41. Probably the larger part of the bonds are held in the United States. The $10,000,000 Great Lakes issue was floated in 1929, in Chicago and Minneapolis, and a Chicago bank is co-trustee. The bonds were probably all taken in the United States.

the *Tribune* most of the output of its 429-ton newsprint mill, the remainder going to a New York paper. Similarly, the *New York Times* obtains most of its 100,000 tons of newsprint from the Spruce Falls Power and Paper Company, Ltd., at Kapuskasing, Ontario, in which it has a 49 per cent interest.[42] That 480-ton mill was built at a cost of $29,000,000 between 1926 and 1929 by the *Times* and the Kimberly-Clark Corporation, which owns the remaining shares.[43] The Spruce Falls Company sells half of its output on the open market. It generates its own power in a 75,000 horse-power hydro-electric plant 50 miles from the mill, owns a 50-mile standard gauge railroad, and has 4,700 square miles of Crown timber leases.[44]

The other American-owned mills are in British Columbia. One of them, the Powell River Company, Ltd., is owned by the Brooks-Scanlon Lumber Company, which, in 1910, came across a "bargain" in a pulp lease and power site which the owners were unable to develop. A 50,000 horse-power power plant and a newsprint mill were built, the mill having, by 1934, a daily capacity of 650 tons. The parent company produces no paper. The Powell Company sells about 70 per cent of its newsprint in the United States (in the southwest, east as far as Kansas City, and on the Pacific Coast). The chief producer of paper on the Pacific Coast is the Crown Zellerbach Corporation, which in 1928 supplied about three fourths of the newsprint used in California, Washington, and Oregon.[45] The Corporation can produce about 1,000 tons of newsprint a day, of which its Canadian company, Pacific Mills, Ltd., contributes 256 tons. The plant, at Ocean Falls, was apparently acquired in 1914,[46] and also produces some kraft and other papers. It is driven by its own 23,000

42. The Mersey Paper Company, Ltd., supplies the rest of the *New York Times'* consumption. The Spruce Falls Company sells newsprint to the Toronto *Mail and Empire,* owned by the owner of Mersey Paper.

43. *Poor's Industrial Volume,* 1934. Kimberly-Clark supplied $7,500,000, the *New York Times* about $8,000,000, and the remainder of the capital was raised by the sale of bonds.

44. Arthur Pound, "Wood, Water, and Brains," *Atlantic Monthly,* September, 1935, pp. 382–384; and *Poor's Industrial Volume,* 1934.

45. *Newsprint Paper Industry,* Senate Document No. 214, 71st Congress, Special Session (Washington, 1930), pp. 84–85.

46. It existed before then as Ocean Falls Pulp and Paper Company, Ltd., but the ownership has not been traced beyond 1914.

horse-power hydro-electric plant. Of the estimated 10 billion feet of timber owned by the parent company in 1932, 30 per cent was in Canada, and, through the Graham Islands Timber Company, Ltd., a saw mill was operated capable of handling 300,000 feet in 10 hours. The Canadian assets are carried at about $20,000,000.

So much for the American newsprint companies in Canada. It will be remembered that we estimated, at the beginning, that they account for about 40 per cent of the capacity of the industry. Some of them, it must have been noticed, produce pulp beyond their needs; some—notably the International Company—have surplus power for sale; some produce other sorts of heavy or industrial paper. But they are essentially newsprint producers.

It is beyond our province to discuss in detail the independent Canadian companies. But some of them have interesting American antecedents. Abitibi, the largest, until recently had as its chairman G. H. Mead of Dayton, Ohio, and as its president Alexander Smith of Chicago. It is believed that the "Mead interests" have had a large investment in Abitibi, which would account for the presence of the Americans on the Board. In November, 1934, Abitibi bought the G. H. Mead Company, a sales organization, which presumably means that Abitibi will do its own selling in the United States. In 1932 Abitibi was declared bankrupt and a permanent liquidator appointed.[47] The Consolidated Paper Corporation has one American on its board, but there is no indication of predominant American influence. However, two of its subsidiaries—St. Maurice, and Quebec Pulp and Paper—were at one time American-owned. Donnacona Paper Company, Ltd., organized and long owned by Americans, was bought by Price Brothers in 1927. A few years later it reverted to the security holders, who are largely Americans. Abitibi's Thunder Bay mill was once American-owned.

The maze of complications in the newsprint market[48] cannot be

47. Senate Document No. 214, pp. 77–78; *Moody's Manual of Investments, Industrial Securities,* Weekly Summary, November 3, 1934. We have been discussing, above, the "entrepreneurial" interests of Americans in Abitibi. Of course, there are large holdings of Abitibi securities by American investors who had no "control" intentions.

48. The price and competitive situation in newsprint was the cause of the Federal Trade Commission investigation which resulted in Senate Document No. 214, from which we have been drawing information.

fully traced here. But the existence in Canada of both American and Canadian mills brings certain aspects of that market within our limits. It has been stated many times that the International Company, is the most influential factor in setting newsprint prices. In describing the price reduction on January 1, 1926, the United States Federal Trade Commission said:

The building program which had started during the high price period was constantly increasing the production capacity of Canada. . . . Production . . . in the United States reached its highest figures during 1926. These conditions brought another price reduction . . . in spite of . . . rapidly increasing consumption. . . . The International Paper Company [announced its reduction in] October, 1925. . . . All of the United States mills east of the Rocky Mountains made the same reduction. . . . The leading Canadian mills also followed the International Paper Company. . . .[49]

In 1934 the vice-president of the Anglo-Canadian Pulp and Paper Company, Ltd., said that the prices of his company would be raised as a result of the decision of the International Paper Company to add $2.50 per ton to existing contract prices for the first six months of 1935 and not more than an additional $2.50 in the last six months. He further explained[50] that only such companies as the International in Canada and the Great Northern in the United States can set their own prices. The prices of other companies reflect the judgment of these leaders.

Before beginning the account of the post-war newsprint market it is pertinent to take a look at the relative efficiency of the mills in Canada. Canadian plant capacity has recently been rated as follows: 50 per cent as "efficient"; 38 per cent as "less efficient"; 12 per cent as "high cost."[51] Dividing the mills into the two groups—American-owned and independent—with which we have been dealing, the following situation is revealed:

	Efficient	Less efficient	High cost
American-owned[52]	70%	29%	1%
Independent[52]	35%	48%	17%
All	50%	38%	12%

49. Senate Document No. 214, pp. 35, 81–82.
50. *New York Times,* November 14, 1934.
51. C. P. Fell, *op. cit.,* p. 51.   52. See Appendix III.

In November, 1920, the contract price for newsprint f.o.b. mill generally prevailing in both countries reached the peak of $135 per ton. A year later it had dropped to $70. In January, 1924, American contract prices f.o.b. mill were $77.60,[53] with most Canadian mills $2.00 less. By 1926 prices drifted down to a uniform $69 in both countries, and weakened to $65 by June, 1926. Though that price collapse caused much distress and excitement, it was by no means the end. During the depression progressive cuts brought official prices to $40, with some contracts as low as $36. Late in 1934 and early in 1935 strenuous but unsuccessful efforts were made to add $5 a ton to the official price. The price situation in 1935 has continued to be confused. Though $40 remains the official price, the mills are absorbing delivery costs, many unofficial discounts and rebates are in effect, and generally speaking newsprint mills are getting, on the average, not much better than $30 a ton, f.o.b. mill.[54]

Until 1927 there was no influence on the market other than the competitive weight of the big companies, of which, to repeat, the International was the most important. In May of that year the independent mills in Canada, alarmed by steadily weakening prices, organized the Canadian Newsprint Company, Ltd., to market their product, control output, allocate tonnage, and set prices. There were no American-owned mills in that group.[55] They entered a tentative agreement to deliver newsprint to the Hearst papers at $65 on a 10-year contract. Early in 1928, however, they decided not to execute the contract. Consequently the Hearst interests signed contracts with two of the constituent companies, and soon afterwards Canadian Newsprint Company, Ltd., dissolved.

The International Company obtained a Hearst contract for 1929 at prices from $7 to $10 below those prevailing, which meant that the new price would be extended to all International's customers. The Canadian manufacturers protested against using the Hearst price as a base, and in November, 1928, the Provincial governments

53. Pacific Coast mill prices had usually been about $5 more per ton.

54. It is important to note that before 1929 prices quoted were f.o.b. mill; since then they have included delivery, which reduced the mill price by about $6 per ton in the Grand Mère area and proportionately less or more in other areas.

55. Senate Document No. 214, p. 36.

intervened. The Prime Minister of Ontario wrote a letter to the Nipigon Company, Ltd., an International subsidiary, warning it that the Province could not permit the industry to collapse.[56] The Canadian companies, excluding Canadian International Paper, the Spruce Falls Company, and the two British Columbia mills, had joined the Newsprint Institute of Canada, formed under the guidance of the Provincial governments of Ontario and Quebec, and had agreed to curtail production and pool orders.[57] Late in November, 1928, Premier Taschereau, of Quebec, urged the International Paper Company to adhere to that agreement, but President Graustein refused. Early in December Mr. Taschereau came to New York and at a conference with Hearst and International officials "told [them] in vigorous language that the price . . . specified in that October contract with Hearst must be raised. He spoke of pressure, and he was insistent in his attitude."[58] The Premier had a copy of the telegram by which, five days earlier, the International Company had virtually assured its customers that the Hearst price would be extended to them. The Hearst representative told the Premier that they were perfectly satisfied with their contract. Mr. Taschereau replied that he was not satisfied and that something had to be done about it. He warned that the Province could change the timber dues overnight, rebating to the mills who lived up to the Canadian Newsprint Institute agreement.[59] Negotiations continued for three months and finally resulted in an increase of $5 per ton.

In November, 1929, the Ontario and Quebec Premiers began their endeavors to obtain another price increase for 1930. Mr. Graustein was called to Montreal and urged to raise the International Company's price to $60. He refused, and repeated his refusal three weeks later. In December the G. H. Mead Company, agents in the United States for Abitibi, announced a price increase of $5 for July, 1930. But despite threats of penalties, the International Company announced no price increase. As a result, the projected increase failed and the Newsprint Institute collapsed in 1930. Since then the in-

56. The letter is quoted in part in Senate Document No. 214, p. 41.

57. *Ibid.*, pp. 42–43, 86.

58. Testimony of Mr. Graustein before the United States Federal Trade Commission, *ibid.*, p. 43.

59. *Ibid.*, pp. 43, 89.

dustry has been without effective organization. By 1934, as has been stated, prices had declined another $15 per ton.

Despite a consumption that has been fairly stable, considering the depression, 58 per cent of Canadian newsprint capacity is either bankrupt, in receivership, or has gone through reorganization, and that largely during 1931 and 1932, when prices and output had not reached their lowest point. Among those distressed mills are 5 out of 8 of the largest in North America.[60] In October, 1934, Premier Taschereau once more intervened to bring about higher mill prices for newsprint, threatening Provincial control of exports.[61] Early in November an increase in stumpage dues was assessed against the St. Lawrence Paper Mills, Ltd., as a penalty for quoting a price reported by the *New York Times* as $40 to the Scripps-Howard Newspapers for 1935, at a time when the Canadian manufacturers generally were attempting an increase to $42.50 for the first six months. On November 8 a committee of newsprint executives obtained from Premier Bennett a promise of aid if the industry as a whole should request it. It is to be noted that Mr. Graustein was among the petitioners. A few days later the International Company announced its price increase.

Regardless of the penalties imposed on the St. Lawrence Mills, that company did not or could not—it is not clear which—withdraw from its $40 contract with the Scripps-Howard Newspapers. It therefore appears that the maximum price for newsprint in 1935 will be $40 per ton. Premier Taschereau is endeavoring to devise some plan (which would have to be of an inter-Provincial nature) whereby all newsprint companies in Canada can be united in a price-maintenance agreement.[62]

60. C. P. Fell, *op. cit.*, pp. 50–51, and R. S. Kellogg, *op. cit.*, p. 23.

61. For these latest developments see the *New York Times,* October 24, November 5, 7, 8, 9, 12, 14, 19, December 15, 1934.

62. *New York Times,* January 17, February 27, March 5, April 11, April 14, April 27, May 1, 1935. The legislation proposed in Quebec will give the Government power to increase stumpage dues from the $2.70 per 1,000 feet "official" rate at present to $6 per cord, or about $12 per 1,000 feet, if it is deemed necessary. One peculiar factor in the newsprint price situation is the form of selling contract customarily used. "Every contract contains a provision that the price shall not be higher than that charged to any customer by any mill with a capacity of 100,000 tons a year or more. Thus if one company

The distribution of newsprint output between the two groups of companies in Appendix III is shown in the following table.

TABLE VIII

Newsprint production in Canada by independent and by American-owned companies

	1929		1933		1934	
	tons	%	tons	%	tons	%
American-owned	1,027,939	38	1,025,025	51	1,222,294	47
Independent	1,700,838	62	991,717	49	1,376,998	53
Total	2,728,777	100	2,016,742	100	2,599,292	100

The figures are striking. They indicate a remarkable stability in output in the "satellite" American-owned mills, and heavy declines, totaling 700,000 tons, in the independent mills between 1929 and 1933. Of the increased business in 1934, however, amounting to almost 600,000 tons, the independent mills obtained a larger share than did the American-owned mills. Apparently the contracts held by the latter mills were with newsprint users whose requirements did not fall off during the severest months of the depression. Possibly, further, those mills have been more energetic in getting new business. No available information gives any precise answer to those queries.[63]

Pulp mills. It has already been stated that some of the American newsprint companies in Canada operate pulp mills which have a surplus for sale. The Kipawa rayon pulp mill and the Hawkesbury mill selling bleached pulp for other types of paper occupy impor-

uses bad judgment or cuts the price to secure a contract, it may easily bring the whole industry down to its level for an entire year or even longer. . . . This kind of contract makes the newsprint industry probably the most competitive there is, a grotesque caricature of competition." See E. A. Forsey, "The Pulp and Paper Industry," *Canadian Journal of Economics and Political Science,* August, 1935, p. 506.

63. It has already been stated that the American mills have a more than proportionate share of the more efficient mills in Canada. That may partly account for their seemingly greater competitive strength during the depression, but it must be remembered that this is a uniform-price industry.

tant positions. But there are other American companies quite outside the newsprint field operating pulp mills in Canada.

Some of these mills were built or bought to supply the parent company in the United States with needed pulp. The A.P.W. Paper Company built its Nova Scotia pulp mill—The Halifax Power and Pulp Company, Ltd.[64]—in 1923 solely for that purpose. The Brown Corporation in Quebec (1905) and the Vancouver Kraft Company, Ltd. (1928) also ship their pulp to the mills of the parent companies.[65] Those three mills have a daily capacity of about 500 tons of pulp, and have extensive timber reserves. The Brown Corporation, for example, has rights in over 3,000,000 acres, a third of which it owns. The Brown Company values its Canadian property at $25,000,000 and will sometime develop its water power jointly with the Shawinigan Water and Power Company.[66] The Scott Paper Company also looks to its affiliate in Canada,[67] for raw materials. Save for one or two companies which produce nothing but pulp, the other American pulp mills in Canada are those run as adjuncts to newsprint enterprises.

Paper goods factories. At the beginning of this section devoted to pulp and paper it was stated that the American-owned factories in Canada could be divided into two groups. One group consists of those we have been describing, whose chief customers are in the United States, although some of them incidentally supply the Canadian market. The other group—a few more than a score—are true branch companies, manufacturing for sale in Canada the products of their parent companies. As the statistics have indicated, these factories constitute only a small part of the total American investment in the Canadian paper and pulp industry.

Some of these plants bear such familiar names as Butterick, Dennison, McCall, Eaton, Vortex, Stone Straw. Others produce boxes, liners, tissue paper, wall paper, paper cups, and are less well known to the general public. Robert Gair Company, for example,

64. Until recently it was called the A.P.W. Pulp and Power Company, Ltd.

65. The Brown Company, in New Hampshire, and the Columbia River Paper Company, on the West Coast.

66. See below, p. 152.

67. The Nova Scotia Wood Pulp and Paper Company, Ltd.

bought the controlling interest in Firstbrook Boxes, Ltd., in 1932. This old company[68] had had Canadian rights for Gair patents since 1928. In 1932 it defaulted on its bonds and the reorganized company gave 72 per cent of its shares to Gair in return for new machinery. A year earlier, the American company had bought an interest in Maritime Paper Products, Ltd., and in 1934 it leased the four mills of the reorganized Canadian Paperboard, Ltd., and organized Gair Company of Canada, Ltd., to operate them. Another fairly elaborate paper box enterprise is Hinde and Dauch Paper Company of Canada, Ltd., incorporated in 1910 by a similarly named Ohio company. In 1928 it acquired, through an exchange of stock, Thompson and Norris Company and now operates three Canadian plants, valued at more than $4,000,000.

Somewhat similar in position to the branch paper factories we have just been describing, are the 15 or more printing and publishing companies established in Canada by Americans. Most of them, such as the subsidiary of the United States Playing Card Company, are printers and lithographers. They produce playing cards, accounting forms, pictures, and so on. Probably the only one of special interest is the Canadian Bank Note Company, Ltd., owned by the American Bank Note Company. This company with head office, as one might expect, in Ottawa and branches in Toronto and Montreal, divides with the Canadian-owned British American Bank Note Company the business of printing all postage stamps and paper money in Canada.

Saw and planing mills; lumber, wood products. We noted, in passing, that several of the newsprint companies have their own mills to handle the timber unsuited for pulping. In addition, there are 35 or 40 lumber and timber companies operating in Canada under American guidance, and as many more producing wood products. Almost all of the latter are subsidiaries of American corporations. But about half of the American-owned lumber companies are owned by individual Americans who have exploited Canadian timber lands, and are not the offspring of previously existing similar ventures in the United States. A single example will serve as an illustration. The Empire Lumber Company, incorporated in Delaware in 1909, is

68. Founded in 1867. See *Historical Summaries of Consolidations in Canadian Industries.*

directed from Philadelphia and markets lumber from a 30,000-acre Crown grant on Vancouver Island.[69]

The other lumber companies are evidence of the northward extension of American lumbermen. For instance, Bloedel, Stewart and Welch, Ltd., has recently begun a $1,000,000 sawmill in British Columbia which will be able to handle 100,000,000 feet per year. It is closely associated with a somewhat similarly named Washington company. The Shevlin, Carpenter and Clarke Company of Minnesota owns the Carpenter-Hixon Company, Ltd., Blind River, Ontario, and the Shevlin-Clarke Company, Ltd., Fort Frances, Ontario. Those two subsidiaries, with a capacity of 160,000,000 feet of lumber per year, supply much of the northern white pine, western white spruce, and Norway pine which the parent company sells in the United States. It is to be noted that these species of wood are becoming increasingly scarce in the United States. Most of these companies are purely private affairs about which it is almost impossible to obtain information. Consequently, although all of them must be operating from their own timber lands or leases, we have not been able to learn what their total reserves are.

Americans interested in the red cedar shingle industry of the Pacific Northwest have also pushed over into the red cedar region of British Columbia. Americans own or have an interest in 20 shingle mills in that Province, operating 173 shingle machines, representing about 40 per cent of the total machines in British Columbia. Certain of those companies also have investments in standing timber, railroads, and logging equipment.

These are not new developments. As was indicated in Chapter I, American interest in Canadian lumbering goes back fully 100 years. In the years just prior to 1914 Field[70] found much American activity at Salmon River (Bay of Fundy), Miramichi, Restigouche, and Bathurst, in the east. He was told that 75 per cent of the 17,000 timber leases in British Columbia were held by Americans, as well as two thirds of the interior and one third of the coast sawmills. Some of these earlier "deals" were large ones. He mentions several ventures involving apparently as much as $10,000,000. He concluded that,

69. This particular company has its timber sawn by a contract mill. In 1932 it was in financial distress and carried a deficit of over $3,000,000.

70. *Op. cit.* (1914 ed.), pp. 56, 137–142.

so far as British Columbia was concerned, in 1913 there was about $100,000,000 of foreign capital in land and timber, of which three fourths was American and one fourth English. The Americans were interested almost exclusively in timber, while the English were more active in real estate.

Many of these companies—probably most of them—were organized to export lumber to the American market. The 8 lumber companies replying to our Canadian questionnaire sold 77 per cent of their output in the United States. What effect the 1932 lumber tariff has had on these companies, we could not find out. However, 3 of the 8 reported that in 1933 the American market was closed so far as they were concerned.

The wood-working factories can be dismissed with a few words. Half a dozen manufacture furniture; another 4 or 5 make boxes. The rest cannot be summarized, producing as they do a variety of things, such as billiard tables, athletic goods, pencils, cork products, and so on.

Iron and Its Products

Paper mills constitute more than a fourth of the American manufacturing investment in Canadian industry. But most of that investment is in newsprint and, with their dependence on the American market, those mills are scarcely typical branch plants. The iron and steel goods factories, second in volume of capital employed, are much more simply concerned with the Canadian market. The 193 American-owned companies in this field, employing, in 1932, a capital of over $175,000,000, turn out nearly 39 per cent of the iron products in Canada. The percentage varies, however, within that general category. Twelve per cent of the "basic" steel is made in American branch plants as compared with 82 per cent of the automobiles and parts.

Furnaces, rolling mills, castings, forgings. Among these mills—the base of the steel industry—there are few American-owned companies, and of those few little is known. Nearly a score of plants produce rails, bars, castings, and such more highly fabricated articles as brake shoes, automatic stokers, and so on. Some of them, such as the subsidiaries of the American Brake Shoe and Foundry Company, have been in operation 20 years or more.

By far the largest is the Algoma Steel Corporation, Ltd., whose nebulous Anglo-American-Canadian ownership is extremely difficult to track down. If it is Canadian-controlled, it belongs in the next chapter, because it owns mines and quarries in the United States. But there is considerable evidence—historical and recent—that the balance of power lies in the United States. Algoma Steel is one of four iron ore smelting companies in Canada[71] and is the largest of the four.

In 1904 The Lake Superior Corporation was organized in New York as the successor to the Consolidated Lake Superior Corporation of a few years earlier. It was the medium through which a group of Americans were undertaking the development of ore and timber in the Algoma region north of Sault Ste Marie, Ontario. Much of the capital, however, came from England. The man who conceived the group of enterprises subsidiary to The Lake Superior Corporation was F. H. Clergue, born and educated in Maine. An engineer, he constructed the hydraulic canals and power plants on both sides of the boundary at Sault Ste Marie. He organized and was president of the Lake Superior Power Company, the Algoma Steel Corporation (which operated the first Bessemer steel plant and rail mill in Canada), the Sault Ste Marie Pulp and Paper Company, the Algoma Central Railway and the Algoma Eastern Railway.[72]

Ground was broken for the first mill of the Algoma Steel Company in 1901, and in May of the following year the first steel rails were rolled.[73] Despite difficulties and reorganization in 1904, three new furnaces were built in 1907, and in 1912 the Algoma Steel Corporation, Ltd., was incorporated and received from The Lake Superior Corporation all its steel property and mines in Canada, the Lake Superior Power Company, Ltd., the Algoma Commercial Power Company, Ltd., and limestone quarries and coal mines in Michigan and West Virginia. Meantime the Lake Superior Corporation was building two railroads to open up its properties. The Algoma Central and Hudson Bay Railway Company runs north

71. Dominion Steel and Coal Corporation, Ltd., The Steel Company of Canada, Ltd., and Canadian Furnace Company, Ltd., are the others.

72. *Who's Who in Canada*, 1925–1926, p. 1122.

73. "New Era for Lake Superior Corporation," *The Citizen*, January 18, 1929.

from Sault Ste Marie about 340 miles, crossing both main Canadian systems, and connecting the mines and the blast furnaces. The Algoma Eastern Railway extends 88 miles northeast from Little Current on Manitoulin Island, to Sudbury, Ontario, providing a Great Lakes outlet for that mining field. There were large land grants to those railroads, and much timber, but the Algoma Steel Corporation's mills were the focal point of the whole project.

It has not been an altogether happy venture. One reorganization had occurred in 1907. In the two years following 1909 the Lake Superior Corporation spent over $11,000,000, partly on the railroads and the Helen mine, but chiefly on the Algoma mills. In 1912 control shifted to England, and $15,000,000 in bonds were issued in London, under Lake Superior's guaranty, to carry out the Algoma Corporation merger and to complete the railroads. At this time 7 or 8 of the 11 directors were Americans. Frequently in the years thereafter—save for the wartime steel boom—the Lake Superior Corporation complained that the Canadian steel rail market was too small, and that it could not raise the $5,000,000 needed to diversify the Algoma mill's output.

Early in 1929 another shift evidently occurred in the control of the parent holding company which, by then, had seemingly settled in the hands of a few Philadelphians. From a reshuffle of the cards a new board of directors emerged on which sat 10 Canadians and 1 Philadelphian with, for the first time, an all-Canadian group of chief executives. That was in a period of active stock markets. Prices of Lake Superior stock moved, during the first nine months of 1929, from $5 to $40 per share. The *Financial Post* reported[74] that probably during the year the Canadian owners took their profit and control drifted back to Philadelphia. It is probable that the balance of control did revert to the United States, and that it is still there. But in the reorganization of 1930–31 the board of directors retained its Canadian complexion.

Lake Superior's guaranty of the bonds of the Algoma Central and the terminal was, by September, 1929, $9,000,000 in arrears, and was accruing at the rate of $532,000 a year. With that charge added to generally disappointing income statements, the parent company had been unable to borrow the money to modernize Al-

74. September 26, 1929.

goma Steel. But the bondholders—chiefly English—would not agree to accept a 40 per cent interest in both railroads and the terminal in lieu of due payments and future guaranties. A year later, however, the Algoma Eastern was purchased by the Canadian Pacific Railway for $2,200,000 in cash, $1,250,000 of which was used to equip the steel mill to produce 130-pound rails. By that time the assets of the Algoma Steel Corporation, Ltd., were almost $50,000,000.

In 1931 the parent company and its various subsidiaries and their subsidiaries were reorganized with a new "parent," like this:

ALGOMA CONSOLIDATED CORPORATION, LTD.

```
         100%                          51%
  Lake Superior Corp.   33%   Algoma Central and Hudson Bay Ry.
      66%
       |
       v
  Algoma Steel Corp., Ltd.      Northern Ontario Lands Corp., Ltd.

  Fiborn Lime-      Cannelton Coal
   stone Co.,         and Coke
    U.S.             Co., U.S.

        Lake Superior Coal Co., U.S.
```

In addition, Lake Superior Corporation owns $5,800,000, 6 per cent bonds and two thirds of the preferred stock of Algoma Steel. The rest of the preferred belongs to Algoma Consolidated, which also owns 40 per cent ($4,123,400) of the first mortgage income 5's and all ($318,800) of the second income 6's of the railroad. As a result of the exchange of shares whereby these new relationships were created, the new holding company, Algoma Consolidated, issued 600,000 shares of common and 400,000 shares of preferred stock. All of the preferred and 400,000 shares of common went to Lake Superior shareholders. Trust certificates representing the rest of the common, and over $3,000,000 of 5 per cent income debenture, stock were issued on the security of Algoma Consolidated's holdings in Algoma Central bonds, to recompense the Algoma Central bondholders—to repeat, chiefly English—for waiving the Lake Superior guaranty. Those bondholders also received trust certificates representing 49 per cent of the common stock of the railroad.

Our chief concern, even if it has become lost in the history of this collection of companies which compose one of Canada's big enterprises, is the steel company. As the chart shows, it is still controlled by Lake Superior Corporation. Lake Superior in turn is owned by Algoma Consolidated, which in its turn is controlled by the former shareholders of Lake Superior. If the majority of Algoma Consolidated shares are in American hands, as is probable but not certain, then Algoma Steel is American-owned.[75] Its $50,000,000 properties include 160 coke ovens, 4 blast furnaces, an open-hearth plant, a duplex plant, rolling mills, merchant mills, and a power plant, with an aggregate annual capacity of 1,560,000 tons of rails, blooms, structural steel, pig iron, and so on, in addition to coke and other by-products. But the Algoma enterprises as a whole are still suffering from inadequate markets. Algoma Steel has had heavy deficits after all charges ever since 1928, and went into receivership in 1932, as did the Lake Superior Corporation. In February, 1935, the Canadian courts approved a proposed sale of the assets of the Algoma Steel Corporation, Ltd., to a new company of the same name. Counsel for the new corporation said that his clients are "ready to go on with the expenditure of $5,000,000 to round out the plant at Sault Ste Marie."[76]

Machinery. Agricultural, industrial, office, and household machinery is produced by threescore American-owned plants whose output, as shown in Table V, is over 40 per cent of the whole Canadian production of such equipment.

Some of the American *agricultural equipment* companies have relatively small plants in Canada producing a few specialized articles. For example, the De Laval Company, Ltd., manufactures separators, and The Hart-Emerson Company, Ltd., a subsidiary of the Hart-Carter Company, makes grain-cleaning devices. The others offer a larger line of farm implements, but only a couple have elabo-

75. The Philadelphia interests are represented by 3 out of 9 directorships on the board of Algoma Consolidated, 4 out of 9 on The Lake Superior Corporation, 3 out of 15 on Algoma Steel.

76. *New York Times,* February 13, 1935.

rate Canadian facilities. Some companies, such as the Caterpillar Tractor Company, sell through independent agents. Others, such as Advance Rumely Company and J. I. Case Company, have their own sales offices in various Canadian cities, but do no manufacturing. The Case Company owned, for many years, a manufacturing site at Fort William, Ontario, but never built a plant. The old M. Rumely Company did have a Toronto factory which, in the 1918 peak, employed 700 men, but it is no longer operated. Deere and Company has 4 subsidiaries in Canada. The three in Winnipeg, Regina, and Calgary are sales companies. The fourth, John Deere Manufacturing Company, Ltd., was organized in 1918 to combine the John Deere Plow Company and the Dain Manufacturing Company, Ltd. The plant in Welland, after being closed for a few years, has since been operating on a small scale. The Dain Company and its Welland subsidiary had been acquired in 1911. For some years thereafter, Deere and Company manufactured harvesters in Canada but not in the United States.

The International Harvester Company of Canada, Ltd., was incorporated in 1903. In 1919 it acquired the Canadian factory and the Canadian patents of the Oliver Chilled Plow Company. It now has three plants, one in Chatham, Ontario, producing motor trucks, and two in Hamilton, one a binder twine mill and the other producing a general line of agricultural implements. It imports certain parts and also some lines of machinery for which the demand is small. As the market develops new lines are manufactured in Canada. In the period 1924 to 1929 about 50 per cent of its Canadian sales were of Canadian manufacture, but since 1930 this figure has risen to between 70 and 80 per cent. The binder twine mill was established in 1925 and supplies this company's entire Canadian market, in addition to exporting considerable quantities. The expansion into this line is of some interest, since binder twine has been duty-free in Canada since 1898. The total assets of International Harvester's Canadian company are about $28,000,000 and its volume of business is from 12 to 15 per cent of that of the parent company. It does a substantial export business, chiefly to countries of the British Empire, amounting in normal years to 15 or 20 per cent of its business. In the years 1926 to 1933, the International Harvester Company of

Canada enjoyed about 40 per cent of the total domestic Canadian agricultural implement business. It has to meet the strong competition of Massey-Harris, Ltd., whose Canadian sales are only about half those of International Harvester of Canada, but whose total sales are about 50 per cent greater.[77]

The principal United States agricultural equipment *sales* companies in Canada—those of Deere and Company, J. I. Case and Company, and Minneapolis-Moline Power Implement Company— between 1926 and 1933 accounted for from 11 to 19 per cent of the value of total sales of such equipment in Canada.[78]

Forty or more American companies operate Canadian *industrial machinery* factories. Many familiar names appear in the list: Canadian Hoffman Machinery, Canadian Ingersoll-Rand, Canadian Ironing Machine, Canadian Laundry Machinery, Canadian Pneumatic Tool (subsidiary of Chicago Pneumatic Tool), Detroit Stoker, Grinnell, La France Fire Engine and Foamite, Link Belt, May Oil Burner, Otis-Fensom Elevator, Pyrene, United Shoe Machinery. But of the history and progress of most of them little is known. Some of them are long-established. The Yates-American Machine Company, the Chicago Pneumatic Tool Company, the Link Belt Company, and the Otis Elevator Company, to mention only 4, entered Canada between 1905 and 1914. Although some of the plants, e.g., Otis-Fensom, are relatively large, many have been severely restricted by the small market. In 1921 the United States Hoffman Machinery Corporation, capable of producing 1,500 garment pressing machines in its American plant, established a Toronto branch with a monthly capacity of 50 machines. And in 1918 the Chicago Pneumatic Tool Company was employing 1,640 men in its 4 American factories and only 10 in the Montreal plant.

Nor is there much of special interest in the two dozen plants making office and household machinery.[79] Most of the better known American products are represented: A B C, Thor, Easy,[80] and May-

77. *Royal Commission on Price Spreads (1934–35), Minutes of Proceedings and Evidence* (Ottawa), pp. 3962, 3968, 4022, 4193.

78. *Ibid.*, pp. 4022–4023.

79. Vacuum cleaners are classified under electrical apparatus.

80. Produced by a licensee of the American company, not by a branch plant.

tag washing machines; Singer sewing machines; National cash
registers; mimeographs; Remington, Royal, L. C. Smith, and Co-
rona typewriters; Toledo and Dayton scales, and so on.

Automotive products. The Canadian automobile industry is not
large in relation to the parent industry south of the Border. In
recent years the Canadian plants have turned out between 4 and 5
per cent of the cars and trucks produced in North America. In the
peak year, 1929, Canadian production amounted to 262,625 vehicles, with a wholesale value of $163,497,676,[81] although by 1932
output had sagged to 60,816 cars and trucks. Since over 83 per cent
of the Canadian output of cars, trucks, and parts are produced by
American branch plants, there is the more reason for a closer
examination.

There are now in Canada the following American motor car companies: Chrysler (including Dodge), Ford, General Motors, Graham Paige, Hudson Essex, Hupp, Packard, Studebaker, Pierce
Arrow (sales only), and Willys-Overland. The Durant and Reo
have been produced by the now-bankrupt Dominion Motors, a
Canadian firm.

Four American motor trucks are at least assembled in Canada:
Federal, International, Stewart, and White.[82] Throughout the past
30 years, right up to 1932, American automobile companies have
established Canadian plants. Ford, in 1904, was probably the first.
Buick (jointly with the McLaughlin Motor Car Company, Ltd.) in
1910, and Everett-Metzger-Flanders (later merged with Studebaker) in 1909, were the other early arrivals. Before 1917 Hupp,[83]
Willys-Overland, Chalmers and Dodge had begun at least to assemble cars in Canada.

The Ford Motor Company of Canada, Ltd., was founded by a
Canadian, Gordon MacGregor.[84] Of its initial capitalization of
$125,000, 51 per cent was given to the Ford Motor Company of De-

81. Figures by National Automobile Chamber of Commerce, as quoted in
The World Almanac, 1934, p. 372.

82. The light trucks such as Dodge, Ford, and Chevrolet are also assembled or partially manufactured in Canada.

83. Which later closed its Canadian plant and did not resume production
until 1931.

84. *Financial Post,* May 20, June 3, 1927.

troit in return for all Ford rights and processes in perpetuity in Canada, New Zealand, Australia, India, South Africa, and British Malaya. The output of its factory at East Windsor, Ontario, reached 2,805 in 1911, 15,657 in 1914, 50,173 in 1917, and 100,614 in 1926. That "Model T" peak has never been regained. In 1929, 87,000 "Model A" cars were produced, and in 1933, 26,398 "V8" models. Sales, which amounted to just under $60,000,000 in 1929, were $17,359,085 in 1933. The original capitalization had grown, through reinvestment of earnings, to $10,000,000, of which $7,000,-000 was issued by 1915. In 1929 the company's capital structure was changed to 1,900,000 non-voting "A" shares and 100,000 voting "B" shares. Each holder of old shares received 19 "A" and 1 "B" shares. At that time 100,000 "A" shares—the first public issue —were sold in Canada "to create a larger number of interested stockholders in Canada."[85] Similar efforts were simultaneously made in other countries to recruit local bodies of shareholders for the various Ford subsidiaries abroad. Just what the American interest in the Canadian company was during those years is not a matter of public record. In 1915, when Henry Ford owned 26 per cent, there were 200 shareholders. John and Horace Dodge sold their 510 shares that year to two Detroit investment houses for $1,500 per $100 share.[86] In 1927 the *Financial Post* expressed the opinion[87] that American buying had carried 85 per cent of the shares to the United States, but that no one group controlled the company. After the creation of "A" and "B" shares in 1929 it was stated that Henry Ford owned 51 per cent of the voting shares.[88] Both Henry and Edsel Ford are directors of the company, which had, in 1933, 22,500 shareholders.

Although in recent years the Canadian Ford Company has not been paying dividends and, indeed, had net *operating* losses of $5,206,737 in 1932 and $620,701 in 1933, it has been almost fantastically profitable throughout most of its history. On an initial capitalization of $125,000, only part of which was paid in cash, the

85. See *Poor's Industrial Volume,* 1932, pp. 1469–1470, from which much of the above is taken.
86. *Commercial and Financial Chronicle,* November 27, 1915, p. 1810.
87. May 20, 1927.
88. *Commercial and Financial Chronicle,* March 30, 1929, p. 2098.

would require about 7,000 employees. (The McLaughlin-Buick, Chevrolet, Pontiac, and Oldsmobile are almost completely produced there.) The Walkerville factory was built in 1919 and makes engines for those 4 cars and Chevrolet front axles. At capacity it would employ 2,000 workers. The Regina, Saskatchewan, assembly plant can handle 30,000 Chevrolets and Pontiacs a year. These facilities, plus the materials and parts supplied by other companies in Canada, enable a very high percentage of "Canadian content" to be reached on the more popular cars. Thus, to take the Canadian Chevrolet to pieces and examine its origins: the chassis springs come from companies in Gananoque and Oshawa; the front axle and engine from the Walkerville plant; the third member assembly and differential from the St. Catherines factory; the body and radiator are built completely in the Oshawa plant. Castings, bumpers, glass, wiring, trim, paint, hardware, and wheels are purchased from many companies in Canada.[90]

Output of General Motors of Canada has been roughly parallel to that of Ford. In 1916, 9,915 cars were produced; in 1920, 22,408; in 1928, 75,000. In 1932 General Motors of Canada sold 39 per cent of all passenger cars sold in Canada. The foreign market, as also in the case of Ford, has been important. Evidently, however, there is no definite market allotment made by the parent company, since as many as 65 countries have been served from Oshawa. Overseas shipments began in 1921, and from then till 1925—a period for which exact figures are available—almost half of the Oshawa plant's output was exported. During the last year or so exports have declined relatively, but even in 1932–33 all Buicks for the United Kingdom were shipped from Canada.

The other American motor car companies in Canada can be described in fewer words. The Willys-Overland Company, now no longer a factor of importance in either country, merged its Hamilton plant, in 1916, with the vehicle branch of the Russell Motor Car Company, Ltd., in Toronto. The resulting company, Willys-Over-

90. It is probable that the Ford plant is the most nearly capable of any in Canada of manufacturing a complete car. See, e.g., C. H. Aikman, *The Automobile Industry of Canada*, McGill University Economic Studies, No. 8 (Toronto, 1926), in which it is mentioned that virtually no imported parts go into the Canadian Ford.

land, Ltd., assembles cars for the Canadian and some export markets. Mr. Russell is president, and his company has an interest in Willys-Overland, Ltd., but 72 per cent of the shares are owned by the American company. Durant Motors entered Canada in 1921, and owned, until about 1930, a 58 per cent interest in Durant Motors of Canada, Ltd. The manner in which that subsidiary company changed into independent Dominion Motors, Ltd., and its later collapse is described in Chapter VI.[91] In 1932 Dominion Motors began the assembly and partial manufacture of Reo cars on some sort of license arrangement. A report in 1934 stated that the Reo Motor Car Company would lease a part of the closed Dominion plant through Reo Motor Car Company of Canada, Ltd. The Chrysler Corporation of Canada, Ltd. (and a half dozen sales companies—De Soto, Plymouth, Dodge, and so on) had its beginnings in the Chalmers plant in Walkerville, 1916, leased a year later by Maxwell Motor Company. The other companies which were mentioned at the beginning of this section have various plants, usually in Walkerville and Windsor, Ontario. They are all assembly plants, rather than factories, although some of them, of course, produce more or less of the vehicle. One of those companies reported that in 1932 its car had a Canadian content of 60 per cent. But at the present time only the Ford, the Chevrolet, the Buick—and possibly other General Motors cars—can make that claim.

Quite apart from the motor car and truck companies are the 20 or more American accessory and parts firms which have Canadian plants. Most of these factories, producing motor lamps, shock absorbers, wheels, radiators, piston rings, lubrication systems, springs, and so on, need no special description. Some of them are almost as old as the automobile companies. The McCord Radiator and Manufacturing Company established its Canadian branch before the war, and in 1928 built a new plant with a capacity of 125,000 radiators a year. The Kelsey Wheel Company, Ltd., was organized in 1914. Compared with the parent factories, many of these plants are probably very small. For example, the Perfect Circle Company, which can produce 4,000,000 piston rings a month in its 3 American plants, built a Canadian plant in 1932 with a monthly capacity of 100,000 rings. But many of them occupy positions of prominence in the in-

91. p. 257.

dustry in Canada. The Skinner Company, Ltd., purchased in 1929
by the Houdaille-Hershey Corporation, had, for many years, produced two thirds of the bumpers in Canada.

This whole American-controlled automobile industry is closely
linked to the Canadian tariff. The Ford and McLaughlin-Buick factories were evidently established with relatively little regard for
tariffs, but even in those cases the continuous tariffs since 1907—
never less than 20 per cent, with 25 per cent drawbacks on imports
to be used on cars of 40 or 50 per cent Canadian content, and 99 per
cent drawbacks on cars later exported—have no doubt increased
their independence of imported parts. Few other American automobile companies would have done more than assemble and most of
them not even that except for the tariff.[92]

Miscellaneous iron products. Seventy or more American companies still remain to be at least mentioned. Half a dozen make engines, boilers, or tanks. Here are Johnson outboard motors, Bowser
pumps, Foster Wheeler oil refinery and steam generating equipment, and, probably largest, Canadian Fairbanks, Morse, Ltd. This
30-year-old company, with assets of $4,649,673, provides gas en-
gines, pumps, scales, and so on, and has been moderately profitable.
It handles the Canadian sales of Fairbanks, Morse and Company,
with which it has a close working arrangement. In all probability
the American company has a large financial interest in the Canadian
enterprise. At any rate, 5 of the 9 directors are Americans. Four
American-owned plants make railway rolling stock—notably the
two subsidiaries of the American Locomotive Company. In 1904 it
acquired the Locomotive and Machine Company, Ltd., renamed the
Montreal Locomotive Works, Ltd., which has a 66-acre plant in
Montreal. The other subsidiary, Canadian Steel Tire and Wheel
Company, Ltd., has a plant on a 6-acre site, also in Montreal.

Another dozen companies manufacture heating and ventilating
equipment. Of these makers of stoves, heaters, and so on, two groups
are interesting enough to warrant special description, even though
several of the constituents are in other categories than iron products.
The American Radiator and Standard Sanitary Corporation, making heavy, bulky products, has subsidiaries in Canada, as well as in
other foreign countries.

92. See Aikman, *op. cit.,* and Pound, *op. cit.*

AMERICAN RADIATOR AND STANDARD SANITARY CORPORATION

American Blower Co.	Heating and Plumbing Finance, Ltd., Toronto
Canadian Sirocco Co., Ltd. Plant: Windsor	

Standard Sanitary Manufacturing Co., Ltd. Plant: Toronto	Dominion Radiator and Boiler Co., Ltd. (1923) Murray Radiator Co. of Canada, Ltd. Plants: Brantford, Toronto

Some indication of the importance of these subsidiaries may be gained from the fact that in 1925–26 the Standard Sanitary Manufacturing Company received $1,900,000 in profits accumulated by its Canadian plant in the previous decade. Crane Company likewise has several plants in Canada to produce the plumbing and sanitary goods its subsidiaries sell in that market through 21 branch houses. Both of those American companies began Canadian operations before the war.

CRANE COMPANY

Canadian Potteries, Ltd. Plant: St. Johns, Que.	Port Hope Sanitary Manufacturing Company, Ltd. Plant: Port Hope, Ont.

Crane, Ltd.
Warden King, Ltd.
Patterns and Tools, Ltd.
Plant: Montreal

Nearly 30 American-owned plants manufacture hardware and tools bearing names such as Simonds, Stanley, Disston, Sargent, Yale. The Stanley Works has 3 subsidiaries in Canada, while the Simonds Saw and Steel Company operates a tool plant in Montreal and has a crude abrasives works which supplies the parent company. Two of the later entrants in this group—Sargent and Company and The American Hardware Corporation—purchased (1931) already existing companies in Belleville, Ontario. Finally, there are many, probably over 30, miscellaneous factories producing wire goods, chains, bolts, tin cans, bottle caps, metal furniture, pipe, etc. Probably of most interest among them are the United States Steel Corporation subsidiaries, charted below. When, in 1913, the $20,000,-000 plant of the Canadian Steel Corporation was built at Ojibway,

UNITED STATES STEEL CORPORATION

| Essex Terminal Railway Company (1918) | Canadian Steel Lands, Ltd. |

Canadian Steel Corporation, Ltd. (1913)

| Canadian Bridge Company, Ltd. | Canadian Steel and Wire Company |

Ontario, there was widespread newspaper comment in Canada at this invasion by the giant from the south. Little, however, can be learned of the volume of its operations in the last 20 years, nor of the bridge works at Walkerville, Ontario. Blast furnaces were never put in operation at Ojibway, but a wire mill, galvanized sheet plate and tin plate mill were operated for some years. The tin plate plant has been closed for over a year. They are, at any rate, only 2 of the 136 plants of the parent company. Even older is the Truscon Steel Company of Canada, Ltd., established in 1907, with a plant capacity of 15,000 tons per year. In 1929 the parent company sold part of its holdings—on which no common dividends had been paid since 1914 —and now has only a 30 per cent interest.

Glancing back over these many American-owned plants in the Canadian iron and steel industry, it is apparent that while in all sections of that industry there are individual companies of importance, the greatest aggregate strength lies in the automotive field, which is very largely American, and in machinery manufacturing, where American-owned plants turn out about 40 per cent of the total production.

NON-FERROUS METAL PRODUCTS

In this industry the American-owned companies—about a hundred, employing a capital of almost $84,000,000—produce about

63 per cent of the total output. In the manufacture of electrical apparatus, in which more than half of the companies and the capital are engaged, over 68 per cent of the gross value of products is accounted for by the American plants.

Most of the electrical apparatus factories produce only a few specialized articles. Six or more make batteries; others turn out spark plugs (Champion, Defiance), vacuum cleaners (Hoover, Premier), radio sets and parts (Stewart-Warner, Philco, Sparton, Stromberg-Carlson), meters, railway signals, motors, and a dozen other products. But two—the subsidiaries of Westinghouse Electric and Manufacturing Company and General Electric Company—have much more elaborate facilities.

Canadian General Electric Company, Ltd., was organized in Canada in 1892 largely through the efforts of Mr. (later Senator) Frederick Nicholls. The merger included Edison Electric Company, Edison Electric Light Company, Thomson-Houston International Electric Company, and Toronto Construction and Electric Supply Company. The first three companies were the Canadian subsidiaries of American companies of similar names which at the same time were being merged into the General Electric Company. The capital stock of Canadian General Electric was $2,000,000, of which $1,250,000 was subscribed by the American companies, $250,000 by the Toronto company, and $500,000 raised in Canada by Mr. Nicholls and his friends. Under the original agreement the Toronto company held an option to purchase $450,000 of stock from the American companies, and shortly after organization this option was exercised, giving the Canadian group majority control. Sometime about 1895, General Electric in the United States was financially pressed and Senator Nicholls offered to buy the bulk if not all of the American-owned shares in the Canadian company. This offer was accepted, and thus from 1895 to 1923 the relationship between the Canadian and American companies was purely an affiliation based on agreements covering technical coöperation and exclusive manufacturing arrangements. In 1911 the Canadian company acquired the Canadian Sunbeam Lamp Company, Ltd., and in 1913 Canadian Allis-Chalmers, Ltd., with all Canadian rights for Allis-Chalmers products. By 1933 its $38,434,124 in assets were chiefly invested in a series of plants: general electrical works in Toronto and Peterborough, Ontario; lamp works and architectural bronze and iron plant in Toronto; and the Allis-Chalmers division in Toronto and Montreal. In 1923, after the death of Senator Nicholls, the American company purchased the majority of the common stock of Canadian General Electric for $62.50 cash for each common share, plus one share of new $50, 7 per cent preferred stock. By 1929 over 90 per cent of the stock of the Canadian company had been acquired at a total cash cost—assuming prior holdings by the American company to have been negligible—of about $12,000,000. The directors of the Canadian company explained that this change in ownership was necessary to provide for closer and more effective coöperation than had been obtained under contractual relations. The American company, a little later, stated that it intended "to preserve essentially the Canadian character of [the] company. . . ."[93] From 1897 to 1933 the Canadian General Electric Company, Ltd., paid dividends on its common stock at an average rate of 6.6 per cent.

The Westinghouse Manufacturing Company, Limited, was organized in Canada in 1896 by the Westinghouse Air Brake Company of Pittsburgh to take care of its rapidly expanding air brake business in the Dominion. The original plant, which was a small one employing about two hundred men, was located at Hamilton, Ontario.

In 1903, the Company was reorganized under the name of the Canadian Westinghouse Company, Limited, and additional land was acquired adjacent to the original plant, and a modern electrical factory put up. In the reorganization, the Westinghouse Electric and Manufacturing Company and the Westinghouse Air Brake Company took practically equal shares, each company's holdings representing about one third of the entire capital stock, the remaining one third being held by individual Canadian shareholders. This relationship remains practically undisturbed today, although the Company has grown substantially in both physical size and assets, and at the present is one of the largest industrial manufacturing establishments in Canada. It manufactures at Hamilton practically all of the products of the various Westinghouse interests in the United States and supplies every requirement of the Canadian mar-

93. *Commercial and Financial Chronicle,* November 3, 1923, p. 1996; April 19, 1924, pp. 1907–1908.

ket, and has been a profitable enterprise ever since its inception. It has paid regular dividends of about 7 per cent throughout its existence, as well as bonuses in 21 years—bonuses which were usually 1 or 2 per cent, but which were 25 per cent in 1917 and $30 per share in 1927. The present capital of the Canadian Westinghouse Company is $9,100,000 and its total assets exceed $17,000,000. All of the executive and active officials, with one exception, are Canadian citizens.

The leaders in the electrical field in Canada are Bell Telephone and its manufacturing subsidiary, Northern Electric,[94] Marconi,[95] General Electric, and Westinghouse. In many fields of production these companies pool and exchange patents, and in the radio business they, together with Rogers-Majestic Corporation, have set up a patent holding company, Canadian Radio Patents, Ltd., which controls all the principal patents covering the manufacture of radio receiving sets and issues licenses on a royalty basis to the 15 or 20 radio manufacturers in the Dominion.

The rest of the makers of non-ferrous metal products are an even more miscellaneous group. In the aggregate they produce just less than 50 per cent of the aluminum, brass, copper, lead, tin, zinc, and precious metals products.[96] Of the twoscore companies, half produce brass and copper products. Largest of those plants is probably that of Anaconda-American Brass Company, Ltd.,[97] which first leased and later acquired the mill of Brown's Copper and Brass Rolling Mills, Ltd., near Toronto. Incorporated in 1922, it is the only complete brass works in Canada and supplies from 80 to 90 per cent of the rolled brass in the Dominion. A much older company is Jenkins Brothers, Ltd., organized in 1906 to manufacture high pressure steam valves and given virtually all foreign markets by the parent American company. In 1924, when it offered for sale $500,000 in first mortgage bonds in Canada, the Canadian company had assets of $1,883,366 and had had net earnings in the previous 9 years which averaged $101,481. Another of these American-owned com-

94. See pp. 129 f.   95. See p. 132.
96. It should be recalled that we are here still describing the manufacture and not the mining, smelting, and refining of metals.
97. Owned by the American Brass Company, which is a subsidiary of the Anaconda Copper Mining Company.

panies is the Eugene F. Phillips Electrical Works, Ltd., which, owned by the Associated Telephone and Telegraph Company,[98] is the only factory in Canada producing certain sorts of insulated copper wire. It owns the controlling interest in Canadian Rock-bestos Products, Ltd. There are only 5 American-owned companies producing lead, tin, and zinc products in Canada. One of them, National Lead Company, set up National Lead Company of Canada, Ltd., in 1929, to own its 4 subsidiaries operating factories in Vancouver, Winnipeg, Toronto, Montreal, and St. John. The American-owned plants which work up precious metals are, save for 2 gold refiners and a few jewelry makers, branches of silverware firms—especially Oneida Community, Ltd., and International Silver Company of Canada, Ltd. At least one of the divisions of the latter company was among the pioneer American branch plants which entered Canada in the Seventies.[99]

NON-METALLIC MINERAL PRODUCTS

Thirty-nine American companies turn out about 44 per cent of the Canadian production of asbestos, glass, graphite, carbon, and petroleum products, and so on. One interesting group is the 6 abrasive companies, subsidiaries of such companies as Simonds Saw and Steel, General Abrasives, Norton, and Carborundum. These companies, organized in the cheap-power Niagara area in Ontario, manufacture crude abrasives which are shipped to the parent factories in the United States for completion. The Norton furnace at Chippewa was established before the war. Eight or 10 plants make fire brick, tile, and such building products. And a miscellaneous dozen produce bath tubs and such wares, e.g., the Standard Sanitary Manufacturing Company, Ltd., mentioned previously;[100] optical goods; porcelain insulators; etc. Here may be mentioned the plant of the Canadian Libbey-Owens Sheet Glass Company, Ltd., opened at large expense in 1921, and closed permanently 18 months later because of Belgian competition.

98. See pp. 130–131.
99. Aluminium, Ltd.'s output of utensils, etc., should be considered in this group, but since the bulk of its activities are classified as mining and smelting, it is postponed to a later section. See pp. 102 ff.
100. See p. 69.

Among the non-metallic mineral companies are two groups which divide their activities between mining and manufacturing. The asbestos companies are so much more largely mining than manufacturing concerns that any description of them will be postponed to the later section devoted to mining.[101] The American petroleum companies in Canada, although they do produce some domestic crude oil, are chiefly oil refiners and merchants and an account of their participation in the development of Canadian oil fields is likewise postponed to the mining section of this chapter. But their other activities are better described here.[102]

The petroleum manufacturing industry is eleventh in importance in Canada. It consists of the refining and distribution of petroleum products made from crude oil, 95 per cent of which is imported— approximately three fourths from the United States and one fourth from Latin America (Peru, Colombia, Venezuela, Trinidad, Dutch West Indies, Mexico) and Russia. The imports are supplied largely by companies with which the Canadian concerns are closely affiliated. The Canadian industry has since the early Eighties been dominated by Imperial Oil, Ltd., subsidiary of the Standard Oil Company of New Jersey. The largest independent Canadian companies are British American Oil Company, Ltd., and McColl-Frontenac Oil Company, Ltd. The other American-owned companies are Canadian Oil Companies, Ltd., Sun Oil Company of Canada, Ltd., Cities Service Oil Company, Ltd., Union Oil Company of Canada, Ltd., White Star Refining Company, and Quaker State Oil Refining Company of Canada, Ltd. Of the latter 5 companies only the first has a refinery; the others are merchandising concerns. For many years Imperial Oil operated the only important refineries in Canada. Now however, British American, McColl-Frontenac, Shell, and Canadian Oil have their own refineries, although some of them may, in regions far from the refinery, buy from Imperial. The other American-owned companies either import from their parent companies or buy from Imperial; the other independent Canadian companies are largely, but not entirely, supplied by Imperial. The increase of independent refineries has decreased Imperial's share of Canadian

101. See p. 109.

102. As far as possible the statistics on output and investment have been calculated on the basis of the same division of function.

gasoline sales to about 55 per cent,[103] from almost 80 per cent at the end of the war. The other American companies sell about 11 per cent of the gasoline, but to the extent—unascertained—that it has been bought wholesale from Imperial it is included in Imperial's 55 per cent. Probably, making a rough adjustment, about 60 per cent of the gasoline in Canada is supplied, but not necessarily sold directly to the motorist, by the branches of American companies.

The briefer history of the lesser American companies can be quickly told. What early American oil marketing may have taken place, excepting Imperial, it is difficult to ascertain. Canadian Oil Companies, Ltd., was founded in 1908 and had, in 1914, a refinery in Marietta, Ohio. The National Refining Company had an interest in it by then and may have participated in its organization. By 1934 its assets were $10,441,370, consisting chiefly of its refinery at Petrolia, Ontario, and its some 200 filling stations. The other companies confine their activities to marketing, partly through their own stations but more largely through independent "outlets." The long life of Imperial Oil, Ltd., is much more complicated. It began in 1880, when the Standard Oil Company of New Jersey incorporated the Imperial Oil Company, Ltd., to which, in the next 15 years, it assigned 3 other oil companies in eastern Canada. Imperial was already operating oil wells in the first Canadian field in the region around Petrolia, and before 1900 had built a refinery at Sarnia, Ontario. The parent company owned about 60 per cent of the stock in this growing enterprise, which by the beginning of this century almost completely controlled the market in eastern Canada.[104] For the first 20 years of the century Imperial Oil, Ltd. (which dropped the "Company" in 1919) expanded quietly, absorbing some small companies, and building its coast-to-coast system, unmatched by any competitor.

In 1914 the International Petroleum Company, Ltd., was incorporated,[105] and acquired oil lands in South America. Ten years later

103. Its direct sales are about 33 per cent; the balance is sold to independent distributors.

104. *Select Standing Committee of Banking and Commerce*, Minutes, March 8, 1932 (Ottawa), p. 17; *Imperial Oil Review*, September–October, 1933.

105. Presumably by Standard Oil, but that is not certain. See *Poor's Industrial Volume*, 1920, p. 3000.

it was taken over by Imperial Oil, Ltd., in which by then Standard Oil had a 75 per cent interest.[106] Further year-by-year account is unnecessary. In 1934 Standard Oil in Canada was organized as shown on page 79.

The properties of Imperial Oil are clearly in three groups. One, on the left of the chart, consists of companies drilling for and pumping crude oil in the Canadian fields. They will be described later. The companies on the right carry on the business of pipe-line transportation and oil refining in Canada. The foreign oil reserves and facilities, owned by International Petroleum, complete the organization. The Sarnia refinery has since 1913 been connected by Imperial's own pipe line with the American pipe-line system at Cygnet, Ohio. By its 24 (180,405 d.w.t.) tankers Imperial is linked with International's Peruvian-Colombian wells, which in 1933 produced about 25,000,000 barrels. The refineries in Peru and Colombia have a capacity of over 20,000 barrels a day, and ship not only to Canada but to South American and European markets. The Canadian refineries have a daily capacity of about 100,000 barrels, and produce approximately 10 per cent of Standard of New Jersey's total output, domestic and foreign. And, to repeat, Imperial supplies about 55 per cent of the gasoline sold in Canada. In 1930 it handled 75 per cent of the fuel oil and 85 per cent of all lubricating oil business in the Dominion.[107]

Imperial Oil, Ltd., is probably the most highly developed of all the Standard Oil Companies outside the United States. A $270,-000,000 company, it is virtually self-contained, with its own oil reserves, its own tankers, tank cars, refineries, and service stations and pipe-line connection with friendly American sources. In the 11 years following 1913 it paid common dividends averaging 12 per cent on an authorized capital which during that period increased from $10,-000,000 to $50,000,000. The shares were converted to no-par in 1925 and in the next 7 years dividends averaged about 95 cents.[108]

106. See *Historical Summaries of Consolidations in Canadian Industries,* from which most of this chronological account can be verified. Imperial Oil owns 58 per cent of the common and almost all of the preferred in "International Pete," which is one of the most actively traded stocks on Toronto and Montreal exchanges.

107. *Commercial and Financial Chronicle,* June 14, 1930, p. 4252.

108. On shares which between 1917 and 1930 had been quartered three times.

STANDARD OIL COMPANY OF NEW JERSEY

Pan-American Foreign Corp.

Lago Petroleum Corp.

Lago Oil and Transport Co., Ltd. (Canada)

Lago Shipping Co., Ltd. (England)

Colonial Beacon Oil Co.

Beacon Transportation Co. of Canada, Ltd.

Gilbert and Barker Mfg. Co.

Gilbert and Barker Mfg. Co., Ltd. (service station equipment)

Imperial Oil, Ltd., 1880 (75%) 670 filling stations, 1900 marketing stations, 3000 tank cars, etc.

CANADIAN PRODUCING COMPANIES

Northwest Company, Ltd., 1927 (100%)
Foothills Oil and Gas Co., Ltd., 1928 (85%)
Southwest Petroleum Co., Ltd., 1930 (64%)
Royalite Oil Co., Ltd., 1921 (79%)
Dalhousie Oil Co., Ltd., 1926 (51%)
Southern Alberta Oils, Ltd., 1928 (100%)
Southern Alberta Refineries, Ltd., 1928
Maryland Oil Co., Ltd., 1930
Southern Lowery Oils, Ltd., 1932
Sterling Pacific Oil Co., Ltd., 1934
Benton Oils, Ltd.
Drilling agreements with 9 independent companies.
And other affiliates.

Imperial Oil Refineries, Ltd., 1927 (100%) 7 refineries.

Imperial Pipe Line Co., Ltd., 1927 (100%) pipe line to United States.

International Petroleum Co., Ltd., 1914, 1920 (58% common, 95% preferred)
Peru, Ecuador, wells, refinery, can factory.

Tropical Oil Co., Ltd., 1916 (100%)
Colombia, wells, refinery, can factory.
Andean National Corp., pipe line.

The New Jersey Company still owns the controlling interest; the remaining shares are widely traded. In 1927, when Standard Oil held 73 per cent of the common stock, it sold 84,876 shares—1.3 per cent of the total—to the Sun Life Assurance Company of Canada at $55 "in pursuance of the Company's policy to have strong Canadian institutions interested in the Company's business."[109]

CHEMICAL PRODUCTS

These factories are extremely difficult to describe summarily. There are 153 American-owned companies in the industry, classified under 14 census sub-heads. Most of them are small plants. The average capital employed is $356,528 as compared with $1,035,146 for all American plants in Canada. In the aggregate they produce slightly over 41 per cent of the chemical goods in Canada.

Nearly 90 of these factories manufacture drugs, proprietary preparations, cosmetics, soaps and washing compounds. They account for 55.92 per cent of Canadian output of such articles, but the capital employed, on the average, is only $233,370. Especially in the last 5 years many American drug and cosmetic companies have rented or purchased small factories or several thousand square feet of floor space in order to compound their products inside the Canadian tariff wall. Very often such ventures involve an investment of no more than $50,000. The list of companies and of products is a long one. Most of the American drug houses are represented: Bauer and Black, Bristol-Myers, Johnson and Johnson, Lambert, Merck, Parke-Davis, Sterling, and United Products. Many well-advertised proprietary articles are made in Canadian branch plants. Here are such names as Bromo-Seltzer, Tanlac, Vaseline, Vicks, Ex-Lax, Listerine, Lavoris, Pepsodent, Mentholatum, Lydia E. Pinkham, Bayer, Castoria. Most elaborate of these organizations is that of the United Drug-Sterling Products group, until recently controlled by Drug, Incorporated. Since before the war those affiliated American companies have owned drug stores,[110] factories and sales companies in Canada, as shown in the following chart.

Those drug and pharmaceutical firms compose one of the largest groups of American-owned companies in Canada—in number, not

109. *Commercial and Financial Chronicle,* October 1, 1927, p. 1852.
110. See pp. 155 ff.

SHAREHOLDERS OF FORMER DRUG, INCORPORATED

United Drug Company

United Drug Co., Ltd.,
 factory, Toronto

Louis K. Liggett, Ltd.,
 drug stores

Life Savers Corp.

Life Savers, Ltd., | Beech-Nut Co. of
Prescott, Ont. | Canada, Ltd.
 | Hamilton, Ont.

Life Savers and Beech Nut
Sales Co., Ltd.

Vick Chemical, Inc.   Bristol-Myers, Inc.

Canadian branch   Bristol-Myers, Ltd., Montreal

Sterling Products, Inc.

Household Prod- | General Drug | Antidolor Mfg. | Chas. H. Phillips
ucts, Inc. | Co. | Co. | Chem. Co.

Scott and | Canadian branch | Canadian branch | Canadian branch
Turner, Ltd. | | |
(Eng.)

Scott and
Turner, Ltd.

Centaur Com- | Three in One | Wells Richard- | The Bayer
pany | Oil Co. | son Co. | Company

Centaur Co., | Canadian branch | Wells Richard- | The Bayer Co.,
Ltd., Windsor, | | son Co., Ltd., | Ltd., Windsor,
Ont. | | Windsor, Ont. | Ont.

Sterling Products, Ltd.,
Windsor, Ont.

Cook Laboratories, Inc.

Cook Laboratories of Canada,
Ltd., Windsor, Ont.

in importance. The makers of toilet preparations have not been as
assiduous in breeding Canadian offspring: only half as many have
Canadian plants. But here, also, the advertisements reproduce themselves, as American enterprise helps to beautify Canadians through

the services of Elizabeth Arden, Harriet Hubbard Ayer, Helena
Rubenstein, California Perfume, Hinds, Hopper Kissproof, Hud-
nut, Maison Blanche, Mennen, Noxema, Parfumerie Melba, and
Pompeian. The list is incomplete, but some are less famous. And, to
keep Canadians and their belongings clean, we have Colgate-Palm-
olive-Peet, Procter and Gamble, Andrew Jergens, J. B. Williams,
B. T. Babbitt, Gold Dust, Annette's, and half a dozen other makers
of soap and washing powders. Palmolive, Colgate, and Procter and
Gamble are not newcomers in Canada. Gold Dust, with a soap plant
in Montreal, a shoe polish factory in Hamilton, and a cereal plant in
Ayr, Ontario, has in both countries had the active direction of G. K.
Morrow, a Canadian.

The important American affiliates in the Canadian chemical industry produce industrial chemicals, paint and varnish, ink, dyes,
and so on, although their share—31.21 per cent—in the total Canadian output of those products is not as large as was the case in the
articles we have just discussed. But the individual plants are, on the
average, more than twice as large as those of the drug and cosmetic
companies. Chief of these companies are the producers of industrial
chemicals and gases, and paints and varnish.

While the Du Pont interests in Canada overshadow the other
American-owned industrial chemical plants, several of the latter are
large. For example, Union Carbide and Carbon Corporation, opera-

UNION CARBIDE AND CARBON CORPORATION

Electro-Metallurgical Co.		National Carbon Co.	
Electro-Metallurgical Co. of Canada, Ltd., Welland. (ferro-silicon and carbon electrodes)		Canadian National Carbon Co., Ltd., Toronto.	
Electric Furnace Products, Ltd. (ferro-manganese)	Union Carbide Co. of Canada, Ltd., Welland. (calcium carbide)	Dominion Oxygen Co., Ltd. (oxygen plants, Toronto, Montreal, acetylene plants, Merriton, Shawinigan, Winnipeg)	Prest-O-Lite Co. of Canada, Ltd., Toronto. (dissolved acetylene)

tor of 168 plants on this continent and in Norway, has subsidiaries which overlap this and several other of the classifications which have been used. Its Canadian organization is charted above. Some of those plants are 20 to 30 years old. In 1930 the Liquid Carbonic Corporation acquired, through an exchange of shares, a 92 per cent interest in Liquid Carbonic Canadian Corporation, Ltd. (then Canadian Carbonate, Ltd.). Now, of its 31 carbonic gas plants 7 are in Canada.

Several American companies have owned Canadian explosives plants. Aetna Explosives Company, in receivership long ago, built a powder plant in Drummondsville in 1915 at a cost of almost $3,-000,000. But now, except for the small plant of North Star Explosives Company, Ltd., most of the others have beeen merged in Canadian Industries, Ltd. The first unit of what is now Canadian Industries, Ltd., was the Hamilton Powder Company, formed in 1862. In 1876 this company and the Windsor Powder Mill were acquired by the American Powder Trust. Later Nobel Explosives Company, Ltd., of England acquired an interest in the Hamilton company. It is not clear how early the E. I. du Pont de Nemours and Company built a powder plant in Canada, but in 1910 the Du Pont Company and Nobel Explosives Company formed Canadian Explosives, Ltd., to acquire the 4 or 5 Canadian explosives companies in which they were interested.[111] During the war Canadian Explosives, Ltd., was tremendously successful in the manufacture of gun cotton, cordite, TNT, etc. But, like its two parent companies, it was faced with the need of either retrenching to the peace-time proportions of the explosives market or finding other peace-time outlets for its energies. And like its parent companies it decided to branch out. In the 9 years following 1919, Canadian Explosives, Ltd., always the largest explosives producer in Canada, became the largest producer of industrial chemicals. Changing its name to Canadian Industries, Ltd., in 1927, it acquired, during those years, at least 10 companies, sev-

111. For that and other information on Canadian Industries, Ltd., see *Historical Summaries of Consolidations in Canadian Industries; Financial Post*, March 15, 1929, June 6, 1929, May 15, 1930; *Poor's Industrial Volume*, 1932, 1934; *Commercial and Financial Chronicle*, February 8, 1913, p. 422, July 25, 1931, p. 646, July 18, 1931; *Monetary Times*, January 19, 1877.

eral of which (Grasselli, and Giant) had been American-owned. In most cases it dissolved them and operated their properties as divisions. By 1933 its assets were $49,000,000. It owns 19 plants in 8 divisions: explosives, ammunition, paint and varnish, fabrikoid, pyralin, salt, heavy chemicals, and fertilizer. Using familiar explosives raw materials, it first, about 1920, began to produce "Duco" paints, fabrikoid, and nitrocellulose plastics. It then bought the Canadian Salt Company and the Grasselli Chemical Company, which gave it a commanding position in the salt industry, important salt by-products, and—through Grasselli—a plant and a selling organization to handle its heavy chemical department. Its niter-cake plant at Copper Cliff supplies International Nickel,[112] and from the fumes of that company's smelter it manufactures sulphuric acid. More details could be added, but those are sufficient to reveal the close post-war parallel in the development of Canadian Industries, Ltd., Du Pont, and Imperial Chemical Industries, Ltd. (post-war outgrowth of Nobel Explosives). That parallelism was most recently evidenced by the building of a $1,500,000 plant by the Canadian company in 1931 to produce cellophane, latest Du Pont "headline" product.

It is difficult to ascertain where the controlling shares in Canadian Industries, Ltd., are. The Du Pont Company and Imperial Chemical Industries combined undoubtedly hold the majority shares, but it is also probable that their separate interests are minority interests. It is noteworthy that the Du Pont interest in General Motors Corporation finds its counterpart in a block of General Motors shares in Canadian Industries' treasury. In 1928 Canadian Industries, Ltd., sold part of its General Motors stock for $10,415,152, which provided funds for its expansion during that year. How it happened to acquire the motor stock is uncertain. In 1922 Du Pont-Nobel Company was organized in Canada—owned 51 per cent-49 per cent by the E. I. du Pont de Nemours and Company and Nobel Explosives Company, Ltd., of England—to hold 89,000 shares of Canadian Explosives common and 400,000 shares of General Motors which Canadian Explosives, Ltd., had previously held for the joint account of the American and English companies. A year later the holding company was dissolved and Du Pont Company held its

112. See pp. 95 ff.

share in the assets directly.[113] Why that maneuvering went on and whether some of those General Motors shares found their way back into the treasury of the Canadian company, or whether it bought its shares in the open market, are matters for speculation.

The American-owned paint and varnish companies can be more briefly treated. Unquestionably largest among them, and the largest paint company in Canada, is the Sherwin-Williams Company of Canada, Ltd. The others—about 10 in number—are chiefly single branch plants owned by such companies as Pratt and Lambert, and Glidden. Some of them are recently created, but others have produced in Canada for years. The Glidden Company, Ltd., for example, which "does a large Canadian business,"[114] was organized in 1909 and began to manufacture about 1912.

The Sherwin-Williams Company entered Canada in 1887. Ten years later the Canadian branch was merged with Walter H. Cottingham Company, Ltd., which had a plant in Montreal. Mr. Cottingham then or sometime later became president. When, in 1911, Sherwin-Williams Company of Canada, Ltd., was incorporated to take over the Sherwin-Williams business in Canada, Lewis Berger and Sons, Ltd. (an English company, which had been associated with the American company since 1905), and Canada Paint Company, Ltd. (an 1893 consolidation of three large works), the new company was certainly the largest in the industry. What financial interest the American company had had in it up to this time is not a matter of public record, but apparently it held only about 10 per cent of the shares of the new 1911 company. In 1911 $300,000 of 7 per cent preferred stock of the Canadian company, with a 20 per cent bonus in common, was offered in Canada, and the next year a New York house underwrote $1,200,000 of its first and refunding 6 per cent bonds. During the years that followed—up to 1928—four other companies were acquired[115] and the English company was sold, save for a minority interest.

During these years the company, although using the name and

113. *Commercial and Financial Chronicle,* March 11, 1922, p. 1956; February 17, 1923, p. 715.

114. *Poor's Industrial Volume,* 1932, p. 308.

115. Martin Senour, International Varnish, Carter White Lead, and Winnipeg Paint and Glass.

formulae of its American associate, was definitely Canadian-controlled. Evidently about 50 per cent of the shares were owned by W. H. Cottingham, and possibly 40 per cent were held by the public, presumably chiefly Canadians. After the death of Mr. Cottingham in 1930, however, his shares were offered for sale. After rumors of possible acquisition by Canadian Industries, Ltd. (already producing "Duco" paints and varnishes), it was finally made known that the Sherwin-Williams Company of America had purchased them,[116] in that way gaining a 60 per cent interest. The president of the American company became president of the Canadian concern after having been on its board since its formation in 1911. It is a case not unlike that of Canadian General Electric, in which, after years of minority ownership, the American company decided to purchase a controlling interest. The *Financial Post* remarked that possibly Sherwin-Williams Company was unwilling to let the 20,000 formulae in the files of the $14,000,000 Canadian company pass into competitive hands.

The other American-owned chemical companies in Canada can be dismissed with a bare mention. Several make disinfectants and insecticides. Three, in addition to Canadian Industries, Ltd., manufacture fertilizer. One of these, curiously, was established chiefly to import crude (duty free) materials and export finished fertilizer to Maine which could be reached more easily from Quebec than from the parent factory on the Middle Atlantic coast. Six or eight produce inks, dyes and colors; another dozen make adhesives, flavoring extracts and polishes. In the aggregate, to repeat, the whole 153-odd produce about 41 per cent of Canada's chemical goods.

MISCELLANEOUS PRODUCTS

This brings the story of American manufacturing in Canada to the "miscellaneous" category seemingly inevitable in any classification. Here are twoscore factories producing about 40 per cent of the brooms, brushes, refrigerators, buttons, fountain pens, aircraft, scientific equipment, and so on—40 per cent, that is, in the aggregate. Of individual products the percentage may be more or less. Many of the names are well-known: Fuller Brush, Rubberset, Kel-

116. *Poor's Industrial Volume,* 1932, p. 133; the *Financial Post,* May 14, June 18, December 5, 1931.

vinator, Parker, Sheaffer, Wahl and Waterman pens, Bissell Carpet Sweeper, Victor Talking Machine, and so on. But most of them are private companies whose operations are not publicly recorded. There is Canadian Kodak Company, Ltd., for instance, which, wholly owned by the Eastman Kodak Company, has a dominant position in the camera and photographic supplies industry. Yet its 20 or more years of development are not detailed in published accounts.

Five American companies have, in recent years, built aircraft assembly plants or factories in Canada. One, Fairchild Aircraft, Ltd., was organized in 1929 jointly by Canadians and Americans. Before then Fairchild planes had been produced under license by Vickers, Ltd. The next year Consolidated Aircraft Corporation associated with Canadian capital in the incorporation of Fleet Aircraft of Canada, Ltd., at Fort Erie, Ontario. A few years earlier the Boeing and the Pratt and Whitney companies—both controlled by United Aircraft and Transport Corporation—formed Canadian subsidiaries which, from plants in Vancouver and Montreal, supply Canada and some Empire markets. As long ago as 1916 the Curtiss Aeroplane and Motor Company had a Toronto plant. It may not have been operated continuously since then, but in 1928 the American company acquired a 51 per cent interest in Curtiss-Reid Aircraft Company, Ltd., now, apparently, known as Montreal Aircraft Industries, Ltd.

MINING AND SMELTING

ANOTHER volume in this Series will be devoted to the Canadian mining industry.[117] Consequently such matters as Canadian-American interchange of capital and mining methods, the early history of American prospecting and mining in Canada, and so on, cannot be repeated here. But there must be included in this chapter at least a glimpse of Canadian mines financed by American capital, and some account of their history and operations. Our records include 49 companies, employing a capital of $236,598,656. Collectively they produce 38.71 per cent of the minerals in Canada, including gold, silver, nickel, copper, aluminum, lead, zinc, coal, asbestos, gypsum, and petroleum. But, as reference to the table at the beginning of the

117. See forthcoming volume by E. S. Moore.

chapter will show, the Canadian and other non-American interest in them is 30 per cent.

Many of these companies have United States executive offices, testifying to the American investment and participation in direction. Some, as will be illustrated, are the offspring of American mining and smelting companies. Others supply raw materials to the factories of American parent companies and their Canadian branches. But the majority of them do not have parent companies. They are, rather, independent mining ventures in which there is sizeable American ownership. Most of them are small affairs, with assets running from a few hundred thousand to a million dollars. But there are among them great and famous mines developed only after heavy cost. Outstanding, of course, is the International Nickel Company of Canada, Ltd., of which much will be said later.[118] Although much of its almost $200,000,000 assets are in the form of smelters, refineries and rolling mills in Canada and abroad, a good share of them is accounted for by the huge Frood and the lesser mines. Eleven other important companies,[119] most of which appear in the following pages, had assets, in 1933, totaling $122,970,246. The assets of the smallest were $2,299,150 and of the largest, $33,501,897.

Most of these companies were incorporated in the years 1910 to 1918, but most of them also acquired then-existing mining ventures. To trace back each of those predecessor mines to find out whether it, too, had American antecedents is a task which has been left to the volume on the mining industry just mentioned. In many cases American prospectors and American mining promoters and engineers would be found even at the roots of the big companies now known to have American affiliations. As explained later, the distant beginning of the present International Nickel Company is found in the purchase of a mine in Quebec in 1877 by W. E. C. Eustis of Boston, and of a copper claim in the new Sudbury field in 1885 by Samuel J. Ritchie of Cleveland.

Some indication has been given in Chapter I of American interest

118. See pp. 95 ff.
119. Premier Gold, Crow's Nest Pass Coal, Dome, Kerr Lake, Granby, Hudson Bay, Noranda, Teck-Hughes, Wright-Hargreaves, Britannia, and Nipissing.

in Canadian mines in the early days. Field gives some illuminating examples of American activity in Canadian mines in the decade preceding the war.[120] San Francisco interests purchased controlling interest in 21,000 acres of timber and coal on Graham Island for $1,000,000. In a further influx into the Kootenay district of British Columbia, Minneapolis and Spokane men opened coal mines on Mc-Gillivray Creek, Crow's Nest Pass; New York people acquired the Highland-Buckeye-Highland-United group near Ainsworth, British Columbia, and the Fife mines; Duluth interests bought the Queen mine; and Spokane capitalists purchased the Lucky Jim. St. Paul interests had bought coal and iron deposits near Cowley, Alberta, and planned to build a railroad from Calgary, Alberta to Butte, Montana—a project which was evidently still-born. Duluth money purchased a half-interest in the Durham Collieries (6,000 acres) north of Lethbridge, Alberta. Field estimated that $61,000,000 of American capital had gone into British Columbia mines, or about half the total mining capital in the province. Among the important undertakings backed by American money he includes the Crow's Nest Pass Coal Company, the British Columbia Copper Company, the Dominion Copper Company, the Britannia (owned by the Howe Sound Company), the Marble Bay mines, the investments of James Cronin and F. A. Heinze (whom he later describes as the Montana copper king) on the Bulkeley, and the Guggenheim interest in Atlin-Ruffner.

In the Northern Ontario mining boom of 1904 to 1914 American capital played an important part. Of the 15 largest dividend-paying mines in the Cobalt field in the period 1904–10, 5 were clearly "American" companies—Nipissing, Kerr Lake, Buffalo, Timiskaming Mining, and Cobalt Central. The other 10 were definitely Canadian in organization and control.[121] The 5 American companies accounted for nearly half the dividends paid, due chiefly to the extraordinary richness of the Nipissing properties, which provided in these six years 30 per cent of all dividends paid. The Cobalt field, however, provided the bases for several Canadian fortunes that were

120. *Op. cit.* (1914 ed.), pp. 53–54; 59–60.
121. Compiled from the Annual Reports of the Ontario Bureau of Mines, 1904–11. Two of the "American" companies had a few Canadian directors and two "Canadian" companies had three American directors.

in large measure reinvested in the Porcupine gold field which began opening up in 1910. Timmins, Dunlap, Leonard, Trethewey played leading rôles in the Cobalt development and were in the Porcupine field from the beginning. American capital, though present in the early days of Porcupine, was on the whole overshadowed by Canadian and British interests in that field. It is not our task, however, to trace this history but rather to examine the presently existing relationships, and to that we now turn.

GOLD AND COPPER

Almost 40 per cent of the gold and copper-gold production in Canada is mined by American controlled or affiliated companies. It is very difficult to discover, in many cases, what the nature of the American interest is. Consequently the statistics may include some companies in which, although in a majority, the American shareholders are so scattered that they exercise no control, and never intended to exercise control. There has been a veritable wave of such buying of mining shares by Americans during 1933 and 1934. Such firms should, if known, be removed from our list of "American companies in Canada" and the American share ownership regarded merely as a "portfolio" investment. We have been careful in using as illustrative cases in the text only those mining companies in which the interested Americans have seemingly occupied an actively entrepreneurial position. In at least 7 of the important Canadian gold and copper-gold companies there is active American participation in management. The largest is the Hudson Bay Mining and Smelting Company, Ltd., a large producer of copper and zinc and of some precious metals. In 1915 six Canadian prospectors stumbled on a sulphide ore deposit in the Flin Flon district of northern Manitoba.[122] John E. Hammell, who had grubstaked them, undertook to promote the claim, which was in the wilderness, 87 miles from the nearest railroad. About half a million dollars were sunk in the Flin Flon claim in the next five or six years with small results. In the early 1920's Hammell interested Cornelius Vanderbilt Whitney, and through him his father, Harry Payne Whitney. In 1927 the Hudson Bay Mining and Smelting Company was organized with the Flin

122. *Time,* July 29, 1935, p. 47.

Flon claim and $17,500,000 in cash. Cornelius Whitney is chairman of the board.[123] The Canadian National Railroad built an extension to Flin Flon which made possible the development of the mine. Hudson Bay Mining and Smelting's subsidiary, Churchill River Power Company, Ltd., built a 44,550 horse-power power plant on the Churchill River, 59 miles from the mine. By 1930 Flin Flon had a population of 5,000, the mine was opened, and another $5,000,000 was raised by a bond issue floated in New York. Unprecedented low prices for copper, silver, and zinc from 1930 to 1933 kept Hudson Bay Mining and Smelting in difficulties. But higher prices since 1933 have turned losses to profits. In 1934 the company produced 99,000 ounces of gold, 1,300,000 ounces of silver, 37,000,000 pounds of copper, and 49,000,000 pounds of zinc. In July, 1935, the company paid off the last of the 1930 bond issue and declared its first dividend.

In British Columbia the chief copper deposits are near Anyox, at Britannia Beach, and at Copper Mountain. Probably the largest American-controlled mine is the Howe Sound Company's at Britannia Beach. At Anyox is the Granby Consolidated Mining, Smelting and Power Company, Ltd., the deposits of which are approaching depletion. The Howe Sound Company organized the Britannia Mining and Smelting Company in 1908 to work 25,517 acres of claims. Its mill, built in 1922, can handle 7,000 tons of ore a day but in 1933 was operating at only 20 per cent capacity. It owns the Torbrit Mining Company, Ltd. The Granby Consolidated is a much larger company, organized in 1901 to acquire for $12,000,000 properties known as the "Phoenix Mine," which were worked until exhausted in 1919. In 1910 it acquired the Hidden Creek Copper Company in the Cassiar District of British Columbia, and it is that property, with the town, concentrator, blast furnaces (2,500 tons daily capacity), converters, and so on, that is responsible for the bulk of the company's output, which can reach 60,000,000 pounds of copper a year, requiring 2,000 employees. In 1930 it closed the Allenby plant, acquired 8 years before. It also has an interest in the important Crow's

123. At his death in October, 1930, Harry Payne Whitney owned 30 per cent both of the bonds and the common stock. The common which he held, valued at $3,707,500 in 1930, had appreciated to $10,381,000 by 1934. *New York Times,* July 20, 1934.

Nest Pass Coal Company, Ltd., described later.[124] Granby Consolidated has a board of directors on which Americans are heavily in the majority, and its annual meetings are held at the New York office. Charles Hayden and J. R. Dillon, 2 of the 6 American directors, are members of the banking firm of Hayden, Stone and Company. The other four are evidently not associated with any other companies. Granby has been moderately profitable. Its dividends, to be sure, have averaged only 3.2 per cent during most of its existence and none have been paid since February, 1932. But, with millions of shares outstanding, the actual cash payments have been large. In the 5 years 1927–31, for example, dividends totaled $7,967,367, although net income available for dividends during those years was only $2,797,351.

Those British Columbia mines produce some gold, but are essentially copper mines. Probably largest of the gold mines under American control in that Province is the Premier Gold Mining Company, Ltd. The Premier or Bush mine, near Alaska, 14 miles from Stewart, was located in 1910. Whether the discoverer was an American, and whether in the first 10 years of its history any Americans were associated with it, we do not know. But in 1919 the American Smelting and Refining Company purchased an interest in order to insure to its smelters the refining of the ore from that mine.[125] The mine has been managed by the American company since 1919. The Premier Mine has been a good producer. On a capital of 5,000,000 $1 shares, it made dividends and capital distributions of about $16,512,000 in cash between 1921 and 1932.[126] In 1933, however, it was announced

124. See p. 111.

125. There seems to be some disagreement concerning the size of that interest. Early in 1921 it was reported (*Commercial and Financial Chronicle,* January 15, 1921, p. 254) that the American company bought 12½ per cent of the shares and that the Guggenheims (directors of the American company) bought an equal share. *Moody's Manual of Investments, Industrial Securities,* 1934, in its account of American Smelting and Refining Company, states that it owns 12½ per cent of Premier shares. But in the account of Premier it is stated that 52 per cent of the shares are owned by the American company. *Historical Summaries of Consolidations in Canadian Industries* cites Premier as controlled by the American company.

126. Distributions for 1928–32 were approximated and may be, at most, 10 per cent too high.

that the mine was nearing exhaustion. Preparing for that eventuality the company had been acquiring other claims. Chief of those are the Tough-Oakes-Burnside gold properties in the Kirkland Lake, Ontario, field. Those claims, staked out in 1912, had been acquired by English interests in 1916 and had reverted to the bondholders (also probably English) in 1928. Premier had formed the Toburn Gold Mines Company, Ltd., to work the mines. Among the assets of Premier is a 38 per cent interest in B. C. Silver Mines, Ltd., an adjoining property. The most of the remaining shares are—or at least were in 1928—held indirectly by the Selukwe Gold Mining and Finance Company, of England. During 1927 and 1928 there was much jockeying, not altogether harmonious, between the American and English groups to reach an agreement for the joint working of the mine.[127]

Dome Mines, Ltd., is another big Canadian mining corporation with a majority of Americans on its board. The 6 American directors (including two partners of J. S. Bache and Company of New York, bankers), not linked with any of the great American mining corporations,[128] are scattered in New York, Rochester, Buffalo, and Detroit. The executive and financial departments are in New York, and Jules S. Bache is president and a large shareholder. There are, however, over 5,000 shareholders. The mine is in the Porcupine field, Ontario. In its 24 years' existence the Dome Mines, Ltd., has long since repaid the investment. Save for 1918 and 1919, it has always paid dividends; disbursements on its 953,334 shares—changed to no-par from a former $10—have exceeded $10,000,000 since 1925. The company's mill was destroyed by fire in October, 1929, and the resulting delays and expenses reduced 1930 earnings to 9 cents a share. Omitting that year, however, the earnings for 1927–33 averaged $1.67 per share, reaching $3.21 in 1933.

Many another American-controlled gold mine in Canada could be described without coming to the end of the list. There is Noranda Mines, Ltd., organized in 1922 to develop several groups of claims in eastern Canada. Some of the gold properties did not prove up, but its Horne mine, smelter and concentrator in Noranda, Quebec,

127. See the 18th Annual Report of the English company.
128. So far as is revealed by their other directorships and positions.

can turn out upwards of 60,000,000 pounds of copper yearly, with sizeable amounts of gold and silver. How "American" or how "Canadian" it may be is not easy to discover. S. C. Thomson and H. W. Chadbourne, New York mining engineers, have managed the property[129] and are among the 4 Americans who sit on the nine-man board of directors. There are, however, over 18,000 shareholders, and since 1928, when 4 Canadians joined the board, control may be in Canada. The bulk of the American investment in Noranda is probably more nearly a "portfolio" than a "direct" or managerial investment. It does have another American connection. It is, jointly with British Metal Corporation, Ltd., the majority owner of Canadian Copper Refiners, Ltd., which owns the 75,000-ton refinery at Montreal, second only to that of the Ontario Refining Company, Ltd.[130] The refinery is managed by the Nichols Engineering and Research Corporation of Canada, Ltd. (which has a minority interest), wholly-owned by the Nichols Copper Company, of New York, which is in turn a subsidiary of the Phelps Dodge Corporation.[131] More unquestionably American is Wright-Hargreaves Mines, Ltd. (1916) with executive offices in Buffalo and a 1,000-ton-per-day gold and silver mine at Kirkland Lake. But to prolong the list is merely to repeat generally similar case histories which belong more properly to the volume on the mining industry in this Series. Yet of these predominantly American gold and copper mines—which, to repeat, produce about a fourth of Canada's output—still another must be included for special reasons.

Teck-Hughes Gold Mines, Ltd., began operations in 1913, although the present charter dates from 1923, when the Orr Gold Mines, Ltd., was merged with the original Teck-Hughes Company. In 1933 it acquired a 70 per cent interest in Lamaque Gold Mines, Ltd., and an option on Vicour Gold Mines, Ltd., both in northwestern Quebec. It also owns a number of minor claims. In 1933 the Ontario properties produced 241,000 ounces of gold bullion. The Lamaque properties are being developed and its mill is expected to

129. *Commercial and Financial Chronicle,* April 2, 1927, p. 1990.

130. See below, International Nickel, pp. 100–101.

131. Nichols Copper Co. also has a minority interest in the Canada Wire and Cable Co., Ltd. (in which Noranda is the chief shareholder), which has a copper-rolling mill and wire-drawing plant adjacent to the refinery.

be in operation in 1935. This is another company with widely held shares. In 1928 there were 8,000 shareholders. But there has been heavy concentration in the hands of some few investors—notably Charles Denison and associates in New York and the Wettlaufers in Buffalo—which no doubt explains the presence in 1933 of 6 Americans on a board of 9 members.[132] In October, 1934, the Commissioner of Securities of Ontario charged two Buffalo directors—Conrad Wettlaufer and W. W. Reilly—with selling part of their holdings while announcement of a dividend reduction was withheld, sales which resulted in "utter demoralization of the market and rapidly falling prices," and asserted that their action "cannot be too severely censured."[133] At the meeting of stockholders on November 20, attended by 2,000, the board was reduced from 9 to 7, all members being reëlected except Messrs. Wettlaufer and Reilly.

A much larger number of American-owned companies produce the other minerals: silver, lead, zinc, nickel, copper, coal, aluminum, asbestos, etc. Together they account for almost 40 per cent of Canada's output. But it must be reiterated that the non-American (chiefly Canadian and English) interest in these mining and smelting companies amounts to 30 per cent of their total capital.

NICKEL

Among all the mining companies in Canada, American-owned or other, the largest and, in its impact on world markets, the most important, is The International Nickel Company of Canada, Ltd. It produces not only most of Canada's but most of the world's nickel. With an output of 200,000,000 pounds of copper a year it is also clearly the premier copper company in Canada.

In 1877 W. E. C. Eustis of Boston became interested in nickel ore located in Orford Township in the Province of Quebec. The following year he incorporated the Orford Nickel and Copper Company,

132. Even the presence of a majority of Americans on the board of directors of a Canadian company does not invariably indicate that the enterprise is an American affair. Often it merely results from the insistence on control of the board by the American bankers to whom the company has turned for financing. That very probably explains the presence of two Hayden, Stone and Company representatives on the board of Granby Consolidated.

133. *New York Times,* October 23, 1934. See also November 7 and November 21, 1934.

which purchased the Crown Mine, later known as the Eustis Mine. In 1879 the Orford Nickel and Copper Company acquired an adjoining copper sulphide mine and reduction works owned by the Canadian Copper and Sulphur Company, a Glasgow, Scotland, concern. The latter company in 1881 was reincorporated in the United States as the Orford Copper and Sulphur Company and built a reduction works at Constable Hook, New Jersey. The president of this company was R. M. Thompson, an American who had carried out the negotiations for the purchase of its Scotch-owned predecessor. The Orford Copper and Sulphur Company was changed in 1887 to the Orford Copper Company, which in 1902 was absorbed by the International Nickel Company of New Jersey, predecessor company of The International Nickel Company of Canada, Ltd.

The other side of the family tree of present-day International Nickel was not concerned with nickel in the beginning. A Cleveland manufacturer, Samuel J. Ritchie, had become enthusiastic about iron deposits at North Hastings, Ontario, while on a trip searching for wood for wagon spokes. Associated with Senator Payne, Henry McIntosh and others, he built the Central Ontario Railway to open up the Coe Hill mine, only to discover that the ore was not suitable for smelting. Consequently he was immediately interested, in 1885, by the reports of rich copper finds at Sudbury, within 200 miles of the end of his railway. In 1886 he bought 10,000 acres in the new field—including the now-famous Frood mine—at a cost of about $35,000, and organized the Canadian Copper Company, becoming its president. The offices were in Cleveland. Strangely enough, those two *copper* companies begat International Nickel.

The chief ore shipments from the new mine went to the Orford works, at Bayonne, on a five-year contract. It became at once evident that the ore contained too much nickel to produce good copper unless a cheap separation method could be devised. This desperately needed development was supplied by Colonel Thompson through one of the happy accidents of chemical research. The Orford niter-cake process, neatly separating copper and nickel, solved the production problem.[134] All that was needed were markets for this almost unknown metal, nickel.

134. Colonel Thompson was astounded to find, one day, that a few of the

In 1888 Dr. E. D. Peters, who had been chief metallurgist at Bayonne, built at Copper Cliff a smelter and later a converter which, by 1892, was shipping matte[135] to Cleveland for experimental refining. The Canadian Copper Company, meanwhile, had weathered a financial storm and resisted purchase offers by the Société de Nickel of France and the Krupp interests.[136]

Colonel Thompson had managed to push his way into European markets through Baron Rothschild in France and Henry Wiggin and Company in England, and in 1901 he built his own furnaces at Copper Cliff because the Canadian Copper Company would not supply him with matte instead of ore at Bayonne. The Canadian Copper Company, although gaining some independence in production, was still largely dependent on the Orford Company for the merchandising of nickel.

In 1902 the direct predecessor of the company of today first appeared. The International Nickel Company of New Jersey was formed and absorbed the Canadian Copper Company, the Orford Copper Company, Wharton's American Nickel Works, the Vermillion Mining Company of Ontario and another small Canadian mine, and two small companies in the New Caledonian nickel field. This new company, with Colonel Thompson as chairman and Ambrose Monell as president, had Charles M. Schwab among its organizers. In the same year the Mond Nickel Company, Ltd., of England (later to join the International Company) began mining in Canada, shipping matte to Wales to be refined under the Mond process. And in 1902 R. C. Stanley, the present chief executive of International Nickel, entered the company as assistant superintendent of the Wharton Works.

The company at this time was beyond any question American in its ownership, management, and financing. The next 30 years, how-

pots of one batch, instead of yielding the usual unwanted nickel-copper alloy, was nickel on the bottom and copper on the top. But no one knew what had, by chance, got into that batch to produce the long-sought result. By patiently trying everything in the shop, it was finally discovered that niter cake was the key to these age-long refractory nickel-copper ores.

135. Concentrated but unrefined nickel-copper.

136. Judge Stevenson Burke, Senator Payne, and Frances Cornell pledged their fortunes to retain control.

ever, were to see marked changes. There was to be increased Canadian and British participation, increased dependence on the American nickel market, and a decided shift in the center of smelting and refining.

The mines, greatly improved, remain the foundation of the company. The great Frood (developed since 1926), the Creighton, and the Garson and Levack (Mond) mines have reserves of more than 200 million tons, sufficient for at least another hundred years at an annual output of:

Nickel	180,000,000 lb.
Copper	240,000,000 lb.
Gold	40,000 oz.
Silver	1,500,000 oz.
Platinum metals	300,000 oz.

International Nickel is, with those resources, the largest nickel, the sixth largest copper, and the largest platinum metals producer in the world.

During the war there began a reorientation of the company's production facilities which was to leave in the United States only executive and financial offices, a rolling mill, a research laboratory, and a foundry. The gigantic importance of nickel in time of war had led the Canadian Government, in 1916, to request the company to refine in Canada all nickel needed by the Empire. Consequently in August of that year International Nickel Company of Canada, Ltd., was incorporated, with a capital of $5,000,000 owned by the New Jersey company. By 1918 the new refinery had been opened at Port Colborne, Ontario, at a cost of over $5,000,000, all provided out of the treasury of the American company. In that year, also, the new Canadian company increased its capital to $50,000,000 and took over all Canadian assets of the International Nickel Company of New Jersey. The old Orford Works were closed permanently in 1922. All refining was transferred to Canada and all rolling operations to a new mill at Huntington, West Virginia. A foundry was built in Bayonne, New Jersey, near the research laboratory.

In 1926 the company undertook a program of expansion, largely in Canada, which cost $52,000,000 before its completion in 1933. Seventy-one per cent of the capital was provided by the sale of securities and the rest out of earnings and reserves. The Frood mine was prepared for use; the new smelter and Orford process refinery was built at Copper Cliff, Ontario; and the electrolytic copper refinery of the Ontario Refining Company, Ltd., was completed. The copper refinery, largest in Canada, has a capacity of 240,000,000 pounds a year.

During these same years the corporate structure also underwent a change. Partly as a concession to increased Canadian shareholding, partly to avoid any anti-trust complications in the United States, and partly to facilitate the acquisition of the English Mond Nickel Company, Ltd., the Canadian subsidiary became the parent company. The older New Jersey company disappeared and a new but subsidiary company, International Nickel Company, Inc., was formed to own the American properties. The whole organization may be charted as follows:

INTERNATIONAL NICKEL COMPANY OF CANADA, LTD.

IN CANADA	IN GREAT BRITAIN
Mines, Copper Cliff	Refineries, Acton, England,
Smelters, Copper Cliff,	Clydach, Wales
Coniston	Rolling mills, Birmingham,
Refineries, Copper Cliff,	Glasgow
Port Colborne	Research, Birmingham
Power plants	Colliery, Wales

International Nickel Co., Inc.
Offices, New York
Rolling mill, West Virginia
Foundry and research, New Jersey

With that organization[137] there is carried on a strangely international business. There is virtually no market in Canada for nickel and only a limited market for copper, and the American market for copper has been closed by tariffs since June, 1932.[138] Further, the

137. Including the information bureaus in France, Belgium, Germany, Italy, and Japan, which have been omitted from the chart.

138. Before that time most of the company's copper had been sold in the United States.

American tariff imposes some barriers on rolled and fabricated nickel. Consequently the movement of ore and metal looks something like this:

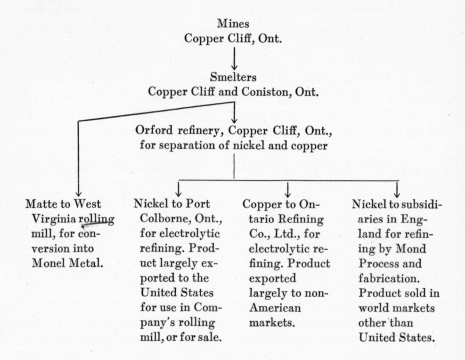

Mines
Copper Cliff, Ont.

Smelters
Copper Cliff and Coniston, Ont.

Orford refinery, Copper Cliff, Ont.,
for separation of nickel and copper

Matte to West Virginia rolling mill, for conversion into Monel Metal.

Nickel to Port Colborne, Ont., for electrolytic refining. Product largely exported to the United States for use in Company's rolling mill, or for sale.

Copper to Ontario Refining Co., Ltd., for electrolytic refining. Product exported largely to non-American markets.

Nickel to subsidiaries in England for refining by Mond Process and fabrication. Product sold in world markets other than United States.

Nickel is the chief product and over 99 per cent of it is sold outside of Canada. In the five years ending 1933, 53.5 per cent was sold in the United States and 33.5 per cent in England, Germany, France, and Russia. The natural alloy "Monel Metal" is produced from the Creighton ore which is smelted at Coniston and is shipped to the West Virginia mill for refining and rolling. Since the acquisition of Monel-Weir, Ltd., in 1932, much of this output is exported, semi-finished, to England for rolling at the company's Birmingham mill. The rest of the ore is smelted and separated by the Orford process at Copper Cliff. The nickel is either refined at Port Colborne and shipped from there, chiefly to the United States, or is sent to England for refining and fabrication. The copper is sold under contract to the Ontario Refining Company, Ltd. The International Nickel

Company now owns 90 per cent of this refinery, organized mainly to refine its blister copper.[139]

That is the story of the International Nickel Company of Canada, Ltd. It mines, smelts, and refines its metals in Canada. It fabricates in the United States and England. It sells to all the world, but it finds the United States its largest market, and Canada—for sheer lack of population—one of the smallest. In its history, its management and its financing Americans have played large rôles. But its shares are listed on exchanges in Canada, the United States and England. In 1934, 44 per cent of the shareholders were Canadian, owning 21 per cent of the shares; 18 per cent were British, holding 33 per cent; and 37 per cent were American, with 42 per cent of the shares. On its board of directors, at the present time, that Anglo-Canadian-American body of stockholders is represented by 13 Americans, 7 Canadians, and 5 Englishmen and Scotsmen. The enterprise means much to Canadian economy. With a little short of $200,000,000 in assets, in the 5 years following 1927 it paid $133,000,000 for wages, upkeep, freight, power, and taxes in Canada, and dividends of $12,000,000 to Canadian shareholders.

Partly by historical accident this company, producing most of the world's nickel, is directed from a New York office. Chiefly by virtue of the greater carrying power of the American capital market it has looked more to the United States for the funds with which to expand. But it remains as completely and inextricably Canadian-American as any company in North America.

SILVER, LEAD, AND ZINC

The dozen American silver and silver-lead-zinc mines in Canada do not occupy a very important position in the mining picture. Keno Hill, Ltd., for example, owned by a subsidiary of the Pacific Tin Corporation, holds the claims which were acquired in 1919 in the Mayo district of Yukon Territory. The results have been disappointing and no work has been done since 1930. Nor had the Base Metals Mining Corporation, Ltd., subsidiary of Gold Field Consolidated Mines Company, of Nevada, been particularly profitable

139. The remaining shares, on which the International Company has an option, are owned by the Canadian subsidiary of the American Metal Company, which operates the refinery.

up to 1933, when it, together with its two mines at Field, British Columbia, the Kicking Horse and Monarch, were sold to Frank Eichelberger of New York and his Toronto associates for $700,000 cash. Two Spokane groups own British Columbia silver mines: Slocan Silver Mines, Ltd., and Silversmith Mines, Ltd., the former since 1910 and the latter since 1918. Between 1912 and 1917 the Slocan Silver Mines paid dividends averaging 23½ per cent, but since then it has paid none. Reproducing its history a few years later Silversmith paid its owners 24 per cent a year (average) from 1921 through 1926. The mine was closed most of the time thereafter until 1934. Then there is Nipissing Mining Company, Ltd., which was owned from 1906 to 1917 by Nipissing Mines Company (Maine) and since then by Nipissing Mines Company, Ltd. (Ontario). Its mines in the Cobalt district have been largely idle during the silver doldrums. And there is Treadwell Yukon Company, Ltd., a Delaware company directed from San Francisco, with silver mines in Taku River, British Columbia; and in the Yukon; and a gold mine in Quebec, acquired since 1928. It also spent considerable money developing the Errington mine near Sudbury, Ontario, which is now closed down. Probably largest of all these companies is Kerr Lake Mines, Ltd., which acquired the properties of the Kerr Lake Mining Company of New York, which had owned them from 1905 to 1917. It is chiefly a holding company, subsidiary of the General Development Company, owners of the Miami and Tennessee Copper Companies. Its $3,084,685 in assets are invested in 7 or 8 companies largely in the Kerr Lake field (silver and cobalt). Between 1906 and 1928 it paid, on its issued capital of $3,000,000, $10,000,000 in dividends and $600,000 in capital distribution. Since then both its operations and its income have been negligible. If these have been fair examples, they lead to the conclusion that silver mines controlled by United States capital are much less important than the gold, copper, and nickel ventures of Americans in Canada.

ALUMINUM

Only less interesting than International Nickel, among the nonferrous metals mining and smelting companies in Canada with American affiliations, is Aluminium, Ltd., associate of the Aluminum Company of America.

It is not quite certain when the American company first entered Canada. The Northern Aluminum Company, now the Aluminum Company of Canada, Ltd., was apparently formed in 1902 and was probably the first Canadian subsidiary of Aluminum Company of America. Shortly after it was formed it became a party to the aluminum association or cartel that was terminated in 1908. The parent company apparently depended upon its Canadian offspring to represent it in the cartel. In 1913, testifying before a Congressional Committee, President A. V. Davis said that the Aluminum Company of America "owns Canadian Aluminum Company [Aluminum Company of Canada, Ltd.], which in turn has agreements with all the 6 or 7 foreign aluminum companies covering the world except the United States, which was excepted because there is a law here preventing it."[140] The company then announced that it would add to its Toronto plant by building a new one at Shawinigan Falls, Quebec, instead of one planned for Tennessee. By 1917 the production of aluminum in the United States was 90,700 metric tons and in Canada was 11,800 tons.[141] It is probable that, although minor production of other companies may be included, those figures reflect the relative size of Aluminum Company of America and its Canadian subsidiary at that date.

Continuously from 1908 until the present time Northern Aluminum Company, its successor company, Aluminum Company of Canada, Ltd., and, on its formation, Aluminium, Ltd., have been members of the successive world aluminum agreements or cartels culminating in the formation of Alliance Aluminium Compagnie in October, 1931, in which Aluminium, Ltd., owns approximately 30 per cent of the stock.

The most complicated and obscure chapter in the history of Aluminium, Ltd., is the part played by James B. Duke (of tobacco and Duke University fame). Apparently about 1914 he became interested in a power site in Quebec. In 1924 in association with Price Brothers and Company, Ltd., already mentioned as a newsprint producer and consequently a big power user, the Duke-Price Power Company, Ltd., was created. By the end of the year the Duke-Price Company had practically completed the construction of the Ile

140. *Commercial and Financial Chronicle,* February 15, 1913, p. 489.
141. As reported in *Metal Statistics,* 1925, p. 427.

Maligne Station, on the Upper Development of the Saguenay River, at a total cost of approximately $35,000,000. This station had a capacity of approximately 350,000 horse-power. The power was ample for the production of aluminum, and Mr. Duke, in association with Mr. George D. Haskell, president of the Baush Machine Tool Company (which, as a user of virgin aluminum, was anxious to be freed from dependence on the Aluminum Company of America as a source of supply), had organized the Quebec Aluminum Company, Ltd., and was attempting to purchase bauxite deposits abroad.

It apparently did not fit in with the policy of the Aluminum Company of America to tolerate the establishment of an independent aluminum smeltery in Canada. Duke-Price Power Company, Ltd., was owned by Quebec Development Company, Ltd., 62½ per cent of the stock of which was owned by Mr. Duke and the bulk of the remainder by the Price Brothers and Company, Ltd. During 1925 the Quebec Company conveyed what later came to be known as the Lower Development of the Saguenay River to a newly formed Canadian corporation, Chute à Caron Power Company, Ltd., now known as Alcoa Power Company, Ltd. All the stock of Chute à Caron was then transferred to a Pennsylvania corporation, Canadian Manufacturing and Development Company. Under an agreement dated July 9, 1925, and by some corporate juggling, which is not relevant here, the Chute à Caron power site was sold to Aluminum Company of America for shares in the latter company amounting to about one ninth of the entire capital stock, both common and preferred.[142] The total amount paid for this undeveloped water power site ranged from about $17,000,000 to $30,000,000 depending on what value is placed on the common stock received. The shares were, of course, distributed among Mr. Duke, Price Brothers and Company, Ltd., and certain unnamed minor interests in proportion to their holdings in Duke-Price Power Company, Ltd.

Mr. Duke, who, subsequent to these transactions, became a director of Aluminum Company of America, died in the fall of 1925. In 1926, in connection with the settlement of his estate, the Aluminum Company acquired his 53 per cent interest in the Duke-Price Power

142. Aluminum Company formed Alcoa Power Company, Ltd., to hold that power site. It is still owned directly by the American Company. See *Moody's Manual of Investments, Industrial Securities,* 1934.

Company, Ltd.[143] Already, in 1925, at the time it bought out the Duke interest in the Lower Development of the Saguenay, the Aluminum Company had begun the construction of a $15,000,000 reduction plant at Arvida, Quebec, which, by 1932, was using 185,000 horse-power. Haskell sued Duke and the Aluminum Company for damages on grounds of a conspiracy in restraint of trade, but lost the suit.

In May, 1928, Aluminium, Ltd., was organized, and a few days later the Aluminum Company of America transferred to it virtually all of its foreign properties and subsidiaries in return for 490,875 shares of Aluminium, Ltd., common stock. In Canada, Aluminum Company of America directly retained only the Alcoa Power Company, Ltd., owning the undeveloped site on the lower Saguenay, and the Cedar Rapids Transmission Company, Ltd., which owns the line transmitting power from the Cedar Rapids Manufacturing and Power Company hydro-electric plant on the St. Lawrence to the plant of the Aluminum Company of America at Massena, New York. The only important foreign property outside of Canada which it retained is the rich bauxite deposits in Dutch Guiana.[144] Aluminum Company of America then distributed its shares in Aluminium, Ltd., among its stockholders. At the conclusion of these shifts the North American virgin aluminum industry had a corporate structure approximately like that outlined on the following page.[145]

Whether any written agreement exists between Aluminium, Ltd., and Aluminum Company of America is not known. But it is a matter of record that Aluminium, Ltd., sells aluminum in the United States only to the Aluminum Company of America.

There is no certain explanation of that segregation of foreign and domestic properties by the American company. The most reasonable guess is that it provided a means of association with foreign pro-

143. Shawinigan Water and Power Company bought a 20 per cent interest; most of the remaining shares were retained by Price Brothers and Company, Ltd.

144. Surimaamsche Bauxite Mattschappij.

145. Most of the information in this section has been obtained from the record in the recent case of the Baush Machine Tool Company vs. Aluminum Company of America, in the United States District Court, Hartford, Conn.

A GROUP OF AMERICAN SHAREHOLDERS

Aluminium, Ltd. (69%)

Aluminum Company of America (73%)

IN CANADA

Aluminum Company of Canada, Ltd.
    Smelters: Arvida, Shawinigan; plant: Toronto.
Duke-Price Power Company, Ltd. (53%), Quebec.
Saguenay Electric Company
    Chicoutimi Electric Co.
    Hebertville Electric Co.
    St. Prime Electric Co.
Saguenay Transmission Co.
Saguenay Terminals, Ltd.
Alma and Jonquière Railway Co.
Roberval and Saguenay Railway.
Aluminum Goods, Ltd. (55%; balance by Aluminum Goods Mfg. Co., Wisconsin)

ABROAD

Great Britain
    Northern Aluminium Co., Ltd.
    Alfloc, Ltd.
Norway
    Electro Chemisk
    Norske Aluminium Company
    Nordisk Aluminium Industri
    Det Norske Nitrid ($33\frac{1}{3}$)
    Inservik Company Laatefos
France
    Aluminium Meridional
    Bauxite du Midi
    Forces Matrices du Bearn
    Carrière d'Arboussas
    Fonderie du Precision
Germany
    Aluminiumwerke Goettingen
    Aluminiumwerke Nuremberg
Switzerland
    S.A. d'Aluminium Coire (liquidated)
    Aluminiumwerke Rohrschach
    Folien A.G.
Italy
    Aluminio Italiano
    S.A. Italiana Conduttori Aluminio
    Prodotti Chimici Napoli
    S.A. Minerari Triestina
    Leucita Italiano
Jugoslavia
    Primoski Bauxite Company
    Jadranski Bauxite Company
    Aluminj D.D.
India
    Jeewanlal, 1929, Ltd.
Japan
    Aluminium-Sumitomo-K.K.
    Asia Aluminium Company
South America
    Demerara Bauxite Company, Ltd.
    Sprostons, Ltd.

Canadian power companies

Alcoa Power Company, Ltd., 1925, Racine, Que.
Cedar Rapids Transmission Company, Ltd., 1914, Ontario, Quebec.

ducers of aluminum without the risk of prosecution under the Anti-Trust Law. As a previous paragraph indicated, the old Canadian subsidiary was a member of the pre-war cartels and agreements among world producers. Aluminium, Ltd., is a member of Alliance Aluminium Compagnie. Haskell, in 1931, again sued the Aluminum Company, charging, among other things, that through Aluminium, Ltd., it exerted an undue influence on the cartel price. In March, 1935, the Federal District Court in Hartford, Connecticut, awarded the Baush Machine Tool Company damages of $2,868,900. Judge Howe's instructions to the jury included four major points at issue. The second point was: ". . . after the Aluminum Company of America had transferred its foreign properties to Aluminum of Canada in 1928, did the American company then monopolize trade by conspiring with companies outside the United States to fix prices here?"[146]

It is not publicly known how actively the American company controls Aluminium, Ltd. Directly, of course, it has no financial influence, since it owns no shares. In 1928, however, the shareholders of the two companies were identical. On December 31, 1931, a small group of shareholders held 69.2 per cent of the common stock of the American company and 73.3 per cent of the common stock of the Canadian company.[147] The presidents of the two companies are brothers. At least it may be presumed that the relations between the two companies are friendly.

The latest expansion of Aluminium, Ltd., is the million dollar plant to be built in Arvida to obtain aluminum from bauxite by a process hitherto not used in Canada. The plant, to be opened in 1936, will use bauxite imported from British Guiana.[148]

PETROLEUM

About 5 per cent of Canadian oil consumption is supplied by Canadian oil wells. All of it, save for a very small field in New

146. *New York Times,* March 10, 1935. On September 16, 1935, the verdict was set aside by the United States Circuit Court and a retrial ordered. *Ibid.,* September 17, 1935.

147. See National Recovery Administration, *Report on the Aluminum Industry* (Washington, 1935); and "The Aluminum Company of America," *Fortune,* September, 1934, pp. 46–52, 100–111.

148. *New York Times,* June 27, 1935.

Brunswick, comes from Ontario and Alberta. The Ontario field is centered at Petrolia, where Imperial Oil at its formation in 1880 inherited a strong position.[149] The Turner Valley field in Alberta began producing in 1913. Its importance began when Royalite's Number 4 came in with 550 barrels of naphtha and 20,000,000 cubic feet of gas in 1924. By 1925 Turner field passed the older Ontario district and now Alberta produces almost 90 per cent of Canada's petroleum. Calgary is close enough to Turner Valley to provide a commercial outlet for part of its natural gas, though a very large proportion goes to waste. The dominant companies in Alberta are the Royalite Oil Company, Ltd., and Foothills Oil and Gas Company, Ltd., both controlled by Imperial Oil. The Imperial companies own 59 wells in Alberta. The new absorption plant opened by Royalite in 1933 reclaimed 185,781 barrels of natural gasoline in that year. In 1934 the total production of Imperial and its subsidiaries[150] was 572,726 barrels, of which, however, 70 per cent is absorption plant production. Imperial's output is over half of the whole Canadian production. Royalite also owns a 25-mile pipe line to Imperial's refinery in Calgary, and a gas scrubbing plant. The Imperial group in the Turner field sold 6.2 billion cubic feet of gas to a public utility company in Calgary in 1933. Most of the gas produced in the Turner field cannot be used. Even with the annual flow held down to 100 billion cubic feet, more than 90 per cent is burned off in huge pits, entirely useless.

Imperial Oil, Ltd., is the only large American-controlled petroleum producer in Canada but other companies have at least made an attempt to produce. In 1928 the *Financial Post* reported that the 4 "really big" companies operating in Alberta were Imperial Oil; Canadian Western Natural Gas, Light, Heat and Power Company; The Alberta Fuel and Gas Company (now out of business) ; and the Hudson's Bay-Marland Oil Company (now Hudson's Bay Oil and Gas Company). The second and third of the 4 are natural gas rather than petroleum companies and are included in a later section of the chapter.[151] The fourth is owned by the Hudson's Bay Com-

149. See pp. 77 ff. for Imperial Oil, Ltd.
150. Including some "custom" production, under drilling and absorption contracts.
151. See pp. 139 ff.

pany and the Continental Oil Company (Oklahoma). It was organized in 1926 to drill on Hudson's Bay lands in Alberta. The American company manages the drilling. It has not struck oil, but supplies gas to a utility company from 2 wells. In a number of other companies in the field American, Norwegian, and English capital was interested in 1928.[152] The smaller American ventures included the Frontier, developed by Denver capital in Wildcat Hills; the now inactive International at Lesser Slave Lake, financed in New York; Eagle Butte at Cypress Hills, in which there was Kansas money. Beginning in 1927 the Canadian Exploration Company, backed by Colorado, Texas, and Wyoming operators,[153] spent $100,000 or more in exploring Alberta and obtained leases on over 16,000 acres. Sixty per cent of the stock of the company was said to be held in the United States. The Seaboard Oil Company of Delaware, through its Canadian subsidiary, Canadian Seaboard Oil and Gas, Ltd., holds 120,000 acres, but has found no oil. Nor has the Nordon Corporation of Alberta, Ltd., on its 50,000 acres in Alberta. It is the subsidiary of the Nordon Corporation, Ltd., incorporated in Delaware in 1930 to take over the California, Texas, and Alberta oil lands of the Nordon Corporation, Ltd., of Canada. Equally devoid thus far of actual oil are the 4,033 Alberta acres of the Burnham Corporation of Canada, Ltd., owned by the Dominguez Oil Fields Company, which has about 750 acres in California and Texas. There has been, it seems, much American interest in the Alberta field. But as far as can be learned the only company among the American group which is producing oil in commercial quantities is Imperial Oil, Ltd. In the natural gas industry, which is treated in a later section, the American companies are more numerous.

ASBESTOS

In the Eastern Townships of Quebec lies one of the most famous asbestos deposits in the world. From this area, at one time, was produced between 85 and 90 per cent of the world's supply of asbestos,

152. *Financial Post,* November 30, 1928.
153. A. E. Humphries (Humphries Oil Company, Wyoming and Texas); Dines, Dines and Holmes (Denver attorneys identified with Midwest Refining Company); H. D. Roberts, S. J. Sackett (Chicago); etc. *Financial Times,* June 7, 1929, and *Financial Post,* June 20, 1929.

though in recent years improved productive technique and new discoveries in Russia and in Rhodesia, combined with the financial difficulties of the Canadian producers, have now reduced the Canadian share of the world's output to a bare 50 per cent. While asbestos was known to exist in Canada as early as 1860, the important discoveries were made in 1876 in connection with the construction of the Quebec Central Railway.

In the early years English, Scottish, Canadian, and American capital were all extensively interested in the development of the Eastern Townships deposits.[154] Many of these properties have passed to and fro among British, Canadian, and American owners. Finally, during the years 1908 and 1912, the Asbestos Corporation of Canada emerged, which combined nearly a dozen producing companies of various ownership. It is not necessary to pursue the checkered financial career of this company. In 1924 it was drastically reorganized and extended through Dillon Read and Company of New York, and became Asbestos Corporation, Ltd. This merger included practically all producers except Johnson Asbestos Company (Canadian-owned) and three American-owned companies: Johns-Manville, Keasbey and Mattison Company, and the Quebec Asbestos Corporation. It is now Canadian-controlled, though there is a substantial minority of American shareholders and of American bondholders.[155]

At the present time Asbestos Corporation, Ltd., is the largest company. It includes in its present properties six or eight which were at some time or other American-owned.[156] Canadian Johns-Manville, Ltd. (1918), however, is almost as large, and in 1932 produced about 40 per cent of the Canadian output. Its modern mines with electric locomotives and a 5-mile railroad to the Canadian Pacific can produce asbestos at $35 a ton. All of its output goes to the parent company in the United States or to its Canadian branch

154. *Monetary Times,* January 7, 1887.

155. M. M. Mendels, *Asbestos Industry of Canada,* McGill University Economic Studies, No. 14 (Montreal, 1930).

156. e.g., Black Lake Asbestos and Chrome Company, Ltd., later Asbestos Mines, Ltd. For earlier years of Asbestos Corporation, Ltd., see *Commercial and Financial Chronicle,* May 11, 1912, p. 1318; March 12, 1921, p. 1027; June 7, 1924, p. 2827; August 1, 1925, p. 589; September 12, 1925, p. 1350; November 28, 1925, p. 2641; and June 23, 1926, p. 484; and Mendels, *op. cit.*

plant. Its history goes back many years. Exactly when T. F. Manville bought his first Canadian asbestos properties is not clear, but the Johns-Manville group acquired control of the large Asbestos and Asbestic Company, Ltd., some time prior to 1910.[157] The other American asbestos mines in Quebec also produce chiefly for their own use. The Keasbey and Mattison Company has been dominated by Dr. Mattison, who, now over 80, was a pioneer in asbestos. It was bought in January, 1934, by an English company (Turner and Newell), whose chief mines are in South Africa and Rhodesia. The other is Quebec Asbestos Corporation, Ltd., owned by Philip Carey Company, of Cincinnati, an asphalt company, which presumably uses asbestos in the manufacture of roofing and similar products.

COAL

Most of Canada's coal reserves, which are estimated at 17 per cent of world reserves, are in Alberta. Present production is chiefly centered in the Maritimes, Alberta, Saskatchewan, and British Columbia, and in those Provinces are located the few American-controlled coal companies. Certainly most important among them is the $5,807,319 Crow's Nest Pass Coal Company, Ltd. Its mines (250,-000 acres) near Fernie, British Columbia, have been operated since 1897, and it now owns a power company and a railroad. How old and how large the American interest may be is not publicly recorded. Granby Consolidated owns a large block. But the more definitely American holdings in the Crow's Nest Pass Coal Company are those of the Northern Securities Company and the Great Northern Railway. The Great Northern's representatives hold 4 of the 5 American directorships. Field reported in 1913[158] that both the Great Northern and the Northern Pacific railways had decided that it would be better to own their own mines in British Columbia to supply coal for their northwest lines than to purchase coal under the contract system. Not much smaller than the Crow's Nest company is the International Coal and Coke Company, Ltd., with its mines and ovens at Coleman, Alberta. It is now a Canadian-controlled enterprise, organized in 1919 to succeed an American company which had owned

157. *Poor's Industrial Volume,* 1932, pp. 812–813; *Fortune,* March, 1934, pp. 82–89, 128–146; Mendels, *op. cit.*

158. *Op. cit.* (1914 ed.), p. 60.

the property since 1903. The lone American (Boston) director is evidently a vestige of that earlier period.

Practically all of Saskatchewan's coal is mined in the Estevan district. There the Truax-Traer Coal Company (which has mines in West Virginia, Illinois, and North Dakota) owns 1,010 acres of coal lands. They are operated by the North Dakota subsidiary.

The largest and possibly the only American-owned coal company in eastern Canada is the Maritime Coal, Railway, and Power Company, Ltd., which was purchased by the Utilities Power and Light Corporation in 1930.[159] The coal properties of that company cover 22 square miles and are mined by 5 collieries.

And with that, this account of American mining ventures is almost complete. America's share in Canadian gypsum mining is largely held by the United States Gypsum Company, which in the last few years has acquired 4 mines located in Nova Scotia, New Brunswick and Ontario, managed by Canadian Gypsum Company, Ltd. In 1930 it was stated that the parent company shipped a million tons of gypsum a year from the Canadian mines to its mills in New York, Philadelphia, and Boston.[160] Its mills in Canada supply the Canadian market. The Bon Ami Company owns a feldspar mine in Quebec; here also Sherwin-Williams operates an iron oxide (ochre) mine. But these and a scattered 8 or 10 other American-owned mines—soapstone, silica, quartzite, lime, etc.—though possibly individually important, do not bulk large in the Canadian mining industry as a whole.

PUBLIC UTILITIES

Over 80 American-controlled companies operate railroads or supply heat, light, gas, telephone and other related services. Collectively they employ a capital of $707,751,033, and the gross value of their products is almost 18 per cent of the Canadian total. As the table at the beginning of this chapter indicates, the American-owned gas companies are most important, relative to the natural gas industry as a whole. But the electricity producers have involved the heaviest investment, with the railroads and telephone companies next (the latter included in utility companies not elsewhere specified).

159. See pp. 150 f.
160. *Commercial and Financial Chronicle,* July 12, 1930, p. 288.

RAILROADS

The American-owned railroads in Canada do not loom up large in comparison with the 2 great and the several lesser systems under Canadian control: they render about 7.4 per cent of the railway service, measured in terms of value. Nor are they as extensive as the Canadian-owned lines in the United States which are described in the following chapter.[161] Whereas the 2 Canadian systems operate or control about 6,600 miles of road in the United States, the American mileage in Canada (excluding trackage rights) is about 1,550 miles. If the Algoma Central and Hudson Bay is added, the total mileage is raised to about 1,850. But the interesting history of American railroad expansion in Canada, together with the more than $122,-000,000 invested in it, are reasons enough for its description.

Field remarked in 1913 that the Canadian railroad system from first to last had been financed by the British investor.[162] That is not quite correct. While a large part of the money came from British investors, a considerable amount was raised in Canada, and probably not far short of $50,000,000 of American money was invested in Canadian railroads prior to 1885. American enterprise, even more than money, was also present in Canadian railroad development in the Seventies and Eighties. To give a few examples: The Canada Southern Railway, running from Detroit to Buffalo, was an American enterprise from beginning to end. Begun in 1870, it was completed in 1873, at an initial investment of from $12,000,000 to $15,000,000.[163] In 1875 Commodore Vanderbilt became its president,[164] and in 1882 it was leased to the Michigan Central, a move made necessary by the Grand Trunk–Great Western merger.[165] In 1871 the Midland Railway (Port Hope, Peterborough, Beaverton) was sold to a new company in which American capital was largely represented; and Adolph Hugel, an American, became its president.[166] The Belleville and North Hastings Railway had an American president in its early years, and later Adolph Hugel joined its

161. See pp. 187 ff.

162. *Op. cit.* (1914 ed.), pp. 9, 14–15.

163. *Monetary Times,* October 24, 1873. The bulk of its $22,500,000 Consolidated 5's was sold in the United States. See below, p. 119.

164. *Ibid.,* December 31, 1875.

165. *Ibid.,* November 17, 1882.   166. *Ibid.,* August 11, 1871.

directorate.[167] The early history of the Canadian Pacific Railway shows many American connections. Even the great Canadians, Stephen, Angus, Shaughnessy, Smith, Van Horne, had acquired much of their training and experience in the American Northwest.[168] The early financing of the Canadian Pacific was made difficult in London due in part to the bitter opposition of the Grand Trunk interests. Its first bond issue of $10,000,000 was handled by a Montreal–New York syndicate, and its first public issue of stock, through New York and Amsterdam underwriters.[169] St. Paul capitalists were largely back of the old Manitoba and Southwestern, but sold out to the Canadian Pacific in 1884.[170] American enterprise and, to a lesser extent, American money thus played an important part in the early history of Canadian railroad building. It should be added that a part of the American railway investment in Canada in the Seventies and Eighties no doubt came indirectly from London through borrowings by the parent groups.

The American railroads in Canada—past and present—have two sorts of origins. Most of them were either built by or ultimately purchased by American railroad companies to be added to systems already partly developed. But others were developed as part of an industrial or mining venture or were bought to aid such a venture. It is sufficient briefly to cite some examples of this latter sort. Largest are the two roads—Algoma Central and Hudson Bay Railway, and Algoma Eastern Railway—built by The Lake Superior Corporation as part of its effort to develop the region north and east of Sault Ste Marie. Practically all of the money used to build those roads came from England, but, as an earlier section of the chapter stated,[171] there has been much American entrepreneurial activity in the whole Algoma project. The Algoma Eastern is now owned by the Canadian Pacific. Another railroad which was rather similar in its origin was the Central Ontario, whose early history was described in connection with the International Nickel Company.[172] Then there

167. *Monetary Times,* June 30, 1876, October 4, 1878.

168. H. A. Innis, *A History of the Canadian Pacific Railway* (London, 1923), chap. iii.

169. *Ibid.* See also *Monetary Times,* December 2, 1881, January 19, 1883, February 2, 1883, and *passim.*

170. *Ibid.,* June 13, 1884.   171. See pp. 57 ff.

172. See p. 96.

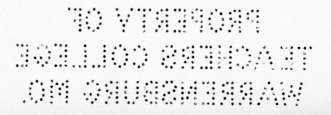

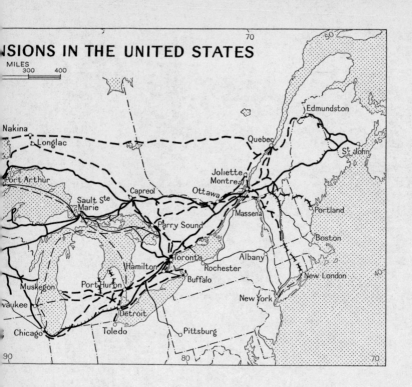

MILES
300   400

Nakina
Longlac
Port Arthur
Sault Ste Marie
Capreol
Parry Sound
Muskegon
Port Huron
waukee
Detroit
Chicago
Toledo
Hamilton
Toronto
Buffalo
Pittsburg
Rochester
Albany
New York
New London
Boston
Portland
Massena
Ottawa
Joliette
Montreal
Quebec
St John
Edmundston

70
50
45
40
90
80
70

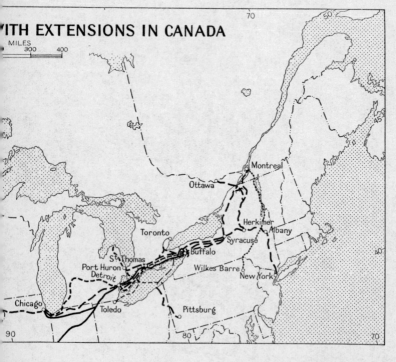

ITH EXTENSIONS IN CANADA

MILES
300   400

Chicago
Toledo
Port Huron
Detroit
St Thomas
Toronto
Buffalo
Wilkes Barre
New York
Syracuse
Herkimer
Albany
Ottawa
Montreal
Pittsburg

70
50
45
40
90
80
70

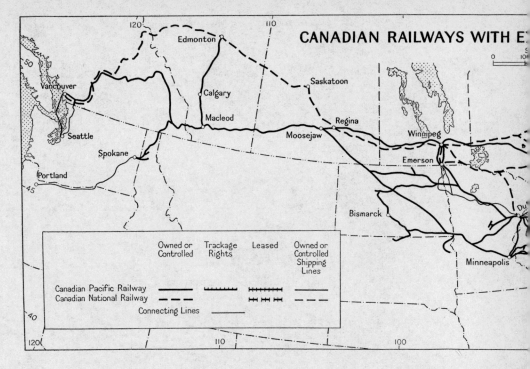

CANADIAN RAILWAYS WITH E

Legend:

	Owned or Controlled	Trackage Rights	Leased	Owned or Controlled Shipping Lines
Canadian Pacific Railway				
Canadian National Railway				
Connecting Lines				

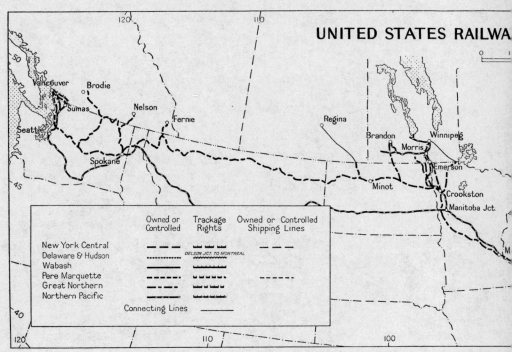

UNITED STATES RAILWA

Legend:

	Owned or Controlled	Trackage Rights	Owned or Controlled Shipping Lines
New York Central			
Delaware & Hudson		*DELSON JCT. TO MONTREAL*	
Wabash			
Pere Marquette			
Great Northern			
Northern Pacific			
Connecting Lines			

is the 50-mile standard gauge railroad owned by the Spruce Falls Power and Paper Company, Ltd.,[173] the 21-mile Essex Terminal Railway[174] (a belt line in the Windsor area owned by the United States Steel Corporation), the 15-mile line in New Brunswick owned by the Utilities Power and Light Corporation,[175] and the railroad operated by Aluminium, Ltd.[176]—all good examples of lines which are adjuncts of American-owned companies whose chief purpose in Canada is not railroading. There are, of course, many logging railroads and mine short lines that are of no particular interest.

It is the much larger group of lines, comprising approximately 1,585 miles of owned or leased track and operated by 7 of the larger American railroads, which will engage most of our attention.[177] It can be regionally subdivided into the 3 sections appearing on the adjoining map:

Ottawa-Montreal	132.84 miles
Southern Ontario	681.93 miles
Winnipeg and west	666.56 miles

The "Manitoba lines" of the Northern Pacific have been leased to Manitoba and have been operated by the Canadian Northern (now Canadian National) since 1901. In point of actual American operation, then, the lines across the Ontario peninsula are most important. Trackage rights are not included in the figures given above.

The first rail connection between the two countries was in 1851, when communication was established between Montreal and Boston *via* Rouse's Point.[178] Two years later the St. Lawrence Atlantic–Atlantic St. Lawrence lines began a hesitant Montreal-Portland service.[179] Seemingly the earliest actual extension into Canada, however, was in 1869–70, when the Massawippi Valley Railway was built from the Vermont line at Beebe Junction to Lennoxville (31 miles) with rights over the Grand Trunk for the remaining 4 miles into Sherbrooke, Quebec. It was immediately leased to the Connecti-

173. See p. 46. It is not a common carrier.
174. See p. 71.   175. See p. 150.
176. See p. 106.
177. The organization, economy, and detailed history of the Canadian-American railroads form the substance of a forthcoming volume in this Series. Consequently this section is confined largely to a brief account of development and present ownership.
178. See p. 188.   179. See p. 188.

cut and Passumpsic Rivers Railroad, which in turn leased it to the Boston and Maine Railroad, thus providing a Boston-Sherbrooke route. Now, however, both the Massawippi and the Connecticut and Passumpsic are leased by and are part of the Canadian Pacific System, forming, as can be seen on the map, its connection with the Boston and Maine at Wells River.[180]

The Delaware and Hudson was the next American railroad to obtain a Quebec entrance. The first entry of this company into Canada was by through passenger service between New York and Montreal, inaugurated on December 1, 1875, the trains operating *via* Mooers Junction, thence *via* the Ogdensburgh (now the Rutland) to Rouse's Point, and the Grand Trunk from Rouse's Point, *via* St. Johns, Quebec, to the Bonaventure Station, Montreal. On September 18, 1876, upon the completion of the road from Chazy Junction (now Chazy) to Rouse's Point, direct connection was made with the Grand Trunk at the latter point.

Delaware and Hudson passenger trains continued to operate into Grand Trunk's Bonaventure Station, Montreal until October 1, 1917. But the use of the Grand Trunk tracks between St. Lambert and Rouse's Point was discontinued in 1907, and the tracks of the Quebec, Montreal and Southern and the Napierville Junction railroads were used between St. Lambert and Rouse's Point.

The Delaware and Hudson bought the 143-mile Quebec, Montreal and Southern for $1,212,929, in 1906. This gave it a line from Noyan, at the Border, to Belleville Junction. Later it extended the Quebec, Montreal and Southern 50 miles east to Fortierville at a cost of $2,067,237. In 1907 the Delaware and Hudson bought the Napierville Junction Railway for $615,680.

The Napierville Junction Railway Company was chartered on July 12, 1888, under Quebec laws, to build from some point in St. Remi, Napierville County, through that County and La Prairie County to St. Cyprian, Napierville County, with the right to extend the line to St. Johns. Its incorporators and first board of directors were independent of the Delaware and Hudson and were, presumably, all residents of Canada. In 1900 its charter was amended to include the right to build instead from St. Constant, Quebec, to the international boundary line at Rouse's Point, New York. In 1904 a

180. See p. 192.

further amendment constituted 5 residents of Canada and one of Plattsburg, New York, a provisional board of directors. The records of the first meeting of shareholders, on January 17, 1905, show that this stock was held as follows: 40 shares by 4 residents of Canada and 4,960 shares by 3 residents of New York. None of them were connected with the Delaware and Hudson. On April 30, 1906, the board of directors authorized the execution of a contract with the Pacific Construction Company, Ltd., for construction of its road from St. Constant, Quebec to the line near Rouse's Point—27.2 miles. The construction, started by the Pacific Company, was later taken over and completed by the Napierville Company, which, on April 9, 1907, sold its entire property to the Delaware and Hudson Company. The road was opened for traffic May 20, 1907.

Beginning on October 1, 1917, and continuing to the present, the through passenger service to Montreal of the Delaware and Hudson has been operated over the Napierville Junction from Rouse's Point to Delson Junction and thence over the tracks of the Canadian Pacific to its Windsor Station in Montreal under a trackage agreement. It is that route which is shown on the map. No longer needing the Quebec, Montreal and Southern, the Delaware and Hudson sold it to the Canadian National in 1929 for $6,000,000.[181]

Another early cross-Border connection—wiped out in 1925—was that of the Hereford Railway which was opened in 1888 from Beecher Falls, Vermont, to Cookshire, Quebec (on the Grand Trunk), and extended 13 miles to meet the Quebec Central in 1889. After a year under lease to the Upper Coos Railroad it was leased to the Maine Central for $64,500 a year, representing 4 per cent on both bonds and stock. In 1925, however, the Maine Central bought the stock for $476,520 and sold the tracks—not the Company—to the Canadian Pacific for $46,378, with the proviso that the actual connection across the Border be dismantled. In recent years, then, of those 4 Quebec connections 1 has been cut off and 2 others are under Canadian operation.[182]

181. From *A Century of Progress, History of the Delaware and Hudson Company, 1823–1923* (Albany, 1925), pp. 339 ff., and from information supplied by the Company.

182. The American connections of the Canadian roads are described below, pp. 187 ff.

The other American lines in eastern Canada are owned by the New York Central. In 1892 the St. Lawrence and Adirondack Railway opened its line from the Border to Valleyfield, Quebec. In 1896 it acquired the American line running to Malone, New York, and leased the section from Valleyfield to Beauharnois, Quebec (from the Grand Trunk) to connect with the line which had been built from there to what is now Adirondack Junction. The final 9 miles into Montreal are over Canadian Pacific tracks. This route, shown on the map, has been operated by the New York Central since 1898 and owned by it since 1905. The last American railroad to seek entrance to Montreal was the Rutland, which satisfied itself with arrangements for its passenger trains. From 1901 to 1917 it apparently operated its own trains into Montreal over the tracks of the Quebec, Montreal and Southern and the Canadian Pacific. Since then, however, it has had a traffic agreement with the Canadian National whereby Rutland passenger cars are carried to Montreal *via* Rouse's Point, and the Canadian company keeps all revenues collected and bears all expenses incurred beyond the boundary.

Not far west of those Border crossings is the Ottawa and New York Railway, by which the New York Central enters Ottawa. It was built in 1882 and operated by the New York and Ottawa Railroad until the New York Central absorbed that company in 1913 and with it acquired the controlling interest in the 57-mile Canadian line. Since the New York Central also is most important among the American lines in the Ontario peninsula sector, to which we now turn, its Canadian subsidiaries are summarized below.

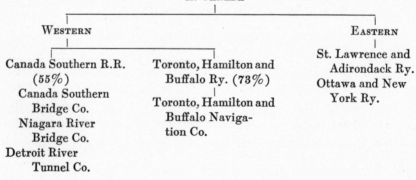

NEW YORK CENTRAL LINES
IN CANADA

WESTERN

Canada Southern R.R.
(55%)
Canada Southern
Bridge Co.
Niagara River
Bridge Co.
Detroit River
Tunnel Co.

Toronto, Hamilton and
Buffalo Ry. (73%)

Toronto, Hamilton and
Buffalo Naviga-
tion Co.

EASTERN

St. Lawrence and
Adirondack Ry.
Ottawa and New
York Ry.

Three American railroads run trains across Ontario from Buffalo or Niagara to Detroit or Sarnia by the routes shown on the map. Earliest was the Canada Southern, which evolved in 1869 from the Fort Erie Railway (1857), and one or two other short lines. Its main line from Fort Erie and Niagara to Windsor was opened in 1873.[183] The Toledo, Canada Southern and Detroit, which it acquired in 1872, gave it entrance to and a belt line in Toledo, Ohio. In 1882 the Canada Southern system was leased by the Michigan Central. In 1904 the lease was changed to an operation agreement whereby the Michigan Central guaranteed Canada Southern bond interest as well as 3 per cent dividends. In 1913 the Toledo line was turned over to the Michigan Central—a New York Central subsidiary—which now owns 55 per cent of Canada Southern common stock. Acquisitions and additions since 1888 have expanded the Canada Southern to the 382-mile system shown on the map. In 1893 the New York Central, the Canada Southern and the Canadian Pacific arranged for the completion and joint operation of the Toronto, Hamilton and Buffalo, in which the Canadian Pacific now has the only shares—27 per cent—not owned by the New York Central Lines. The 103 miles of that line appear on the map as three sides of a square touching the Canada Southern at two points, reaching the ferry line at Port Maitland to provide a connection to Pittsburgh *via* Ashtabula, Ohio, and meeting the Canadian Pacific main line to Toronto north of Hamilton.

The second American railroad to obtain the use of a route across the peninsula was the Wabash Railway, which, in 1897, was granted the right to joint use of the Grand Trunk tracks whereby it could run trains from Chicago or Kansas City to Buffalo. The original terms of the contract provided for a rental of $275,000 a year and a proportionate contribution to maintenance and operation costs. The Wabash still uses that strategic short cut to Buffalo, but it has neither leasehold nor ownership of any tracks in Canada. Six years later the Pere Marquette bought a route to St. Thomas, Ontario, by acquiring the Lake Erie and Detroit River Railway Company. That company and its later acquisitions were financed and constructed between 1885 and 1898 by Thomas Walker and his Canadian associates and was operated by them until the Pere Marquette purchased

183. See p. 113.

it and also entered an agreement with the Canada Southern and Michigan Central covering trackage rights from St. Thomas to Niagara. The Lake Erie and Detroit River cost the Pere Marquette $2,870,000 in its own bonds in addition to the guaranty of the $3,000,000 Lake Erie 5's.[184] It had been a profitable road under Walker management. Until 1915 it leased the 23-mile London and Port Stanley Railway, which is owned by the City of London.

The American-owned railroads in Canada which have been described were acquired to reach the Montreal-Sherbrooke region in Quebec, to enter Ottawa, or to cross Ontario. The remaining American mileage north of the boundary resulted from attempts by the Great Northern and Northern Pacific to obtain a share of the freight traffic in the Prairie Provinces and British Columbia. The Northern Pacific made its first investment in Canada in 1887, followed in 1891 by the Great Northern. By 1900 the "Manitoba lines" consisted of the 355 miles appearing on the map in the Winnipeg-Brandon area, crossing the Border at Emerson, Minnesota. The Manitoba government no doubt welcomed the competition provided by these lines with the Canadian Pacific whose grain rates it felt were too high.[185] Premier Norquay's government in Manitoba, against Canadian Pacific protests and a veto from the Parliament in Ottawa, had authorized a line from Winnipeg to connect with the Northern Pacific at the Border in 1887, but the money ran out and the Norquay government fell. The Northern Pacific, obviously, took over that project. In 1900 D. D. Mann, of the rapidly growing Canadian Northern, asked J. J. Hill to sell the Manitoba lines to his company. Hill is said to have replied that "no railway ever sells branch lines to another railway," but added that it might sell them to a government.[186] Mann then persuaded Premier Roblin of Manitoba to buy the lines and turn them over to the Canadian Northern. In effect that was done in 1901. But rather than actually sell them, the Northern Pacific leased the lines to the Manitoba government for 999 years at a rental now amounting to $300,000 a year with a purchase option at $7,000,000. The government immediately as-

184. Paul Ivey, *The Pere Marquette Railroad Company* (Lansing, 1919), pp. 275 ff.

185. D. B. Hanna, *Trains of Recollection* (Toronto, 1924), pp. 105 ff.

186. *Ibid.*

signed the lease to the Canadian Northern (now the Canadian National), which has since operated the lines. Now Northern Pacific's only active interest in Manitoba is its half share in the Midland Railway of Manitoba which will be presently described.

In 1913 the Northern Pacific obtained trackage rights over the Vancouver, Victoria and Eastern Railway and Navigation Company (a Great Northern subsidiary) from Sumas into Vancouver, but except for a few months in 1918 it never used that route; and in 1931 it agreed to the abandonment of the line in return for rights over the section of the Vancouver Company's road nearer the coast. Since 1917 the Great Northern and the Northern Pacific have jointly developed the terminal in Vancouver which they own through the Northern Pacific and British Columbia Railway—a terminal company. Despite its early beginnings, the Northern Pacific Railway now operates no tracks in Canada except those of the terminal companies it owns in Vancouver and Winnipeg jointly with the Great Northern.

The Great Northern, however, still owns and operates the stub lines which the map shows running into Canada at a number of points from Winnipeg to Vancouver. Its first entry, however, was not in Manitoba but in British Columbia. In 1887 the New Westminster Southern Railway Company had been chartered by Canadian interests to build a line from Blaine, Washington, to Brownsville, near Vancouver, with the object, of course, of providing a Seattle route. But after 9 miles had been graded and 25 miles cleared funds were exhausted. The contract for completion of the line was sold to the Great Northern in 1890, it acquired the New Westminster Company and by 1891 had completed the line. In 1924 the property was sold to the Vancouver, Victoria and Eastern Railway and Navigation Company.[187]

That latter railroad was chartered in 1897 by British Columbia and Ontario interests, but during the following few years very little cash was expended. In 1900 the Great Northern acquired the company and built the lines appearing on the map.[188] A year earlier the

187. In 1916 an 8-mile section north of Brownsville had been sold to the Canadian Pacific.

188. Much of this information was supplied by President W. P. Kenny, of the Great Northern.

Spokane Falls and Northern Railway System was acquired which owned two short Canadian sections: the Red Mountain Railway and the Nelson and Fort Sheppard Railway. In 1921 the former was discontinued, but the Nelson line is still operated as is the Crow's Nest Southern, running, as the map shows, to Elko and from there 4 miles over Canadian Pacific tracks to Fernie. During the years several of the British Columbia extensions have been abandoned or disposed of.[189] The present mileage is chiefly that of the Vancouver, Victoria and Eastern, the Nelson and Fort Sheppard and Crow's Nest Southern being mere cross-Border extensions. On these roads, largely built by the parent company, there is no mortgage debt.

In Manitoba there is the same story of partial abandonment of early tracks, but the Great Northern, in contrast to the Northern Pacific, still operates lines in that Province. The earliest of these roads was the Brandon, Saskatchewan and Hudson's Bay Railway Company chartered by Canadians in 1903. Here again lack of capital hampered construction, and the company was sold in 1905 to the Great Northern, which provided the funds to build it as far as Brandon. That road is still operated. About the same time the Midland Railway of Manitoba was organized, built lines to Morden and to Portage La Prairie, and bought a terminal site in Winnipeg. Consequently, although crossing into Manitoba at three points instead of one, the Great Northern tapped almost the same territory as did the Northern Pacific before 1901. In 1909 the Midland Railway transferred its lines to the Manitoba Great Northern—a new subsidiary of the parent company—and retained only its Winnipeg terminal site. Since then the Great Northern and the Northern Pacific have invested over $5,000,000 in developing a freight termi-

189. Latest was the 35-mile Colebrook-Sumas section of the Vancouver, Victoria and Eastern, which though not operated has not been dismantled. One may mention the unhappy Victoria and Sydney Railway (see *Moody's Manual of Investments, Railroad Securities,* 1914, p. 1174, and Norman Thompson and J. H. Edgar, *Canadian Railway Development* [Toronto, 1933], chap. xi). The Great Northern built its 17 miles of line on Vancouver Island, connected with Washington by ferry, aided by a bond issue guaranteed by the Province and by the City of Victoria. In operation soon after 1892, its 3 second-hand locomotives carried its portion of the scanty traffic shared with 2 parallel lines. It was abandoned in 1919.

nal and tracks to connect with the Winnipeg–United States line, which, as was explained a few pages back, though owned by the Northern Pacific is leased and operated by the Canadian National. The train crews of the Midland operate the freight and passenger trains of both its parent companies over that route to their main lines at Emerson, Minnesota. Since 1927 the Great Northern has not operated the line to Portage La Prairie.

With that the bare recounting of the cross-Border connections of American railroads is completed. Read in conjunction with the corresponding section of the next chapter, and compared with the two maps, it provides at least a bird's-eye view of the links which bind together Canada and the United States with "ringing grooves" of steel.

TELEGRAPHS

There is now no American company supplying commercial land-line telegraph service in Canada. Consequently the Canadian-American telegraphs are, from the American side, chiefly the story of earlier Western Union subsidiaries in Canada and the present-day interconnections—both cable and telegraph—between the two countries.

The first telegraph link across the Border was from Queenston, Ontario, to Buffalo in 1847.[190] In 1852 that line was acquired by the Montreal Telegraph Company, later purchased by a predecessor of Western Union. Meantime efforts were being made to build lines in Canada from Quebec to the Atlantic, and in the United States north along the coast from Washington, D.C. to Halifax, Nova Scotia, where steamers from Europe could drop news-packets. Frederick Gisborne organized the British North American Electric Association and in 1847 managed to build a line 112 miles eastward from Quebec City.[191] The next year Americans pushed a line from Calais, Maine into New Brunswick, and John Torney of New Brunswick

190. Between the Toronto, Hamilton and Niagara and St. Catherines Electro Magnetic Telegraph Company and Theodore S. Faxton's Springfield, Albany and Buffalo line.

191. F. N. Gisborne (1824–92) came to Canada in 1845 and took charge of the Quebec office of the Montreal Telegraph Company. In 1847 he or-

extended Gisborne's line to meet it. He also opened the line to Montreal. About that time the Montreal Telegraph Company acquired
the Gisborne-Torney company. The Montreal Telegraph Company
absorbed a number of early Canadian lines, including, in 1866, the
Western Union wire from Buffalo to Quebec.

The telegraphs along the Atlantic Coast north of New York were
begun in 1846 when F. O. J. Smith built a line to Boston and then
on to Portland, where the Maine Telegraph Company extended it to
Calais, in 1849, to join the New Brunswick–Quebec system men-
tioned above. But Halifax was the goal. Lawson R. Darrow, agent
for the Morse patentees, in 1848 constructed a telegraph line from
Calais to St. John, New Brunswick, a project which had the backing
of the Associated Press of New York. In 1849 his company, the New
Brunswick Electric Telegraph Company, began service. New
Brunswick refused Gisborne's request for permission to build a
Halifax-Quebec line, as also did Nova Scotia. By that time the New
Brunswick Electric Telegraph had reached Amherst; and Nova
Scotia commissioned Gisborne to build the final 125 miles to Hali-
fax, which completed the New York connection by 1850. The only
other pioneer Canadian-American line seems to have been a Troy-
Montreal service opened in 1849.

Somewhat later, on the other side of the continent, Western
Union, convinced that an Atlantic cable was an impossibility, was
pushing forward an ambitious project for a telegraph up through
British Columbia and Alaska, across the Bering Straits to join a

ganized and became manager of the British North American Electric Telegraph Association to connect Canada and the Maritime Provinces. From 1849
to 1851 he was superintendent of government lines at Halifax. He became
interested in connecting Nova Scotia and Newfoundland by a submarine
cable. After a great deal of difficulty he finally succeeded in interesting both
New York and Canadian capitalists, and the project was completed in 1856.
Among the Americans who backed Gisborne's Newfoundland project was
Cyrus W. Field, and Gisborne's enthusiasm and detailed plans for an Atlantic cable from Newfoundland to Ireland played an important part in
launching Field on that hazardous, heartbreaking but finally successful un-
dertaking. From 1879 to 1892 Gisborne was superintendent of the Dominion
Telegraph and Signal Service. See *Proceedings and Transactions of the
Royal Society of Canada* (Ottawa, 1893), II, 67–68.

line to come east across Russia and Siberia. In western Russia connection was to be made with European lines. The Canadian section, crossing at New Westminster, had been extended several hundred miles when the completion of the Atlantic cable put a stop to the whole affair. Local service was continued, however, in British Columbia.[192]

During the Sixties and Seventies Western Union's leading associate in eastern Canada was the Montreal Telegraph Company, which has already been mentioned. In 1868 the Dominion Telegraph Company (now owned by Dominion Telegraph Securities, Ltd.) was formed to develop a system in the Ontario-Quebec area. In 1879 the American Union Telegraph Company, organized in that year by Jay Gould to carry on his struggle with Western Union, leased the Dominion Telegraph Company for 99 years at $52,000 (now $62,-500) a year—sufficient to cover all bond interest and 5 per cent on the common stock. This transaction, and later rumors that Jay Gould was manipulating the market for Montreal Telegraph stock in order to buy it up cheaply, caused a good deal of concern in Canada. The *Monetary Times* stated editorially that "if American interests try to get control of the Montreal Telegraph Company's wires as they have the Dominion Telegraph, it will result in an insistent demand that the Government take over all telegraph lines."[193] In 1881 Western Union acquired the American Union and with it the Dominion Telegraph Company, and proceeded to organize the Great Northwestern Telegraph Company to consolidate the two Canadian companies. The majority of the stock of the Great Northwestern was held in Canada, but its president was Erastus Wiman of New York, a prominent and loyal ex-Canadian, and one other of its 10 directors was American.[194] Beginning in 1915, the telegraph lines

192. It is said that the Siberian section, extended down into China, etc., played an important rôle in communications in Asia, but no particular search was made for such by-products of this curious Russo-Canadian-American venture.

193. January 28, 1881. For other comment on Jay Gould's operations see *ibid.*, July 4 and October 10, 1879.

194. In 1881, of the 5,000 shares of Great Northwestern stock, 4,025 were held in Canada and 975 in the United States. In 1883, of the $1,000,000

of the Canadian Northern Railway were operated as part of the Great Northwestern System.

When the Canadian National Railways were created in 1923, the Canadian Northern, Grand Trunk, Great Northwestern, and some government lines were grouped in the Canadian National Telegraphs; and Western Union retained only some land lines in the Maritimes. In 1927 and 1929 it sold all its commercial lines in those provinces to Canadian National Telegraphs except the 1,185 miles which connect its Nova Scotia and Newfoundland cable terminals with its land lines in the United States. Its guaranty of the rentals on the leased properties of the Dominion and Montreal companies still holds, however, although in normal course the rentals are paid by Canadian National Telegraphs.

The Canadian National Telegraphs and Western Union have an exchange agreement covering the traffic of the 2 systems. There are also agreements concerning the connection between Canadian National Telegraphs and the Western Union transatlantic cables in Nova Scotia and Newfoundland. Of those cables 2 belong to the Anglo-American Telegraph Company, Ltd., of London, which is operated by Western Union on a long-term lease. Through this company, Western Union offers to Canadians an all-British cable route between Canada and Europe.

The activities of the other American telegraph companies in Canada are even more contractual and less financial than those of Western Union. We have discussed 2 of the 4 chief North American telegraph systems. The Canadian National Telegraphs, to summarize, was built of units some of which had previously been part of the Western Union system. The Canadian Pacific Railways telegraph service, however, grew as the railway grew. Its lines join the Postal system[195] at the American border. The Canadian Pacific cable service is obtained through Commercial Cables to England and the

stock of the Montreal Telegraph Company, $825,000 was held in Canada, $153,000 in Great Britain, and $22,000 in the United States. *Monetary Times,* June 17, 1881; August 19, 1881; September 2, 1881; December 2, 1881; January 18, 1884.

195. Operated by Postal Telegraph and Cable Corporation, a subsidiary of International Telephone and Telegraph Corporation.

Far East and through All-America Cables to the West Indies.[196] The Commercial Cables Company owns, in Canada, only its cable stations in Canso, Nova Scotia, and the lines connecting them with the United States.[197]

TELEPHONES

The American railroads in Canada, to repeat, represent efforts of American systems to cross the Ontario peninsula, or to reach north to the larger Canadian cities. They have done no "system building" in Canada. The American participation in Canadian telephone development was partly directed by a similar effort to provide for intercountry communication. But a well-developed Canadian system has been the chief objective of those ventures.

There are in Canada half a dozen fairly separate telephone companies linked through American connections and, since 1932, by a trans-Canadian long-lines system. Moving from the east, there are the Maritimes and the New Brunswick companies, the Bell of Canada in Ontario and Quebec, the 3 government-owned systems of the Prairie Provinces, and the British Columbia system. We cannot spare space for even a brief survey of all those companies; we are here, as throughout this chapter, concerned only with their past and present American relations.

The account begins with the Bell Telephone Company of Canada —largest in the Dominion. The company was incorporated in 1880, uniting the scattered services undertaken as a side-line by the telegraph companies. The American Bell Telephone Company, which had bought the Canadian rights from Professor Melville Bell, father of the inventor, supplied a third of the $500,000 capital for the Canadian company. To quote an official of the present Canadian Bell: "Such were the doubts of the future of the telephone that only two thirds of that amount could be raised in Canada." The issued

196. Both of those companies are subsidiaries of International Telephone and Telegraph Corporation.

197. Probably some mention, in connection with telegraphs, should be made of the private wire system maintained by E. A. Pierce and Company from New York to Montreal *via* Albany, to Hamilton, Toronto and Ottawa *via* Buffalo, and to Vancouver *via* Seattle. See *Fortune,* October, 1931, p. 68.

capital of the company is now about $77,000,000. But the American company—now the American Telephone and Telegraph Company —has not always subscribed for the later stock issues. Consequently in 1934 the ownership was distributed[198] as follows:

	Per cent
Canada	66.5
United States	
A.T. and T.	24.2
Other	4.4
Other foreign	4.9

In 1888 the lines in Nova Scotia and Prince Edward Island were sold to the Maritime Telephone and Telegraph Company and those in New Brunswick to the New Brunswick Telephone Company. The Bell Company, however, now holds a majority of the stock of the New Brunswick Company although the operations continue to be provincially directed. In 1908 and 1909 the Prairie Provinces bought the Bell lines within their borders, largely in return for Provincial bonds. Consequently the chief income of the Bell of Canada is derived from the approximately 750,000 phones in Quebec and Ontario.

The American Telephone and Telegraph Company has a fourth interest in the Canadian Bell—a block of shares which, though the largest held by any single owner, "is in every sense a minority interest." Only 2 of the 15 members on the board of directors are Americans. But there are important relations between the two companies.

The Canadian Bell has, by contract, the widest possible access to the results of all research and priority rights on all patents of the American company. The terms of that contract are not fully known, but the Canadian company seems to pay a percentage of its income and not a fixed amount. In 1927 the Canadian Bell applied to the Board of Railway Commissioners for an increase of rates. At the hearings it was stated that payments on the service contract with the American company were $330,000 in 1924 and $420,000 in 1926. Although there was some feeling that the payments were excessive, the board made no criticism of the terms of the contract.

198. See the *Toronto Globe,* November 16, 1934.

Recent financial transactions between the 2 companies illustrate perhaps as well as any other the working of the friendly relations between them. "During 1931 plant additions and betterments were financed by short term loans at low interest rates in New York. At maturity these were repaid through borrowings from the American Telephone and Telegraph Company. At the close of the year their advances to [the Canadian Bell] amounted to $9,075,000."[199] In 1932 "The policy was continued of borrowing New York funds from the American Telephone and Telegraph Company."[200] These borrowings, however, were for bond interest and other indebtedness payable in New York funds. In its report of 1933 the Canadian company stated: "On December 31, 1932, the amount of United States funds owed by [the] Company to the American Telephone and Telegraph Company was $12,245,000. By the end of December, 1933, this indebtedness had been reduced to $235,000, which has since been repaid. To effect this result United States funds were purchased from time to time at premium rates on a continuously declining scale and finally at a discount. The average premium cost was 5.84 per cent. . . . To aid in financing [these] purchases of United States funds, advances of Canadian funds were obtained from the Company's bankers [in Canada] to a maximum amount of $7,000,000. . . ." During those years the annual interest charge on outstanding Canadian Bell bonds were $3,375,000, nearly all payable in New York funds. With American dollars at a large premium, the American company loaned available funds at the regular bank interest, thus saving the Canadian Bell much of the premium.

The equipment used by the two companies is largely uniform.[201] In 1906 the Bell Company bought the controlling shares of the Northern Electric and Manufacturing Company, Ltd., in which the Western Electric Company[202] had an interest. The Imperial Wire

199. The Bell Telephone Company of Canada, Annual Report, 1931.
200. *Ibid.*, 1932.
201. The same is true of general policies and even advertising, although the uniformity is in no sense imposed on the Canadian company.
202. Which manufactures virtually all the equipment for the "Bell System" in the United States, and is almost wholly owned by the American Telephone and Telegraph Company.

and Cable Company was similarly jointly owned by the two companies. When, in 1914, the two manufacturing companies were merged into the present Northern Electric Company, Ltd., the American interest was about 44 per cent.

The Canadian telephone system as a whole is connected with American lines at 8 points.[203] Until a trans-Canadian service was opened in January, 1932, calls to the west were routed through the Bell System in the United States. In July, 1932, all-British trans-Atlantic radio-telephone service was established *via* Montreal. Between 1927 and 1932 Bell of Canada had offered that service only *via* the United States.[204] The Canadian Bell has, since 1927, provided connections with Mexico *via* New York, Chicago and San Antonio.

The relations between the Canadian and the American Bell companies are simple enough. They began almost at the beginning of the industry and have continued during years of parallel development of the 2 systems. The investment of the Associated Telephone and Telegraph Company in the British Columbia system seems to be in a rather different category. The Associated Company operates virtually no telephone lines in the United States.[205] Consequently its Canadian expansion is not to be explained as a linking of systems. It is rather an owner of telephone patents which it exploits through its own factories in Chicago, Canada, England, and Belgium. Its telephone companies—in South America, Portugal, Santo Domingo, Jamaica, and British Columbia—are probably partly an outlet for its equipment and partly an additional source of income.[206] Its Canadian properties must be regarded from those points of view. They may be charted thus:

203. Montreal, Niagara, Detroit, Fort William, Winnipeg, Regina, Calgary, and Vancouver.

204. See p. 133.

205. The National Telephone and Telegraph Corporation (see the chart in text) owns the small Point Roberts and Gulf Telephone Company in Bellingham, Washington.

206. Compare the International Telephone and Telegraph Corporation, manufacturing "Bell" equipment in foreign countries other than Canada, and operating foreign systems using that equipment.

ASSOCIATED TELEPHONE AND TELEGRAPH COMPANY

National Telephone and Telegraph
  Corp. (1926, Del.)

British Columbia Telephone
  Co., Ltd. (99.9%)
Northwest Telephone Co., Ltd.
Kootenay Telephone Co., Ltd.
Chiliwack Telephone Co., Ltd.
Mission Telephone Co., Ltd.
Dominion Directory Co., Ltd.
  (publishes directories)

Canadian Telephones and
  Supplies, Ltd. (sales,
  Vancouver, Toronto)

Eugene F. Phillips Electrical Works, Ltd.
  (plant, Brockville, Ont.)
Canadian Rockbestos Products, Ltd.
  (plant, Montreal)

The factories supply the British Columbia system, operating about 109,000 phones in 1933, with equipment, and presumably get what business they can elsewhere in Canada. The gross income of the British Columbia Company amounted in that year to $4,479,079, compared with total earnings, both manufacturing and telephone operations, of $9,148,632 for the Associated properties as a whole. The British Columbia assets and earnings bulk large in the Associated System.[207] Operating through a non-competitive charter in British Columbia, the Company's lines are linked with the Trans-Canada System[208] and with the American long distance lines. Of its $20,000,000 in securities, the common is all held by the parent company. The bonds and preferred stock have been publicly floated in both countries.

Radio Communication and Broadcasting

If this book were concerned solely with the movement of capital and the resulting ownership and control of cross-Border companies

207. Assets, British Columbia system, about $30,000,000; Associated assets as a whole $80,000,000 in 1933. The Philippines system, with about 20,000 phones, is the next largest.

208. In which it built the difficult 625-mile western stretch over the Rockies.

by Canadians and Americans this section might be omitted. There is almost no American capital invested in either of these two phases of wireless telegraphy in Canada. But there are interesting inter-company relationships which cannot be ignored without leaving a gap in the record of Canadian-American industry.

Within Canada the Canadian Marconi Company offers the only direct international wireless communications. It was organized in 1903[209] and has an exchange of patents agreement with Canadian General Electric Company, Ltd., Canadian Westinghouse Company, Ltd., Bell Telephone Company of Canada, Northern Electric Company, Ltd., and the International Western Electric Company. All of those companies in turn have close working arrangements with American corporations.

In 1927 the controlling shares in Canadian Marconi were vested in Canmar Investment Company of England. The control of that company, in turn, is in the hands of a voting trust of 3 men, 2 appointed by Lazard Brothers and Company, Ltd., of London, and 1 by the British Marconi Company. Minority and, in consequence of that arrangement, non-voting interests are held by the 2 Canadian railways and by the Radio Corporation of America. There is no doubt a scattering of Canadian Marconi shares in other American hands, but, from the "control" point of view, that R.C.A. holding is the only American financial interest in radio telegraphy in Canada.[210]

That is the whole story of American financial influence in Canadian wireless telegraphy. But there are "hook-ups" with American systems which deserve mention. In 1927 the Radio Corporation of America established wireless telephonic service between England and the United States, linking the American Telephone and Telegraph system with the British Post Office system. Gradually, be-

209. As the Marconi Wireless Telegraph Company of Canada, Ltd.

210. See *Poor's Public Utility Volume*, 1932, pp. 151–152; *Montreal Standard*, September, 1929. In November, 1928, a flurry of trading in Canadian Marconi on the New York Curb carried it from $3 to $28 at a time when it was earning only 1 cent a share. It was rumored that R.C.A. was doing the buying, but *Financial Post* dismissed the reports as without foundation, since R.C.A. had acquiesced, only a year before, in the forming of the voting trust. See *Commercial and Financial Chronicle*, December 1, 1928, p. 3035.

tween 1927 and 1932, the Canadian Bell Telephone Company offered that service (through its system tie-up with American Telephone and Telegraph) throughout Canada. Now wireless telephonic messages are routed out of Canada to other parts of the world by the Canadian Bell either *via* the United States or through Canadian Marconi as it chooses. The Canadian Pacific Railroad telegraph system uses the facilities of the Mackay Wireless Company, a subsidiary of the International Telephone and Telegraph Corporation of New York. The Canadian Marconi Company uses Radio Corporation of America service to the West Indies and South America and in turn provides facilities to Australia for R.C.A.

Canadian-American radio broadcasting inter-relationships are more complicated, although here, too, there is seemingly no investment of capital by any of the American broadcasting companies in Canadian stations. The first radio broadcasting stations in Canada, as in the United States, were operated as advertisements by newspapers and radio equipment companies. Among these early stations was one in Toronto owned by the Wireless Dry Cell Company of New York. But as soon as commercial broadcasting developed, the larger resources and greater income of the American stations gave their more elaborate programs a competitive advantage in winning listeners in Canada. By that time Canada and the United States had agreed on a distribution of the available wave channels whereby 78 were to be used by the United States, 11 were to be shared, and 6 were to be exclusively Canadian.[211] As will presently be described, the 2 main companies obtained re-broadcast outlets through certain Canadian stations, but there is no evidence that they have any financial interest in those stations.[212]

The National Broadcasting Company entered Canada in 1929 through 2 affiliated stations: CKGW (now CRCT) in Toronto and

211. In December, 1934, the Federal Communications Commission ordered WLW (Cincinnati) to reduce its power at night to 50 kilowatts because of protests from the Canadian Government that it had been blanketing Canadian stations. WLW is seeking a permanent injunction restraining the F.C.C. from enforcing its order. *New York Times,* December 23, 1934; *Evening Star* (Washington, D.C.), February 10, 1935.

212. In 1931, however, a charge of American financial interest in a Canadian station was made in Parliament in Ottawa. A station was opened in Windsor obviously to cover the Detroit area. Although the manager was a

CRCF in Montreal. Such an extension of service to Canada involved ordering from the American Telephone and Telegraph Company and the Bell Telephone Company of Canada special wires from the test boards in New York and Buffalo to the test boards in Montreal and Toronto, at the expense of National Broadcasting. Over that wire CRCT and CRCF are given any sustaining (non-commercial) program they wish. Each station pays $1,500 a month for that service. In return the American company pays $50 per hour to the Canadian stations for each commercial night program they take.[213] The Canadian stations are not obligated to carry the programs. The Columbia Broadcasting System has 3 associated stations in Canada: CFRB (Toronto), CKAC (Montreal) and CKLW (Windsor). It has a written contract with those stations providing that they shall handle Columbia programs exclusively.[214] Those stations cannot provide Columbia programs for any other Canadian stations.

The growing predominance of American radio programs in Canada in the latter part of the last decade led to a growing agitation for a government-sponsored chain of stations. "Canadian programs for Canadians" and "Resist foreign invasion of our homes" reveal, in slogan form, the general ideology of this campaign. A Royal Commission, in 1929, headed by Sir John Aird, and later a select Parliamentary committee made recommendations which, among other things, urged the formation of a Canadian Radio Broadcasting Company to operate a coast-to-coast chain of stations. In 1932 the Canadian Broadcasting Act was passed providing for a Canadian Radio Commission which was to operate stations and to

Canadian and the company was said to be Canadian-owned, it had a Detroit studio and carried Detroit advertising. The exclusively Canadian wave length it used had previously been refused to the *Border Cities Star*. Charges of political favoritism were made in the House of Commons on the ground that the president of the company was a prominent Windsor Conservative. It was reiterated that the station was 51 per cent Canadian-owned. There was pretty clearly some Detroit capital in this company.

213. At first glance it may seem strange that N.B.C. charges for the sustaining programs it provides and pays for the commercial programs. But it should be remembered that by re-broadcasting the commercial programs the Canadian stations are "rendering a service" to N.B.C. by enabling it to reach a wider area.

214. The N.B.C. has no such contract with its two Canadian associates.

control all radio programs in Canada. By the end of 1933 there were 48 hours of Canadian Radio Commission broadcasting each week.

There are in Canada now 2 groups of programs: those of the Commission and those—to a considerable extent American re-broadcasts—of the private stations. The Commission has no financial interest in the 3 Columbia associates or in the Montreal station affiliated with National Broadcasting. But there are definite relations between the Commission and the 2 American systems.

The Commission has ruled that no more than 5 per cent of any radio program shall consist of advertising. It immediately called both American companies to a hearing on that ruling. The National Broadcasting Company offered the Commission all of its sustaining programs for re-broadcast through the Canadian stations.[215] N.B.C. commercial programs, however, go into Canada not through the Commission but only over CRCF and CRCT, as has been described. In return the Commission provides without charge any Canadian program National Broadcasting Company wants (*via* Toronto or Montreal). American commercial programs re-broadcast in Canada must be accommodated to the 5 per cent rule, but since a recent modification there has been little trouble. The Columbia Broadcasting System has a similar arrangement, but does not offer the Commission its full sustaining service free of charge. As a result of these arrangements the Commission, over a recent period, gave 50 concerts to the United States chains and received about 70 broadcasts from United States and England.[216]

AIR LINES

There have been gestures by Canadian and American air transport companies in the direction of Canadian-American service, but the actual developments have not been important. There is virtually

215. And even gave the American Tobacco grand opera broadcasts as sustaining programs.

216. This sketch of Canadian-American radio relations has been drawn from *Poor's Public Utility Volume,* 1934; the *Report of the Aird Commission;* the *Interim Report of the Canadian Radio Commission,* 1933; Canadian newspaper files; and from information supplied by Mr. Donald Withycomb, National Broadcasting Company. It is expected that other volumes in this Series will stress political and sociological aspects of the subject.

no financial inter-relationship between the air lines of the two countries.

"The first operation was across Puget Sound which started in 1919. It has been conducted, not so much for traffic between Canada and the United States, but in order to serve the steamers sailing from Canadian ports to the Orient and get United States mail to them in shorter time. . . ."[217] Similarly, an American line crosses Canada from Detroit to Buffalo, but does not pick up mail or passengers. In October, 1934, the Canadian Government gave permission to the Pacific Alaskan Airways, a branch of Pan American Airways, to use its field at White Horse, Yukon Territory. The initial service will fly from Fairbanks, Alaska, across Canadian territory to Juneau, Alaska. But none of these companies provide Canadian-American service and none of them involve American investment in Canada.

Airplanes cross the Border at 3 points to carry mail and passengers between the 2 countries.[218] A daily round-trip mail service is maintained between Winnipeg and Pembina by the Canadian Postal Service, through Canadian Airways, Ltd. The same schedule has been flown since 1928 between Montreal and New York via Albany, the Canadian Government paying for the southbound and the American Government for the northbound mail. The American operative on this line is the Canadian Colonial Airways, a subsidiary of American Airways, Inc.[219] The remaining service is operated by an American company between Seattle and Vancouver.

Part of the impetus behind the financial support of Canadian Airways, Ltd., largest airline in Canada, was evidently due to a desire to keep American companies out of that field. One of its constituent companies is Aviation Corporation, which took over bankrupt In-

217. Leighton Rogers, Aeronautical Chamber of Commerce of America, Inc., in a letter to the authors.

218. Before 1931 Canadian companies gave a service from Montreal to Toronto, Detroit, and Buffalo, and a daily mail service between Toronto and Winnipeg via Detroit and Pembina (on American planes over that stretch). But the 1931 reduction in air mail subsidies by the Canadian Government caused the withdrawal of those lines.

219. In November, 1934, the United States Post Office asked the cancellation of this contract on the ground that the 96 cents per mile rate was excessive. Another company has made a lower bid for the service. *New York Times*, November 16, 1934.

ternational Airways. Americans were interested in buying that company, which has the Montreal-Toronto contract, until it was made clear that the air mail contracts would not be given to an American-owned company. Transcontinental Airways, operating east of Montreal, was taken over by Canadian Airways to prevent American Airways from acquiring it as a St. Lawrence outlet. Canadian Airways was formed in 1929 with investments by both Canadian railways, whose presidents are among its officers. Its president said, in commenting on that fact: "The Canadian Airways has successfully, up to this time, kept American Airways interests out of Canada, but Canadian companies with American money where American manufacturing interests were in the background have confronted us from time to time. It was thought desirable to have a board of directors for Canadian Airways that would impress American interests with the fact that the Company was financially in an impregnable position."

Bus Lines

Buses cross the Border on regular routes at 13 points from Vancouver to Montreal.[220] It is extremely difficult, however, to trace the ownership of the lines operating over those routes. The crossings to Vancouver, Kamloops, Nelson, and Fort William are merely short runs over the Border terminating in those cities. It is probable that the operators on the American section also hold the franchise for the Canadian run. The Seattle-Vancouver and the Duluth–Fort William routes are reported by the Greyhound Lines as part of their system. The Puget Sound Power and Light Company controls the North Coast Transportation Company, which operates a bus service from points in Washington to Vancouver. The Checker-Greyhound Lines (Saskatchewan) connect with an American line—but not with the Greyhound system—at North Portal, to complete the run to Fargo, North Dakota. The Canadian section of the Calgary-Spokane route is operated by Central Canadian Greyhound Lines, Ltd. Although both of those companies use the name "Greyhound," they are evi-

220. Seattle-Vancouver, Wenatchee-Kamloops, Spokane-Nelson, Spokane-Calgary, Fargo (*via* Minot)-Regina, Fargo-Winnipeg, Duluth–Fort William, Port Huron–Sarnia, Detroit-Windsor, Hamilton (*via* Niagara)-Buffalo, Ogdensburg-Prescott, Plattsburg-Montreal, Burlington-Montreal.

dently not part of the Greyhound Lines and are probably Canadian-owned.

The only bus connection between Manitoba and the United States is over the Canadian-American Lines, Inc., from Winnipeg to Fargo, where it connects with Northland Greyhound to Minneapolis. Canadian-American Lines was formerly a Royal Transportation line which was sold in 1931 to Grand Forks, North Dakota, residents and is probably part of the Greyhound system. Its Canadian franchise does not permit it to pick up passengers within Canada, except in Winnipeg. Against the opposition of existing operators in Canada, Northland Greyhound has for several years been trying to obtain a franchise to operate directly from Minneapolis to Winnipeg over United States Highway 75. In summarizing the bus lines in the Prairie Provinces, an attorney for a Winnipeg bus company concludes: "There is absolutely no control of Manitoba, and so far as I am aware, of Saskatchewan or Alberta Bus Companies, by American capital, and as I have intimated before, our main thought in the past has been to keep American capital out of all local lines, having simply a working arrangement for operating connections."[221]

The remaining United States–Canada bus connections run into Ontario and Quebec. Canadian Greyhound Lines, Ltd., and Toronto Greyhound Lines, Ltd., operate buses from Windsor and Detroit to Buffalo *via* Niagara, and from London to Toronto. Both of those companies appear on maps as part of the Greyhound Lines. Greyhound Management Company, Cleveland, controls Canadian Greyhound, which in turn has a considerable interest in Toronto Greyhound. Another Detroit-Buffalo line, Canadian-American Coaches, Ltd., which is Canadian-owned, runs buses on American territory from St. Catherines through Niagara Falls, New York, to Buffalo. Gray Coach Lines, Ltd., also Canadian-owned (by the Toronto Transportation Commission), maintains a route from Toronto down the west side of the Niagara River into Buffalo at the bridge. Central Ontario Bus Lines, Ltd., still another Canadian venture, links its lines with the United States by a Sarnia–Port Huron connection with Eastern Michigan Coach Lines. Running out in various directions from Hamilton, the Highway King Buses, Ltd., a subsidiary of the Ontario Hydro-Electric Commission, has a line which follows

221. In a letter to the authors.

the same route as Canadian-American Coaches into Buffalo. So
much for the Toronto-Buffalo-Detroit area. The 2 Greyhound
companies are closely linked with the American Greyhound system.
The other companies are distinctly Canadian-owned and 2 of them
operate a few miles of route in northwestern New York.

Farther east the situation is simpler. The main Quebec system is
the Provincial Transport Company of Montreal, which is probably
associated—through Montreal Tramways—with Montreal Light,
Heat and Power Company. Jointly with the Fifth Avenue Coach
Company (New York) it has an equal interest in 2 subsidiaries
which provide Montreal–United States service. The Frontier
Coach Lines, Inc., operates buses from Montreal down the east
shore of Lake Champlain to Burlington, Vermont, and thence to
Boston. Champlain Coach Lines, Inc., maintains a service from
Montreal down the west shore of the lake to Albany and from there
to New York. A little farther west the Greyhound Lines run buses
to Ogdensburg, New York, where passengers may cross to Prescott,
Ontario, by ferry and board Colonial Coach Lines buses, a subsidiary of Provincial Transport. Canadian Hydro-Electric Corporation
owns the Gatineau Bus Company operating north from Ottawa.[222]

In the Canadian bus system as a whole there is evidently very
little American capital and, in general, few American-owned buses
cross the Border, except at 3 or 4 western points. In Ontario and
Quebec the only American operation—and even there the control
may be Canadian—is in the Ontario Greyhound lines.

POWER, LIGHT, GAS, AND SIMILAR UTILITY COMPANIES

American enterprise did not participate in the development of the
Canadian gas and light industry as early, probably, as it did in
that of telephones, telegraph, and railways. Nevertheless, in the 20
years before the war there had been several American ventures in
those utilities. Field[223] remarks that Philadelphia capital developed
the power and industries around Sault Ste Marie and that Boston
capital and enterprise were active in Shawinigan Water and
Power.[224] The present Great Lakes Power Company, Ltd., owned
by the Middle West Utilities Company, includes the old Algoma

222. See pp. 146 ff.   223. *Op. cit.* (1914 ed.), p. 22.
224. See p. 152.

District Power Company, Ltd., at the "Soo" to which Field refers. The hydraulic canals on both sides of the St. Mary's River were planned and built by F. H. Clergue, founder of the Lake Superior–Algoma enterprises.[225] Most of the American companies presently operating natural gas properties in the old southern Ontario field are newcomers, themselves not long in existence. But among the many small Canadian operating companies they have acquired in the last decade are some which were already American-owned. All the great American hydro-electric plants in Canada, with the exception of Canadian Niagara, have been built in the post-war period, although the plans for some of them had been long in the making.

Practically all of the American power, light, and gas enterprises in Canada are owned by the 12 public utility holding companies listed below:

Associated Gas and Electric System
Central Public Service Company
Cities Service Company
International Paper and Power Company
International Utilities Corporation
Iowa Southern Utilities Company
Middle West Utilities Company
National Fuel Gas Company
Niagara-Hudson Power Corporation
North American Gas and Electric Company
North Continent Utilities Corporation
Utilities Power and Light Corporation

There is a second group of companies in which the American financial interest is pronounced but which are largely or entirely Canadian-controlled. In the histories of some of them there have been much closer American associations than is now the case. Those 5 companies are the following:

Canadian Public Service Corporation, Ltd.
London Street Railway Company
Montreal Light, Heat and Power Consolidated
Shawinigan Water and Power Company
Union Gas Company of Canada, Ltd.

225. See pp. 57 ff. for the history of those companies.

Only the second and fifth of those companies are included in the power or gas statistics of American-owned companies in Canada in this chapter.

A third, hodge-podge collection of companies completes the American interest in the industry. Here is Duke-Price Power Company, Ltd. Here also are the power companies owned by American branch plants, paper mills, or mines in Canada in order to provide power for their works. Of these latter—and there are at least 6—only one sells excess power. The power subsidiary of the Minnesota and Ontario Paper Company has, for at least 18 years, supplied light and power in the cities of International Falls, Minnesota, and Fort Frances, Ontario.

The distinctly and definitely American-owned companies in Canada supply 34 per cent of the electricity (in terms of kilowatt hours) and 74 per cent of the natural gas (in terms of cubic feet). Together, those gas and electric companies employ a capital of $335,791,875. The electric companies produce, to repeat, a third of the total current generated in Canada. But the gross value of their product is only 17 per cent of the Canadian total. In all probability that apparent discrepancy is to be accounted for by the fact that a large proportion of the power generated by the American-owned companies is sold wholesale or to big mills at industrial rates. The gross value of product of the natural gas companies is over 88 per cent of the total for that industry.

The portions of Canada served by the American companies are indicated in Table IX. The gas companies are centered in the 3 natural gas fields of Canada: in the vicinity of Moncton, New Brunswick; in southern Ontario; in Alberta. As the previous paragraph together with the table indicate, those regions are largely supplied by American-owned systems. In addition, Sault Ste Marie is supplied with gas. The electric light services are more widespread. They tend to follow the hydro-electric resources of the country, although some of them depend on steam-generated power. In Quebec the retail services are chiefly in the Ottawa-Gatineau river valley, in the vicinity of Rimouski, and in the East Townships. Part of the Duke-Price output indirectly reaches Montreal. Unlike the gas companies, the American electricity companies have largely passed by Ontario, where, of course, the Ontario Hydro-Electric Commis-

TABLE IX

Communities Served by American-Owned Public Utility Companies in Canada

Province; name of American company	Gas	Electricity	Other
Maritime Provinces			
International Paper and Power Company		Wholesale to Dalhousie and Grand Falls, N.B.; also to paper mills	
Utilities Power and Light Corporation	Moncton, N.B.	Amherst, N.S. and vicinity, Moncton, Sackville, N.B.	Moncton, N.B., street railway
Associated Gas and Electric System		Fredericton, St. Stephen, N.B., Bridgeton, N.S., Charlotte-town, P.E.I., and 10 or more other towns	
Cities Service Company	St. John and vicinity	St. John and vicinity	St. John, street railway
Central Public Service Company		Campbellton, Andover, Perth, N.B.	
Quebec			
Central Public Service Company		Rimouski and 42 nearby towns	
International Paper and Power Company		Area between (and north of) Ottawa and Montreal (no service to Montreal); La-prairie south to United States line	
Duke-Price Power Company, Ltd.		To large factories and to Shawinigan Water and Power	
Ontario			
Utilities Power and Light Corporation	Belleville and Oshawa		
North Continent Utilities Corporation	Sault Ste Marie		
National Fuel Gas Company	Niagara, Welland, Fort Erie, Bridgeburg, Sherkston		
Niagara Hudson Power Corporation		Power wholesale to Ontario Hydro-Electric Commission	
Middle West Utilities Company		Sault Ste Marie and 9 other towns; also to mining district	Sault Ste Marie, street railway
Cities Service Company	Galt, St. Cathe-rines, Brant-ford, Hamilton, and 83 other towns		
International Paper and Power Company		Wholesale to Ottawa and to Ontario Hydro-Electric Commission	
Minnesota and On-tario Paper Company		Fort Frances	
Prairie Provinces			
North American Gas and Electric Co.		Assiniboia, Estevan and 29 other towns in southern Sask.	
Middle West Utilities Company		7 towns in Manitoba, including Deloraine and Hamiota	
International Utilities Corporation	Calgary, Leth-bridge, Edmon-ton and 23 other towns in Alberta	Grand Prairie and Drumheller, Alta., Yorkton, Sask., and 79 other towns in both provinces	
Cities Service Company	Locale unknown		
British Columbia			
International Utilities Corporation		Duncan, Ladysmith, Nanaimo	Duncan, water

sion has a virtual monopoly. Several hundred thousand horsepower, however, are sold to the Commission by the American companies, as a glance at the table will indicate. Sault Ste Marie, the nearby towns and the mining district to the north, and Fort Frances, are the only regions in Ontario directly supplied with power by companies controlled in the United States. Three regions in the Prairie Provinces buy their power from American-owned plants: Assiniboia, Estevan and vicinity in southern Saskatchewan; the Drumheller region in Alberta and the towns across the line in Saskatchewan; and 7 communities in Alberta, including Deloraine and Hamiota. The 3 towns, Duncan, Ladysmith and Nanaimo, are the only communities in British Columbia supplied by American power and light companies. And in Duncan is, apparently, the lone American-owned waterworks in Canada. The 5 holding companies noted in the table have fairly extensive electricity systems in the Maritimes, including Dalhousie, Moncton, St. John, Charlottetown, Campbellton, Fredericton, and at least 15 other towns.

Seemingly the only street railways in Canada owned by American *companies* are those in Sault Ste Marie, Ontario, Moncton, New Brunswick, and St. John, New Brunswick (the latter now in the hands of the preferred shareholders). The majority of the securities of the London Street Railway are in American hands.

As a bird's-eye view, that is a fairly accurate picture of the American-owned power, light, and gas companies. But in keeping with the rest of the chapter something of the corporate structure and history of that American ownership must be included. The natural gas properties are quickly described. The New Brunswick field is very small. The only American company in the vicinity, the Moncton Tramways, Electricity and Gas Company, Ltd., supplies the city of Moncton with gas from that field. It belongs to the Utilities Power and Light Corporation whose Canadian organization is charted a few pages further on. The natural gas field in the southwestern part of Ontario is controlled by 3 companies. The Provincial Natural Gas and Fuel Company of Ontario, Ltd., supplies Niagara Falls, Welland, Fort Erie and a few nearby communities. The parent company, National Fuel Gas Company, now owns 70 per cent of the shares and has controlled it for at least 15 years. The Dominion Gas Company, incorporated in the United States in

1912, serves a much larger area. It is owned by Cities Service and although it includes one power subsidiary the whole Canadian organization is charted here:

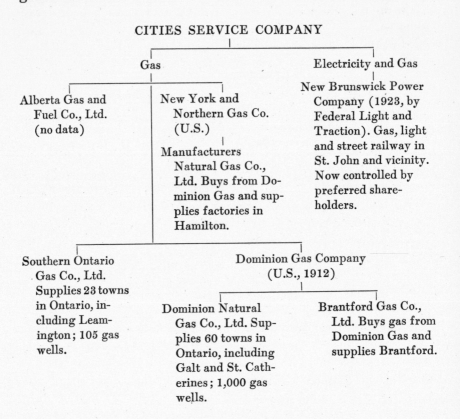

CITIES SERVICE COMPANY

Gas

Alberta Gas and Fuel Co., Ltd. (no data)

New York and Northern Gas Co. (U.S.)

Manufacturers Natural Gas Co., Ltd. Buys from Dominion Gas and supplies factories in Hamilton.

Electricity and Gas

New Brunswick Power Company (1923, by Federal Light and Traction). Gas, light and street railway in St. John and vicinity. Now controlled by preferred shareholders.

Southern Ontario Gas Co., Ltd. Supplies 23 towns in Ontario, including Leamington; 105 gas wells.

Dominion Gas Company (U.S., 1912)

Dominion Natural Gas Co., Ltd. Supplies 60 towns in Ontario, including Galt and St. Catherines; 1,000 gas wells.

Brantford Gas Co., Ltd. Buys gas from Dominion Gas and supplies Brantford.

The third of the important Ontario gas producers and distributors is the Union Gas Company of Canada, Ltd. Two of the officers and 3 of the directors are Americans, but they represent American bankers and not public utility companies. Although there is evidently a heavy American financial interest in this company (which supplies the largest cities in the gas fields: Windsor, Hamilton, London, etc.), it is probably Canadian-controlled. The other American gas companies in Ontario may be located on the table.

The newest Canadian natural gas producing areas are in Alberta. One is near Medicine Hat; 2 others (Bow Island and Turner Valley) supply Calgary; a fourth (Viking) serves Edmonton; and the last is near Foremost. The International Utilities Corporation is the only American public utility company with subsidiaries in those fields.

INTERNATIONAL UTILITIES CORPORATION

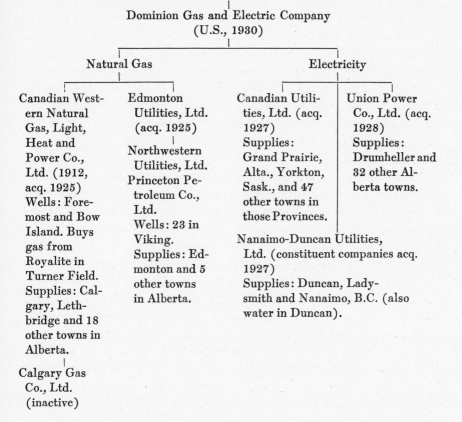

Dominion Gas and Electric Company
(U.S., 1930)

Natural Gas		Electricity	
Canadian Western Natural Gas, Light, Heat and Power Co., Ltd. (1912, acq. 1925) Wells: Foremost and Bow Island. Buys gas from Royalite in Turner Field. Supplies: Calgary, Lethbridge and 18 other towns in Alberta.	Edmonton Utilities, Ltd. (acq. 1925) Northwestern Utilities, Ltd. Princeton Petroleum Co., Ltd. Wells: 23 in Viking. Supplies: Edmonton and 5 other towns in Alberta.	Canadian Utilities, Ltd. (acq. 1927) Supplies: Grand Prairie, Alta., Yorkton, Sask., and 47 other towns in those Provinces.	Union Power Co., Ltd. (acq. 1928) Supplies: Drumheller and 32 other Alberta towns.
Calgary Gas Co., Ltd. (inactive)		Nanaimo-Duncan Utilities, Ltd. (constituent companies acq. 1927) Supplies: Duncan, Ladysmith and Nanaimo, B.C. (also water in Duncan).	

Canadian Western's wells are in the Foremost and Bow Island fields and, having been operated since 1912, are meeting with falling pressure. Consequently it is now conserving its resources there and is buying from Royalite in the Turner field.[226] These subsidiaries, which supply the important Prairie cities of Calgary, Lethbridge, and Edmonton, together with many smaller communities, are the most important distributors of natural gas in Alberta and serve

226. See pp. 107 ff. for a description of the gas and petroleum operations in that field by Royalite and other companies.

almost 34,000 customers. Northwestern Utilities, Ltd., buys the output of the two wells of the Canadian subsidiary of the Continental Oil Company.[227] The International Utilities Corporation acquired those companies in the 3 years following its own organization in 1924. In 1930 they were transferred to the newly-organized Dominion Gas and Electric Company, which was then sold to American Commonwealth Power Corporation. When that short-lived boom promotion collapsed in 1932–33 International Utilities Corporation accepted 93 per cent of the common and all of the preferred shares in Dominion Gas and Electric in lieu of its claims as a note holder. Most of the remaining common is held by Commonwealth Distribution, Incorporated, which is engaged in the dismal task of trying to salvage something for the security-holders of defunct American Commonwealth.

Unquestionably the most imposing American power developments in Canada are those of the International Paper and Power Company, which have been summarized earlier in this chapter.[228] Almost all of the original International paper mills had generated water power for their own use, but the present power systems of International in both countries[229] have been developed since 1924. The Canadian power plants are based on the Gatineau and Ottawa sites which were acquired in 1925 when the Riordon properties were purchased.[230] By the end of 1931 the hydro-electric installations had reached 679,519 horsepower.[231] Canadian Hydro-Electric Corporation, Ltd., owns the Canadian properties. The 3 plants on the Gatineau River, north of Ottawa, have an installed capacity of 470,000 horsepower. The Paugan plant, with its 204,000-horsepower generators, is one of the largest in the world. Practically all of Paugan's output is sold to the Ontario Hydro-Electric Power Commission and transmitted to Toronto, 230 miles distant, over the first 220,000-volt

227. See p. 108.   228. See pp. 40 ff.
229. It owns the New England Power Association, largest light and power system in New England.
230. See the references cited above, p. 42, and the Annual Reports, 1928 to date, of Canadian Hydro-Electric Corporation, Ltd.
231. There has been no increase since. The New England hydro-electric installation is 568,280 horsepower. There is also in Canada one 9,000-horsepower steam plant (at Dalhousie), whereas in the United States the Company's steam plants have a capacity of 555,950 horsepower.

line in the British Empire. The water for the Paugan plant is impounded by the Mercier and Cabonga dams on the upper Gatineau, which together have a combined capacity of 145 billion cubic feet, considerably more than that of the Assuan Dam on the Nile River. There are 3 plants on the Ottawa River (near Ottawa) which feed 87,600 horsepower into this same power system. A 24,000-horsepower hydro-electric plant at Kipawa supplies the rayon pulp mill there, and at Grand Falls on the St. John River, which divides Maine and New Brunswick, a big plant generates 80,000 horsepower and transmits most of it 104 miles to the International's newsprint mill at Dalhousie, the remainder supplying light to Dalhousie and Grand Falls and power to the Fraser mills. The general area served by the International's power plants is shown in greater detail on the table with which this section began.[232] In 1933 Gatineau Power Company, Canadian Hydro-Electric Corporation's chief subsidiary, had operating revenues of $9,279,641, which were derived as follows:

Hydro-Electric Power Commission of Ontario	$4,572,697
International's paper mills (sale of power to)	2,798,636
Other public utilities and municipalities (sale wholesale to Ottawa, Hull, Grand Falls, Dalhousie, etc.)	449,393
Retail sales	824,742
Other wholesale industrial users (Canada Cement, Fraser, Eddy, etc.)	634,173

Although power is retailed in well over 100 municipalities, largely in Quebec, retail sales obviously are relatively unimportant as an outlet for the huge power capacity of the system as a whole, which now has assets of $144,711,366.

The very large rôle played by sales of power to the Hydro-Electric Power Commission of Ontario in Canadian Hydro-Electric's earnings explains the alarm among the holders of the bonds of its subsidiary, Gatineau Power Company, when the power contracts were attacked in the Ontario Legislature. Premier Hepburn explained the attitude of his administration in the following words: "The people of Ontario have been shackled by the Gatineau contracts of the former administration. . . . We are paying for power

232. See p. 142.

we do not need on that contract, and will continue to do so for the next forty years unless some steps are taken to remedy the situation . . . the Cabinet now has such steps under consideration. . . ."[233] On April 1, 1935, the Ontario government introduced in the Legislature a bill, the Hydro-Electric Power Commission Act, 1935, which declared contracts with the Gatineau Power Company and 3 Canadian-owned Quebec power companies were "illegal, void and unenforceable." Premier Hepburn explained that Ontario will continue to purchase power from Gatineau Power Company under the existing contract but will not be bound by the terms of the contract.[234]

Two other American-owned companies in Canada likewise were organized not to build up little distribution systems but to develop great hydro-electric resources. The Niagara-Hudson Power Corporation, which owns the power plants on the American side at the Falls, controls, through subsidiaries, the Canadian Niagara Power Company, Ltd., and the St. Lawrence Power Company, Ltd. The first is owned directly by Buffalo, Niagara and Eastern Power, Jacob Schoellkopf's company, which first utilized Niagara Falls as a power producer. The plant on the American side produces 452,000 horsepower. The Canadian plant has a capacity of 127,000 horsepower. Nominally, part of the output on the Canadian side is sold to the Ontario Hydro-Electric Commission, the rest being transmitted across the line to Niagara Falls and Buffalo. Actually, Canadian Niagara and Ontario Hydro exchange a good deal of power as it is needed from day to day. The net result is that very little power on balance is sold to the Ontario Hydro-Electric Commission.

The Duke-Price Power Company, Ltd., is the third of these great hydro-electric ventures in Canada which have been planned and financed by Americans. The early rôle played by James B. Duke and the subsequent participation of Price Brothers and Company, Ltd., and the Aluminum Company of America have already been recounted.[235] Its plant, 8 miles below Lake St. John, Quebec, is now equipped to produce 495,000 horsepower and can be increased by

233. *New York Times*, March 3, 1935.
234. *Ibid.*, April 2, 3, 13, 1935.
235. See pp. 102–107, where an organization chart is also given.

45,000 horsepower. About two thirds of its output is sold to the Aluminum Company of Canada, Ltd., Shawinigan Water and Power Company, Price Brothers and Company, Ltd., and the Port Alfred paper mill.[236] The company is controlled by Aluminium, Ltd., through Aluminum Company of Canada, Ltd., which owns 53½ per cent of the shares. Shawinigan owns 20 per cent, and the rest are held by Price Brothers and the Duke interests. Much of the funds with which the power plant was built, however, was supplied by the $35,291,000 bond issue originally offered in the United States.

So much for the great power plants under American control. The other American light and power companies in Canada are relatively unimportant. They are merely widely scattered distribution systems producing and selling small fractions of the electrical energy produced in Canada. In almost no case do they constitute important segments of the total properties of the parent companies. Cities Service Company's New Brunswick Power is a 1912 merger of St. John's street car and power companies, acquired in 1923 by Federal Light and Traction (a Cities Service sub-holding company). Although it owns a 19,000-horsepower waterpower site, it depends on a steam plant to supply St. John and to run the street railway. In 1934, however, dividend arrearages put the preferred shareholders in control.[237] Another of these small distribution systems, already charted, is that of International Utilities Corporation,[238] which supplies electricity to 13,400 customers in Saskatchewan and Alberta— in 79 communities—and to 4,036 in British Columbia. In southern Saskatchewan, Dominion Electric Power, Ltd., and Biggar Electric, Ltd., serve 4,819 customers in 31 towns in the Estevan and Assiniboia regions. They are both controlled by Dominion Electric Power Company, an American corporation owned by a subsidiary of North American Gas and Electric Company. The population is only 23,000 and is supplied by small steam and diesel plants, with a 138-mile

236. The Aluminum Company of America guarantees the performance of the first of those contracts. See pp. 102 ff., for its relation with the Canadian aluminum industry.

237. See p. 144, for the position of this company in Cities Service's Canadian organization.

238. See p. 145.

transmission line between Shaunavon and Assiniboia. Save for electric companies supplying Sault Ste Marie and Fort Frances, Ontario, and 7 or 8 towns in Manitoba, the rest of the American subsidiaries are in the Maritimes and in Quebec. Largest, probably, are the 5 acquired by the Associated Gas and Electric System from 1926 to 1928, which supply 13,425 customers in Charlottetown, Prince Edward Island, Fredericton, New Brunswick, Yarmouth, Nova Scotia, and 70 other towns with a combined population of about 80,000. These towns, spread over the 3 Provinces, use the power generated by 3 steam and 4 hydro-electric plants with a total capacity of 6,160 kilowatts. In Yarmouth and Fredericton, however, the Associated System distributes current purchased from the Power Commission. The Central Public Utility Corporation—one of the subsidiaries of Central Public Service Company, Chicago—acquired, in 1927, the Lower St. Lawrence Power Company (organized 5 years earlier), which generates 9,586 horsepower at Grand Metis Falls, Quebec, and supplies the Rimouski region—about 42 towns with 5,058 customers. It also transmits power to a subsidiary at Campbellton, New Brunswick. The last of the American public utility holding companies that need be mentioned is the Utilities Power and Light Corporation whose subsidiaries in Canada are shown below. Electricity is supplied by them to 12 communities in New Brunswick, 9 in Nova Scotia and two in Manitoba. Natural gas

UTILITIES POWER AND LIGHT CORPORATION

Central States Utilities Corp. (U.S.)		Utilities Power and Light Corp., Ltd.	
Canada Electric Co., Ltd. (1930) Supplies Amherst, N.S. and vicinity.	Eastern Electric and Development Co., Ltd. (1930) Supplies Sackville, N.B.	Maritime Coal Railway and Power Co., Ltd. (1930) 15 mi. railway and 17 sq. mi. coal lands, N.S.	Ontario Shore Gas Co., Ltd. Supplies Belleville, Oshawa
	Moncton Tramways, Electricity and Gas Co., Ltd. Supplies Moncton, N.B.		Canadian Fuels Ltd. (no data)

is piped to 6 New Brunswick towns and manufactured gas to 6 in Ontario. The $3,737,408 Maritime Coal, Railway and Power Company was suffering from lack of working capital when Utilities Power and Light bought it in 1930 and transferred its 2 electricity subsidiaries to Central States Utilities.

It is not easy to discover, in every case, the motives which prompted these investments.[239] The 3 great power companies present no difficulties. Canadian Hydro-Electric is a reasonable by-product of a paper company whose mills are huge power consumers. Duke-Price owes its American relations, in the first instance, at least, to James Duke's interest in power development. Since Aluminum Company of America also needed cheap power for its Canadian smelters it is not difficult to understand why it was willing to support the project. Niagara-Hudson Power, of course, in developing its site on the Canadian side was merely completing a project already begun nearby on the American side. The others are more obscure. It is understandable that natural gas resources of Ontario should have attracted Cities Service and the National Fuel Gas Company. Probably the Alberta natural gas investments are as reasonable. But some of the electric light companies must be suspected to be part of the nervous aggrandisement of rapidly expanding holding companies not much concerned with the geographical relevancy of the units in their "systems." Associated Gas and Electric System has placed its Maritime subsidiaries under the management of the New England Gas and Electric Association. Although in 1933 they accounted for only about 4 per cent of the electricity sales of the Association, they are at least understandably related to a system covering Massachusetts, New Hampshire, and Maine. Similarly, Central Public Service Company's modest systems in the lower St. Lawrence and New Brunswick—especially the latter—represent a natural push across the Border. Middle West Utilities' older subsidiary in the "Soo" district seems much more adequately correlated with its American properties than does its later, unprofitable, isolated assets in Manitoba. Defunct American Commonwealth Power Corporation's venture into Canada was purely a promotion.

At the beginning of this account of gas, light, and power com-

239. See also pp. 213–215.

panies 5 were listed as having closer past than present relations south of the Border. Of one of them, Union Gas of Canada, enough has been said.[240] The 2 most important Canadian power companies are Shawinigan Water and Power and Montreal Light, Heat and Power Consolidated. Much of the financing of the latter has been done in the United States. But so far as can be learned it is now and always has been Canadian-controlled. Shawinigan has had closer American relations. In 1933 only 11 per cent of the shares were held in the United States. But J. E. Aldred, an American, is chairman of the Board and it is said that the Baltimore capital supporting the Aldreds was the largest early factor in its development.[241] Dominion Lighting and Traction Company, Ltd., operates in the Windsor area, which probably suffices to explain the presence of its Michigan vice-president. Canadian Public Service Corporation, Ltd., in which there is still a large American financial interest, is an amalgamation of scattered units—largely in western Canada—several of which (especially Canadian Western Telephone Company, Ltd.) were controlled in the United States.

MERCHANDISING

Two sorts of American direct investments are to be found in this field of commercial activity in Canada. There are the offices or separate companies maintained by American factories to handle Canadian sales. There are also the various kinds of American-owned stores.

To the first group we need give but scant attention. Many of them are exactly comparable with the unincorporated sales offices maintained in the larger American cities by manufacturing companies. They represent an effort to follow the market more aggressively than might be possible from the often isolated factory. The Canadian sales office is frequently separately incorporated; for example, Allis-Chalmers Rumely, Ltd., with head office in Winnipeg and half a dozen sub-offices. It is not particularly important closely to examine these sales companies. They have a modest advantage over

240. See p. 144.
241. See p. 139 for Field's reference to Boston money in that company before the war.

the unincorporated sales office in that goods may be shipped to them by the parent company's factory and the sales results kept separate from the American accounts. They may also, by adopting a Canadianized name, eliminate some sales resistance. Most of them are not supported by branch factories—the parent company has not yet decided that the Canadian market warrants manufacturing on the spot. But there are cases of that sort. The Associated Telephone and Telegraph Corporation and the Brunswick-Balke-Callender Company, for example, have separately incorporated their Canadian factories and their Canadian sales offices. It is probable that there are certain accounting advantages here, too, since it permits both the parent and the branch factory to "sell" goods to the sales company in cases where the branch plant does not produce a complete line. Many American-owned manufacturing subsidiaries in Canada were at one time merely sales companies.

Outstanding cases of distribution in Canada through branch houses are the American agricultural implement companies. Their branches have, in periods of agricultural prosperity, carried inventories worth millions of dollars.[242]

But more interesting are the American-owned stores in Canada. Among them the Canadian links of American chain store systems are outstanding. But before describing them, the other wholesale and retail ventures of Americans north of the Border may be more cursorily mentioned. Half a dozen American manufacturers have carried into Canada their habitual practice of selling at least a portion of their products direct to the public through their own sales outlets. Here are the 670 gas stations of Imperial Oil, the 150 stores of the Singer Manufacturing Company (some of which are owned by agents), the half dozen Kodak stores, and the 3 belonging to A. G. Spalding and Brothers.[243] The Kodak stores, several of which

242. See Field, *op. cit.* (1914 ed.), p. 25. International Harvester, for example, carried its Canadian branch house inventories at $7,200,000 in 1921. See also above, pp. 60–62.

243. There are a few others. The Ground Gripper Shoe Company, Inc., has retail outlets in Canada, as have Grinnell Brothers, and Keith Shoe Company (Walk-Over). A few years ago two American candy companies operated stores in Canada, but these have either withdrawn or been absorbed into Canadian enterprises.

were bought from former owners years ago, are separately incorporated.

Several American wholesalers have pushed into Canada. The Marshall-Wells Company has 6 hardware branches in the Northwest states, and 9 in the 4 Western provinces. A separate corporation owns the real estate occupied in Winnipeg, Vancouver, and Edmonton,[244] and a factory in each country supplies some of the goods sold. The Gamble-Robinson Company operates a chain of 65 branch houses wholesaling fruit, vegetables, and groceries in 7 Middle Western states and in Ontario and Quebec.[245] During and just after the war, the Nash Shareholders' Company of Minneapolis built up a large fruit and vegetable jobbing and brokerage business in Western Canada. So extensive did it become that it threatened a complete monopoly, and complaints were filed against it under the Combines Investigation Act. After lengthy legal proceedings, four individuals and four corporations were convicted and fines totaling $200,000 were imposed.[246]

There are miscellaneous cases. In one or two the retailing activities are an unplanned outgrowth of other activities. A few companies—notably J. R. Watkins Company and W. T. Rawleigh—do a considerable house-to-house canvassing business, chiefly in rural areas. Occasionally individual Americans—as contrasted with corporations already engaged in merchandising in the United States—have interested themselves, either in the beginning or later, in retailing ventures in Canada. Several small chains of retail lumber yards in the Prairie Provinces were started by Americans a number of years ago. One of those companies, over 30 years old, began as a land-selling enterprise, then started a private bank, and finally, as opportunity offered, opened lumber yards. The outstanding case of this sort, however, although one where the Americans entered subsequent to the beginning of the company, is Dominion Stores, Ltd., 71 per cent

244. And in 6 American cities.

245. It is not known what proportion are in Canada. Each branch house has complete warehouse refrigeration and other equipment. The Canadian property is held through wholly-owned subsidiaries.

246. See Annual Report of the Registrar of the Combines Investigation Act for 1925 and 1926.

of whose shares are held in the United States.[247] The shares are widely distributed among over 3,000 shareholders in both countries, no one of whom holds more than 5 per cent,[248] but of the 16 largest blocks, which amount to 21 per cent of the total, 9—comprising 15 per cent—are held by Americans. Among those large American shareholders are the chairman and one of the members of the board. It must be kept in mind, however, that this American influence in an important Canadian chain store company is in a distinctly different category from that to which we now turn, where American chain store companies have quite naturally opened Canadian units.

Six American "chain" companies have some of their hundreds of stores in Canada: Woolworth, Kresge, H. L. Green, Mercantile Stores, Liggett, and the Great Atlantic and Pacific Tea.[249] Mercantile Stores Co., Inc., or its predecessors, now operating 19 dry goods stores in the United States has owned Thomas C. Watkins, Ltd., in Hamilton, since before the war. The others—3 variety chains, a grocery, and a drug chain—had 551 Canadian stores at the end of 1933.[250]

Chain stores of all sorts in Canada in 1930 comprised about 7 per cent of the *total*[251] stores, and accounted for 20 per cent of the sales. The variety store field is dominated by chain stores, and the grocery and combination meat and grocery and drug chain stores bulk larger in Canadian merchandising than does the chain store on the average.

247. *Proceedings of Royal Commission on Price Spreads,* November 14, 1934, pp. 782, 789–791.

248. Of the shareholders, 1,786, or 54 per cent, were American; 4 of the 10 members of the board are Americans.

249. In 1929 the Safeway Stores, Inc., operating 3,527 grocery stores in the West, merged Kirkham Groceterias, Ltd., in British Columbia, and its own British Columbia subsidiary into Safeway Stores, Ltd., but we do not know how many—if any—of its stores are in Canada. See p. 256, for mention of repatriated stores.

250. Most of the information in the rest of this section was obtained from *Proceedings of Royal Commission on Price Spreads,* pp. 597–1311, except financial data for the parent companies, which are from *Moody's Manual of Investments, Industrial Securities,* 1934.

251. Chain and independent combined. For the purposes of this study the so-called "voluntary chains" are considered independent stores.

The American-owned chain stores are in those 3 fields. The following table shows these relationships.

TABLE X

Chain Stores in Relation to All Stores in Canada, 1930[252]

Type of chain	Per cent of total stores	sales
Variety chains in relation to all variety stores	63.5	93.6
Grocery and meat and grocery chains in relation to all such stores	9.0	30.0
Drug chains in relation to all drug stores	8.1	18.6
All *chain* stores in relation to all stores	6.8	20.4
Variety, grocery, and drug chains in relation to all stores	2.2	6.0
Six American-owned chains in relation to all stores	.7	2.5

In 1930 the 921 stores operated by the 6 American-owned companies[253] comprised $\frac{7}{10}$ of 1 per cent of all stores in Canada (independent included) and did 2.5 per cent of the business. The variety, grocery, and drug chains which include those American companies have 2.2 per cent of all stores, chain and unit, in Canada and account for 6 per cent of the sales. But they do most of the variety store business, about 30 per cent of the grocery, and almost 20 per cent of the drug business of the country. The table on the next page, which must be read against this background of the "all-stores" picture, shows a little more exactly the position of the American companies within their respective chain store groups.

Two thirds of the chain variety stores are American. A third of the chain groceries and 14 per cent of the chain drug stores are American-owned.[254]

252. Computed from reports of Dominion Bureau of Statistics, 1930; and *Proceedings of Royal Commission on Price Spreads,* November 12, 1934, and following sessions.

253. In these and subsequent figures in this section Dominion Stores, Ltd., is considered an American company. See p. 154.

254. These figures and the others in Table XI are computed from the same sources as those in the previous table, with the addition of 1933 bulletins of the Dominion Bureau.

TABLE XI

American-Owned Chain Stores in Canada

Type of chain	No. of chains 1933	No. of stores 1930	No. of stores 1933	Per cent American stores 1933	Sales 1930 Value	Per cent	Sales 1933 Value	Per cent	Employees, 1933 Total	Per cent in American stores
Variety										
All	14	327	354		$ 39,383,379		$32,463,300		8,091	
American-owned	3	218	231	65	30,834,271	78	25,885,961	80	6,103	75
Grocery and comb. meat and grocery										
All	67	2,128	2,162		119,843,792		97,277,700		11,214	
American-owned	2	666	782	36	37,859,738	32	35,268,399	36	4,815	43
Drug										
All	29	292	301		13,971,087		11,001,700		1,519	
American-owned	1	37	42	14	2,461,479	17	2,008,206	18	306	20

The 3 American companies, Woolworth, Kresge, and H. L. Green, operating variety stores in Canada, pretty well monopolize the variety chain store business.

In 1897 S. H. Knox and Company opened a store in Toronto. Ten years later E. P. Charlton Company incorporated a Canadian company. When, in 1912, the two parent companies merged with F. W. Woolworth Company they owned 32 Canadian stores and had had sales of $3,115, 674 that year. By 1929 F. W. Woolworth Company, Ltd., the successor company in Canada, sold $21,681,293 worth of goods. In 1933 it operated 136 stores, which were 7 per cent of the Woolworth stores in North America, as can be seen in the table on the next page. The Canadian stores have during recent years accounted for about 7 per cent of Woolworth sales. It is very interesting to note, however, that although the sales per store are a little less in Canada, the profits per store are startlingly larger even after interest payments have been made by the Canadian company and before payment of Federal taxes by the American stores.

The S. S. Kresge Company did not enter Canada until 1928. Its subsidiary, S. S. Kresge Company, Ltd., opened its first store early the next year and by 1933 it operated 44 stores, chiefly in Ontario and Quebec, but with a few in Saskatchewan, Alberta, and British Columbia. The sales amount to about $5,000,000 a year. Table

TABLE XII

Canadian Subsidiaries in Relation to Parent Companies[255]

	Woolworth			Kresge§			Atlantic and Pacific**		
		Canada			Canada			Canada	
	Total	Number or value	Per cent of total	Total	Number or value	Per cent of total	Total	Number or value	Per cent of total
Stores	1,941	136	7.0	678	44	6.5	15,427	277	1.8
Sales, 1929–33	$1,375,414,741	$93,230,444	6.8	$703,383,320	$19,711,694	2.8	$4,964,672,302	$91,640,136	1.8
Average sales per store per year, 1929–33	145,359	137,000†		201,469	107,269		321,817†	††	
Net income,* 1929–33	115,940,295	11,193,062‖	9.5‖	59,856,684	540,695	0.8	152,486,135	def. 141,545	
Average profit per store, per year, 1929–33	12,262	16,460†		17,888	2,140		9,884†	††	
Assets, 1933	177,630,059¶	10,065,364	5.6	119,439,270	11,303,904	9.2	125,747,368	5,391,814‡	4.3

* Sales less costs, depreciation and amortization, for parent companies; net available for dividends, for subsidiaries.

† Computed on basis of number of stores in 1933.

‡ Computed by doubling the assets of the Toronto division, which has 140 stores. The exact assets of the Quebec division, which has 138 stores, are not available.

§ The first Canadian store was opened in 1929, and for three years the chain was rapidly being added to. Consequently many stores were open only a part of a year, although no correction can be shown in these figures. Kresge charges no interest for its loans to the Canadian Company, whereas Woolworth charges 6 per cent. There would be no net profit in Kresge, Ltd., if 6 per cent had been paid on loans.

‖ During those years the Canadian Company paid $2,551,905 to the parent company as interest on loans or advances. Since the parent company has no funded debt, that sum might be added to the profits, which would give a larger percentage to total.

¶ Although the other Woolworth figures have all been adjusted so as to exclude European interests, this includes about $30,000,000 investment in English and German companies.

** A. and P. in Canada began operations in 1927 and was expanding during 1929–1932. It is charged no interest on loans from parent company, and consequently deficit is larger than these figures indicate.

†† Accurate figures are not available to show the number of stores in operation each year. The 1933 sales per store were $56,000.

255. Sources: Moody's Manual of Investments, Industrial Securities, 1934; Proceedings of Royal Commission on Price Spreads, November 12, 1934, and following sessions.

XII reveals the net income, profits, and assets of the Kresge Companies.

Both of those companies have been financed entirely by the parent companies and are little more than Canadian divisions of the chain store systems. The third American chain store presents a contrast. In 1920 Metropolitan Chain Stores, Inc., of New York acquired the Canadian stores previously owned by Canadian Smallwares Company and Variety 5-10-15 Cent Stores. By 1930 Metropolitan Stores, Ltd., which it organized, was operating 52 stores and had assets of $10,000,000, sales of $7,400,000, and a net profit of $423,-000. In 1930 the F. and W. Grand Silver Stores, Inc., which had about 165 variety stores in the United States, bought Metropolitan Stores, Ltd., and 3 years later, when the American company went into receivership, H. L. Green Company, Inc., acquired them both. The Canadian properties have been financed[256] largely through public bond issues by real estate subsidiary holding companies. The organization of H. L. Green Company in Canada may be charted thus:

METROPOLITAN STORES, LTD.

51 Stores, 1933 49 Stores, 1934	Metropolitan Chain Properties, Ltd. Metropolitan Corporation of Canada, Ltd.

The combined 1933 sales, American and Canadian, were about $29,-000,000, of which approximately 20 per cent were in Canada. For the 5 years following 1929, however, the Canadian company, with sales of $32,000,000, suffered a small deficit.

The Great Atlantic and Pacific Tea Company incorporated a Canadian subsidiary in 1919, but not until 1927 did it open its first store. By 1934, however, there were 277 A. & P. stores north of the Border, one third in the Montreal division and the rest in the Toronto division. The Canadian sales reached a peak in 1931–32, at $21,000,000, and dropped to $15,500,000 in 1933–34. As Table XII shows, the Canadian sales are a little less than 2 per cent of total A. & P. sales. The Toronto division has yielded, since 1929, a

256. For further detail on chain store financing by American companies in Canada, see pp. 227–228.

small profit, but after deducting Montreal division losses the Canadian company shows a small loss.

Louis K. Liggett, Ltd., the one American drug chain in Canada, acquired several small Canadian chains as the nucleus for its own organization. It was incorporated in 1916, taking over the Toronto store of Liggett, Ltd., and 3 in Winnipeg owned by the Gordon, Mitchell Drug Company. Two years later Allen and Cochrane, Ltd.'s 6 Ottawa stores were added. In 1920, by further purchases and by opening new stores, its chain reached 39 stores. In 1922 it was reorganized, all unproductive assets written off, and a surplus of $1,000,000 set up by reducing the capitalization. Soon afterwards Messrs. Allen and Cochrane sold their small interests to United Drug Company, Ltd., the Canadian parent company.[257] Sales had reached a peak, not since regained, of $2,824,181. By 1930 the number of stores had been reduced to 37; in the next 3 years, however, 5 more were added. Profits have been negligible,[258] despite cancellations of debts owing the parent company and virtual exhaustion of the surplus set up in 1922.

It should be apparent from the preceding analysis that, save in the variety, grocery, and drug chain stores, and in gasoline filling stations, the American retailing activities in Canada are not very important.

MISCELLANEOUS COMPANIES

Manufacturing, mining, merchandising, communications and public utilities are the broad fields in which most of the American-owned industry in Canada is to be found. But there remain other sorts of businesses where enough American companies have entered to make it worth while examining them. In most cases, however, we have no measuring rod by which the relative importance of the American contingent may be estimated.

Motion Picture Industry

The motion picture industry in Canada is almost entirely confined to the distribution of imported films and the ownership or

257. Itself owned by the United Drug Company of Boston.

258. Tamblyn, Ltd., a competing chain with 59 stores, has been more successful.

management of theaters. Such small producing organizations as exist have no American connections. All the larger American producing companies have incorporated subsidiaries in Canada and distribute their films from coast to coast through chains of exchanges. Collectively they supply about 90 per cent of all feature pictures shown in Canada, and an even larger percentage of the shorter films. There is nothing peculiar or unique about their Canadian business except the overwhelming share of the market which they hold.[259]

In this volume we are interested primarily in economic and industrial relationships and it is not our task to discuss the cultural effects of this dominance of American films. It may be noted, however, that the feeling against this virtual monopoly has at times been formidable and has led to the passage of modified quota laws and to much agitation for more stringent regulation of the "movies."

While Loew's and Radio-Keith-Orpheum own theaters in Canada —the former has 4 theaters in Montreal, Toronto, and London, and the latter has some 8 theaters in 6 cities, from Calgary to St. John— yet the dominant corporation in the Canadian motion picture field is Famous Players Canadian Corporation, controlled by Paramount Publix Corporation.[260] The theaters of the Radio-Keith-Orpheum (Canada), Ltd., are largely but not entirely linked up with Paramount's Canadian theaters by an agreement made in 1929. Some of them have quite a long history going back to the Orpheum Circuit in

259. Much of the information in this section is taken from the Report of the Commissioner in the *Investigation into an Alleged Combine in the Motion Picture Industry in Canada* (Ottawa, 1931).

260. In earlier years other American theater owners had property in Canada. Field (*op. cit.* [1914 ed.], pp. 62–63) found, in 1913, that the Gayety was owned by the Columbian Amusement Company, New York; Shea's Theater by Buffalo people; the Princess by a Detroit man (under contract) who purchased it from the Canada Life Insurance Company; Loew's Theater was controlled by Canadians, but Marcus Loew Company, New York, owned 20 per cent stock and $100,000 bonds; and there was Seattle money in an Edmonton, and American money in two Vancouver, theaters. There may still be some American capital in theaters other than those mentioned in the text. For example, Consolidated Theaters, Ltd., was organized in 1928 to acquire the 11 theaters in Toronto, Montreal, and Sherbrooke which had been owned by Consolidated Theaters Corporation, incorporated in 1927 by New Yorkers and Canadians.

Manitoba, Alberta, and British Columbia, and the B. F. Keith theater in Ottawa.

Famous Players Canadian Corporation was created in 1920 and entered into a contract with Famous Player's–Lasky Corporation (predecessor of Paramount Publix) which gave it for 20 years "first run" in Canada of all pictures of the parent company. Regal Films, which distributed for Metro-Goldwyn-Mayer, Pathé, and other, including some British, producers, is also controlled by Paramount Publix. In 1928 Famous Players Canadian Corporation made a 5-year contract with Columbia Pictures of Canada, Ltd., which gave it first choice of all Columbia pictures in 13 principal cities in Canada. In 1930 Famous Players Canadian Corporation virtually controlled the distribution of 50 per cent of all films released in Canada.

Commencing business in 1920 with 13 theaters, Famous Players Canadian Corporation steadily expanded its chain of owned or controlled theaters until in 1934 the number reached over 200, or about 20 per cent of all theaters in Canada. Its dominating position is not, however, made clear by this figure of 20 per cent. In 1931, at the time of the Combines Investigation, it owned the only theaters in 25 Ontario cities with a total population of almost 300,000. In 11 other Ontario cities, including Windsor and 5 others with populations of over 20,000, it operates the only first-run houses. And in the 4 important cities of Hamilton, London, Ottawa, and St. Catherines its theaters were the leading first-run houses. Its only important competition in central Toronto was Loew's Downtown, also an American-operated theater. Famous Players Canadian has not been as energetic in Quebec. But in 1931 it controlled about half the seating capacity of the theaters in Montreal. Nor has the rest of Canada been neglected. The company, for example, owns the largest theater in Halifax, the 3 largest—containing a third of all theater seats—in Winnipeg, almost 80 per cent of the seating capacity of the theaters in Edmonton, and so on. The Combines Investigation concluded that Famous Players Canadian Corporation occupied an exclusive, or a dominant, position in all but 8 cities of 10,000 population or over in Canada—one each in Nova Scotia and New Brunswick, two in Ontario, and four in Quebec. Through its dominance or monopoly of first-run business throughout Canada, Famous Players is in a peculiarly favorable competitive position in dealing with those producers and distributors of films in Canada which it does not directly control.[261]

In March, 1929, "control of Famous Players Canadian Corporation was brought to Canada with much pomp and panoply."[262] It was the opinion of the Combines Investigator in 1931 that at no time during the company's history have Mr. Zukor and his associates in Paramount lost substantial control. Whatever may have been the reason for the juggling of shares during 1929–30, Paramount bought back, in 1930, 96 per cent of the shares by an exchange of its own stock.

INSURANCE

In 1932 there were 20 American life insurance companies operating in Canada. They held $2,044,024,535 in life insurance, which was 32 per cent of the total in force in Canada. It represented, however, only about 2 per cent of the total life insurance held by United States companies. In the other insurance fields there were over 130 American companies operating in the Dominion.[263] Together they wrote fire, accident, indemnity, and other kinds of policies amounting to $3,013,356,793, which was 32 per cent of the total non-life risks in force in Canada. Many American insurance companies invest some of their American reserves in Canadian securities. Consequently their total investment in Canada is much more than proportionate to their Canadian business. In 1932, for example, the United States legal reserve life insurance companies had 4 per cent of their total assets in Canada, although, as stated above, only about 2 per cent of their business was in the Dominion.

The average American insurance company does business in Canada under its own name through an unincorporated branch which makes the required deposits with the Canadian authorities. A few, however,

261. It should be noted that Famous Players Canadian Corporation was finally acquitted in the courts on charges laid under the Criminal Code and arising out of the Commissioner's investigations.

262. *Financial Post*, May 29, 1930. See also May 15, 1930, and March 27, 1930, and Report of the Commissioner, *op. cit.*, pp. 16–17.

263. Although 113 companies write fire insurance and 132 issue casualty policies, giving an apparent total of 235, most of the casualty companies are identical with the fire companies.

have separate Canadian subsidiaries. The American Surety Company and the Hartford Steam Boiler Inspection and Insurance Company, for example, own, respectively, the Canadian Surety Company and the Boiler Inspection and Insurance Company of Canada. There are at least 5 other such subsidiary companies. Why those few companies chose to operate in Canada through subsidiaries rather than branches is not very clear. One of them explained that, after 20 years of doing business through a Canadian agent, it decided to form a limited company which would both protect its business more adequately and provide a better sales appeal. There is, in this case, a common president and an interlocking directorate. All large risks are submitted to the parent company for approval and the parent company audits the subsidiary. The parent company is also licensed in Canada for some purposes.

It is the common testimony of both the companies and the insurance associations that, to quote the vice-president of one of the largest, "you will find practically the same general type of [agency] organizations in the two countries. In both countries, some companies operate on the managerial system while others operate through general agencies. The forms of insurance offered in the two countries are practically uniform, any variations being of a minor character."

FINANCE

Some American manufacturing companies maintain their own finance organizations to support the sales organizations of their Canadian branch plants. The General Motors organization has already been referred to,[264] in which Canadian branches of General Motors Acceptance Corporation and General Exchange Insurance Corporation finance wholesale distribution and retail sales and insure cars until fully sold. In addition several of the American finance companies have quite naturally included Canada in their field of operation. The Commercial Credit Company, certainly one of the largest, controls, through subsidiaries, the Continental Guaranty Corporation of Canada, Ltd., Montreal (which purchases various sorts of commercial paper) and the Credit Alliance Corporation, Ltd. (especially financing purchases of machinery and equipment). The Continental Guaranty Corporation, even in 1931, purchased

264. See pp. 65–67.

almost $10,000,000 worth of commercial paper. A similar venture is the Canadian Acceptance Corporation, Ltd. (owned by the Commercial Investment Trust Corporation), which finances manufacturers and merchants by purchasing the notes and accounts arising out of their sales. A third, probably smaller, is the Paramount Finance Company, Ltd., of Windsor, a subsidiary of the Union Investment Company, Detroit.

In the period between 1919 and 1931 several billion dollars' worth of Canadian bonds were publicly issued in the United States. In the 5 years 1927–31 about $1,300 millions were floated. Usually, though not invariably, the underwriting of these issues involved some sort of tieup between Canadian and United States investment dealers, though this was not invariably the case. There were some instances where an issue payable in New York only was handled entirely by a United States firm.

The arrangements between the houses in the two countries were of a very informal nature, though custom tended to stereotype the procedure. Once certain houses had worked together in tendering for and marketing an issue an account was opened which tended, except in unusual circumstances, to bring the same houses together again to handle future issues for the same borrower. Nevertheless, the arrangement did not obligate any firm to continue in the account. If at the consultation arranging for the bidding price for the security the views of one firm could not be reconciled with those of the others, that firm was at liberty to withdraw. It is safe to say that the discussion almost invariably brought about general assent as to terms.

The associations between United States and Canadian houses developed gradually. It is known that certain Canadian firms had a Canadian staff in some of the United States houses to handle Canadian securities in the over-the-counter trade. In this way strong links with United States houses were formed. This arrangement later gave place to New York branches of the large Canadian investment dealers. Moreover, it became necessary for United States houses to have branches in Canadian cities such as Montreal and Toronto, though since 1931 the number of these has diminished. When the New York market became the source of so much Canadian financing, the associations were developed further, though still informally, to meet the new situation. It became the custom for loans payable in both Canadian and New York funds to be handled by a syndicate including both Canadian and United States houses. One firm either in Canada or the United States, though usually in the United States unless the United States share was small, became manager of the whole account. A sub-manager of the Canadian or United States group, as the case might be, was also appointed. This type of arrangement prevailed also in the Canadian participation in United States and foreign issues.

There was a substantial volume of such bonds marketed in Canada: bonds of South American and European governments, French, German, and Italian corporations, and some United States corporations such as National Cash Register and North American Edison. Sometimes in connection with these issues Canadian houses were members of the originating group or of the banking group, but more often were probably only included in the selling group. However, the volume of this business, substantial as it was, was small when compared with that of Canadian new issues placed in the United States and bonds of old issues which flowed to that market.

In general it may be said that the bonds of Canadian governments and municipalities, including guaranties by such borrowers, were disposed of by public tender, while industrial and utility corporation issues were arranged by negotiation. In periods of emergency or distress financing, when the assumption of large commitments on new issues by a syndicate becomes practically impossible, there is of necessity a temporary modification of the tender system. Due to the conditions existing in 1931, particularly those in the latter half of that year, such a period of emergency in Dominion financing developed. A considerable volume of financing had to be done for Canadian Provincial and Municipal borrowers, and at the beginning of the year it appeared that all of this money would have to be raised in the Dominion. It was evident that if the requirements of the various borrowers were to be met adequately, these borrowers should be brought to the market in an orderly manner, for amounts which the domestic market might reasonably be expected to absorb. With this end in view, the larger investment banking firms coöperated to form an orderly marketing organization, which included and had the active support of the Canadian chartered banks, and provided for wide-spread participation by all the recognized security dealers throughout the Dominion in all the important issues of Canadian governmental borrowers. By this means Canadian borrowers were able to satisfy their more pressing capital requirements during the first eight months of the year, after which the improvement then evident in security prices, and the general outlook, seemed to warrant a discontinuance of the orderly marketing arrangement.

Since the Conversion Loan of May, 1931, there has developed a new technique of handling the domestic issues of the Dominion Government: the various dealers report their sales directly to the Dominion Government officials, who exercise the functions of what might be called syndicate managers.

During the period of heavy flotation of Canadian issues in New York the following procedure, though subject to variations, was typical. A Provincial government desiring to raise a loan payable in Canadian and New York funds called for tenders. The investment house which happened to be the continuing manager of a particular group of houses which had an informal arrangement for bidding together for issues of that particular borrower, would communicate with the other United States and Canadian investment firms who were members of the group, and set out the participations arranged for each member for the particular issue. The representatives from each of the member houses would then meet to determine what the group would bid for the issue. Similarly other groups of houses would agree on a bid.

In large issues the originating group, having purchased an issue, might be desirous of distributing the financial responsibility involved by the formation of a banking syndicate of slightly increased membership. The members of the banking syndicate would then form a selling group which would in turn accept a commitment, thus still further reducing the financial liability of the members of the originating group.

The selling terms were set out in detail in a letter to selling group members. The highest price was the retail selling price; the lowest price was that at which the member of the selling group bought bonds from the originating or banking group. Purchasers of very large amounts received a concession off the retail price. Usually there was also included a list of exempted institutions, which would be specially canvassed by banking group or originating group.

Following is an example of the actual offering terms in Canada for a Canadian–United States issue:

Retail price	$98.25
Price to dealers	97.75
Price to purchasers of $25,000 to $249,000	97.75
Price to purchasers of $250,000 or more	97.50
Price to selling group	97.25
Price to exempted institutions	97.25

The procedure for marketing corporation securities was substantially the same, except for the fact that due to the complex character of various industrial credits and the wide range of variation which is possible under the terms of corporation securities, as compared with the more or less stereotyped form of securities issued by public borrowers, the issues made by corporations were usually effected by negotiations with the underwriting house, rather than by public tender. In the case of a corporation issue, one large firm might purchase the issue and form a banking syndicate of which it would be a member also. This banking syndicate would purchase the bonds at some advance in price, and then form a selling group, of which firms in the banking syndicate would also be members. This selling group would purchase the bonds from the banking group at another advance in price. In this way, the liability was gradually split and distributed, and the various firms compensated in proportion to their interest in the account.

Many United States and Canadian firms engage in the international trade in securities described above. Canadian chartered banks and investment dealers carry on regular day-to-day trading, either with agents in the United States or through their own offices in New York. Similarly, in new issues, these institutions with their associated United States firms place such issues in Canada and the United States. It is the Canadian dealers and banks, with their agencies, offices, or associates in the United States, which maintain the trading markets for most Canadian funded obligations, since only a small fraction of Canadian bond issues which are active in over-the-counter trading are handled by the regular stock exchanges. Possibly most elaborate among the American brokerage branches in Canada are those of E. A. Pierce and Company in Toronto, Ottawa, and Hamilton, which extend to Canada the private wire system of the parent company.[265]

Scarcely financial organizations, and yet closely associated with them, are the credit rating organizations. There may be more than a few Canadian subsidiaries of such companies. But Dun and Bradstreet of Canada, Ltd., is no doubt the largest. R. G. Dun and Company commenced busines in the United States in 1841. In 1857 it opened a Montreal branch, chiefly to provide its American customers with credit information regarding Canadian companies. Later, of course, it supplied Canadian companies with that sort of information. During the years many Canadian offices have been opened. A somewhat similar organization, but providing Canadian exporters with insurance against the insolvency of foreign buyers, was organized in 1932 as the Canadian Foreign Credit Underwriters, Ltd. It involved the extension to Canada of the facilities of the American Foreign Credit Exchange.[266]

HOTELS

The history and corporate relations of an industry of this sort are extremely difficult to discover. As near as can be determined, 14 Canadian hotels have, within the last 10 years, been at least nominally American-owned. One burned down, 2 have not been traced, and 3 are now evidently Canadian-owned. The others are probably still American.

The most ambitious attempt at Canadian hotel operation was made by the United Hotels Company of America.[267] It is not an organization which publishes much information concerning its business relations, but apparently its almost invariable practice in Canada has been to assist in the organization of companies to build hotels. It may have supplied some capital in return for the 51 per cent of

265. See p. 127.

266. The ownership and later fortunes of the Canadian company were not traced. See *Commercial and Financial Chronicle,* June 18, 1932, p. 4412.

267. Mr. George H. O'Neill, of Toronto, is said to have been instrumental in bringing United Hotels to Canada. See *Monetary Times,* Mar. 14, 1930.

the common shares which it usually received. Most of the capital, however, was raised by the sale of the bonds and preferred stock of the Canadian companies. The King Edward Hotel Company, Ltd., for example, floated bonds apparently largely in the United States, amounting to over $6,500,000. The 51 per cent interest of United Hotels, before the shares were reduced to no-par, amounted to $510,-000 par value. The United Hotels company also had a contract to operate the hotels. In 1927 it operated 24 hotels, including the following in Canada:

> Mount Royal, Montreal, 1,060 rooms
> King Edward, Toronto, 861 rooms
> Clifton, Niagara Falls
> Prince Edward, Windsor, 250 rooms
> Admiral Beatty, St. John
> Royal Connaught, Hamilton

In 1929 there was an unsuccessful attempt to form a new holding company, United International Hotels, Inc., to operate the Canadian and some of the American hotels. After 9 years the largest of the hotels, the Mount Royal, went out of United Hotels operation in 1930, when a Montreal syndicate bought the majority of common shares. Most of the bonds of that hotel were issued in Canada. The Clifton burned down. The King Edward was foreclosed in 1933 by the Metropolitan Life Insurance Company, holder of $2,150,000 first mortgage bonds, plus arrears. The Prince Edward is still operated by United Hotels but it is Canadian-owned. The remaining two are now owned and operated by Canadians.

Most of the other American hotels are more obscure. The 700-room Windsor in Montreal, built in 1902, was controlled by the Boomer-Dupont Properties Corporation (which operated an American chain) from 1924 to 1927, when control was repurchased by a Canadian banking group. Ford Hotels Company, Inc., which owns a hotel in Erie, Pennsylvania, also owns, subject to mortgages, two moderate price 750-room hotels in Toronto and Montreal, opened in 1929 or 1930. The Prince of Wales Hotel in Alberta, partly owned by the Great Northern Railway through the Canadian Rockies Hotel Company, Ltd., is opened in the summer months if the tourist traffic warrants. Of the other hotels almost nothing save their name is known to us.

RESTAURANTS

Few of the American restaurant chains have established Canadian units. The Childs Company is the only case of importance, and only 7 of its 111 restaurants are in Canada. The first one was opened in 1910. There are now 3 in Toronto, 3 in Montreal, and one in Winnipeg. The Canadian business is operated through an unincorporated branch as one of 8 geographic groups. A subsidiary, Childs Company of Manitoba, Ltd., owns the largest building in Winnipeg. Childs' departure from a white tiled restaurant first occurred in Winnipeg. As far as is known only two other American companies operate Canadian restaurants. The Home Dairy Company, which confines its operations largely to northern New York, owns two cafeterias in southern Ontario, and Stewart's Cafeterias have at least a Montreal establishment.

OTHER

We have come at last to the tag end—the last few miscellaneous companies which complete this long account of American companies in Canada. For very many years American construction companies have undertaken special jobs in Canada. A St. Paul firm did much of the grading when Van Horne was rushing the Canadian Pacific across the Prairie Provinces to the Rockies; and a Pennsylvania company laid tracks for Galt's St. Lawrence and Atlantic Railway before the Grand Trunk acquired it. But not many contracting and engineering companies have established permanent Canadian organizations. Of those which have, the United States Realty and Improvement Company is the largest. It owns the George A. Fuller Company, which in turn owns the George A. Fuller Company of Canada, Ltd., organized in 1909. The Canadian company has carried on a general construction business in Canada. In 1921, for example, it was building a hospital in Fredericton, New Brunswick, paper mills for the St. Maurice and Fraser companies, a dam in Quebec, and pulp mills at Kipawa (now owned by Canadian International Paper). In 1928 $750,000 in preferred stock, guaranteed by the parent company, was issued in Canada "in order to have certain Canadian interests identified with the company."[268] During the depression, however, the preferred has been taken up to relieve the parent company from the payment of dividends when the subsidiary was unprofitable. The Canadian company controls the Richelieu Development Company, Ltd., which holds title to Montreal real estate —27 buildings in 1931. Three other companies—Thompson-Starrett Company, James Stewart and Company, and Stone and Webster, Inc.—have had Canadian subsidiaries doing construction and engineering, but little is known of them. In 1929 the famous salvage firm, Merritt-Chapman and Scott Corporation, organized a Canadian company to engage in the general contracting business, but as nearly as can be learned it withdrew as the depression in the building trades intensified.

A further development of some interest may be noted. On September 1, 1931, there came into effect a special tariff on magazines, as a result of which more than 50 American magazines are now printed in Canada, with a circulation of over 900,000 per issue or more than 20,000,000 per year. The largest are *Liberty*, *True Story*, and the *Pictorial Review*. In nearly all cases the magazines are identical reproductions of the American editions, though in the advertising columns names of Canadian branch houses are usually substituted for those of the parent companies. *Liberty*, however, substitutes for its editorial page a special editorial page dealing with Canadian affairs, and occasionally runs a special Canadian feature article in its Canadian edition. Practically all of these magazines are sold in Canada at the same price as in the United States. Most other American magazines, not printed in Canada, sell from 5 to 10 cents higher in Canada. None of the magazine publishers have established plants in Canada to print their Canadian editions. All use existing Canadian printing establishments on a contract basis. In most cases only the printing is done in Canada, the American office looking after circulation, subscriptions, distribution, and so on. The Maclean Publishing Company, however, not only does the job printing for 8 or 10 magazines, but also looks after new subscriptions, special advertising, and distribution. It should be added that many American magazines with very large circulation in Canada prefer not to print in

268. *Commercial and Financial Chronicle,* February 4, 1928, p. 733.

Canada, and seem to find that the added price to their Canadian readers has not seriously impaired their sales. These include the *Saturday Evening Post, Time, Literary Digest, Ladies Home Journal, Good Housekeeping, Life,* etc.

The rest can be dismissed with a word or two. There are half a dozen fishing companies; a ranching company or so; several ice and refrigerating companies; the ever-present railway station news stands of the American News Company's subsidiaries; a few realty companies and advertising agencies. If fields were included in which only one American-owned company is operating, the list could be much extended.

SUMMARY

RECAPITULATION of such a mass of case histories and hasty bird's-eye views can scarcely go beyond the page of statistics with which the chapter began. Almost a fourth of the manufacturing in Canada is done by American-controlled companies. The concentration of American companies is largest in rubber goods, 64 per cent; pulp, paper and lumber, 34 per cent; machinery, 42 per cent; automotive goods, 82 per cent; electrical apparatus, 68 per cent; non-ferrous metals, 50 per cent; non-metallic minerals, 44 per cent; chemicals, 41 per cent; and miscellaneous manufactures, 40 per cent. Of the following manufactures, on the other hand, American branch plants produce less than 20 per cent of total output:[269] all vegetable products except rubber goods, all animal products, all textiles, miscellaneous wood and paper products other than newsprint and pulp, iron smelting, rolling, casting, and forging. The Americans evidently control more than a third of the mining output, a third of the output of electric power, and two thirds of the natural gas output. But the railways, telegraphs, telephones, air lines, radio, and bus lines are predominantly Canadian. In the purveying of financial services insurance is the only field (except, possibly, installment financing) in which American companies compete actively, and even there they do only about a third of the business. In the motion pic-

269. There may be certain small subdivisions within these groups in which the American share is larger, just as in the previous ones there may be subfields in which the Canadian share is larger than the gross percentage indicates.

ture business the American-owned companies are powerful, and in the variety store business they dominate. But in merchandising as a whole, in restauranting, hotel-keeping, and so on, Canadians control the field. And it should be reiterated that even in the industries in which American control is pronounced, there is frequently a Canadian minority interest of considerable proportions.[270]

270. See p. 26 and Table V.

CHAPTER III

THE EXTENT OF CANADIAN INDUSTRY IN THE UNITED STATES

INTRODUCTION

WE turn in this chapter to the obverse side of the picture drawn in such detail in the preceding one. Every Canadian and every American who has any knowledge of Canadian economy is aware of those hundreds of American-owned factories, mines, public utilities, or what not in the Dominion of Canada. But few Canadians and fewer Americans realize that in proportion to Canada's wealth and population her direct investment in the United States is even larger. The following table is as nearly complete a record of Canadian companies in the United States as the available information affords.[1]

Financial companies have been excluded from this table. Five of the Canadian banks have United States branches or agencies, and one—the Canadian Bank of Commerce—owns two commercial banks on the Pacific Coast. Of Canadian insurance companies 22 are licensed to carry on business in the United States. The larger Canadian investment bankers, especially A. E. Ames and Company, Ltd., Wood Gundy and Company, and Dominion Securities, have New York offices. And 92 Canadian investment trusts hold American securities.

Excluding the investment trusts, it is estimated that 110 Canadian companies maintain some sort of permanent organization in the United States. Not counting branch factory sales offices, and elimi-

---

1. The information concerning Canadian subsidiaries in the United States is scattered and difficult of access. Table XIII is based on lists of companies compiled by the authors and by economists in both countries. It is believed to be substantially complete and correct, but verification is extremely difficult in some marginal cases. Chapter III as a whole is written on the basis of the same lists and on the detailed information concerning a good many companies thereon. But no questionnaires, such as those mentioned in pp. 25–26 above, were sent out to Canadian companies controlling companies in the United States. It was felt by the authors that the number of companies involved was not large enough to make it possible to observe a pledge of confidence.

TABLE XIII

Canadian-owned Companies in the United States*

| Industry | Parent companies | United States subsidiaries or branches† | | |
		Factories	Mines and petroleum	Transportation and other utilities	Sales and miscellaneous
Paper products	11	17			6
Iron, steel and other mineral products	9	17			3
Other manufactures‡	27	29			5
Mining, etc.	16		17§		
Transportation	4			34¶	
Other utilities	1			2	
Other companies	8				8‖
Total	76	63	17	36	22

* Excludes banks, brokers, insurance and investment trusts. See text.
† Including minority interests and leased companies—about 10 in all.
‡ Including meat packing, breweries and distilleries.
§ Including a pipe-line company and a storage company.
‖ Including a chain store and a tea packer.
¶ Largely excluding a number of smaller companies controlled by the subsidiaries.

nating duplications as far as possible, those subsidiary or branch organizations and offices number between 165 and 170. Since banks, insurance, and brokerage branch offices have not been included in the accounting in the previous chapter, they may be segregated here —subsequently some attention will be paid to them. Which returns us to the 76 companies and their 138 branches and subsidiaries as shown in the table.

The investment in those companies, so many of which publish no financial statements of any sort, is very difficult to estimate. The two Canadian railroads hold stocks and bonds in their American subsidiaries amounting to about $210,000,000. The Dominion Bureau of Statistics records "capital employed" by the two parent companies in their American lines amounting to $202,000,000. For the other subsidiaries an estimate of $60,000,000 seems, on the basis of a considerable number of known cases, to be a reasonable total.

Canadian-owned companies in the United States are from 10 to

12 per cent of the number of American companies in Canada and employ 12 per cent as much capital. In population and volume of investment, Canada is less than 10 per cent the size of the United States. The Canadian industry in America is therefore larger, proportionately, than is American industry in Canada. It is, of course, obvious that, because of the much greater economic size of the United States, it does not at all follow from these percentages that the impact of Canadian industry in America on American economy is comparable with that of American industry on Canada. But we have been at some pains in the previous chapters to reveal these cross-Border outreachings not as aggrandisements but as the generally normal accommodation of mobile capital and enterprise to barriers of all sorts. That point of view is greatly strengthened when it becomes evident that Canada, within the limits of her resources, has followed an identical process in the course of her industrial and commercial relations with the United States.

It is definitely worth while describing these scores of Canadian companies in the United States about which so little has been written. And in that description the same industry-by-industry procedure of Chapter II will be used.

Wood and Paper Products

Three Canadian companies now operate paper mills in the United States.[2] The most important is Fraser Companies, Ltd. In 1925 that company organized Fraser Paper, Ltd., New Brunswick, to build a mill at Madawaska, Maine, with a capacity of 51,000 tons of high-grade sulphite papers and 39,000 tons of paperboard per year. Across the St. John River, in Edmundston, New Brunswick, is the main bleached sulphite pulp mill of the parent company. Half of its output is piped in slush form to the American mill. That is probably the closest physical relationship between parent and branch factory of any of the hundreds of recorded cases. Fraser Companies, Ltd., owns all of the $1,000,000 stock of Fraser Paper and 62.5 per cent of its $4,000,000 bond issue. In 1929 Fraser Companies signed a

2. The Canadian Paperboard Company, Ltd., owns the Tidewater Paperboard Company in Norwich, Conn., which manufactures paperboard and containers. But Gair Company of Canada, Ltd., an American-owned company (see above, p. 54) now operates the Canadian Paperboard mills.

10-year contract to supply Sears, Roebuck and Company with catalog paper—in all probability from the American mill. One of the largest Fraser Companies' subsidiaries is Restigouche Company, Ltd. (originally Stetson, Cutler and Company, Ltd.) which owns the Ashland Company (a lumber company in Sheridan, Maine) and two Stetson, Cutler sales companies in Boston and New York. In 1932 Fraser Industries, Inc., was formed to handle Fraser products in the United States.

In 1924 it was announced that the Brompton Pulp and Paper Company had acquired 140,000 acres of freehold timber in Maine which would be shipped to its mills in Quebec.[3] It seems rather like carrying coals to Newcastle for a Quebec paper company to seek pulpwood in the United States, but, although the *Chronicle* did not seem aware of it, the Brompton Company had owned, since 1918, 4 paper companies[4] close to the Border in New Hampshire. By 1926, 2 had evidently been sold, but the 2 remaining American mills had a daily capacity of 70 tons kraft and 85 tons of bond and other paper. In 1927 the Groveton Paper Company was sold to its bondholders, but Brompton (now controlled by St. Lawrence Corporation, Ltd.) still owns the Claremont Paper Company which produces kraft paper at 2 mills. The parent company is chiefly a newsprint producer. In the Northwest the Pacific Coast Paper Mills, Inc., was established in 1926 by the Westminster Paper Company, Ltd., to provide for its increased business in the United States and to evade the import duty.[5] The American mill, at Bellingham, Washington, produces several kinds of paper.

The most interesting group of Canadian companies in the United States is that now controlled by or affiliated with Moore Corporation, Ltd., which occupies a very strong position in the sales and manifold book business. Mr. S. J. Moore came to Canada as a boy, learned the printing trade, and in 1879 opened a small printing shop in Toronto. A few years later he made the acquaintance of a Toronto shop clerk who had worked out a scheme for a counter check sales book. Mr. Moore managed to raise $2,500 and organized a

3. *Commercial and Financial Chronicle*, January 12, 1924, p. 206.

4. Claremont Paper Company, Wyman Flint and Sons Paper Company, Odell Manufacturing Company, and Groveton Paper Company.

5. *Commercial and Financial Chronicle*, November 20, 1926, p. 26.

company, the Carter-Crume Company, to produce and sell these books. Some time during the Eighties he opened a factory in Buffalo and soon his American business greatly exceeded the Canadian. In 1893 Mr. Moore became interested in a young silverware salesman, William A. Rogers, who had developed the idea of manufacturing and selling souvenir spoons. As a result, the Niagara Silver Spoon Company was organized in 1893. In 1901 under Mr. Moore's leadership this company was merged with various silverware companies in Massachusetts and Connecticut to form William A. Rogers, Ltd. These companies were later—about 1927—sold to an independent group.

Again, some time prior to 1909, Mr. Moore through his Buffalo connections became interested in the F. N. Burt Company, manufacturers of small paper boxes. In 1909 the F. N. Burt Company, Ltd., was organized to acquire F. N. Burt Company, Inc., and three of Mr. Moore's Canadian companies. In the succeeding years it acquired or organized a number of other companies.

The largest unit in the Moore group of companies is the American Sales Book Company, Ltd., incorporated in Ontario in 1911 to consolidate a number of separate Moore units. It is probably the largest manufacturer of sales books in the world and in 1934 employed 1,090 persons.

In 1928 the Moore Corporation, Ltd., was incorporated to consolidate all the sales-book and business-forms business carried on by the various companies in which Mr. Moore was interested. The F. N. Burt Company, Ltd., sold its business in these lines to the Moore Corporation for stock in the new company. It continues as a manufacturer of paper boxes in both countries. In 1934 the Moore companies operated 11 plants in the United States and 4 in Canada, and employed more than 2,200 persons. The present organization is shown in the chart below.[6]

The remaining Canadian wood and paper companies in the United States are less important. A Vancouver company owns a paper box factory in Seattle; a New Brunswick lumber firm controls the Calais Box and Lumber Company in Maine; and a Buffalo plant is in Canadian hands.

6. Niagara Fold, Inc., and Moore Research Company, Inc., do not appear any longer in the lists of Moore Corporation subsidiaries.

INTERLOCKING DIRECTORATES

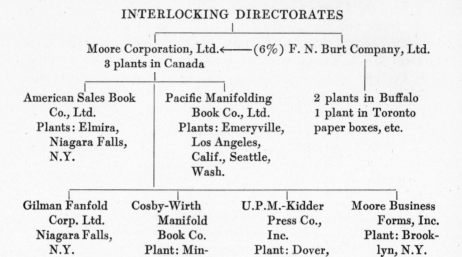

Moore Corporation, Ltd.◄———(6%) F. N. Burt Company, Ltd.
3 plants in Canada

| American Sales Book Co., Ltd. Plants: Elmira, Niagara Falls, N.Y. | Pacific Manifolding Book Co., Ltd. Plants: Emeryville, Los Angeles, Calif., Seattle, Wash. | 2 plants in Buffalo 1 plant in Toronto paper boxes, etc. |

| Gilman Fanfold Corp. Ltd. Niagara Falls, N.Y. | Cosby-Wirth Manifold Book Co. Plant: Minneapolis | U.P.M.-Kidder Press Co., Inc. Plant: Dover, N.H. | Moore Business Forms, Inc. Plant: Brooklyn, N.Y. |

MINERAL PRODUCTS, CHIEFLY IRON AND STEEL

The most interesting Canadian venture in this section of American industry is that of International Metal Industries, Ltd., one of the youngest Canadian combines. It came into existence very humbly as Clear Vision Pump Company in 1922 to develop a gasoline pump for service stations. In 1927 it changed its name to Service Station Equipment Company, Ltd., and in the next year acquired 2 American companies: Bennett Pump Corporation and Service Station Equipment Company. The Bennett Corporation is one of the largest in its field. During the following few years it acquired several other plants. By 1934, under a new name, it controlled 4 companies in Canada and 1 in England. Its American organization assumed the proportions shown in the chart below.

Whereas in 1932 the predecessor company, Service Stations, Ltd., had assets of almost $16,000,000, by 1934 they had been reduced to $6,414,034, evidently by cutting off unprofitable factories. That process may account for the seeming disappearance of plants in Bryan, Ohio, and Boston, Massachusetts. The subsidiaries remaining in this holding company produce all sorts of service station equipment, as well as water-heaters, electric refrigerators, etc. It is said that the British American Oil Company, Ltd., is interested in

INTERNATIONAL METAL INDUSTRIES, LTD.

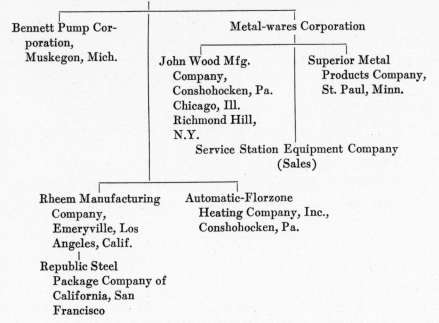

Bennett Pump Corporation,
Muskegon, Mich.

Metal-wares Corporation

John Wood Mfg.
Company,
Conshohocken, Pa.
Chicago, Ill.
Richmond Hill,
N.Y.

Superior Metal
Products Company,
St. Paul, Minn.

Service Station Equipment Company
(Sales)

Rheem Manufacturing
Company,
Emeryville, Los
Angeles, Calif.

Automatic-Florzone
Heating Company, Inc.,
Conshohocken, Pa.

Republic Steel
Package Company of
California, San
Francisco

International Metal Industries, Ltd.; at least the same man is president of both companies.

Two important Canadian metal goods manufacturers have, for a number of years, operated branch plants in the United States. Massey-Harris Company, Ltd., with antecedents extending as far back as 1857, is one of the largest producers of agricultural equipment in the world.[7] It apparently first entered the United States as a producer in 1911 when it purchased the Johnson Harvester Company, at Batavia, New York, for a sum between $2,000,000 and $3,000,000. Two years later the Deyo-Macey Engine Company, Binghamton, New York, was acquired.[8] What happened to the latter company is not apparent, but the Johnson Harvester Company was evidently changed to the Massey-Harris Harvester Company in 1917. Although the parent company owns 3 big factories in

7. See p. 62.
8. *Commercial and Financial Chronicle,* January 14, 1911, p. 122; November 29, 1913, p. 1087.

Canada, it imported certain articles from Batavia until latter-day Canadian tariffs made it unprofitable.[9] In 1928 Massey-Harris purchased the plant of J. I. Case Plow Works, Inc., in Racine, Wisconsin, for $1,262,000 cash and the assumption of a first mortgage of $1,111,200. That plant and the older Batavia factory were merged in the present Massey-Harris Company (United States) which, in 1929, had assets of $12,452,120.[10] The 2 factories, covering 59 acres, are supported by 14 American sales offices.

The other important company is Page-Hersey Tubes, Ltd., which began operations in Canada in 1902. In 1915 it purchased the Cohoes Rolling Mill Company, which had been in existence in Cohoes, New York, since 1854. Ten years later another subsidiary was established in Cohoes, the Mohawk Conduit Company, Inc., to supplement the skelp and iron mill with a steel pipe and conduit factory. Consequently Page-Hersey now owns 5 pipe plants, of which 2 are in the United States. American sales are handled by the Page-Hersey Trading Company, Inc.

The other metal-working branch plants in the United States owned by Canadians are much less important. Canadian Bronze Company, Ltd., for example, owns Diamond Bronze Company, Inc., in Vermont. In the past, however, several other Canadian companies have had steel products factories in the United States. The Canadian Car and Foundry Company's New Jersey plant was destroyed by fire in 1917.[11] That plant had been acquired by the Canadian company to assist it in handling its war contracts. Canada Foundries and Forgings, Ltd., lost its Buffalo plant by fire 5 years later. Neither this nor the Kingslands plant was ever rebuilt. The attempt of one of Canada's few independent motor vehicle manufacturers to operate a Detroit plant resulted in disaster. The Gotfredson Corporation, Ltd., guaranteed the bond issue and certain other debts of the Gotfredson Truck Corporation, which ultimately—1930—carried the parent company itself into bankruptcy. The last of these

9. See p. 234.

10. Later figures for the American company are not available.

11. The Kingslands Case is still being appealed, in which Canadian Car and Foundry is suing the German Government in the American courts for over $1,000,000 for damages, on the ground that German agents caused the fire. See *Survey of Corporate Securities, Financial Post,* 1933.

"erstwhile" branch plants was the McKinnon Dash Company of Buffalo, which passed out of Canadian hands when General Motors bought the parent company.

OTHER MANUFACTURES

There are somewhat more than 30 factories, breweries, and packing plants in the manufacturing industries which are closely affiliated with Canadian parent companies. But they are scattered in so many fields that analysis is difficult.

The largest group consists of the 12 breweries and distilleries which have been acquired or built in the United States by Canadian corporations since the end of prohibition. Most widely publicized of these ventures is the Peoria, Illinois, distillery of Hiram Walker–Gooderham and Worts, Ltd., which has cost over $5,000,000.[12] It began operations in July, 1934, and, with a daily capacity of 100,-000 gallons of whiskey, it is said to be the largest in the world. Late in 1933 and early in 1934 another big Canadian whiskey maker, Distillers Corporation-Seagram, Ltd., acquired, through an exchange of shares, 2 American whiskey companies. One, the Rossville Union Distilleries, Inc., transferred its Indiana plant and almost $3,000,000 in cash to a new company, Joseph E. Seagram and Sons, Inc. Later the Maryland Distillery, Inc., was acquired. The vendors of the two companies received a 16 per cent interest in the Canadian company, whose largest shareholder is Distillers Company, Ltd., Scotland. The 2 Seagram distilleries have a combined daily capacity of 60,000 gallons. Three Canadian brewing companies have purchased interests varying from a third to complete ownership in 7 American breweries in Montana and on the West Coast. Another has granted its rights in return for 25,000 shares to the Peerless Corporation, which at one time produced the Peerless Motor Car.

Several other plants produce drugs and chemicals. Shawinigan, for example, has a third interest in Niacet Chemical Corporation, the largest producer of synthetic acetic acid in the United States. International Proprietaries, Ltd., owns Enos Fruit Salt factories in the United States and throughout the world and also controls the Genotherm Company in New York. But in October, 1934, its assets

12. See p. 224.

and business were sold to English interests. The Dominion Tar and Chemical Company, Ltd., has a subsidiary in Duluth, but most of its plants are in Canada.

Half a dozen companies manufacture food products. The most conspicuous of these is the Fanny Farmer Candy Shops, Inc. Laura Secord Candy Shops, Ltd., was established in Canada in 1913. Six years later the Fanny Farmer company was incorporated. Until 1932 the 2 companies had a common president, and the secretary-treasurer of the Canadian company still serves the American firm in the same capacity. A few years ago, when negotiations were under way for the refinancing of the American company, the controlling shares were clearly in Canada. But in its testimony before the Price Spreads Commission in November, 1934, the Laura Secord Company stated that in October its remaining interest—3,133 preferred shares—was redeemed for $119,054, and that "as far as the company itself is concerned" there is no connection between the two. It is probable, however, that the shareholders of Laura Secord are also interested in Fanny Farmer.

Canada Packers, Ltd., was incorporated in 1927 to control several meat packing companies. One of them was Canadian Packing Company, which had been owned by Allied Packers, Inc. Another was William Davies Company, Inc., which had been in the meat packing business since 1854. Though an Illinois corporation controlling subsidiaries in Canada and in England, William Davies Company, Inc., has always been Canadian-owned and controlled, though at times there has been a substantial American minority stock interest. In 1922 its retail stores were sold to A. Martin, Ltd., which later became part of Stop and Shop, Ltd. Its Chicago plant has a storage capacity of 25,000,000 pounds of meat. The other food companies are simpler. George Weston, Ltd., largest Canadian-owned biscuit maker, sold its American rights to George Weston Biscuit Company, Inc., in return for a minority interest. By 1933 the Canadian company and its associate was in control of Weston Biscuit Company, Ltd.—the reorganized American subsidiary. Orange Crush, Ltd., through its control of Honey Dew, Ltd., operates several not overly successful sandwich shops in the United States and in England.

There are a few other scattered factories. Toronto Carpet owns 2; Woods Manufacturing Company operates a jute and cotton mill in

Ogdensburg. And, as widely advertised as any, the Salada Tea Company, Inc., is Canadian-owned.

MINING AND PETROLEUM

Canadian activity in the mining and petroleum industry in the United States is relatively much less important than it has been in manufacturing. There are, as nearly as can be learned, 7 Canadian companies directly engaged in mining in the United States.[13] Two are interested in American coal mines as a source of fuel for the operations of the parent company. The Canadian Pacific Railroad has at least a bondholder's interest in Cambridge Collieries in Ohio. The Steel Company of Canada has both coal and ore properties in the United States. In 1917 it acquired an interest in two ore properties, and in 1924 and 1926 in two additional ore properties, all in the Lake Superior region. In 1918 it purchased 1,617 acres of coking coal in Pennsylvania for $1,090,000, but in 1919 these were consolidated with other holdings so that it has a one third interest in 4,438 acres. Another company, Sterling Coal Company, Ltd.—incorporated in Canada in 1910—owns a mine in Ohio and controls two West Virginia coal mining companies. The Ohio mine was abandoned in 1932. Of the metal mines—one in Nevada, another in California, a third in Colorado—nothing more than their names and ownership could be discovered. It is probable that the Colorado venture is defunct.

Seven or 8 Canadian corporations own petroleum properties in the United States. Most active is British American Oil Company, Ltd., which, through two subsidiaries, owns wells and pipe lines in Texas and Oklahoma and ships the crude oil to its refineries in Canada.[14] The other companies do not have such a well-developed refining and distribution system in Canada to dispose of their output. Seemingly the largest, although no recent information is available concerning its operations, is Atlantic Keystone Petroleum Company, Ltd., which has a string of subsidiaries in both countries drilling in Alberta, Wyoming, and Texas. In 1931 it had 10,000 shareholders —evidently Canadians, Englishmen, and Americans, if one could

13. The Algoma Steel Corporation, Ltd., is classed as an American-controlled company, and its 3 mines in the United States are not included here. See pp. 57 ff.

14. See p. 76.

judge from the board of directors. Four others—Ajax, Acme, Bethel, and Alberta Pacific—have small interests in wells and lands in Oklahoma, Texas, and Montana. Two of them produced 278,102 barrels of oil in 1932–33. None of them are important enough to justify further detail.

MISCELLANEOUS COMPANIES

Of the miscellaneous companies, consisting so largely of sales companies and grain export offices, only one is of special interest—the post-war American offspring of Loblaw Groceterias Company, Ltd. The parent company operates 111 self-service stores in Canada, all but 6 established since 1921. The American subsidiary, Loblaw Groceterias, Inc., at its peak in 1932, operated 132 stores: 77 in Chicago, 32 in Buffalo, and 23 elsewhere in western New York. In March, 1932, the Chicago stores were sold to the Jewel Tea Company for cash and preferred stock. The New York stores are still operated, but without conspicuous success. Evidence before the Price Spreads Commission indicated that: "The Canadian company has not received rentals, royalties, interest, dividends, or other income of any nature whatsoever from the Buffalo company. . . ." Whereupon the following cursory discussion took place.[15]

Chairman: This is a case where the Canadian company controls the American company?

Mr. White: The Canadian company has not actual control, but has effective control.[16] In that respect we are unique.

Chairman: Yes, I notice that.

Mr. Sommerville: You are not unique in this respect; having gone into another country, you are not making any money.

Mr. Young: In that respect you are in the same class as the A. and P. Company.

Mr. White: Only they came in here.

Mr. Young: They are here, but they are not making any money.

Hon. Mr. Stevens: You might have a saw-off with the A. and P.

15. *Royal Commission on Price Spreads (1934–35), Minutes of Proceedings and Evidence,* November 20, 1934, p. 1136. Mr. White was representing Loblaw, Mr. Sommerville was counsel for the Commission, and the other speakers were members of the Commission.

16. It was explained earlier in the hearings that the Canadian company is the largest shareholder, and the estate of T. P. Loblaw the second largest. The two combined have a clear majority.

Mr. White: Do you suggest amalgamation, Mr. Stevens?

Hon. Mr. Stevens: No, I suggest a saw-off, and both be left to their own country.

The Chairman: A saw-off at the border line. Continue.

That dialogue does not, of course, have any particular importance. But it illustrates the point earlier made, that it is generally considered "unique" if a Canadian company is found to be the owner of an American subsidiary. The reader of this chapter should, by now, have discovered that it is not, in fact, a particularly rare phenomenon.

TRANSPORTATION AND OTHER UTILITIES

A half dozen or so Canadian companies render such services in the United States, but overwhelmingly most important are the two Canadian railroad systems. However, as was suggested in Chapter II, it is doubtful that much of the American mileage was acquired for the sake of the traffic it could originate. Rather it has provided for the two Canadian systems either more direct routes or has given them access to cities and seaports in the United States. The map in the preceding chapter[17] illustrates that fact. The Canadian Pacific crosses Maine as the shortest route from Montreal to a Canadian salt water port. It reaches a few miles south into Vermont to connect with American roads to New York and Boston. It has trackage rights over the Michigan Central from Detroit to Chicago. By its control of the Soo Line, Wisconsin Central, and Duluth South Shore it gains access to Chicago and Duluth for its traffic from the whole Regina-Winnipeg district and incidentally obtains North Dakota–Minnesota traffic. In the Northwest the Spokane International gives the Canadian Pacific an outlet through the American northwest. The Canadian National's United States mileage serves a similar function. In New England its trains can reach Portland and New London over owned or leased tracks and can connect with the New York Central Lines at Massena, in northwestern New York. The old Grand Trunk pieced together the Michigan-Indiana-Illinois tracks shown on the map. Again, despite the incidental acquisition of local lines in Michigan, it was the need of American termini—Chicago in this case—that was behind the development, as it was, too, in the purchase of the Winnipeg-Duluth line.

17. See p. 114.

Refer back, for a minute, to the map of the American lines in Canada. The contrast is sharp. Save for the path worn by the American railroads across the Ontario peninsula on their way from Detroit to Buffalo, all the other mileage now *operated* by those companies across the Border consists of spurs running up to 8 Canadian cities. It may be said that except for the Ontario tracks, the American lines in Canada are appendages to the parent systems, whereas the American lines of the Canadian railroads provide several indispensable outlets for their traffic.

The history of the acquisition of their present American lines by the Canadian railroads is difficult to compress into a few pages.[18] The first Border crossing by rail seems to have been at Rouse's Point, New York, in 1851, when the Champlain and St. Lawrence Railroad was extended that far. That little railroad is owned by the Canadian National, whose American history may therefore as well precede that of its rival. Before the Canadian National was ever more than dreamed of, and about 7 years before the old Grand Trunk was created, A. T. Galt and his associates in the Eastern Townships of Quebec were striving to build a Montreal-Portland railroad in preference to one to Boston which would pass by west of them. Out of their plans came the St. Lawrence and Atlantic and the Atlantic and St. Lawrence, both chartered in 1845: one to build the Canadian section and the other the American section of a Portland-Montreal line. The first train ran over this route on July 18, 1853. Two years earlier British promoters and contractors had forestalled Galt and persuaded Ottawa to charter the Grand Trunk Railway of Canada, and it leased the Atlantic and St. Lawrence for 999 years the year it opened.

We cannot loiter over the woeful tale of Grand Trunk vicissitudes.[19] The present-day American subsidiaries of the Canadian National are shown below in order to aid a swifter telling of the story.

18. Here, as in the previous chapter, the reader is referred to the forthcoming volume on Canadian-American communications for the early history of much of this phase of the subject, and for the economy of Canadian-American railroads in general.

19. See H. A. Lovett, *Canada and the Grand Trunk* (Toronto, 1924), Norman Thompson and J. H. Edgar, *Canadian Railway Development* (Toronto, 1933), for brief convenient accounts; also the volume in this Series previously referred to.

CANADIAN NATIONAL RAILWAY COMPANY

AMERICAN SUBSIDIARIES

CENTRAL VERMONT GROUP

Central Vermont Ry., Inc.
  New London Northern
    R.R. (leased)
  The Centmont Corporation
    Bethel Granite Ry.
  Vermont and Province Line
    R.R. Co.
  Central Vermont Transporta-
    tion Co.
  Brooksay Realty Co.
Montreal and Providence Line
Montreal and Vermont
    Junction Ry.
Stanstead Shefford & Chambly Ry.

GRAND TRUNK GROUP

EASTERN
  Champlain and St. Lawrence R.R.
  Atlantic and St. Lawrence R.R.
    (leased)
  United States and Canada R.R.
  Canada Atlantic Transit Co. of
    U.S.
  New England Elevator Co.

WESTERN
  Grand Trunk Western R.R.
    Muskegon Ry. & Navigation Co.
    Cincinnati, Saginaw & Macki-
      naw R.R.
    Detroit and Toledo Shore Line
      (50%)
    Grand Trunk Junction Railway
  St. Clair Tunnel Co.
  International Bridge Co.
  Portland Elevator Co.
  Toledo Terminal R.R. Co.
    (minority)
  Detroit Terminal R.R. Co.
    (50%)

CANADIAN NORTHERN GROUP

Duluth, Winnipeg and Pacific Ry.
  Duluth, Rainy Lake and
    Winnipeg Ry.
  Minnesota and Manitoba R.R.
Minnesota and Ontario Bridge Co.
Duluth and Virginia Realty Co.

OTHER SUBSIDIARIES

Chicago and Western Indiana R.R.
  (20%)
The Belt Railway of Chicago ($\frac{1}{12}$)
Chicago, New York and Boston Re-
  frigeration Company
Grand Trunk Pacific Dock Co.,
  Seattle

By 1860, people connected with the Grand Trunk, a predecessor of the Canadian National, had built a 60-mile line from Port Huron, Michigan, opposite Sarnia, Ontario, to Detroit and leased the resulting Chicago, Detroit and Canada Grand Trunk Junction Railway to the Grand Trunk. Not until 1877 did there seem any need to acquire tracks any farther toward Chicago, since the Michigan Central provided Detroit-Chicago facilities. But when W. H. Vanderbilt added the Michigan Central to the New York Central the Grand Trunk administration[20] determined to buy or build its own line to Chicago. Consequently between 1878 and 1879 it acquired, for about $1,500,000, 7 stretches of track, which bridged the 330 miles from Port Huron to Chicago. The only section which was built by the Grand Trunk was the 30 miles from Valparaiso to Thornton. Most of the other 6 were small bankrupt railroads. These lines, with the later Michigan acquisition shown on the map, were ultimately consolidated as the Grand Trunk Western Railroad. By 1891 the Grand Trunk had completed the St. Clair tunnel (6,026 feet long, Sarnia to Port Huron), but despite that improvement the Michigan lines showed heavy losses. In 1882 the Great Western was absorbed. That pioneer Canadian railroad had pushed its Buffalo-Detroit line across Michigan to Grand Haven, an unlucky venture which did not improve the appearance of the income statements of the Grand Trunk's American lines.

In the east the Montreal-Portland route had been disappointing. Consequently in 1899 the Grand Trunk bought the Central Vermont to provide other eastern outlets. That, with later lesser additions, completed the American mileage of the old Grand Trunk. Its acquisition had been financed in London, but probably more than two thirds of the original tracks had been laid down by local companies with American capital. Once under the Grand Trunk, money for further expansions was provided largely by London. In 1913, for example, work on the Providence branch of the Central Vermont was suspended because the Balkan War had shut off London capital.[21]

Meantime in the west another part of the present-day Canadian National had been acquiring an entrance into Duluth. The Cana-

20. As is commonly known, the Grand Trunk from its beginning to its acquisition by the Canadian National in 1923 was controlled in England, largely financed in England, and governed by a London board.

21. *Annalist,* 1913, January 27, p. 62; February 10, p. 126; February 24, p. 190.

dian Northern Railway Company was building a system west and
north from Winnipeg.[22] Between 1899 and 1909 it acquired the 3
companies shown on the chart which operate the 215-mile American
section of the track connecting Winnipeg and Duluth, thus giving
Canadian Northern's wheat traffic access to the water route to
Chicago.

The Canadian Pacific Railway has a much more extensive railway
system in the United States—over 5,000 miles, as against the 1,778
miles controlled by the Canadian National. But its investment
therein is less than that of the Canadian National. It is very difficult
to determine the actual investment made by the Canadian companies
in American properties. Certainly to total the assets of all the various subsidiaries would be far from acceptable. In the first place the
Canadian claim on those assets is very often only that of a residual
equity. In the second, much of the capital sunk in those assets was
expended by prior owners and much of it, also, has long been unproductive. It has seemed reasonable to accept the total of all securities
—stocks and bonds—held by the two Canadian companies in their
American subsidiaries as a fair index to their investment in the
American mileage. On that basis, at the end of 1933 the Canadian
National held approximately $134,000,000 and the Canadian Pa-
cific about $65,000,000 face value in those securities.

Like the Canadian National—in its Grand Trunk days—the Ca-
nadian Pacific's first American lines were in northern New England.
Between 1872 and 1879 the International Railway of Canada had
built a line from Lennoxville, Quebec, to the Maine Border near
Megantic. In 1886 the Canadian Pacific organized the Atlantic and
Northwest Railway, which purchased the International Railway of
Canada and the International Railway of Maine. By 1888 the
Maine company had completed its line from the end of track at the
Border 144 miles across Maine to Mattawamkeag (presumably
with funds provided by the Canadian Pacific). From there to the
New Brunswick Border the Canadian Pacific, then, as now, used the

22. Hays, who went from the Wabash to become manager of the Grand
Trunk in 1895, tried to buy the Canadian Northern in the early 1900's. Fail-
ing that, the Grand Trunk embarked on its costly project to build its own
route to the Pacific.

Maine Central tracks to get its trains to its St. John line. A few years earlier (1881) the Montreal and Atlantic—a Canadian Pacific subsidiary—had leased the Newport and Richford Railroad by which Canadian Pacific trains could penetrate far enough south in Vermont to reach American lines to Boston and New York. To those eastern acquisitions the Canadian Pacific has, since then, made few additions. The most important was the 32-mile electric Aroostook Valley Railroad, running through the potato country from Presque Isle, Maine. These various properties appear on the left in the chart below.

CANADIAN PACIFIC RAILWAY COMPANY
AMERICAN SUBSIDIARIES

NEW ENGLAND	WESTERN
Atlantic and Northwest Ry.	Minneapolis, St. Paul and Sault
Montreal and Atlantic Ry.	Ste. Marie Ry. Co. [Soo Line]
(in Canada)	(51%)
Newport and Richford R.R.	Wisconsin Central Ry. Co. and
(in U.S.)	minor lines
Aroostook Valley R.R.	Duluth, South Shore and Atlantic
New Brunswick Ry. (in Canada)	Ry. Co. (51%)
Aroostook River R.R. (in U.S.)	Mineral Range R.R.
Houlton Branch R.R. (in U.S.)	South Shore Dock Co.
Connecticut and Passumpsic Rivers	Spokane International Ry.
R.R. Co. (leased from Boston	Coeur d'Alene R.R.
and Maine)	Pend d'Oreille Ry.

At the same time the across-Maine route was being acquired to shorten the distance to St. John, the Canadian Pacific was purchasing its west-of-Chicago lines. "To secure a larger share of traffic from the northwestern states, control was secured of the Minneapolis, St. Paul and Sault Ste. Marie Railway Company [in 1888], . . . and of the Duluth, South Shore and Atlantic Railway Company. . . . The Canadian Pacific line was extended . . . to Sault Ste. Marie [Ontario] . . . and connections were made . . . with the [Soo Line] at that point . . . in 1888, and with the Duluth Railway in 1889."[23] Both of those railroads had been built by Ameri-

23. H. A. Innis, *A History of the Canadian Pacific Railway*, pp. 138–139.

cans, but many extensions were subsequently made under Canadian
Pacific management. In 1893 the Great Northern opened its St.
Paul–Seattle line, which closed to the Canadian Pacific the St. Paul
connection it had been using *via* Winnipeg. It consequently hur-
riedly extended the Soo Line from St. Paul to the Canadian Pacific
main line near Moose Jaw.[24] Between 1909 and 1913 over 1,000
miles were added to the Soo Line, much of which was built rather
than purchased. In 1909 the Soo bought 51 per cent of the common
shares and acquired most of the preferred shares in the Wisconsin
Central Railway Company which, in addition to local lines in Wisconsin, gave the Canadian Pacific its own tracks into Chicago and
Milwaukee.[25] By 1913 Soo Line mileage was 2,943—all owned but
22—and that of the Wisconsin Central 1,032. The 550-odd mile
Duluth, South Shore and Atlantic was acquired to obtain its main
line from Superior—near Duluth—to Sault Ste Marie, Michigan.

The Canadian Pacific lines in the Far West of the United States
consist of the 163-mile Spokane International, whose junction is
clearly shown on the map. It was built in 1905–6 under arrangements that one eighth of the cost was to be borne by the Canadian
Pacific on condition that it be granted an option on a further 52
per cent of the common to be exercised by 1917. It now owns 93 per
cent of the common but none of the $4,200,000 bonds.

Taking as a whole the capitalization of the American subsidiaries
of the Canadian Pacific, it is apparent that although it owns a voting majority of the common stock,[26] it owns only a minority of all
securities. In other words, the general public has financed the building of the lines. Especially is that true of the Soo Line, which has
over $147,000,000 in stocks and bonds outstanding, of which the
Canadian Pacific owns less than $24,000,000—including, as has
been said, 51 per cent of the common. However, the bulk of the indebtedness incurred prior to the war was at a time when the Cana-

24. *Ibid.*, pp. 206–207.

25. The common cost $3,661,121, but the preferred (to the amount of
$11,169,000) was acquired in exchange for Soo Line Leased Line Certifi-
cates. In 1924 the rest of the common was bought for $43 a share.

26. The Wisconsin Central is in receivership now and is being operated
by the Canadian Pacific for the receivers.

dian Pacific was looking chiefly to London for financing.[27] Since most of the bonds carried a Canadian Pacific guaranty, many of them probably were taken up by British investors, already so familiar with American railway securities.[28]

It must be left to the later volume of this Series to describe the position of these Dakota-Wisconsin lines in the Canadian Pacific system. But one shift in traffic may be mentioned, since it caused a rearrangement of Soo Line mileage. In its annual report of 1921 the Canadian Pacific explained that the United States tariff on wheat and the practical shutting down of the iron mines in Michigan and Minnesota had seriously affected Soo Line earnings. In 1910 the Soo Line purchased the 37-mile Cuyuna Iron Range Railway which connected with its line at Lawler, Minnesota. The Cuyuna was extended to reach new mines and the first ore shipments to Superior began in 1912. During the following decade they reached a peak of 1,800,000

27. Ever since its completion the main financial interest in the Canadian Pacific Railroad has been overwhelmingly British. The following table gives the geographical distribution of the ownership of the common stock for selected years.

Year	Canada Per cent	United Kingdom Per cent	United States Per cent	Elsewhere Per cent	Total amount outstanding
1906	10.58	60.83	15.03	13.56	$106,000,000
1915	14.14	62.64	9.86	13.36	260,000,000
1923	21.14	50.73	20.69	7.44	260,000,000
1926	19.43	53.96	18.74	7.87	260,000,000
1929	18.07	42.90	32.68	6.35	330,000,000
1934	17.26	52.50	24.40	5.84	335,000,000

The preference stock has full voting rights, and of the $137,250,000 outstanding 97 or 98 per cent has always been held in Great Britain, so that in 1934 the total voting strength of all American-owned shares was 17 per cent; of British shares, 66 per cent; and of Canadian shares, 12 per cent. Of the $291,000,000 of consolidated debenture stock all but $65,000,000 is held in Great Britain. Probably less than half of the $205,000,000 of bonds and notes are held in the United States. All the presently outstanding bond issues placed in the New York market were issued between 1926 and 1930.

28. Recent traffic losses of some of these roads have made the guaranty a burden to the Canadian Pacific. In 1932 it was necessary to advance $1,-400,000 to the Soo Line to meet the guaranty on its first consolidated mortgage. The funds were provided by loans from the National City Bank of New York and the First National Bank of Chicago. See *Commercial and Financial Chronicle,* April 2, 1932, p. 2553.

tons but declined to 246,000 by 1921 and were only 538,950 in 1931. In 1929 the Interstate Commerce Commission approved a contract with the Northern Pacific Railway Company,[29] to divide the iron ore and coal traffic previously handled separately by the two companies from the mines to their docks in Superior. Now each company hauls its share of traffic at its own expense and retains the revenues. Ore cars are pooled, and the Soo Line uses Northern Pacific tracks from the mine to its line and has abandoned 32 miles of the Cuyuna from Lawler west. Arrangements permitting it to use Northern Pacific docks at Superior saved the Soo Line (and the Canadian Pacific) the $2,500,000 which new docks would have cost.

The other Canadian-owned public utility companies in the United States are relatively unimportant. The Provincial Transport Company, Ltd., has a half interest in the Frontier Coach Lines, Inc., and Champlain Coach Lines, Inc., which operate from Montreal to Boston and New York. The remaining shares are owned by the Fifth Avenue Coach Company.[30] Also in the field of communication there is the Niagara Lower Arch Bridge Company, Ltd., which owns and operates the bridge used by the Canadian National and by motor vehicles across the Niagara River; the Canada Steamship Lines, Ltd., which controls at least 2 American subsidiaries operating boats on the Great Lakes and in the Thousand Island area; and the Twin City Rapid Transit Company which provides street car service in St. Paul and Minneapolis. Canadians are heavily interested in the latter company and have several representatives on the board. Their interest is, however, more financial than managerial. More clearly Canadian is the International Electric Company of Vermont, which is a subsidiary of Southern Canada Power Company, Ltd., and supplies Beebe and Derby Line.[31] A more striking instance of Canadian-managed communications in the United States is that of the telegraph lines operated by the Canadian Pacific and by the Canadian National Telegraphs. The Canadian Pacific telegraph system is operated in connection with the company's railroads through

29. See pp. 120 ff., for other of its Canadian relations.
30. See p. 139.
31. Southern Canada Power is in turn a subsidiary of Power Corporation of Canada, Ltd.

Maine between Sherbrooke, Quebec, and St. John, New Brunswick.[32] Canadian National telegraph lines in the United States comprise the Grand Trunk Pacific Telegraph Company and the Great North-western Telegraph Company.[33] The lines are chiefly on the Portland Division of the old Grand Trunk between Island Pond, Vermont, and Portland, Maine, and in the northern part of New York—in the vicinity of Massena Springs and in the Lake Champlain area. Although owned by Canadian National Telegraphs, these lines are now operated by Western Union.

FINANCIAL SERVICES

In the first pages of the chapter the Canadian banks, insurance companies, brokers, and investment trusts operating in the United States were summarized. Only concerning banking and insurance will any further detail be given.[34]

It is very difficult to discover the importance of the insurance written by Canadian companies in the United States relative both to the total business of those companies and to all insurance in the United States. A number of Canadian fire and casualty companies do business in various American states, but the bulk of Canadian insurance written south of the Border is in the life field. In 1932, 14 Canadian life insurance companies were licensed in from 1 to 40 states. They had in force insurance amounting to $1,500,000,000, which was about 22 per cent of their total business and about 8 per cent of total life insurance in force in the United States. Overwhelmingly the most important of those companies is the Sun Life Assurance Company, Ltd., one of the largest holders of common stocks in North America.[35] Its assets in 1933 were $624,452,991 and its total insurance in force was $2,770,453,871. While the insurance in force is not geographically segregated, $1,278,508,728 was payable in

32. The Soo Line, a Canadian Pacific subsidiary (see above, pp. 192 ff.) owns the telegraph lines along the railroad and has an arrangement with Postal to operate them.

33. See pp. 125–126.

34. See pp. 165–169 for discussion of Canadian-American investment banking.

35. See annual *Report of the Superintendent of Insurance of the Dominion of Canada* for detailed list of its portfolio.

United States dollars, which probably indicates with fair accuracy the volume of policies outstanding in the United States. Similarly, although there is no published statement of assets held in the United States, the company showed assets in 1933 payable in United States dollars as follows:

Mortgages	$ 1,892,243
Policy loans	35,711,460
Securities	325,018,985
Other assets	23,754,662
Total	$386,377,350

Assuming that assets payable in United States dollars were largely United States mortgages, loans, securities, and so on, it appears that more than half of Sun Life assets were American. Sun Life owns the Federal Life Assurance Company, the Mutual Life Assurance Company of New York, and the Cleveland Life Insurance Company, acquired between 1916 and 1926.[36]

Four of the Canadian chartered banks maintain a total of 13 branches in the United States. These offices do a large foreign exchange, call loan, bill and acceptance business. With one exception, they do not do a general commercial banking business. The Canadian Bank of Commerce in its branches in Portland (Oregon), San Francisco, and Los Angeles (the two latter separately incorporated under the laws of California) carries on today a general banking business begun as branches of the Bank of British Columbia in 1864.[37] In 1925 the Portland branch absorbed the business of the Pacific Bank of Portland. From 1900 to 1915 the Canadian Bank of Commerce held a controlling interest in the Commercial National Bank of New Orleans.[38]

36. *Moody's Economist Service*, London, England.

37. Victor Ross, *History of the Canadian Bank of Commerce* (Toronto, 1920), I, 303, 308.

38. *Ibid.*, pp. 125, 336.

CHAPTER IV

MOTIVES

THE existence, in any country, of foreign-owned enterprises has always excited a public curiosity which seems to be based on the half-expressed assumption that these alien ventures were established under the stimulus of peculiar motives. Yet there is nothing unusual about the acquisition by business men in one country of interests in another country. The profit motive is a sufficient explanation. It is the extent and diversity of these foreign-controlled corporations as between Canada and the United States, rather than their mere existence, which arrests attention.

The development has been inevitable. Here are two adjacent nations with territory along their common border in some cases interpenetrating, both rich in natural resources and possessing in the main the same language, the same racial and cultural characteristics. Practically the only barriers are man-made; and even these are of such a nature, as the preceding chapters have abundantly shown, as to promote reciprocal investment rather than to retard it. Apart from the man-made incentive to United States investment in Canadian branch and subsidiary activities, there is the normal attempt of business in one country to obtain natural resources so easily accessible in the adjacent country and the search by transportation systems for the most direct route to markets, irrespective of boundary lines. All this, and familiarity in each country with conditions and opportunities in the adjacent country, has given rise to direct capital investment which in many cases would have taken place even in the absence of tariff barriers.

But the more curious enquirer will wish to examine the picture with greater attention to detail, suspecting that in looking behind the search for profits in a near-by land the meaning of so diverse a migration may be made the clearer.[1] It is altogether to be expected

1. See the discussions in *American Branch Factories Abroad,* Senate Document No. 258, 71st Congress, 3rd Session, and Document No. 120, 73rd Congress, 2nd Session; *American Direct Investments in Foreign Countries,* Trade Information Bulletin No. 731; Louis Domeratzky, "Ameri-

that the reasons which induced a producer of heating equipment to build a Canadian plant might prove to be unconvincing in persuading a manufacturer of pumps. Again, it might well happen that the Middle West Utilities Corporation and the F. W. Woolworth Company, each seeking profitable trade in Canada, would adopt wholly different methods of approach.

BRANCH FACTORIES

Why have many hundred American, and several score Canadian factories taken the risks involved in crossing the Border and building or buying branch factories? Two answers at once suggest themselves. These companies may believe they can place their goods before the consumer at lower prices than could be quoted on the basis of importation.[2] Or they may have discovered that consumer resistance to imported goods is sharply reducing sales volume. In either case the company expects, in taking such a step, to make a larger profit than it could if it continued to serve foreign markets by exporting across natural and artificial barriers.[3]

Tariffs. Import duties unquestionably occupy first place among barriers to Canadian-American trade.[4] With Canadian tariff rates steadily, and since the war sharply, increasing, and in view of the preferential treatment accorded to Great Britain, it was inevitable that American companies should find it increasingly difficult to export to Canada. On the other side of the picture Canadian producers

can Branch Factories Abroad," *Commerce Reports,* December 9, 1929, pp. 587–591; Frank A. Southard, Jr., *American Industry in Europe* (New York, 1931), chap. iii; Kenneth Taylor, "Branch Plants of Outside Companies are Builders of Canada," *Financial Post,* December 23, 1933.

2. Although even then, if tariffs have entered in, or if transportation is expensive or other costs higher, the price may be considerably higher than in the home market.

3. But if costs are higher in a branch plant, the sales and the profits may be lower than they were earlier when importing was still feasible. The above analysis still holds, however.

4. "It is safe to state that in the case of Canada, where probably the greatest number of branch plants are located, the tariff is the most influential factor, as shown most strikingly by the fact that the automotive production centers of the two countries are located within a few miles of each other." Senate Document No. 258, p. 12.

have been handicapped by increased tariffs in exporting to the United States.

In 1932 a Canadian trade journal[5] reported that 42 companies in Canada had increased the extent of their manufacturing operations as a direct result of higher tariffs and a discount on the Canadian dollar. Seventy-six per cent of the companies replying to the American questionnaire[6] stated that tariffs played an important part in their decision to produce in Canada; as did 63 per cent of those who replied to the Canadian questionnaire. In December, 1932, the first Canadian plant for mercerizing cotton yarns was established by an American company which had had a good market in Canada for years, despite tariffs, because of its ability to make quicker delivery than its English competitors, and on account of a Canadian preference for American yarn. But the discount on the Canadian exchange, and the still greater discount on sterling exchange in terms of American dollars, added to an increasing preferential tariff on British goods, forced the price of the American article 40 per cent above the British.

In 1931, to cite further examples, the Canadian Industries, Ltd. —an affiliate of E. I. du Pont de Nemours Co., and Imperial Chemical Industries, Ltd.—built the first cellophane plant in Canada (at a cost of $1,500,000) because the Canadian duty was increased from 5 to 18 per cent with a promise of a further increase as soon as an advance in domestic output should occur. In 1925 the Prophylactic Brush Company had built a Canadian plant in order to avoid a 33 per cent duty, and as a result its Canadian sales increased 300 per cent the first year. As early as 1916 the Goodyear Tire and Rubber Company organized its Canadian subsidiary "to handle Canadian and such other foreign business as can be shipped advantageously from Canada rather than from the United States owing to tariff conditions."[7]

To an extent Canadian tariff policy—especially since the war—

5. *Industrial Canada,* March, 1932.
6. See p. 25, for a description of the "American" and "Canadian" questionnaires which were sent out in connection with this study. Copies of them are reprinted in Appendix IV.
7. *Commercial and Financial Chronicle,* January 15, 1916, pp. 254–255.

has been designed, at least partially, to encourage the influx of branch plants. The publication, by the Dominion Bureau of Statistics, of a list of foreign companies established in Canada between August 15, 1930, and December 31, 1933, may be taken as indicative of a belief on the part of the Canadian Government that a relationship exists between that influx of foreign companies and the tariff policy sponsored by the Bennett administration, which took office in 1930. In the United States, on the other hand, foreign branch plants—although they exist in fairly large numbers—have never been of enough importance to be influential in guiding American tariff policy.

There can be no question that in Canada during the last few years tariffs have been of overwhelming importance in the branch plant movement. Dozens of small American plants in Canada established during the past decade would never have been built but for the sharp post-war increase in tariff rates. It is not as easy, however, to estimate the effect of tariffs in earlier years. The companies which, answering the Canadian questionnaire, feel that the influence of tariffs has been important, began manufacturing in Canada as noted in the following table:

Before 1889	3
1889–1898	5
1899–1908	11
1909–1918	32
1919–1928	28
1929–1934	23

Clearly, for many years tariffs have played a rôle in branch plant policy.[8] In 1913 the *Monetary Times* (Toronto) remarked that "Americans are planting branch factories in Canada one after the

8. It should be explained, however, that it was noticed, in tabulating the questionnaires, that some companies were not careful to distinguish between factors originally responsible for their decision to enter Canada and factors now effective in keeping them there. Thus a company might find tariffs important now, although earlier, when for other reasons it entered Canada, they were relatively unimportant. It must also be remembered that most of the companies did not list the various "motives" in order of importance. Of the 40 in the Canadian questionnaire which did, however, 17 put "Tariffs" first, with "Adaptation of product to Canadian tastes" next, with 7 firsts.

other. If the tariff is absorbing too much of the profits of goods produced in the United States and sold in Canada, they shove a subsidiary plant over the tariff wall."[9] Referring to a still earlier period, another writer says: "The expansion into Canada had an early
phase between 1885 and 1890. This phase was exceptional and was
not followed by other manufacturing establishments until 1899,
when the real beginning was made. This date coincides well with the
beginning of the preferential tariff in Canada which was a part of
the tariff revision of 1897."[10]

While such data are fragmentary they do establish two significant
facts. First, tariffs have been a factor in the Canadian-American
branch plant movement for more than 50 years. Second, tariffs have
increasingly stimulated the erection of new branch plants and the
expansion of old ones, as their scope and severity have increased.
Many sales companies have been converted into manufacturing
plants[11] and many assembly plants have manufactured an increasing
percentage of the product.[12]

In recent years the advantage of operating inside the British Empire preferential tariff system has added to the attraction of branch
plant undertakings. Twenty-four per cent of the American questionnaire replies and 15 per cent of the Canadian replies referred to
Empire tariffs as an additional motive; but it is to be noted that this
was not a motive *originally* operative in the case of the older companies. Franklin Johnston found,[13] in 1932, that 15 per cent of the
American companies in Canada had been influenced by Empire tariffs. A further indication of the importance of Empire trade in the
calculations of the American company considering Canada as a producing point is found in the fact that, excluding those whose Canadian branches export only to the United States, about 40 per cent of
the companies questioned replied that they were serving foreign—
chiefly Empire—markets from Canadian plants. It is thus made evi-

9. Quoted in the *Annalist,* January 17, 1913, p. 43.

10. Senate Document No. 258, p. 34.

11. e.g., the Maytag Company, Ltd., which, after 20 years of sales activity, began to manufacture in 1930.

12. See pp. 231 ff.

13. "While Ottawa Confers," *The American Exporter,* September, 1932,
pp. 9–11, 39–40. The total number of companies interviewed is not given.

dent that although the majority of American plants in Canada were
established primarily to cater to Canada, the prospect of a wider
Empire market has been attractive to an important minority.[14]

Beyond this it is difficult to go. Few American factories in Canada
have been uninfluenced, as to their establishment, by tariffs. But
what proportion of them would not have been established at all if
tariffs had remained low cannot be determined with any exactness.
Probably a majority of the branch plants established since the war,
especially the smaller and more recent ones, are solely creatures of
the tariff. Many of the older and larger branch factories established
in years when tariffs were a lesser, though always present, factor
probably would have been established as soon as the market war-
ranted, even in the absence of customs barriers. Nor may we assume
that factories put in operation for the purpose of evading tariffs
would be dismantled if those tariffs were removed. This would occur,
no doubt, in cases where high costs and small markets have combined
to produce disappointing results. But in many other cases, once the
investment has been made it will be maintained as long as it is reasonably profitable. Furthermore, it might well occur that a branch
plant, although not established until after tariff pressure had come
into play, would develop a larger and more profitable business than
the parent company had been able to develop, on an export basis, before the tariff became a hindrance.

Consumer preference. If the Canadian and American consumers
had perceptibly different tastes, many companies might decide that
the best way to accommodate those peculiarities would be to set up a
local factory and a local sales organization in each country capable
of making the necessary changes both in the product and in the sales
program. In this connection it is to be noted that American companies have often found such radical differences in European tastes
that only a plant at the point of sale could cater to them.[15]

But it is generally agreed that the differences between the Canadian and American markets are trivial. Only 10 per cent of the companies which replied to the American questionnaire reported market

14. It is difficult to determine how largely that factor has increased in importance. The Canadian Trade Commissioner in New York believes much
export diversion has taken place in the past three years. See pp. 241 f.

15. See Southard, *op. cit.*, pp. 124–126.

differences calling for modifications of their product in Canada. A hosiery producer makes minor style changes in his Canadian product; a manufacturer of phonographs and radios varies the cabinet styles, and meets the requirements of the Ontario Hydro-Electric Commission as to electric apparatus. A producer of felt for paper-making finds that Canadian users desire a somewhat different product; while makers of gasoline pumps are, of course, obliged to modify their product to suit the Imperial liquid measure. In response to the same question on the Canadian questionnaire, however, 21 per cent of the companies stated that some sort of modification in their product had been found necessary. The discrepancy between the two sets of replies is probably to be accounted for by the fact that the Canadian managers, close to the situation, are more sensitive to differences of taste than are the executives of the parent companies. The Canadian replies make it clear that the greatest variety of taste was exhibited in the matter of style and color, and that these differences were most common in printing, furniture, salesbooks, silverware, scientific equipment, trucks, automobiles, radios, tires, brushes, and batteries. The makers of equipment are, of course, obliged to make modifications to suit Canadian power conditions. Notwithstanding all this, the two markets are so nearly alike that few American companies have crossed the border chiefly in order to produce a different product for a different market.

However, as the by-product of the same campaigns which have produced high tariffs in Canada, there has been created, over a period of years, a perceptible preference for Canadian-made goods. An American producer of foodstuffs states that, after a good export business to Canada from 1896 to 1932, a Canadian preference for Canadian-made goods combined with a tariff made it necessary to build a branch factory. Similarly, a manufacturer of motor trucks reports that in 1920 its salesmen found that there would be less sales resistance in Canada if the product was Canadian-made. Two American manufacturers of refrigeration and ventilating equipment stated, in 1931, that they were contemplating establishing Canadian plants because more and more of their contracts were calling for "Made in Canada" goods.

Almost 70 per cent of the companies replying to the American questionnaire listed "consumer preferences" among the forces urg-

ing the establishment of a Canadian company. That precise phrase-
ology was not used on the other questionnaire, but 32 per cent of
those companies cited "adaptation of product to Canadian tastes"
and "desire to use 'Made in Canada' label" as important factors.
The extensive advertising campaigns conducted in England and
throughout the Dominions in favor of Empire-made goods have created a consumer preference for certain types of Canadian goods, and
thus combine with the actual tariff preference in giving a Canadian
plant value as an export base.

A minor but common production modification is widely required
by the consumer in the case of packaged goods. Nearly 30 per cent
of Canada's population is French-speaking, and though nearly half
of these can read and speak English there is a very strong loyalty to
the French-Canadian language and culture. If packaged goods are
to obtain a wide sale in the Province of Quebec, they must carry bi-
lingual labels, descriptions, instructions, and so on.

This demand for Canadian goods cannot be exactly weighed, but it
is safe to assume that it is an added factor of influence at a time when
Canadians are being subjected to appeals to "Buy Canadian" and to
patronize Empire products. More specifically, this preference ex-
presses itself in requirements that goods must contain a certain definite percentage of "Empire content" if they are to receive the benefits of the British preferential tariff rates.[16]

It is not clear how much Canadian companies have been influenced, in establishing their American branch plants, by their desire
to publicize the fact of American manufacture. Hiram Walker whiskey advertisements have, to be sure, drawn attention to the new
plant in Illinois. But, on the whole, it is doubtful if American consumers, accustomed as they have been for generations to high tariffs, are much influenced by such appeals. In a vast market, in which
goods of foreign origin do not bulk large, the mark of foreign origin
may actually be an effective advertisement.

Factory costs: raw materials, labor, transportation. Except for
a few minerals (asbestos, nickel, aluminum), timber, pulpwood, and
fish, raw materials may be disregarded as a factor in branch plant
establishment. As has been pointed out in Chapter II, some American
companies, such as Johns-Manville, have gone to Canada in search of

16. See the fuller discussion of this point on pp. 233, 241 ff.

raw materials to supply the home factory and, once there, serve the Canadian market from a smaller, local factory. But very few companies found raw materials so much cheaper in Canada as to make that consideration the chief reason for supplying the Canadian market from a Canadian plant.

Only 11 per cent of the answers to both questionnaires listed raw materials as important in inducing the companies to enter Canada as producers. Most of these were paper and lumber companies who would never have entered Canada but for the possibility of exporting to the United States. Several others (including a lobster packer and some producers of asbestos and abrasive) also sell their product largely outside of Canada. Of branch plants chiefly engaged in serving the Canadian market only a trivial few find raw materials an important advantage of Canadian manufacture.

In the case of wages, again, there is little evidence that actual labor cost has been, in the field of manufacturing, low enough in Canada to account for the influx of American branch plants. An American company considering establishment of a Canadian plant may, indeed, be encouraged by the discovery that both raw materials and labor can be had at advantageous rates in Canada. But virtually none of our sample of more than 300 companies cited low wages as a decisive influence in setting up their Canadian branches. Further, only 40 per cent of the companies replying to either questionnaire reported that wages in their Canadian plants were any lower than they were in the parent factories. Wages generally are lower in Quebec than in Ontario; but of 965 branch plants whose locations were known, only 159 were located in Quebec, as against 636 in Ontario.[17]

When we turn to transportation cost, however, we find more cases —although still only a minority—in which American companies have gone to Canada and Canadian companies to the United States because their products were bulky enough to make decentralized production advisable. Eighteen per cent of the replies to both questionnaires list transportation economies among the factors making Canadian production attractive. Among these we find such clear cases as a cotton bag company with a plant in Winnipeg catering to the grain trade, a plumbing manufacturer, producers of automatic stokers, oil burners, office equipment, chains, marine motors—all

17. See pp. 220 ff.

bulky products. But there are also included the producers of relatively light goods, such as drugs, fountain pens, cotton gloves, overalls, confections, etc. Furthermore, many manufacturers of very bulky and heavy goods—such as, for example, rubber tires, elevators, hardware, telephone equipment, forgings, batteries, steel tanks, vacuum cleaners—do not include transportation costs among the barriers they sought to avoid by producing in Canada.

Although the data are confusing, it is evident that some American companies in Canada and some Canadian companies in the United States have found transportation costs high enough to be influential in the creation of both foreign and domestic branch plants. It is doubtful, however, if more than 15 or at most 20 per cent of Canadian-American branch factories owe their existence in any measurable extent to transportation savings. Yet, where tariffs have created a disposition to establish a branch plant if it is feasible, the saving in transportation may be an important element in the decision.

In general, the factory costs of American companies in Canada are no lower than, and are in most cases definitely higher than those of the parent company.[18] Consequently the most that can be said is that the American company planning to enter Canada hopes that its labor, transportation, and raw material costs will average something near those in the parent plant. If that is the case, tariffs, consumer preferences, and the general advantage of being "on the spot" may tip the balance in favor of a branch plant. Only a small minority[19] have found Canadian costs low enough to be independent inducements to manufacture north of the border.

Auxiliary subsidiaries. Some of the American-owned companies in Canada owe their existence to a contribution they make to the main product of an associated company.

In some cases the main product is produced chiefly in the United States for American consumption, the auxiliary enterprise in Canada falling more properly among the "source of raw material" companies, to be discussed later. The Canadian paper mills owned by the *New York Times* and the *Chicago Tribune* are examples, as are the asbestos mines of Johns-Manville Company, the feldspar mines of the

18. See pp. 236 ff. for further discussion of this point.
19. Ignoring the pulp and paper factories, which are separately considered.

Bon Ami Company, and the abrasives plant of the Simonds Saw and Steel Company. In this class belong, also, the American coal and limestone mines owned by the Algoma Steel Corporation, Ltd., and the Cambridge Collieries Company, in Ohio, affiliate of the Canadian Pacific Railway.

But in other cases these branch organizations are auxiliary to parent branch plants serving the Canadian market. Here, for example, we find the Roberval and Saguenay Railway and the Essex Terminal Railway, owned, respectively, by Aluminium, Ltd., and the United States Steel Corporation. Here, also, are the St. Maurice Power Corporation, Ltd., partly owned by the Brown Corporation, and the Peterborough Hydraulic Power Company, Ltd., subsidiary of the Quaker Oats Company. The Canadian Forest Products, Ltd. —an International Harvester subsidiary—and the Goodyear Cotton Co., Ltd.—belonging to the Goodyear Tire and Rubber Company of Canada, Ltd.—make obvious contributions to the Canadian operations of their parent companies.

Other American-owned branch plants in Canada are auxiliary in a somewhat different sense. If, for example, a company in the United States has been supplying parts or semi-fabricated material to another company which begins branch plant operations in Canada, there may be a strong inducement for the producer of parts to do likewise. Or, suppose that a company has done a profitable business supplying one of the larger chain store organizations. The possibility of supplying the Canadian units in the chain may persuade the company to set up a branch plant in Canada. In other words, a number of American companies have been strengthened in their decision to begin producing in Canada by the fact that familiar customers in the United States have already established branch plants in the Dominion which may supply attractive initial orders.

Servicing. Markets of such extent as those of the United States and Canada create sales and after-sales problems almost unknown in smaller countries. Such companies as International Harvester and Massey-Harris cannot permanently sell agricultural implements in the countries north and south of their respective head offices without maintaining the elaborate sales and service organizations for which they are well known. Many a firm has found that a foreign organiza-

tion with at least a warehouse for replacements adds many dollars to
foreign sales.

Almost 40 per cent of the companies replying to the American
questionnaire, and 46 per cent of those answering the Canadian, included "after-sales services" among the reasons for which they began
producing in Canada. While there is no way of proving the point, it
is probable that the service that a subsidiary in the foreign market is
capable of rendering has sent more American companies across the
border than any other factor save tariffs. It has unquestionably influenced the Canadian companies entering the United States. Better
control over the sales force, better adjustment to the market, closer
association with the consumer, and quicker delivery of goods are all
more surely obtainable through the medium of a local subsidiary.[20]

In general. The branch plant, whether it is Canadian or American,
represents an attempt to conquer the handicaps imposed by law, custom, or distance.[21] In the absence of tariffs the remaining barriers
would be insufficient to explain the establishment of many—probably
the majority—of the plants now in existence. But in many cases,
where the demand for the product is relatively large, there is as much
justification for the establishment of foreign branch plants as there
is for the establishment of branch plants in the domestic market.

In every case the parent company has been guided in its decision
to operate a foreign factory by the variety of factors we have discussed. Such a company must calculate the value of the market which

20. It must be granted, however, that in the absence of tariffs and consumer preferences, a well-established *sales* subsidiary will suffice for those
purposes.

21. Mention should be made of the effect of the "working clause" in the
Canadian patent law on the establishment of branch plants. While only a
few companies replying to our questionnaires cited that as a factor in their
case, Mr. E. L. Bacher, Manager of the Foreign Trade Department of the
United States Chamber of Commerce, is of the opinion that in the United
Kingdom and Canada the working clause has been a real influence in bringing branch plants to those territories. (See a speech delivered in Buffalo
March 6, 1930.) Louis Domeratzky grants this, but points out that in the
case of Canada there are other factors of so much more importance that the
working clause drops into the background. (See Senate Document No. 258,
pp. 16–17. Mr. Domeratzky wrote the text of this pamphlet, although no
author is cited.)

may be lost against the cost of saving it. It must expect new and unforeseeable influences to arise in the future which may make the branch either more or less profitable than it was in the beginning. The experience of a single company will supply an example of these changing conditions. This enterprise, manufacturing tools, operated its own factory in Canada for many years and finally merged with a Canadian competitor to form a company in which it has an interest.

We originally started our plant there in 1909 shortly after the promulgation of the Canadian tariffs which were prohibitory. Up to that time we were able to compete. At that time Empire preferential tariffs were not operative. Within the last few years they have become distinctly operative.

At the time we started our plant there wages in our industry in Canada were fully fifty per cent lower than in the United States. Wages are now about on a par. Within the last few years there has been a distinct preference in Canada for Canadian made products. Furthermore, in some lines of our business after-sales servicing was quite necessary.

Our reason for merging [with a Canadian firm in 1928] was owing to the fact that in 1927, which was a reasonably active business year in Canada, the total volume of business in the Dominion of Canada [in this field] from a manufacturing standpoint amounted to only $2,100,-000 divided among five manufacturing institutions. . . . The result of this overexpansion of the industry in Canada resulted in a very meager, if any, profit.

MINES, FORESTS, AND FISHERIES

Here, still pursuing the trail of motivation, two groups of enterprises emerge.

The supply of some resources is more plentiful and consequently cheaper in one country than in the other. It is, therefore, quite natural that both Canadian and American companies should cross the border in search of those resources, either to supply the home— and, incidentally, the foreign—market directly, or to provide the home plant with raw materials.

Among the Canadian organizations of the American paper companies, for example, will be found ownership of everything from pulpwood reserves, as in the case of the Hammermill Paper Company, to elaborate and almost colossal forest reserves, paper mills,

and power plants, such as those of the International Paper and
Power Company. In most of these cases the parent factories look to
the Canadian company for at least a portion of their raw material.
Similarly the Canadian mines of the Johns-Manville Company and
the International Nickel Company of Canada, Ltd., are the chief
source of supply for the American mills. A slightly different case is
that of the American Smelting and Refining Company which, in
1921, made a substantial investment in the Premier Silver and Gold
Mine, in British Columbia, in order to insure that it would get the
smelting work from that mine.[22] The search of the Portland Packing
Company for lobsters along the shores of northeast Canada because
of a scarcity on the Maine coast, and the sardine plants of the Booth
Fisheries Company in New Brunswick, are typical of the same sort
of efforts to supplement American supplies from a Canadian source.

Canadian companies have ventured south in search of raw materials to supply the home market. The Algoma Steel Corporation,
Ltd., owns two West Virginia coal mines and a Michigan limestone
quarry;[23] the Steel Company of Canada owns coal properties in
Pennsylvania and ore properties in Minnesota; while half a dozen
Canadian-owned oil companies look to subsidiaries in the United
States for petroleum. The chief motive, at least in the case of the
steel companies, has been to obtain uninterrupted supply of raw
materials. The Steel Company of Canada on two occasions had to
close down partially, due to inability to buy sufficient coal in the
open market during the periods of shortage following serious coal
strikes.

But other American companies have been attracted to Canadian
forest and mineral resources not in order to supply an associated
American plant but purely by the promise of financial return. The
story of American participation in Canadian mining and lumbering
has already been told. Here it need only be repeated that dozens of
such companies, unassociated with any save an American executive
office, for decades have had their share in the development of Canada.

22. *Commercial and Financial Chronicle*, January 15, 1921, p. 254.
23. The Algoma Steel Corporation is an American-controlled company.
(See pp. 57 ff.) But it is an example of a Canadian producer which has acquired mines in the United States.

COMMUNICATIONS

Almost all of the American companies that have had a stake in the development of Canadian communications have been motivated by a desire to push northward the service they were already rendering in the United States. More than that, most of them probably regarded their Canadian extensions merely as a completion of the service they were offering to Americans.

In this class, for example, are to be included the American railroads which either cut across Canadian territory between two American points—as does the New York Central in southern Ontario—or bought or built lines to connect their American systems with Canadian cities such as Montreal, Toronto, Ottawa, and Winnipeg.[24] The history of the Canadian-American telegraph and telephone systems and of radio communication and broadcasting[25] supplies additional examples of the completion of communication systems which would have been at least partially truncated had they stopped at the Border.

Nor do the Canadian railroads present any different picture.[26] A glance at maps of the Canadian National and Canadian Pacific systems indicates clearly enough that their American mileage has, on the whole, been acquired either for the purpose of crossing Maine to Canadian seaports, or of reaching south to Portland, Chicago, New York, Duluth, and Spokane.

In a few cases, however, American participation in Canadian communication companies cannot be ascribed to an effort to complete a system. The Associated Telephone and Telegraph Company, for example, must certainly regard its ownership of the British Columbia Telephone Company as an investment rather than as an integral part of a closely-knit telephone system.[27] The American ownership of a few scattered Canadian railroads and tramways[28] is to be accounted for either as the chance interest of American entrepreneurs in earlier years, or as the post-war "invasion" of Canada by the American

24. See pp. 113 ff.   25. See pp. 123 ff.
26. See pp. 187 ff.
27. Although, of course, the British Columbia company is connected with the Canadian and American long-lines systems.
28. Such as the East British Columbia Railway, the London Street Railway, the Moncton tramways, and a few others.

public utility holding companies, to be described presently. These "sports" in the progression of American investment in Canada are scarcely to be thought of as part of the development of Canadian-American communication.

LIGHT, POWER, AND GAS

A few companies close to the border in both countries naturally supply gas or electricity to communities across the line. For example, the Power Corporation of Canada, Ltd., supplies power to Tongass, Alaska, and the Maine and New Brunswick Electric Power Company, Ltd.,[29] serves near-by communities in both State and Province. But such instances of an actual transmission of power or gas across the border are not typical of this phase of Canadian-American development.

Two groups of American companies have purchased or built power and gas companies in Canada.[30] The first group includes those which acquired hydro-electric power sites in Canada, usually in connection with industrial enterprises, and subsequently developed them. In some cases the power is generated solely for intra-plant use.[31] But two important American ventures in Canada sell power both wholesale and retail. The Niagara-Hudson Power Corporation organized and owns the Canadian Niagara Power Company, Ltd., producing power in a 127,000-horsepower plant on the Canadian side of Niagara Falls. Most of the power is sold to the Ontario Hydro-Electric Power Commission, the rest being transmitted to Niagara Falls and Buffalo. The other case is that of the International Paper and Power Company, which developed the huge Gatineau system.[32] The Niagara-Hudson Corporation's operations are the quite natural development of properties immediately adjacent to its own. The International Company's investment in Canada is due to different conditions. The company went into Canada before the war to safeguard its position when newsprint was placed on the free list by the United States. Undertaking the production of newsprint in Canada on a large scale soon after the war, it built the power plants that

29. A part of the Central Public Service Corporation system.
30. See pp. 139 ff.
31. See the two cases mentioned earlier in this chapter, p. 208.
32. Canadian Hydro-Electric Corporation, Ltd., see pp. 146 ff.

supply its mills with the cheap power so essential in that industry. The power beyond the needs of its own mills is sold, and provides an income which has done much to carry the company through the black days of the newsprint industry since 1929.

But the second group of American-owned power and gas companies in Canada cannot be accounted for on any such grounds as development of adjacent properties or the by-product of industrial operations. Rather, in the aggregate, they represent a part of the "elephantiasis" suffered by the public utility holding companies of the United States during the pre-1929 era.

These Canadian appendages to American public utility holding company "systems" have already been described.[33] Here we only review the considerations which led to their acquisition. The natural gas properties of the Cities Service Company and the National Fuel Gas Company can probably be accounted for as cross-Border development in the easily accessible Ontario peninsula. But the interests of the remaining companies in the Canadian power and gas industry owe their existence to motives which are more difficult to isolate. Some were acquired by holding companies which were rapidly and almost promiscuously adding subsidiaries to the base of their sub-structures with little or no regard to the possible lack of integration between them. The widely scattered Canadian properties of the American Commonwealth Power Corporation—before its recent reorganization—probably belong in this "promotional" group, as may also those of the North American Gas and Electric Corporation. Others may represent the acquisition of what appeared to be at least potentially profitable properties. It is claimed that the Associated Gas and Electric Company entered Nova Scotia simply because a group of companies were for sale which, although in financial difficulties and in need of much rehabilitation, gave promise of a fair return.

It is impossible to state with precision whether investment or expansion was the impulse uppermost in any particular case. But in a period during which, within the United States, amazing collections of widely scattered public utility companies were being grouped together and called systems, it would have been a matter of surprise if Canada had been ignored in the search for purchasable properties.

33. See pp. 139 ff.

The second group of companies we have just been discussing arrived too late on the Canadian scene to be the result of efforts to develop large power resources.[34] But in a few old and important Canadian power companies, Americans entered at the beginning, in an easily understandable effort to share in the profits of promising ventures. Thus, for example, there was large American participation in the building of both the Shawinigan Water and Power Company and the Duke-Price Power Company, Ltd.[35] But these companies were not the outgrowth of previously existing parent companies supplying power in the United States. They represent, rather, the entrepreneurial activities of individual Americans. Later, however, the Aluminum Company of America became interested in the Duke-Price company.

SERVICES

A large, but miscellaneous, group of American and Canadian companies have crossed the frontier to sell services rather than commodities. In almost every case the motives are simple enough. The parent company, having a profitable business at home, decides that the market either north or south of the boundary is attractive enough to justify an investment.

The insurance companies of both countries have not regarded the Border as a barrier. The banks have, in most cases, not attempted to solicit deposits in the neighboring country;[36] but they have, notably in the case of the Canadian banks, maintained the organization necessary to complete their Canadian-American banking services.

American restaurants,[37] chain stores,[38] hotels,[39] and theaters[40] have for many years considered Canada as scarcely a foreign country. Similarly the Loblaw chain groceries in Canada expanded into Buffalo and Chicago, while the Laura Secord candy stores partici-

34. Although, of course, if they have modernized plants and reduced costs, they may have widened the market for power.

35. See pp. 103–105, 148–149, 152.

36. But the Canadian Bank of Commerce does operate commercial banks in Portland (Oregon), San Francisco, and Los Angeles.

37. Childs, Home Dairy, and Stewart's Cafeterias.

38. Woolworth, Kresge, Metropolitan, Safeway, etc.

39. Ford and United Hotels.

40. Notably the Loew's and R.K.O. groups.

pated in the organization of the Fanny Farmer shops in the United States. In all these cases there is no need to probe beneath the surface in search of any peculiar explanation for the venture in a foreign land.

So, too, advertising agencies, contractors, brokers, and publishers have, in many instances, attempted to obtain their full share of the North American market in the only way possible—by establishing branch organizations or affiliations in both countries.

A few of the American companies, however, were guided by slightly more complex motives in their northward migration. Some chains of American-owned stores in Canada are the sales outlet for the Canadian factories of the parent company, and represent merely the extension to Canada of the same sales system used in the United States. Examples are to be found in the stores of the Singer Sewing Machine Company, the Eastman Kodak Company, the A. G. Spalding Company, and the service stations of Imperial Oil, Ltd.

Summary

It is clear that Canadian-American industry, regardless of which country provides the direction, is of two sorts, and consequently owes its origin to two sets of motives. The first group is composed of mines, timber companies, public utilities, communication enterprises, stores, hotels, financial companies, and so on. The second consists of branch factories.

The companies in the first group, with a few exceptions, owe their origin to the search for raw materials, or to an effort to complete or extend a service. In general it may be accepted that these companies, whether Canadian or American, have been much less concerned with the fact that they were venturing into a "foreign" country than by the existence near at hand of needed raw materials or familiar markets.

The second group "is motivated essentially by the desire to bring the product within the purchasing power of the foreign consumer through saving on transportation and import duty, or to induce him to buy the product of the foreign branch plant when he is prejudiced, for some reason or another, against foreign products. . . ."[41]

The branch plant, whether Canadian or American, is "a more

41. Senate Document No. 258, p. 8.

intensive method of selling . . . products in foreign markets. . . ."[42]
It is, as an earlier study attempted to show, a "new export technique."[43] All too frequently it is made necessary by artificial barriers
in the absence of which simple exporting would be preferred. But for
all that, it is a way of foreign trading that a free-trade world would
not avoid.

42. *Ibid.*, p. 5.   43. Southard, *op. cit.*, pp. 131–132.

CHAPTER V

OPERATIONS

WITH the history and extent of Canadian-American industry well in mind we can turn to the examination of its organization and operation. The factory is, as we have seen, the commonest form of direct investment in both countries. It is the sort of American investment in Canada which attracts the most attention. Consequently, although we will draw some examples from mining, public utilities, stores, and other such non-manufacturing companies, this chapter is chiefly a study of branch factories.

Anyone interested at all in the whole development with which this book is concerned will want answers to certain very obvious questions. How are these foreign subsidiaries organized? That is, how is the decision to enter the country arrived at, what form of organization is chosen, how is the subsidiary financed, and what sort of relations are maintained with the parent company in the United States or Canada? How are they operated? Do they import, assemble, or manufacture? Are their wage scales governed by that of the region around them or of the parent company? How do their costs compare with those of the parent company? What markets do they serve? What selling methods do they use?

It must not be expected that we are going to supply complete answers for all of those questions. This is a subject in which the search for information often yields disappointments instead of results. Seldom will more than 30 per cent of any group of companies answer queries, and even that coöperating minority is reluctant to supply details concerning costs, wages, and sales. But with what information we have some progress can be made in the attempt to look inside of branch factory walls.

Out of the study of hundreds of individual branch enterprises a composite picture can be constructed of a "typical" branch factory. Typically, the American plant in Canada has been established to avoid tariffs and to cater to the consumer preference for "Empire-made" goods. Although it may export some of its output, it has been organized mainly to serve the Canadian market. It is incorporated in Canada as a limited company, is owned by the parent company, financed by it, and closely controlled by it. It is, in terms of numbers, typically a small plant, employing up to $200,000 capital and turning out only a small proportion of the products produced by the giants among American-owned companies in Canada.[1] It is a factory, not an assembly plant, and although it may import some parts from the parent company it tends to produce 85 per cent or more of the product in Canada. It pays the going rate of wages in Canada, which means that its wage scale is a little—but only a little—lower than that of its American associate. Its costs are higher than those of the parent and the price it charges the Canadian consumer is likely to be higher than that paid by the Americans for such goods. But except for the fact that those higher prices limit an already widely scattered market, it finds the Canadian market little different than the one served by its parent company. Finally, the typical American plant in Canada, although hard hit by the depression, has been profit-making.

It is the purpose of a composite picture to blot out individual differences. So, in this case, all the qualifications in the remaining chapters are necessary to prevent this description of a typical branch plant from being misleading.

ORGANIZING THE BRANCH PLANT

Turning from this typical yet non-existent factory to a survey of the hundreds of individual cases out of which it is compounded will help satisfy the doubts that a picture of the "average" should always rouse. We begin by assuming that the parent company has decided to establish a branch factory. Possibly it has been losing a hitherto profitable Canadian market[2] because of tariffs or prejudices against foreign goods and hopes a Canadian factory will save it. One company, for example, says:

At one time we did $25,000 worth of business in Canada. Then the depression, exchange, an additional duty (20 to 40 per cent) and the "Buy Canada" campaign reduced our sales to less than $5,000. We then opened a branch factory and took over one of our Canadian competitors so that our sales have increased to about $75,000 this year, with prospects of considerably more in 1935.

1. See pp. 26–28.
2. Or American market. But most of the analysis is based on branch plants in Canada, since they provide the larger sample.

Or it may be hoped that disappointing Canadian sales will improve after the goods are produced in Canada and offered at a lower price. Or some of the other considerations described in Chapter IV may have been important. At any rate, it has been decided to produce— or at least assemble—in Canada.

Selecting a location. If it is proposed to buy an interest in an already going concern in Canada, the choice of locations is restricted to the probably few purchasable companies. In 1912, for example, the Quaker Oats Company purchased the Saskatoon Milling Company. Similarly, in 1923, the B. F. Goodrich Company acquired an interest—ultimately the controlling interest—in the Ames-Holden Tire and Rubber Company, Ltd., which later became Canadian Goodrich Company, Ltd. Many American companies have made their entrance into Canada in that manner.[3]

If, however, there is to be no such affiliation with a previously existing Canadian company, the problem of location is a little more complicated. Even in cases such as the two just cited, of course, the American company had its choice of all possible locations. In buying an existing firm it is, in a sense, acquiescing in the location selected by that company in earlier years. It has, presumably, decided that no unoccupied location will be any more suitable.

What factors govern the choice of branch plant location? There are a few special localization factors arising out of the fact that the proposed factory will have an American associate. But in general the same considerations must influence the location of both subsidiary and independent factories in Canada. Convenience to markets, both Canadian and export, availability of skilled labor, good transportation, access to raw materials, suitable factory buildings, cheap power, fuel and rent, location of related industries—all are influential in guiding the choice of a factory location.[4]

The Canadian questionnaire asked specifically which of a number of factors guided the choice of a location. The 168 answers are summarized below, showing the number of companies checking each suggested reason.

3. See pp. 224 f.
4. That list of factors, and the order given, is taken from the study of "Industrial Development in the United States and Canada" made by the National Electric Light Association and the Metropolitan Life Insurance Company.

Near domestic markets	91
Convenient transportation	52
Skilled or cheap labor	36
Nearness to parent company	33
Acquisition of an existing firm	31
Low rent factory space	31
Cheap raw materials	22
Near related industries	21
Cheap power	19
Satisfactory factory space (other considerations than low rent)	14

In 1913, of 453 Canadian plants believed to be American-owned 71.6 per cent were located in 7 cities or urban regions[5] as follows:

	Per cent
Toronto	21
Montreal	12
Hamilton	10
Border Cities	10
Niagara Frontier	10
Winnipeg	6.6
Calgary	2

In 1934, an examination of 1,030 American-owned industrial plants in Canada[6] indicated that 70 per cent are located as follows:

	Per cent
Toronto	32
Montreal	13
Border Cities	9
Niagara Frontier	7
Hamilton	5
Vancouver	2
Winnipeg	2

5. Calculated from the list given by F. W. Field, *Capital Investments in Canada* (1914 ed.), pp. 39–52. "Border Cities" includes the whole group of municipalities across the river from Detroit; "Niagara Frontier" includes all the municipalities in the area opposite Buffalo and Niagara Falls; included in Toronto and Montreal are their immediate suburbs. It should be noted that each company is assigned to the city of its head office. Since in a number of cases this is either not the city of its main plant (e.g., International Nickel), or there may be several plants (e.g., Goodyear Tire), there results a slight exaggeration of the concentration in Toronto and Montreal.

6. Made by the authors. It includes a few mines, but is generally comparable with Field's data.

There thus appears to be a somewhat greater concentration in 1914 in the larger industrial centers of Canada. Toronto, however, has markedly increased in popularity as a factory site, probably because the small American-owned plant, producing a product to be sold directly to the consumer, finds it a good central location.

American branch plants tend to settle more largely in Ontario than is true of Canadian manufacturing establishments as a whole. In 1931, of the roughly 24,000 factories in Canada, 42 per cent were in Ontario and 31 per cent in Quebec. But of the 1,030 American-owned plants mentioned above, 66 per cent are in Ontario and only 16 per cent in Quebec. The reasons for this are not hard to find. American managers naturally prefer the familiarity of an English-speaking community. Southern Ontario is of easier access from most of the industrialized northeastern part of the United States. Moreover, Southern Ontario is the area of greatest circulation for American magazines and newspapers with their voluminous advertising of well-known products and brands. The branch plant thus has almost a ready-made market at its doors if it is located in Ontario.[7]

Consequently, reverting to the picture of the typical branch plant, we can add the fact that it is likely to be located in Ontario, with Toronto, the Niagara Frontier, Hamilton, or the Border Cities as its most probable address. Quotations from two questionnaire replies may better illustrate the sorts of decisions that are made on branch factory location.

Our principal reason for locating in Toronto was the fact that over 50 per cent of our production could be delivered by truck, which meant excellent service to our customers and a reasonable transportation cost. We made surveys of a number of places within a radius of a hundred miles and found that power, fuel, wages and rail costs would be practically the same.

It was our desire to locate in a comparatively small city somewhere between Windsor and Montreal. Several other cities . . . might have been quite as satisfactory . . . but in locating here we acquired a going concern, enabling us to get into production at a much earlier date . . . and [gave us] a line allied, though not competitive, to our own.

7. There is, however, a moderate concentration of textile and rubber branch plants in Quebec towns that have, for years, been centers for those industries. But even in these industries Ontario is well represented.

Selecting a form of organization. Most branch plants are incorporated under the laws of the domicile country. Thus the vast majority of American plants in Canada are limited liability companies, with a corporate existence distinct from that of the parent. In 1931 the Dominion Bureau of Statistics reported that of 1,071 American concerns in Canada only 104 were operated as branches, the remaining nine tenths of the total being separately incorporated in Canada.

Separate incorporation provides for a complete segregation of both assets and income of the parent company and the subsidiary. Further,

incorporation under Dominion law entitles a foreign corporation to operate anywhere in Canada. . . . Subsidiaries have to submit their own statements to the authorities, while a branch must submit statements for the parent company as well, and . . . in some Provinces taxation is based on total authorized capital which, in the case of a branch, is the capital of the parent company.[8]

In addition, of course, a branch plant in the form of a limited company permits sharing ownership with Canadians if that is desired, as it often is. It also permits closer identity with the Canadian community by the use of "Canada" or "Canadian" in the name, and so on. Consequently even sales subsidiaries are often incorporated under Canadian law.

The few American companies operating their Canadian organizations as direct and unincorporated branches apparently do so because of the simplicity of that form of organization. Some wish to operate their Canadian plant on exactly the same basis as their American branch plants. The Yale and Towne Manufacturing Company actually dissolved its Canadian limited liability company in 1923 and has since then operated its Canadian plant as "Yale and Towne Manufacturing Company, Canadian Branch."

8. *American Direct Investments in Foreign Countries,* Trade Information Bulletin No. 731, pp. 31–32. Although Dominion incorporation is preferred, some companies choose Provincial incorporation. The Company Acts of the Dominion and of the various provinces differ with respect to information which must be furnished. Sometimes a company can be incorporated in one province when it would meet with difficulty under Dominion laws or the laws of other provinces, especially in the case of mergers. This consideration is probably not relevant in the vast majority of branch plants.

Acquiring a plant. Many American companies, as has been stated, have purchased Canadian companies, using their plants to serve the Canadian market. Later, of course, they may build new plants or acquire still further Canadian companies. Or the initial plant may be leased, an idle factory purchased or a new one built.

An example or two might be selected from among the more important cases. In the years following 1887 the Sherwin-Williams Company built a plant in Canada, which it owned until 1911. In that year Sherwin-Williams Company of Canada, Ltd., was incorporated to acquire that plant; the Canada Paint Company, Ltd., an 1893 merger of 3 of the largest paint companies in the Dominion; and Lewis Berger and Sons, Ltd., of England, which had become associated with the American company in 1905. In this new company the American company acquired a minority interest. Successively, in 1920, 1926, and 1928, four more companies were acquired by Sherwin-Williams of Canada, and in 1931 the American company purchased the controlling interest.

Or, turn to another industry. One American company in the fabricated steel industry began its Canadian operations by having its goods manufactured on an agreement basis by a Canadian company which was later acquired. Still later another Canadian company was purchased, one of its departments dismantled, and the whole Canadian organization moved into that plant.

There are outstanding examples of the building of new and expensive branch factories. Possibly the Canadian mills of the International Nickel Company and the International Paper and Power Company are scarcely branch plants in the truest sense, since their operations bulk so large in affairs of the parent company. At any rate they were built in the early post-war years at a cost of many millions of dollars. But the new distillery built by Hiram Walker–Gooderham and Worts, Ltd., at Peoria, Illinois, is a typical branch plant and cost $5,725,000.[9] Until this plant was completed Ameri-

9. *New York Times,* November 17, 1934. This outlay, plus an addition of $4,800,000 for inventories in the United States, was evidently the chief factor in the passing of dividends on the common stock of the parent company. Outlays for a similar purpose were cited as one reason for heavy accounts receivable item in the Seagram's balance sheet. *Ibid.,* January 9, 1935.

can production was carried on in several leased distilleries in the vicinity of Peoria.

Some American companies—especially since 1932—are serving the Canadian market with products made by independent Canadian companies on license or contract. Such an arrangement, of which there are probably more than a hundred, solves at once the several problems of organization, plant acquisition, management, and so on. Later in the chapter and elsewhere in the book these border-line cases between branch plant and independent company are more fully discussed.

Most American plants in Canada, then, are owned by the operating company. Many of them were at one time Canadian-owned, but the majority were built by the present operators for their own uses. That is probably true even of the scores of small factories which American companies have established in Canada in the past 6 or 7 years. But it is in this latter group that most of the leased plants are to be found. Not only are there small idle factories for rent, but idle floor space may be had, and leasing is attractive to the American company which wants to try its hand at manufacturing in Canada but also wishes to keep the investment as low as possible. Many of these small concerns employ capital of less than $50,000.

Financing the Canadian venture. About 80 per cent of the more than 300 companies replying to both questionnaires stated that the Canadian subsidiary was financed entirely by the parent company. In 1931 the Dominion Bureau of Statistics calculated Canadian and other non-American minority interests in American-owned concerns in Canada as follows:

	Per cent
Wholly owned in the United States	40
90–99 per cent owned in United States	31
70–90 per cent owned in United States	12
50–70 per cent owned in United States	7
Less than 50 per cent owned in United States	10

It may not be strictly accurate to accept those figures as indicating not only degree of American control but also the distribution of the financial load. However, there can be little doubt that the average branch plant—including the Canadian plants in the United States—is financed almost entirely by the parent company.

To the scores of branch plants, large or small, which the parent company finances entirely out of corporate surpluses we need give no further attention. Nor are we concerned with the numerous cases in which the parent company has sold its own securities—chiefly in the American market, although Canadians may buy them—and has used some of the funds for Canadian expansion.

In some of these latter cases, however, it is interesting to notice that the Canadian properties are partial security behind the mortgage of the parent company. For example, the Northern Paper Mill first 5's of 1934–48, offered in the United States and Montreal, have both the Canadian and American assets as security. An older case is that of the Glidden Company's first mortgage 6's, which have the Canadian plant as partial security. The Brown Company has pledged the entire $14,000,000 common of the Brown Corporation (Canada) behind its own $18,000,000 first mortgage of 1946, and has agreed similarly to hypothecate any debt imposed on the Canadian properties.

Exchange of stock has been utilized by some American firms in the purchase of Canadian companies, although it is impossible to know accurately how extensive such exchanges have been.[10] In some cases stock of the parent company has been the medium through which the exchange has been effected. This has been true of the Borden Company; in part of the old Kraft Cheese Company; the General Motors Corporation; the International Paper Company, in acquiring the Riordon properties; the National Biscuit Company, in the acquisition of Christie Brown and Company, Ltd.; the American Laundry Machinery Company; the Otis Elevator Company; and the Liquid Carbonic Corporation.

It is probable, however, that the American company exchanges the common, and very often the preferred, stock of its Canadian subsidiary—rather than its own—in those cases in which the Canadian vendors do not demand cash. For instance, the United States Gypsum Company's subsidiary, Canadian Gypsum Company, Ltd., purchased the Albert Manufacturing Company by an exchange of

10. The Canadian minority interests indicated on the preceding page are partly the result of the purchase of Canadian properties by an exchange of stock.

stock, and the United Drug Company, Ltd., increased its capitalization in order to acquire Allen and Cochrane, Ottawa.

A final method by which some of the financing of American companies in Canada is transferred to Canadians is the public issue of the securities of the Canadian company. Here the credit of the Canadian enterprise is utilized, reinforced in some cases by guaranties by the parent company.[11] Such companies as Sherwin-Williams Company of Canada, Ltd., Canadian Consolidated Felt Company, Ltd., Goodyear Tire and Rubber Company, Ltd., Curtiss-Reid Aircraft of Canada, Ltd., Hinde and Dauch Company of Canada, Ltd., Pacific Mills, Ltd., have offered bonds and stock to the public in both countries. In a good many of these cases the investment underwriting houses have included Canadian firms.

It is difficult to obtain a complete list of such securities, and still more difficult to determine how much of each issue was taken in the United States and how much absorbed by Canada. Appendix I, however, probably includes most of the publicly issued securities of important American-owned Canadian companies.[12] That list indicates that between 1912 and 1929 such firms sold stocks and bonds of a par value of about $150,000,000, of which approximately $110,000,000 was absorbed in the United States.

It is apparent, then, that the capital market in both countries has been directly approached to supply some of the funds with which certain of the larger American-owned companies in Canada have been expanded. But although possibly as much as 10 per cent of the capitalization of such companies has been offered, at one time or another, to the general investor, that is not the way in which most American-owned factories in Canada have been financed.

The American chain store financing in Canada presents interest-

11. e.g., the 6½ per cent debentures of the St. Regis Paper Company, Ltd., issued in New York in 1924, and guaranteed, principal and interest, by the St. Regis Paper Company.

12. Cases such as United Cigar Stores, Ltd., and Bell Telephone of Canada, Ltd., were omitted as not strictly American subsidiaries. Also certain other items were eliminated because although the proceeds from the security sale may have been expended in Canada, the debtor corporation is domiciled in the United States.

ing variations.[13] There are 6 companies concerning which relatively full information is available.[14] One of them, Dominion Stores, Ltd., although American-controlled has no parent company and is financed by sale of its own securities or by bank loans. Another, Metropolitan Stores, Ltd., has sold over $6,000,000 in bonds—its own or subsidiaries'—to buy its properties and build its stores. In 1933, however, the new owner, H. L. Green Company, paid in over $1,000,000 to provide a surplus for development purposes. The remaining 4 have looked to the parent company for funds. F. W. Woolworth Company, Ltd., in 1931, owed almost $9,000,000 to the New York company, on which it was charged, in accordance with a 1912 contract, 6 per cent.[15] Similarly S. S. Kresge Company, Ltd., and the Canadian Atlantic and Pacific Company owed, respectively, $7,412,000 and $2,904,000 to the parent companies in 1933, but no interest is charged on these advances. During the depression the United Drug Company, Ltd., advanced $340,000 to Louis K. Liggett, Ltd., and twice—in 1924 and again in 1928—it canceled earlier loans to the amount of $568,000 which it evidently regarded as uncollectable.

As was noted above, 20 per cent of the companies replying to the questionnaire reported that their Canadian company was at least partially financed in Canada. About a third of these explained that the former Canadian owners were still interested in the company. Others stated that the Canadian security holders, whether officers, employees, or public, provide a good-will element.[16] Most of the larger American-owned companies operating in Canada, however, probably depend on Canadian purchase of the securities of the parent company to provide whatever good-will exists in a consumer ownership. In a number of cases, however, employees are allowed to purchase stock in the Canadian company.

13. See various sections of the *Royal Commission on Price Spreads 1934–1935, Minutes of Proceedings and Evidence,* November 12, 1934, and subsequent days.

14. See p. 155.

15. The capital of Woolworth Canadian Company is nominal, and these advances, on the balance sheet, are the chief offsets to assets.

16. The Ford Motor Company of Canada, in 1929, offered 100,000 "A" shares for sale in Canada "to create a larger number of interested shareholders."

Liaison: policy determination. The final step in the organization of the subsidiary is the devising of some satisfactory manner by which contact may be maintained between it and the parent company. It is possible to imagine, at one extreme, a Canadian subsidiary which, once set up, is allowed complete independence in its operations, being accountable to the parent company only for the dividends it chooses to declare. Such a subsidiary may exist, but we have not found it. At the other extreme is the "factory branch," not separately incorporated, and completely controlled, through all the machinery of reports and conferences, no matter whether it exists in Canada or in the United States. In between those extremes lie practically all of the branch plants.

Here, of course, we are dealing with data which are hard to summarize. Most of the companies briefly indicated in their answers to the questionnaires the nature of the contact maintained between head office and subsidiary. Random quotations from 10 of the more complete answers may be illuminating. These companies operate branch factories in widely scattered industries.

The operation of the Canadian subsidiary is under the control of the Canadian company so far as corporate, manufacturing and other details (except sales) are concerned. Sales policies are controlled by the Home office at Cleveland. . . . In other words, we consider our domestic market covers the United States and Canada.

The entire organization is headed up at Indianapolis with a local management [in Canada], both sales and manufacturing, and a branch manager in Vancouver.

The Canadian managers are responsible to the head office, large transactions are approved by head office, finances are managed by head office, policies are established by head office.

Vice-president in charge of exports supervises operations, with a general manager in Canada.

The operating head of our Canadian business is a director in the parent company and attends monthly meetings of the Board of Directors, and free exchange of visits between the two plants is made in all technical and sales problems by those interested.

Daily reports, copies of all letters written, and of all invoices, deposit slips and check vouchers [are sent to head office].

Actions of Canadian managers directed from office of American company in all matters except regular routine.

Canadian manager is a director of the United States parent company. Occasional visits are made by American management.

Contact is through our International Division, which is organized for the conduct of all business abroad including contact with foreign subsidiaries, affiliated and associated companies.

Engineering is all done by the parent company. Our sales experts are available to help Canadian sales.

Obviously, statements such as these do not lend themselves to anything approximating statistical treatment. But, at the risk of some inaccuracy, the answers to both questionnaires indicating the type of control are summarized below.

	American replies	Canadian replies
Personal visits; reports	49	14
Executive, supervisory, general	30	40
Close supervision	24	33
Interlocking officers and directors	15	12
Handled like other branches	10	
Interchange of data, especially technical		13
None, nominal, or slight	11	33
	139	145

The Canadian questionnaire asked, in addition, whether operations were supervised in detail by the parent company. To that question almost 75 per cent replied in the negative. There is some conflict between the two sets of answers. One would gain an impression of greater independence of action among subsidiary companies in reading the replies of the branch managers than in reading those of the head office executives. But it seems apparent that, on the whole, general policy is determined by conference with the parent company, and that, through regular reports, the parent company is kept closely informed concerning Canadian operations. Probably a fourth of the subsidiaries are completely supervised by the parent company. Another fourth are run by a largely unrestricted Canadian management. The other half are those in which, as we have said, the local manager runs the plant, decides the wage-scale, determines the out-

put, adapts the general policy to local conditions, and only looks to
the parent company for general guidance, and for approval of large
expenditures, radical price changes, and major contracts.

There is much evidence that Canada has been considered more a
division of the domestic market than part of the foreign market.[17] It
is interesting to note that in more cases than not the separate "International" companies formed by many American companies in recent
years to handle foreign business do not control Canadian affairs. The
Crown Cork International Company, it is true, holds shares in the
Canadian subsidiaries of its parent, Crown Cork and Seal Company.
But Johns-Manville International Corporation, General Motors Export Corporation, Bates International Corporation, and International B. F. Goodrich Company, although organized to handle the
foreign business of their parent companies, do not supervise the
Canadian market.

It is natural that the ease of communication, the general convenience of mail, telephone, telegraph, and railroad should result in a
more intimate relationship between parent and subsidiary. Head
offices in the industrial northeast United States are, in many cases, in
easier contact with their Canadian than with some of their more distant American branches.

OPERATING THE SUBSIDIARY

It is important not to forget that throughout this analysis we are
concerned not with these factories as such, but rather with their
affiliation with either Canadian or American parent companies. Consequently our attention should be focused on a comparison between
their operation and those of Canadian and American industry in
general. If there were nothing peculiar about branch plant operation
when viewed either by the parent company or by independent industry, there would be no necessity for this section of the book.

Sales, assembly, or manufacture? We have assumed, in this chapter, that it has been decided to advance operations in the Canadian
—or American—market at least a step beyond the distribution of
finished goods imported from the parent company. But there may

17. An official of one of the chain store companies stated in a conversa-
tion with the authors that only recently had his company become aware that
Canada is a foreign country.

exist an almost infinite variety of production arrangements once that first step is taken.

At the one extreme is the completely integrated and self-contained factory deriving no parts, raw materials, or patterns from the parent company. In fact, even a step beyond that lies the independent Canadian factory producing goods for American companies under license agreements or manufacturing arrangements. Even there, however, there is considerable variation between the amount of production assistance rendered by the American associate.

At the other extreme is the packaging and assembly plant. Strictly defined, such a plant does no fabricating. It imports from the parent company all the parts with which to assemble a complete article, or, as in the case of tooth paste, it may import the paste in bulk, the empty tubes, and the cartons, confining its operations to filling and packaging. Many assembly plants, however, soon began to manufacture simpler parts—or possibly to buy them in Canada—while other plants from the beginning produced sizeable percentages of the product. One maker of proprietary medicines, for example, says that he shipped finished goods from the United States to Canada from 1900 to 1910, bottled a few items between 1910 and 1914, built a factory in 1914, and enlarged it to make a full line in 1919.

From the questionnaire sent to American companies owning subsidiaries in Canada some impressions can be had concerning branch factory operations. One hundred and seventy-one replies were received. Forty-eight per cent report that their Canadian companies completely manufacture. Sixteen per cent largely manufacture the product but import up to 25 per cent of the parts and materials. Another 16 per cent confine their Canadian operations to the assembly of parts chiefly imported. Seven per cent license Canadian companies to produce for them, and the remainder are sales subsidiaries, importing the complete product.

From the Canadian questionnaire more definite information has been gained of the growth and changes in the fabrication facilities of subsidiary companies. From the histories of 151 American-owned branch plants the following facts are summarized:

> 68 per cent entered Canada as factories producing a substantial portion of the product.
>
> 18 per cent entered as sales offices. Half of them added assembly in 5.5

years after entry and all of them began manufacturing 7.3 years after entry, on the average.

8 per cent entered as assembly plants and began manufacturing 4.4 years later.

6 per cent entered as assembly plants and do not yet manufacture.

It is evident that although partial manufacture is by no means uncommon, the pure assembly plant, doing practically no fabricating on the premises, is not a popular method of serving the Canadian market. In Canada, as in most other countries, tariff schedules have increasingly tended to apply virtually the same total charge on an aggregation of parts as that which is levied on the finished article.

Much evidence indicates that subsidiary companies are producing a steadily growing portion of the product in their own plants, and that the companies of recent origin have been, from the beginning, largely independent of the parent factory for parts. The above figures are undated, but other data drawn from the Canadian questionnaire and elsewhere more clearly reveal recent tendencies. Early in 1933 the British Board of Trade issued an order restricting Empire preferential rates to goods containing at least 50 per cent "Empire content"[18] which has probably provided a further impetus to the tendency just mentioned. The Toronto Industrial Commission examined 88 American-owned plants established in the Toronto area 1930–32 and discovered 25 with a Canadian content of 100 per cent, 38 with 75 to 100 per cent, 18 with 50 to 75 per cent, and 7 with less than 50 per cent.[19]

The Canadian content of the products of 112 companies answering the Canadian questionnaire increased from 69 per cent in 1926 to 72 per cent in 1929 and 81 per cent in 1933.[20] Seventeen of the

18. The restriction applied to a long list of manufactured goods, including perhaps one half of the manufactured goods imported by England. It did not include, for example, textiles and clothing unless they had rubber in them. Prior to April 1, 1933 the rule had been 25 per cent Empire content on manufactured goods, including flour and cheese. On what Great Britain calls natural products, such as wheat, it was 100 per cent and remains so.

19. *New York Times,* February 1, 1933; New York *Sun,* January 31, 1933.

20. Lumber and newsprint companies were excluded, since, although the Canadian content of their product is obviously 100 per cent, they are not comparable with the branch factories we are here discussing.

plants were opened subsequent to 1929 and had, in 1933, 80 per cent Canadian content. Of the other 95, 50 show neither increase nor decrease in the Canadian content of their products, while the remaining 45 report increases, 1926 to 1933.

It is not altogether easy to assign reasons for this increased independence in branch plant fabrication. In early 1932, 16 Canadian factories—most of them American branches or licensees—reported that they were increasing the Canadian content of their output or adding to the list of goods produced under the impact of tariffs and related barriers.[21] Another 26 were new companies who attributed their existence to tariffs, or license arrangements arising out of tariffs. Massey-Harris Company, Ltd., stated that it was discontinuing the importation into Canada of several agricultural implements from its American plant. Not all of these increases in branch plant fabrication are directly due to the tariff. Some companies have managed to increase their business to the point where Canadian sales can bear a larger factory overhead. Others have gradually found more Canadian sources of parts and materials—although those new sources in turn may be tariff-supported.

Many of the American questionnaire replies offered explanations of their selection of one or another of the several arrangements—complete or partial manufacture, assembly, licensing, sales—which reveal the considerations lying behind their choices.

One company, producing business machines, says:

For the most part machines and attachments are shipped from the main factory [in the United States] manufacturing at the Canadian plant being confined to supplies, some assembly work, repairs and service, the rebuilding of traded-in machines, etc. The reason that no machines are manufactured in Canada is that the demand is not large enough as yet to warrant tooling up for manufacturing. Furthermore, under present conditions splitting the production between Canada and the United States would automatically increase our costs at the main factory through reduced volume. Outside accessories such as cabinets, ribbons, etc., as well as raw material for the manufacturing of supplies

21. "Some of the new lines added by Canadian manufacturers as the result of tariff, etc.," *Industrial Canada,* March, 1932. Much detail is given in this article.

are purchased directly by the Canadian company from the supplier, either in the United States or in Canada.

Another company in the same field, producing a larger line, explains its Canadian operations as follows:

Complete manufacture where the volume is good and the tool expense low; where volume is smaller the expensive tool part is imported. If the volume is very small goods are imported.

Random selections from the explanations of companies whose Canadian companies import greater or less portions of their final product will illustrate those interesting compromises between assembly and complete manufacture.

All engineering is done by the head office.

At one time we shipped some raw materials and containers to Canada. It is now cheaper to buy in Canada instead of paying duty.

Before tariffs were raised labels, boxes and foil were bought cheaper in the United States by being combined with home office purchases.

The woodwork is mainly made in Canada.

Complete manufacture should be done there [in Canada] but all materials are not available.

Depends on where parts can be made with least cost.

Some products are manufactured complete in Canada; some 75 per cent; some are assembled—it depends on cost and investment required.

Originally we carried on complete manufacture in our Canadian plant because of tariffs. We shifted to assembly three years ago due to reduced volume.

Some products we can manufacture in Canada as cheaply as in the United States. Others we import in bulk.

We carry on further processing of partly manufactured materials. Canadian volume does not justify full processing.

Finally, there are those companies who avoid manufacturing in Canada, turning instead to the sale of imported goods, to assembly, or to manufacturing arrangements with Canadian firms. The following are typical of the replies of such companies to a question concerning their choice of those types of operation.

We confine our Canadian company to sales only. The volume doesn't warrant Canadian production.

We assemble, because all the parts cannot be obtained in Canada.

We have an assembly plant. The volume in Canada doesn't justify complete or partial production.

A manufacturing arrangement with a Canadian firm is more economical in view of the volume available.

A manufacturing arrangement is cheaper. There is no economic reason to duplicate the existing plant and equipment.

Formerly we manufactured in our own Canadian plant, with about 25 per cent imported parts. Now we use a manufacturing arrangement with a Canadian firm.

Through such testimony it is possible to see more clearly where manufacture, partial manufacture, assembly, licensing, and import of finished goods fit into the branch plant economy. Where the market is reasonably large and no insuperable costs exist as hindrances the branch factory is more likely to turn out a complete product. If, however, the market is smaller, or if the investment necessary to tool a factory for independent production is too large for the market, some, or all, of the parts will be imported. For example, we find one company saying:

The original adventure up there did not prove to be satisfactory or successful because of the fact that the Canadian market could not absorb [our product] in quantities sufficient to make manufacture up there by us profitable.

Of course, if the import duties on the finished product or on certain parts are not high enough to be sales barriers, there is an added—and important—reason for assembly or direct export from the parent factory of finished goods.

Costs. In the earlier parts of this chapter some incidental attention was given to the costs under which branch plants operate. In this section we turn directly to that phase of the subject. But it must be admitted that the data are not complete. What we need are "cost per unit of output" and "labor cost per unit of output" schedules for a representative group of American companies, American and Canadian branch plants, and Canadian companies. What we have are fragmentary and not too specific replies to two questions which were asked both of American parent companies and Canadian subsidiaries:

1. What is the difference between your wage scales in the two countries?
2. Can you quote the same f.o.b. price from both plants?

Anyone who has attempted to obtain such information will realize that to ask more specific questions on costs is to run the risk of replies so scattered as to be useless.[22]

About 150 companies answered the second of these two questions in the American questionnaire. Their replies, classified by types of operation, are given in Table XIV.

TABLE XIV

Relation between f.o.b. Prices Quoted by Parent Companies and Canadian Subsidiaries

| | Number of subsidiaries whose prices are | | | |
Canadian activity	Higher	The same	Lower	Some higher, some the same
Sales	8	..	1	..
Assembly	19	2	..	..
75 to 95% manufacture	14	6	3	..
Complete manufacture	32	24	11	..
Licensee	10	1	..	..
Mixed*	9	3	1	7
Totals	92	36	16	7

* Some articles completely manufactured, parts imported for others.

From these figures certain conclusions emerge. First, two thirds of that group of companies are either obliged or disposed to quote a higher price at their Canadian than at their American plants. The

22. See an article on branch plant costs in Europe by Graham W. Parker, "American Branch Plants Meet European Competition," *Factory and Industrial Management,* September, 1932, pp. 355–357; October, 1932, pp. 375–377.

other third are able to quote prices as low or even lower at the Canadian plant. The Canadian questionnaire[23] produced the same number of answers and exactly the same results—66 per cent reporting higher f.o.b. prices and the rest the same or, in a few cases, lower prices. Second, the operation of plants in both countries is no assurance that equally low prices can be quoted in each market. That is, there are more plants, even those producing the entire product, that are unable to make equal quotations than plants that are able to. But it is also apparent that if the branch plant produces the complete article it has a greater chance of quoting lower prices than if it imports even some parts. Evidence of that is found in the fact that nearly all of the American companies who reported f.o.b. prices no higher in Canada produce at least 75 per cent of the product, and 70 per cent of them the entire product, in the branch plant. Or, to put it another way, 78 per cent of the factories which either import some parts or assemble imported knocked-down products quote higher factory prices in Canada;[24] but only 47 per cent of the complete branch plants quote higher factory prices. The data on the Canadian questionnaire provide even less correlation between degree of Canadian content and ability to quote an f.o.b. price as low as that of the parent company. To be sure, practically all of the subsidiary companies who did report equal factory prices were producing 75 per cent or more of the product in their own plants. But scores of companies with similar production facilities were unable to match the prices of the parent factories.

Two other points in the table deserve attention. While the sample is small, it is worth noting that of the 11 companies whose product is made in Canada on license by independent manufacturers, 10 report higher factory prices in Canada, due either to tariffs on imported parts or to the smaller volume. And 7 of the 20 companies who produce some things in Canada and import all or part of others—the "mixed" companies—are unable to quote an f.o.b. price on the latter as low as that quoted by the parent company.

23. It may be recalled that this questionnaire was sent to the Canadian branches rather than to the United States head offices as in the case of the American questionnaire.

24. Including among them the companies designated as "licensee" and "mixed" in Table XIV.

All the companies replying to the Canadian questionnaire cited one or the other of the following reasons why they do not quote the same factory prices as the parent companies:

Raw materials and parts higher	23
Output smaller	22
Both	22
Tariff	17
Costs in general higher	8

Almost identical explanations were offered in the answers to the American questionnaire, save for greater emphasis on tariffs on imported parts. In 1932, to cite an example, an electric motor manufacturer stated that costs in the Canadian plant were higher than in the parent factory because of (1) duty on imported parts; (2) 30 per cent higher cost of materials, chiefly due to the Canadian tariff but partly to smaller volume purchases; (3) considerably higher labor cost due to smaller volume production.

These factory price differentials are reflected in generally higher retail prices in a variety of fabricated goods in Canada as compared with the United States. Random comparisons, in November, 1934, between Hamilton and New York prices, gave the following results. Prices of trade-marked food and toilet articles were about the same. But New York prices were lower by an average of 25 per cent on 4 makes of automobile, 27 per cent on typewriters, 28 per cent on electric refrigerators, 23 per cent on light bulbs, 10 per cent on films, and 7 per cent on cameras.

The conclusion seems inescapable that branch plants in Canada have, on the whole, higher costs than do their parent companies and that, sheltered by a tariff, they pass those costs on to the consumer.[25]

Wages and labor policy. This section is based on general wage comparisons taken from the two questionnaires instead of on labor cost data, which were not obtainable. Most American companies in Canada pay the going rate of wages in their industry. But 27 per

25. Franklin Johnston, in "While Ottawa Confers," *The American Exporter,* September, 1932, pp. 9–11, states that over 60 per cent of the plants he visited said that their costs in Canada were higher—a finding comparing well with the analysis in this chapter. He concluded that the Canadian public is paying from 20 to 35 per cent more for American goods than it might in the absence of high tariffs.

cent reported, in the Canadian questionnaire, that their wage scale is above that prevailing. It may be that those companies are influenced by the possibly higher wages of the parent companies. They may, however, represent merely the always-present minority who go above the general rate to attract better workers.

The story is a little more complicated when the wages paid in Canada are compared with those paid by the parent companies. Fifty-six per cent of the companies answering the American and 50 per cent of those replying to the Canadian questionnaire report approximately the same wages in parent and subsidiary. Seven per cent of the Canadian replies report higher wages in Canada. Thus only about 43 per cent of both groups have found Canadian wages more than slightly lower than those paid by the associated companies in the United States.[26]

It is safe to conclude that while more than a third of the American factories in Canada pay lower wages than do the parent companies, wage savings are not an important element in the Canadian-American branch plant movement. It is probable that much of the seeming wage advantage is canceled by the higher labor costs resulting from less capital investment per worker and lower volume of output.[27]

There is little to concern us so far as the labor policy of the American branch plants in Canada is concerned. It has been difficult to obtain adequate information. But that which is available indicates that most companies find it possible to follow the same labor policy in both countries. No doubt there are cases in which trade unions are stronger in the one country than the other, and of course labor legislation in the two countries is not uniform. Probably the

26. There are some scattered statistics on wage rates in American-controlled plants in the *Report of the Royal Commission on Price Spreads* (Ottawa, 1935). For example, in the meat packing and agricultural implement industries the highest average wage rates were found in American-controlled companies. On the other hand two or three small American branch plants in textiles were found to be paying extremely low wages. See the *Report,* pp. 114, 116, 118, 375, 380, 393.

27. Here again, Franklin Johnston's results are similar. He reported that 50 per cent of the companies he investigated were paying about the same wages in Canada as in the United States; 4 per cent were paying higher wages in Canada, and 46 per cent were paying lower, although often very slightly lower, wages.

chief limitations met by American companies in Canada are those imposed by the immigration authorities to prevent unnecessary competition in the labor market.

It is, of course, almost the rule for subsidiaries—whether Canadian companies in America or American companies in Canada—to have among either their officers or directors representatives of the parent company. Nevertheless Canadian-American companies chiefly employ citizens of the domicile country.

Markets. It will be remembered that the chief concern of the typical branch factory with which this chapter began is the Canadian market. It was stated in Chapter IV that from 55 to 60 per cent of the companies questioned do not serve any other markets from the Canadian plant. The remaining 40 to 45 per cent, however, allot certain foreign markets to their Canadian associates.

From the Canadian questionnaire more detail was obtained. Forty-seven per cent of the 158 replying companies have exported at least some of their output since 1926. Ten per cent confine their exports to the United States. That group, consisting of timber, pulp, newsprint, abrasive, fertilizer, and coal companies, shipped three fourths of their output to the United States, and are not, strictly speaking, branch factories. The other 37 per cent ship to Empire and other non-American markets. In 1926 the 30 companies in the group exported an average of 22 per cent of their output. In 1929 there were 40 companies, but they shipped only 19 per cent of their output. In 1933, 54 companies were exporting, but disposed of only 16 per cent of their total output. There has been, then, a marked increase in the number of branch plants exporting. The decrease in their exports is due chiefly to the fact that most of the newcomers shipped very small percentages of output. Most of the 24 companies which began exporting after 1926 represent actual diversions from the parent company's foreign markets, since all but 5 of them were in existence in 1929 but had not been engaged in exporting.

A few scattered companies export to non-Empire markets from the Canadian plant, but the foreign trade of most of the branch plants is with the Empire—and especially with Australia and New Zealand. The fact that Empire markets are the commonest addition to the field of operation of the branch factory lends circumstantial support to the conclusion that preferential tariffs have caused the diversion of export trade from the parent company to the Canadian branch plant. A number of companies specifically cite such tariffs as a cause of export diversion from the American plant. However, the Canadian plant may find increases in inter-Dominion tariffs a hindrance to exports just as the parent factory earlier found British preferential tariffs a barrier. Four factories, producing corsets, batteries, vacuum cleaners, and locks, exported 36 per cent of their output in 1926. By 1933 their exports had dropped to 8 per cent. Plants had been established in England by the parent companies of two, and in Australia by the parent company of one. The fourth said Australian and New Zealand tariffs had killed those markets.[28] An American-owned radio factory exported half its output in 1933, but in 1934 the parent company opened a foreign plant and the exports stopped. In a few cases the lower costs of the Canadian factory had won its foreign markets. Although in many cases foreign markets have been assigned to branch plants by the parent company, it is not known whether in any instance that has been done in an attempt to reduce branch plant unit costs by increasing output. Mr. Edward Bacher, in the address earlier quoted[29] ventured the opinion that "on the whole . . . branch plants are to hold export trade that would otherwise slip away rather than to divert trade which is securely held." Nor is it in contradiction to that conclusion that the Canadian Trade Commissioner in New York has found scores of American companies, since 1932, interested in a study of the tariff savings to be gained in exporting from Canada.

Advertising and selling. Three fourths of the companies replying to the Canadian questionnaire stated that their sales problem was not noticeably different from that faced by the parent company. Nor do most of the remaining fourth find marked peculiarities calling for vastly different sales policies. The thin market with its great dis-

28. This drop would be due in part to the tariff war which went on between New Zealand and Canada, 1930–32, and to the severe tariff and exchange restrictions imposed by both Australia and New Zealand. The volume of trade between Canada and the Antipodes improved rapidly during 1934 and in the last six months of that year had been very largely reëstablished.

29. See p. 209.

tances has forced economy in selling campaigns; less use of traveling salesmen, more small accounts. Some subsidiaries take a larger line of goods than does the parent company in an effort to get volume.

So far as advertising is concerned the two countries evidently present few differences. For years the leading magazines of the United States have circulated freely in Canada, carrying the same advertisements. Those in Canadian newspapers and magazines present few noticeable alterations of phrasing or design which would mark them as Canadian save for the name of the Canadian company. The McLaughlin-Buick is an interesting example of a change in name. Originally what was substantially the Buick car was made and sold in Canada under the name "McLaughlin." About 1923 the word "Buick" appeared in small letters worked into the border around the large "McLaughlin." Two years later the "Buick" became large and the "McLaughlin" small. Now the word "McLaughlin" has all but disappeared. The Canadian edition of *Liberty* has a maple leaf and "Printed in Canada" on the cover, and in most—but not all—of the advertisements the name of the Canadian subsidiary has been substituted for that of the American company. But the advertisements are otherwise unchanged. There are, no doubt, occasional changes in package design, etc., to divorce the product from part of its Americanism. The statue of Liberty, for example, may give way to a maple leaf. Standard Brands, Ltd., sells the Gillett and Gillex Cleanser brands only in Canada, and the International Paper and Power Company manufactures and sells fibreboard only in Canada and England. The same general observations may be made of Canadian advertising in the United States. The appeal does not appear to be designed particularly for the American readers, with the exception of those, notably in the case of whiskey, which call attention to the existence of an American factory.

CHAPTER VI

RESULTS

PROFITS AND LOSSES

It is extremely difficult to obtain anything like a complete picture of the profits and losses experienced by branch concerns, whether owned by Canadians and located in the United States, or owned by Americans and located in Canada. In only a minority of the cases are financial statements available. From another—and important—fraction of the American-owned companies in Canada information was obtained by direct inquiry by the Dominion Bureau of Statistics. Concerning the income and deficits of Canadian-owned companies in the United States certain general totals, by industrial groups, were supplied by the Bureau of Internal Revenue of the United States. The statistics resulting from these various sources can be considered only rough approximations. But they give a valuable idea of the order of magnitude of the sums involved.

American-owned companies in Canada. It is estimated that during the period 1926 to 1933 inclusive the United States branch and subsidiary firms in Canada had net profits amounting to between $750,-000,000 and $800,000,000, net losses of between $200,000,000 and $250,000,000 and, therefore, on balance, profits of $550,000,000. It is also estimated that between $390,000,000 and $410,000,000 of these profits were remitted to the United States, the balance being paid to Canadian or other shareholders, into surplus, or used for expansion. Against these remittances there is an offset of funds sent to Canadian branches to meet deficits or for expansion, the amount of which is not ascertainable. These conclusions are computed from the table on the following page.

Available records, as shown in the table, account for $660,829,911 profits, $99,144,450 deficits, and $348,559,621 remittances during that period. Using these figures as a basis, the larger totals given above were estimated by the following method. It was assumed that for the firms for which no record is available the proportion of those having profits was the same as for the recorded firms. A profit figure—and for the balance, a loss figure—of roughly from one third to

TABLE XV

Profits, Losses, and Remittances to United States of Branch and Subsidiary Companies in Canada, 1926 to 1933

Year	Estimated number of branches existing each year	Profits		Deficits			Remittances to United States	
		Number of firms known to have profits	Total profits	Number of firms known to have deficits	Number of firms for which amount of deficit was known	Amount of deficit	Number of firms	Amount of remittances
1926–1933		2,853	$660,829,911	2,158	1,017	$99,144,450	1,469	$348,559,621
1926	950	334	69,636,229	151	50	2,280,875	152	35,978,385
1927	975	363	78,238,386	148	45	1,967,921	172	32,476,476
1928	1,000	403	118,737,031	150	44	4,342,869	197	41,525,773
1929	1,050	423	134,883,764	171	57	2,449,047	195	46,933,351
1930	1,100	397	89,929,397	254	105	7,952,688	211	71,026,369
1931	1,150	333	64,959,153	376	198	22,157,058	204	57,014,414
1932	1,177	284	47,118,361	463	265	38,489,314	168	30,513,596
1933	1,200	316	57,327,590	445	253	19,504,678	170	33,091,257

one half of the average for recorded figures was applied. In the case of recorded firms known to have experienced deficits but with the amount unknown, the same method of applying one third to one half the average deficit of the fully recorded firms was used.

Figures for remittances were increased moderately to correspond with the higher figures for profits. Against this sum of $390,000,000 to $410,000,000 remitted to the United States as profits, some mention should be made of the contribution of the branches to Canadian income. In 1932, a year of the depression, 158,000 workers were employed by these firms, the wages and salaries bill being over $189,-000,000. In addition, materials to the value of $215,000,000 were purchased, the bulk of them probably in Canada, thus giving employment indirectly to many more.

All groups of investments have by no means been equally profitable.

In 1929, approximately 80 per cent of the recorded profits occurred in the following groups, the total profits of recorded companies being $134,883,764:

> Prepared foods and confectionery
> Rubber
> Pulp and paper
> Agricultural implements
> Industrial machinery
> Automobiles and trucks
> Electrical apparatus
> Petroleum products
> Industrial chemicals and gases
> Mining and smelting
> Utility companies
> Merchandising
> Miscellaneous

In 1932, the profits of recorded companies were $47,118,361, approximately 80 per cent in the following groups:

> Prepared foods and confectionery
> Electrical apparatus
> Petroleum products
> Industrial chemicals and gases

Mining and smelting
Utility companies
Merchandising

In 1932, 80 per cent of the losses of recorded companies totaling $38,489,314 were incurred by enterprises in the following groups:

Pulp and paper
Furnaces and rolling mills
Agricultural implements
Automobiles and trucks
Non-ferrous metal mining and smelting other than gold and nickel
Merchandising

It is difficult to summarize these income data further without loading the chapter with tedious percentages. It would be interesting to know, for example, whether large factories were more profitable than small ones, to know what the average income or loss is in various groups of branch companies. Most of that information is lacking. It is a striking fact, however, that over 60 per cent of the capital employed by American-owned firms in Canada is in the following 35 companies:[1]

Manufacturing
    Robin Hood Mills, Ltd.
    Dominion Rubber Company, Ltd.
    Goodyear Tire and Rubber Company of Canada, Ltd.
    Ontario Paper Company, Ltd.
    Pacific Mills, Ltd.
    Powell River Company, Ltd.
    Spruce Falls Power and Paper Company, Ltd.
    Minnesota and Ontario Paper Company
    Algoma Steel Corporation, Ltd.
    International Harvester Company of Canada, Ltd.
    Canadian International Paper Company, Ltd.
    Ford Motor Company of Canada, Ltd.
    General Motors of Canada, Ltd.
    Canadian General Electric Company, Ltd.
    Canadian Westinghouse Company, Ltd.

1. See pp. 26–28, where the concentration of investment in the larger companies is discussed.

    Canadian Oil Companies, Ltd.
    Imperial Oil, Limited
  Mining and Smelting
    Hudson Bay Mining and Smelting Company, Ltd.
    The Granby Consolidated Mining, Smelting and Power Company, Ltd.
    International Nickel Company of Canada, Ltd.
    Aluminium, Limited
  Utilities
    Bell Telephone Company of Canada, Ltd.
    British Columbia Telephone Company, Ltd.
    Canada Southern Railway Company, Ltd.
    Toronto, Hamilton and Buffalo Railway Company, Ltd.
    Vancouver, Victoria and Eastern Railway
    Canadian Hydro-Electric Corporation, Ltd.
    Canadian Niagara Power Company, Ltd.
    Duke-Price Power Company, Ltd.
    Middle-West Utilities Company of Canada, Ltd.
    Dominion Gas and Electric Company, Ltd.
  Merchandising and Miscellaneous
    S. S. Kresge Company, Ltd.
    Metropolitan Stores, Ltd.
    F. W. Woolworth Company, Ltd.
    Famous Players Canadian Corporation, Ltd.

Those companies earned approximately $93,000,000 in 1929. It is not easy to estimate what share that was of total profits earned by all American-owned companies in Canada in that year. Table XV shows a recorded profit, less deficit, of about $135,000,000 for 423 American-owned companies in Canada in 1929. If the correction earlier suggested is made to include unrecorded firms, a total profit, again less deficits, of from $180,000,000 to $200,000,000 would result. On that basis the 35 companies listed above accounted for about half of all profits earned by American-owned firms in Canada. That calculation is offered simply as a very rough approximation of the facts. At most it serves only to indicate the very great importance of a relatively few companies among American-owned enterprises in Canada.

Canadian-owned companies in the United States. In the following table is shown the income and losses of a large proportion of Canadian-owned companies in the United States.

TABLE XVI

Income and Losses of Canadian-owned Companies in the United States

Industrial group	Companies reporting for 1926, 1929, and 1932				Companies reporting for 1 or 2 years: 1926, 1929, or 1932			
	Number	Net income	Number	Deficit	Number	Net income	Number	Deficit
Mining and quarrying								
1926	1	$ 5,000*	5	$ 466,799	2	$ 46,982	..	$ ......
1929	1	5,000*	5	259,134	1	5,000*	3	104,074
1932	..	......	6	302,910	3	43,343	4	265,617
Wood and paper								
1926	5	1,013,781	2	132,409	2	173,569	2	43,448
1929	6	1,463,076	1	700,000*	7	354,994	..	......
1932	6	422,303	1	900,000*	4	152,072	3	150
Metal products								
1926	4	187,639	1	400,000*	2	36,439	2	141,298
1929	5	2,417,168	..	......	5	680,509	3	17,252
1932	1	50,000*	4	1,954,926	..	......	4	2,263,864
Other manufactures								
1926	6	68,186	5	94,471	3	6,088	..	......
1929	5	635,422	6	78,124	3	79,682	1	700,000*
1932	3	177,450	8	167,246	1	200,000*	1	5,000*
Transportation and communication								
1926	8	2,403,013	8	1,783,138	6	195,042	2	374,879
1929	9	3,435,063	7	12,858,113	3	178,428	4	4,771,011
1932	5	890,650	11	21,414,111	..	......	2	1,741,473
Construction trade, miscellaneous								
1926	8	394,844	3	12,239	1	10,000*	2	18,659
1929	7	166,331	4	270,895	4	27,853	7	47,887
1932	5	52,260	6	140,474	1	500,000*	5	74,580
Banks, brokers, insurance								
1926	13	4,019,948	2	68,175	1	500,000*	2	26,433
1929	13	6,795,257	2	933,056	3	668,217	..	......
1932	9	461,686	6	5,886,045	1	50,000*	3	86,372
Investment, miscellaneous finance								
1926	10	189,132	5	315,046	8	147,728	3	3,969
1929	14	2,718,048	1	300,000*	46	6,155,915	15	2,381,676
1932	3	39,399	12	2,531,650	16	2,409,611	34	7,691,869
Grand total								
1926	55	8,276,562	31	3,136,231	25	1,064,534	13	608,686
1929	60	17,630,433	26	15,347,487	72	8,147,496	33	8,021,900
1932	32	2,055,903	54	33,224,607	26	3,217,383	56	12,128,905

* Not in excess of amount given.

The data given in the table are divided into 2 groups. The first, on the left, includes those companies for which figures were available in all of the 3 years, 1926, 1929, and 1932. The second includes firms for which information could be obtained for only 1 or 2 of the 3 years.

Obviously the first group of Canadian subsidiaries, those occupied in mining and quarrying, have not been profitable; even in 1929, 8 firms of the 10 included showed deficits, while only 2 had profits. In 1932, 3 firms out of 13 had profits. But the deficits average much higher than the profits.

In the wood, wood products, and paper group are included such firms as American Sales Book Company, F. N. Burt Company, Fraser Paper, Gilman Fanfold, etc. In 1929, 13 out of 14 firms were profitable. In 1932, 10 were still showing net income, while 4 had deficits.

Those engaged in the manufacturing of iron and steel products, non-ferrous metal products, and in manufacturing non-metallic mineral products were profitable in 10 out of 13 cases in 1929, but only 1 firm out of 9 showed profits in 1932. This group includes such firms as Adirondack Steel Foundries Corporation, Bennett Pump Corporation, E. W. Bliss Company, J. I. Case Plow Works, Massey-Harris Company, Standard Paving Company, etc.

Other manufacturing concerns were profitable in 8 cases out of 15 in 1929. In 1932, 9 firms had deficits, while 4 showed profits.

By far the largest amounts involved are shown in the transportation and communication group. These figures, however, can scarcely be taken at their face value. They include branches in which the Canadian Pacific Railway or the Canadian National Railway have only a partial interest. It is probable, also, that there is some overlapping, as where the income of a system and its subsidiary are both included. The actual net income or deficit of Canadian railway investments in the United States are almost certainly considerably at variance with these figures. Information gathered from other sources yields the following figures for railways:

	Net income	Deficits
1926	$1,375,964	$ 578,517
1929	5,578,855	340,831
1932	799,561	10,572,373

Construction, trade, and miscellaneous companies show small profit or loss evenly divided as to number of cases in 1929 and losses predominating in 1932.

Next to the railways in importance are the financial groups. Banks, brokers, and insurance companies show 16 out of 18 having profits in 1929. In 1932, 10 firms still had profits, but 9 firms had much greater deficits. Profits in 1929 exceeded deficits by $6,500,-000. In 1932 deficits exceeded profits by $5,500,000. Investment and miscellaneous finance companies (chiefly investment trusts) show 60 firms with profits amounting to nearly $9,000,000 in 1929, and deficits amounting to some $2,500,000 in 16 firms. In 1932, 19 firms had profits of less than $2,500,000, and 46 firms had deficits of over $10,000,000.

If the figures for transportation companies are deducted, it is possible to gain an idea of the average profitability of Canadian branches in the United States, other than transportation and communication companies. The following table is of interest:

TABLE XVII

Summary of Income and Deficits of Canadian-owned Companies in the United States

Year	No. of firms	Net income	Average	No. of firms	Deficit	Average
1926	66	$ 6,743,041	$102,167	34	$ 1,586,900	$ 46,673
1929	120	22,164,438	184,704	48	5,740,263	119,589
1932	53	4,382,636	82,691	97	22,197,928	228,845

This table shows that in 1926 profits exceeded deficits by some $5,000,000. In 1929 excess of profits amounted to over $16,000,000, while in 1932 deficits were in excess by nearly $18,000,000.

In the mining and quarrying group the average situation was a deficit of around $50,000 in the 3-year period. In the wood products group profits ranging from an average of $170,000 in 1926 to $57,000 in 1932 predominated. In the metal group average profits of around $300,000 were typical in 1929 and deficits averaging $500,000 typical in 1932. In the group of "other manufactures" profits are more or less indeterminate. In the construction, trade, and miscellaneous group it is difficult to find the typical, though the profit side seems to have a slight advantage, especially in 1926 and 1929. Banks, brokers, insurance companies had typical profits of $300,000 in 1926 and $450,000 in 1929. In 1932 deficits of around $650,000 were characteristic. In the investment and miscellaneous finance group small profits dominated in 1926; in 1929 an average profit of $150,000 was characteristic, but in 1932 an average deficit of over $200,000 was outstanding.

Profits and losses, general. It is at least apparent that in normal times subsidiary companies, whether Canadian-owned or American-owned, have been profitable more frequently than unprofitable. Whether they have resulted in larger trade than the parent companies, collectively, might, under other circumstances, have carried on on an export basis is a question which is considered in the next chapter.[2] But it can be noted here that, in mere absolute amounts, branch company earnings have been of considerable importance to parent companies. Imperial Oil, for example, had net profits in 1929 and in 1932 of about $19,000,000 and $5,400,000 respectively. Goodyear Tire and Rubber Company of Canada, Ltd., reported profits of almost $3,500,000 in 1929; International Harvester (Canada), $1,874,430; Ford Motor of Canada, $5,308,220; Canadian General Electric, $4,428,885; F. W. Woolworth (Canada), $1,805,636; and so on. At many points throughout Chapters II and III other examples of the earning power of subsidiary companies have been given.

REPATRIATION AND WITHDRAWAL

We have been describing these scores and hundred of expatriate American and Canadian companies as if they were steadily increasing in size and number and as if, in general, they were reasonably profitable. On the whole, that is the case. There has been much expansion, and many little plants, as the text has abundantly shown, have grown to the utmost limits of the market. And the average branch plant, on both sides of the boundary, has been profitable.

But lost behind the picture of averages and aggregates are two reverse currents in the flow of American and Canadian companies north and south across the Border. One of these currents is composed of companies whose subsidiaries across the Border either have lost

2. See pp. 267 ff., also Chapter IV, *passim*.

consistently or have so drably broken even that it has not been worth
the effort of the parent organization to continue them. The other
current consists of the companies who have sold their cross-Border
enterprises either to Canadians or to Americans, as the case may be.

It has not been easy to obtain an accurate impression of either of
those movements. Naturally there is much less publicity given to the
failure of an old branch plant than to the establishment of a new one.
Nor are the usually private transactions involved in the transfer of
ownership of branch companies unfailingly reported in the press.

In 1919 F. W. Field estimated[3] that there were 388 American
branch factories in Canada. By 1934 there were possibly 900, or say
an increase in 15 years of 500. During the same period Canadians
acquired either entire or substantial ownership in at least 70 companies, and between 75 and 80 other companies were either closed or
liquidated by their American owners. Of that known 150, about 115
were factories, the rest being mining, communications, and other
sorts of enterprises. Now although we intend subsequently to examine the withdrawal and repatriation movements separately, we can
here notice that in both of them the erstwhile parent company cur-
tails or ceases entirely its cross-Border operations. Consequently, the
rate of withdrawal, considering branch factories only, has, in the
past 15 years, been about one fourth that at which new plants have
been established.

Dr. W. H. Carter, Jr., attempted to estimate the mortality rate of
the American branch companies listed by Field[4] in his various studies
of foreign capital in Canada. He concluded[5] that American-owned
companies in Canada in the 20 years following 1909 suffered a 30
per cent mortality in the first 5 years, with eliminations continuing
at a decreasing rate until, with half the original companies left,
relative stability was reached in 20 years. It must be remembered,
however, that there are great difficulties in tracing several hundred
branch companies over 2 decades. Privately owned as they usually

3. *Monetary Times,* May 9, 1919, pp. 18–24.

4. F. W. Field, *Capital Investments in Canada* (editions of 1911, 1914);
Monetary Times, November 13, 1909, pp. 2011–2013, 2025–2026; May 9,
1919, pp. 18–24; October 27, 1916, pp. 5–7.

5. Wm. H. Carter, *American Branch Plants in Canada* (Harvard University, unpublished Ph.D. thesis, 1932).

are, most of these enterprises are not mentioned in the various financial handbooks. Changes in the corporate relations of both parent and subsidiary further complicate such a search. Consequently there is much danger that the rate of mortality is exaggerated.

The sale or abandonment of a branch company does not invariably indicate that the venture has been unprofitable. In many cases—probably in the largest group—it means just that. In others, however, the parent company has sold a still-solvent and even profitable subsidiary, usually to Canadians but sometimes to other Americans. It is worth while to examine these various sorts of withdrawals in greater detail.

In the first group, not only does the parent company withdraw from Canada, but it closes or otherwise liquidates its subsidiary. Many examples are easily available. The Libbey-Owens Sheet Glass Company built a Canadian plant in 1920 only to discover, within 18 months, that costs could not be kept low enough to compete with Belgian glass. Consequently, although the subsidiary still exists, the factory has been leased to other companies since 1921. The questionnaires sent out by the authors in both countries brought replies from several score of companies who reported that their Canadian subsidiaries were no longer operating. Usually no explanations were offered, but in a number of cases it was stated that the Canadian market had not proved large enough to support a branch factory.[6]

Factories have not been the only vulnerable branches. Mines, of course, have been abandoned; timber companies have been pinched, especially by the latter-day increases in the American lumber tariff; construction companies, such as James Stewart and Company, and Merritt-Chapman and Scott Corporation have withdrawn; and oil refineries have been closed.

Often, of course, during the years there have been failures of parent companies, which has meant, usually, that the semi-dependent subsidiary over the Border has been closed. Probably half a dozen now-forgotten motor car companies had Canadian companies. At least one defunct Canadian automobile enterprise, the Gotfredson Corporation, Ltd., had an American branch. Similarly, the Canadian stores of Steel's Consolidated, Inc., were pushed into financial catas-

6. Similarly, several companies reported shifting from manufacturing to assembly, or to a manufacturing arrangement.

trophe by the failure of the parent company. Only the most laborious search of the records of bankrupt companies would reveal the number of foreign branches that perished with their parent organizations.

In at least a few cases American companies left the door open behind them as they began to manufacture in Canada, and were able to retreat more easily when the venture proved unattractive. The J. C. Brill Company, late in 1921, organized the Canadian Brill Company, Ltd., and leased the plant of the Preston [Ontario] Car and Coach Company, Ltd., with a purchase option. Early in 1923 it was announced that the business in Canada did not warrant either the renewal of the lease or the purchase of the factory. Consequently the plant was turned back to the owners and the Canadian subsidiary was dissolved. So, too, the Cities Service Oil Company, Ltd., abandoned, in 1924, the refinery it had leased three years earlier from the Great Lakes Oil Refining Company in Ontario.

There is much evidence that the mortality rate among American-owned companies in Canada has increased during the depression. Branch plants established on the basis of market estimates during years in which purchasing power was higher have found the sales shrinkage since 1929 intolerable. There has not been, of course, anything like a net withdrawal of American companies from Canada during the depression, but for every 4 new American factories established in Canada since 1929, 1 existing plant has been either closed or sold to Canadians.[7]

A very interesting aspect of this phase of Canadian-American industry is the purchase by Canadians of companies previously American-owned. Although the data are incomplete, there have probably been more "failure" withdrawals than "repatriation" withdrawals.[8] But the group of repatriated companies is large enough to constitute an important element in Canadian industrial development.

Several types of repatriations are discernible among the 70 examples discovered. In one a group of Canadians—possibly including a bond house—raise the capital, purchase the property from the

7. Based on an estimate of 200 new plants and 50 withdrawn or repatriated plants in the 5 years 1930–34.

8. It should be noted that the estimate made in the preceding paragraph included all known factory withdrawals, regardless of cause.

American owners, and carry on the company as an independent venture. Belding-Corticelli, Ltd., organized in 1911, was a merger of 3 companies, 2 of which were probably American subsidiaries. One of the latter had been successfully operating in Montreal since 1877. The textile industry also yields two more recent examples of this sort. Cosmos Imperial Mills, Ltd., was organized to own 2 mills purchased from the New England Southern Mills by A. E. Ames and Company, Ltd., for $1,500,000. In this case the Americans evidently retained a minority interest and 2 places on a board of 7.[9] The National Hosiery Mills, Ltd., was incorporated in 1928 to acquire the assets of the Real Silk Hosiery Mills of Canada, Ltd., and the rights to the name and merchandising methods of that well-known brand. In this case preferred and common were publicly sold in both countries, but there is no reason to believe that control does not lie in Canada.

Other cases appear in the food and metal goods industries. In 1927 a Toronto investment house issued securities partially financing the Northern Bakeries Company of Canada, which purchased for $5,000,000 in cash the 10 Canadian bakeries previously owned by the Continental Baking Corporation. A year later Melchers Distilleries, Ltd., acquired the 30-year-old company of similar name which was owned by The Fleischmann Company of Ohio. In 1924 the Walter M. Lowney Company, Massachusetts, sold its Canadian subsidiaries—Canadian Cocoa and Chocolate Co., Ltd., and Walter M. Lowney of Canada, Ltd.—to Canadians for $1,500,000. And in 1927 the Canadian Bronze Company, Ltd., was organized to acquire 3 companies which had since 1896 been American-owned.

In non-manufacturing fields, several repatriations have occurred. Among the components of Stop and Shop, Ltd., grocery chain company, are the 15 stores formerly owned by Montreal Piggly Wiggly Corporation, Ltd. In 1929 the Foundation Company, New York, sold its Canadian company to a group headed by Drury and Company. Three hotels have returned to Canadian control—the Windsor in 1927, the Mount Royal in 1930, and the King Edward in 1932. In 1933 the American-owned chain of restaurants operated under the name of Bowles Lunch Company was purchased by a Canadian

9. The Canadian mills operated 30,000 of the total of 257,000 spindles in the parent company's mills.

syndicate organized by the man who had for years been the general manager in Canada. In this case the principal American shareholder had died and the estate desired to sell the shares. And in the finance business, the Industrial Acceptance Corporation, Ltd., was purchased by Greenshields and Company in 1930.

Before turning to other sorts of repatriation, two companies with interesting Canadian-American backgrounds might be described— Dominion Motors, Ltd., and Consolidated Industries, Ltd. In 1921 Durant Motors of Canada, Ltd., was incorporated. Durant Motors, Delaware, owned 58 per cent of the stock and on a 20-year contract supplied all needed parts and motors. The American company was also to receive 50 per cent of all profits over 8 per cent. In 1927 the York Acceptance Corporation, Ltd., began operations as a finance subsidiary, and two years later the Delaware company borrowed $1,250,000 from it, depositing as collateral the controlling shares in Durant, of Canada. In January, 1931, the loan, in default for some months, was foreclosed, and the York Acceptance Corporation, after much controversy, disposed of the collateral to Canadian interests,[10] who canceled the agreement with the American company and formed Dominion Motors, Ltd., which produced Nash, Frontenac, and Reo cars under varied arrangements. Here, then, is a case in which a Canadian company emerged from an American subsidiary. By 1934, however, the ravages of the depression had suspended Dominion Motors' operations and practically wiped out shareholders' equity. There was some indication that Reo Motors Company of Canada, Ltd., would continue independently, leasing space in the Leaside plant.[11]

We have mentioned several times the many manufacturing arrangements, royalty, and licensing agreements through which some products reach the Canadian market. It happens in some cases that Canadian-owned companies have inherited such agreements from some erstwhile American-owned portion of their assets which remain as evidence of past relations. Consolidated Industries, Ltd., is another variation of that general group of relationships. Organized

10. See *Commercial and Financial Chronicle,* April 11, 1931, p. 2777; April 18, 1931, p. 2973.

11. Although derived from various sources, the above account is chiefly from the *Survey of Corporate Securities, Financial Post,* 1932, p. 107.

to acquire the DeForest Radio Co., Ltd., and operating for a time under a similar name, it became a holding company for several companies[12] holding rights to the names and processes of American corporations. No Americans appeared on the board of directors. In 1933 and 1934 Consolidated Industries became seriously embarrassed, and all its assets, including contracts, trademarks, and goodwill were taken over by Rogers-Majestic Corporation, Ltd., at prices which gave to unsecured creditors 20 cents on the dollar. Rogers-Majestic is continuing the manufacture of DeForest Radios and Norge Refrigerators.

So much, then, for the group of former American subsidiaries which have become independent Canadian companies.[13] Some American-owned branch companies in Canada have merged with already-existing Canadian companies to form new corporations in which the Americans retain only a minority interest. One of the subsidiaries of the Canadian-owned Russell Motor Car Company, Ltd., is the Canadian Acme Screw and Gear, Ltd. Both of these companies have a branch plant history. In 1929 the Canada Wire and Cable Company, Ltd., acquired the Canadian subsidiary of the General Cable Corporation, which received a minority interest and three places on the board of the Canadian company. So, too, to mention other cases, the Hayes Wheel and Forgings, Ltd., Canadian Transit Company, Ltd., and the Canadian Motor Lamp Company, Ltd., are companies in which the American[14] minority is a vestige remaining from earlier years when some part of the present-day company was a branch plant.

Another important example of repatriation in which an erstwhile American controlling interest becomes a minority interest is Building Products, Ltd. In 1905 an American company, Bird and Son, established a plant in Canada to produce industrial paper products. In 1925 the Canadian subsidiary was merged with the Canadian plant of another American firm, Ruberoid Company, to form Build-

12. Hammond Company of Canada, Ltd., Norge Corporation of Canada, Ltd., Condon Corporation.

13. Other examples are to be found in Appendix II.

14. The Canadian Transit Company, Ltd., is jointly controlled by the Canadian Tank Car Company, Ltd., and the General American Transportation Corporation.

ing Products, Ltd., in which the majority interest is in Canadian hands. The new company has 6 plants manufacturing roofing and sheathing paper, wall board, and asphalt shingles. All of the directors save one are Canadians. Out of 120,846 common shares, however, only 4,500 have voting rights, and it is not altogether certain on which side of the boundary line those shares are to be found. In 1932 Bird and Son carried its investment in Building Products, Ltd., at $400,000, compared with total outstanding common of about $1,500,000. Sixty thousand of the non-voting shares were offered to the public by A. E. Ames and Company, Ltd., in 1927.

A final—and the simplest—sort of case in which control has crossed to Canada is the purchase of an American-owned branch plant by an already-existing Canadian company in the same field. These differ from the rather similar examples just described in that there remains here not even an American minority interest. The list in the Appendix is clear enough. Only a few illustrations are necessary. The Western Union Telegraph Company's lines in Canada have been, in various ways, taken over by Canadian National Telegraphs. In 1929 the Delaware and Hudson Company sold the Quebec, Montreal and Southern Railway to the Canadian National Railways. During the past two or three years the British American Oil Company, in its policy of westward expansion, has acquired two small refineries in the Prairie Provinces. One, the North West Stellarene Company, Inc., of Coutts, Alberta, was American-owned. Of the numerous examples among manufacturing enterprises, the purchase by Price Brothers and Company, Ltd., of Donnacona Paper Company (which it lost 5 years later), and the acquisition of Canadian Metal Products Company by Burlington Steel, Ltd., are sufficient to indicate the nature of these cases.

It has not been possible to find out exactly why many of these transactions have taken place. The motives of the Canadian purchasers are usually easy to understand. In many cases Canadian capitalists and Canadian security underwriters have seen an opportunity to purchase a profitable, or potentially profitable, property owned by Americans. In other cases Canadian companies have sought to improve their position by acquiring a previously competing American-owned factory. In some instances where the American company liquidated its small factory, the Canadians acquired the business rather than the physical property.

The story is a little more complicated when we turn to ask why the Americans sold out. Sometimes the Canadian branch has been hardly, or not at all, profitable, and if a Canadian company or individual Canadians think they can do better with the same assets, the American company may be glad to save further losses and get out. Or the purchase price may be more attractive than the prospect of profits. In 1924 Walter M. Lowney Company sold its Canadian subsidiary for $1,500,000. In so doing it lost dividends, which had amounted to $56,500 the previous year. But it used the cash received from the sale to pay off debts, and reduced its interest burden by $90,000 per year. The Continental Baking Corporation used the $5,000,000 received from the sale of its Canadian bakeries to pay off debts and make plant improvements.

Some American companies may have found the prospect of allying their Canadian branch with a well-established Canadian concern just as attractive as did the Canadian company, which may account for the cases in which the American company retained a minority interest in the merger. Or the Canadian situation may have shifted so as to make the American company disinterested. The Republic Steel Corporation, for example, through a subsidiary, had been shipping rolled metal from its mill in Ohio to be finished by its branch in Guelph, Ontario. When the Canadian tariff made that arrangement no longer profitable it sold the Canadian company to Burlington Steel Company, Ltd.

Other cases are not so clear. The sale of half a dozen important paper and pulp mills[15] to Canadians may have been due to the inability of their owners to make them pay or to the attractiveness of the offer. Nor is it possible to go beyond that in explaining the withdrawal of Western Union from Canada. The Delaware and Hudson Company's case is simple enough; it was no longer using the Quebec Central tracks into Montreal and consequently was willing to sell.

During these same years Canadian industry in America, on its part, has had the same withdrawals, the same sales to Americans.

15. Provincial Paper Mills, Ltd., St. Maurice Paper Company, Ltd., Thunder Bay Paper Company, Ltd., Saguenay Pulp and Paper Company, Chicoutimi Pulp Company, Nashwaak Pulp and Paper Company.

Probably about 10 per cent of the Canadian companies operating in the United States have, in the last 15 years, either closed down or sold to Americans. We are dealing with imponderables, but it is probable that the similar back-flow of American industry in Canada which we have just described has been proportionately about the same size.

In both cases, too, there has been an acceleration of the withdrawal during the depression. It appears, however, that whereas what we have called repatriation accounts for about half of the American back-flow from Canada, it has been less important in the case of Canadian industry in America.[16] The simple failures need not be mentioned in detail.[17] But a few of the repatriations are interesting enough to be described. The Alabama Power Company, which had been financed largely in London, had been controlled by a Canadian holding company, Alabama Traction, Light and Power Company, Ltd., with Canadian officers and directors. By 1924 the ownership and financing had so largely shifted to the United States that the Canadian parent company was dissolved. More obscurely, the $20,000,000 pre-war Illinois Traction Company was evidently Canadian-owned and directed, although by 1931 it was a unit in the North American Light and Power Company.

The only other company which, once Canadian, is now American, that need be mentioned is the Canada Dry Ginger Ale Company.[18] The original company was J. J. McLaughlin, Ltd., in Toronto, a small carbonated water factory owned by the McLaughlin family, executives of General Motors of Canada and former makers of the car of that name. A Canadian, P. D. Saylor, was sent to New York to check up on the American subsidiary, which was selling ginger ale without conspicuous success. The managers of the New York branch included John Wanamaker, Jr., and William Rhinelander. Saylor took charge, changed the bottle design, the selling methods, and spent $70,000 on New York advertising the first year. The second year, 1924, Saylor asked for $250,000 for advertising. The Canadian owners were appalled—the sum was greater than the entire

16. Of about 20 Canadian branches which seem to have disappeared from the United States, only 5 or 6 are known to have been purchased by Americans.

17. See p. 182.

18. See "Up from Pop," *Fortune*, August, 1931, pp. 45–47, 120.

gross business of the parent company—but consented. Soon afterwards Saylor and an American, J. M. Mathes, bought the business in both countries, and by 1929 sales had reached 2,000,000 cases. Here, then, the Canadian manager of the New York branch of a Canadian company turned his office into a parent company.

These return movements in Canadian-American industry are worth remembering. True it is that hundreds of American companies operate in Canada, and that they earn enough, through the years, to hang on during periods of adversity. The preceding chapters have given abundant proof of those facts. But these last pages offer two corrections to that picture. The first is that especially during depression many unsuccessful branch companies withdraw. This is the more true in Canada because the thin market has meant that many companies operate, even in good times, on a very small margin of safety. The second, and more striking, lies in the fact that Canadians have always bought control in branch companies. How far, ultimately, this will go cannot be predicted. But just as the Canadian capital market is becoming increasingly capable of absorbing security issues, so, too, it is increasingly able to express its growing maturity by the "nationalization" of previously foreign firms.[19] It is a movement which lends further support to the belief we have expressed that Canadian-American industrial interrelationships, except where distorted by barriers, are mobile and normal.

19. It should be noticed that the analysis of repatriation in this chapter has not taken account of the Canadian minority interest in American subsidiaries in Canada, amounting, as explained in Chapter II, to over 22 per cent.

CHAPTER VII

CONSEQUENCES AND PROBLEMS

WE have now concluded our main task: the survey and detailed description of Canadian-American industry. If we have risked trying the reader's patience, our answer is, first, that the subject is of such importance to both countries that the facts in considerable detail ought to be available; second, that there have in the past been too many easy generalizations currently accepted, both on this continent and elsewhere, with reference to this industrial migration; and, third, that the inaccessibility of much of the data increases the usefulness of their collection in a single book. The task of fully interpreting this complex movement must await a later time and will no doubt employ the minds and time of many other students. But we cannot close this study without drawing together a general summary and without suggesting briefly some of the more important consequences and some of the more immediate problems.

Of Canadian industry in the United States much can be accounted for under two heads—economic necessity and individual personalities. Most of the mining properties owned (coal, ore, and oil) represent attempts to make secure to the parent company in Canada adequate and regular supplies of raw materials. Canadian railways in the United States, and also the offices of Canadian banks are necessary tie-ups to terminal, port, or market facilities. The enterprises associated with individual personalities may be illustrated by those founded in the United States by such Canadians as Moore, Loblaw, Larkin, Ritchie, and O'Connor. It was not that sales-book manufacturing, or self-service chain stores, or the packaging of tea, or the selling of patent medicines had in general reached a state of superior efficiency in Canada, but that these particular men had skill along certain lines, that the eastern Canadian, or more narrowly still the Ontario, market was not big enough for them, and expansion into New York, Michigan, Illinois, or Ohio was easier and more natural than expansion into Quebec or the Canadian West. It may be noted that the Canadian control of these United States properties usually does not long survive the individuals who founded them. Of the remaining Canadian industries in the United States, some are the product of natural geographic conditions (e.g., Fraser Paper); some were the product of war-time necessities (e.g., Page-Hersey, and Canadian Car and Foundry); and in a few cases Canadian companies have acquired genuinely international reputations and organizations (e.g., Massey-Harris).

For American industry in Canada a general summary is more difficult, but the following percentages[1] raise some interesting questions. They show for a group of reasonably specific and homogeneous manufacturing industries the percentage of total Canadian production coming from American-controlled establishments.

	Per cent
Automobiles and trucks, and parts and accessories	82
Rubber products	65
Electrical apparatus	68
Medicinal and pharmaceutical preparations; soaps and toilet preparations	56
Non-metallic mineral manufactures	41
Agricultural, industrial, office, and household machinery	42
Pulp, paper, and lumber	34
Flour and cereals and their preparations	15
Furnaces and rolling mills; castings and forgings	12
Animal products	11
Textiles and clothing	8

Broadly speaking, American enterprise has played a dominant or important part in Canadian industry in only certain types of production. First, there are the industries for which the United States has become particularly noted, and in which American enterprise has not only dominated the Canadian field but has occupied important positions in the industrial economy of the older European countries. The principal of these are automobiles and parts, rubber tires, electrical apparatus, telephone equipment and service, petroleum, and motion pictures.[2] In these industries American expansion into Canada has been part of a world-wide expansion, though since Canada is nearer home and industrially less developed than the principal European countries, it is natural that the percentage of production

1. Abstracted from Table V, p. 24.
2. F. A. Southard, Jr., *American Industry in Europe.*

from American-controlled plants should be larger in Canada than in Great Britain, France, or Germany. In absolute numbers and amount of capital employed, four of these industries—automobiles, rubber, electrical apparatus, and petroleum—account for about one seventh of the American plants and more than one quarter of the direct capital investments in Canadian manufacturing.

Second, American companies have established or acquired plants in Canada to maintain and develop the sales in Canada of well-known, widely advertised, branded or patented articles, the demand for which has been fostered and extended by their familiarity to the Canadian consumer through travel, magazines, radio, and motion pictures. Thus we find scores of small plants producing this or that brand of coffee, hosiery, cereals, toilet preparations, patent medicines, and so on. In this group American expansion into Canada is not paralleled by similar expansion into Europe.

A third class of American companies has entered Canada to obtain control of necessary raw materials or other industrial requirements. Control of resources in Canada has meant that important American companies can be sure of regular and adequate supplies free from the political and economic hazards that so often beset a distant source. Some clearly are in this group, especially pulp and paper, lumber, asbestos mining, and fishing. The economic advantages of vertical combination or integration are well known, and as the best or most accessible reserves of raw materials in the United States become depleted, it is natural that new reserves should be acquired in so convenient a place as Canada. But by no means all American investments in Canadian natural resources are of this sort; many are purely the result of the inherent financial attractiveness of the venture, e.g., gold, silver, and copper mining, and hydro-electric developments. And finally, American enterprise, not directly associated with any existing American organization, has been drawn into Canada by the lure of profits. Conspicuous examples of the two latter groups would include pulp and paper mills (with the hydro-electric power developments so often ancillary to them), lumbering, and mining.

It is quite as illuminating to examine the fields of economic activity into which American enterprise has not ventured to any considerable extent. There are the railways, whose period of active construction preceded that in which the United States had large amounts of capital available for foreign investment. There are the banks, in which American control has been discouraged by the fundamental differences in the banking systems of the two countries and the statutory requirement that a majority of the directors of every bank must be British subjects domiciled in Canada. The airways and radio broadcasting are other examples of activities where the absence of American capital is due to deliberate policy in Canada, either private or public. But even in the sphere of manufacturing there are many fields in which American enterprise has played little part. The more important of these are textiles and clothing, animal products, the primary iron and steel industry, and the flour, cereal, and baking industry. A number of reasons why this is so may be suggested.

In textiles, for example, the primary cotton industry—yarn and cloth—is largely in the hands of old Canadian firms where the family tradition has been strong for several generations. Moreover, Great Britain and not the United States long had technical and financial world leadership, and the American textile industry has been primarily concerned with the home market. In the new and rapidly expanding artificial silk industry we have one of the very few cases in which the "world cartel" in delimiting the "spheres of influence" has not assigned the Canadian market to subsidiaries of American companies. In the secondary textile industry—clothing, etc.—the typical producing unit in all countries is small, and the only occasion for a branch plant is the production and marketing of a particular specialty or widely advertised article.

Why American enterprise has not gone more into animal products and flour and cereal products in Canada is more difficult to explain. In the Canadian meat-packing business the family tradition has been strong in only a few cases, and one might have expected that the great Chicago packers would quite naturally have come to dominate the Canadian trade. Perhaps the explanation lies in the fact that both these Canadian industries have been long established, that they have developed at a fairly normal rate, that they require an elaborate field organization dealing with the likes and dislikes of thousands of individual producers, and that more than most industries they are subject to government investigation and control. Whatever the reasons may be, the American interest is small and very largely confined to food specialties with well-known names.

In the case of the primary iron and steel industry, American interest in world markets has never been great, and Canadian tariff increases, at least since 1890, have stimulated Canadian production at the expense of British and European, rather than American, exporters.

Whatever may be the reasons for the relative concentration of these migrant enterprises in one field and relative lack of concentration in others, the outstanding fact is that in the economy of Canada and the United States mobility of capital has been of tremendous importance. Neither the space nor the data permits us fully to explore the implications and consequences for both countries of this vast group of enterprises which we have termed "Canadian-American Industry." But we must go a certain way with the exploration.

CANADIAN-AMERICAN INDUSTRY AND CANADIAN-AMERICAN TRADE

Foremost in discussions of this subject, particularly in the United States, is speculation concerning the effect of these "alienated" subsidiaries on the commodity trade between the two countries and on employment in the export industries. Alarm over the transplantation of American industry, with the evident loss of employment by American labor, is no new thing. When in 1913 the B. F. Sturtevant Company, of which Governor Foss (Massachusetts) was an official, established the branch plant in Canada which it still operates, he explained:

All over the United States the tendency among principal manufacturing companies is toward the establishment of plants in Canada . . . the movement has now proceeded to a point where corporations which fail to follow are faced with serious embarrassment. . . . This movement of American manufacturers to Canada could be stopped and they could remain intact in this country if it were not for the absurd condition created by tariff regulations.

In commenting on the matter, the *Wall Street Journal* complained that "if capital goes from this country into Canada, . . . labor will go along with it, and . . . the United States will be so much the poorer. . . ."[3] In more recent years certain sections of organized labor in the United States—notably the American Federation of Labor—have feared that the branch plant movement is appreciably reducing American employment. Out of those fears grew Senate Resolutions 128 (September 30, 1929) and 138 (January 15, 1932), which called forth two Department of Commerce studies of that phase of the branch plant movement.[4] The 1929 report concluded that on the basis of existing information "it would be impossible to measure the actual loss to American export trade involved in the establishment of an American branch plant in a foreign country." The 1932 investigation went only far enough beyond its predecessor to calculate the volume of employment provided by American branch plants abroad and then warned that the "employment figures should not be interpreted as representing the amount of potential American labor displaced." With those two conclusions we have no great disagreement. But on the basis of information now available it may be possible to carry the problem of trade and employment displacement a little farther.

When an American company establishes a branch plant in Canada its effects on Canadian-American trade may be several. It will in all probability replace all or a part of the former export trade of the parent company with Canada. It may call for a new export of initial equipment and later replacements from American companies producing it. It may mean continued exports of parts and materials from the parent factory to the branch plant. Similar consequences may result from the establishment of a Canadian-owned plant in the United States. Let us investigate those possibilities a little more closely.

The first one presupposes, or seems to, that the volume of former export trade would still have been maintained under the conditions which, as was developed in Chapter IV, tend to create branch plants. For example, if an American company has been doing a business of $100,000 a year in Canada and finds it shrinking to $25,000—at which point it is scarcely worth while maintaining office or agents—

3. Quoted in *Monetary Times,* July 19, 1913, p. 129; and in Field, *Capital Investments in Canada* (1914 ed.), pp. 27–28.

4. *American Branch Factories Abroad,* Senate Document No. 258, 71st Congress, 3rd Session; Senate Document No. 120, 73rd Congress, 2nd Session.

can the branch plant by which it seeks to restore that business be said to "replace" the export trade? To be sure, the export trade may almost completely disappear, but that still does not answer the question. To quote from Senate Document No. 258, cited in the previous footnote:

. . . if the sale of the branch-factory product depends on the reduced price made possible by the savings in transportation and import duty and other expenses, it would be incorrect to regard the entire value of sales of the branch-factory product as a measure of the loss incurred by the American plant.

When a survey of this problem was being made in Europe a few years ago the International Telephone and Telegraph Corporation pointed out:

It is not possible for any American manufacturer to compete in the foreign markets in the field of telephone equipment with the same article made in foreign countries. If the International Corporation should close up its factories abroad, it would merely mean that German and Swedish factories, our chief competitors, and the other American-owned factories in Europe, would divide the foreign field, and that no more American communication equipment would go from this country than goes at the present time. As a matter of fact, the chances are there would not as much go, for there would be no coördination, as there is today, between the European sales and the export business which we carry on in this country.[5]

What it seems to amount to is this: In the aggregate, branch plants in Canada carry on the bulk of the business which the parent companies might otherwise conceivably care for by direct export. However, it is altogether probable that most of that business (the evidence does not warrant a guess at the percentage) could not, under existing circumstances, be held from a United States shipping point. Many American companies in Canada may have been unwisely established. But most of them do owe their existence to disappointing results in the export trade of the parent company. Consequently, although there has been a displacement of both workers and plant capacity by the branch plant movement, it cannot be considered a "wilful" displacement.

5. Southard, *op. cit.*, p. 199.

There are, to repeat, two possible mitigations of the decrease of American exports to Canada as a result of branch plant operations. One is the trade in supplies and equipment, the other the trade in parts. Unquestionably the 900-odd American factories in Canada provide a large and continuing market for machinery, raw materials, semi-fabricated iron and steel, etc., although it is utterly impossible to determine from the trade statistics how large that trade is.[6] However, it must be remembered that just as the branch plant deprives the parent company of a certain section of its potential or prior markets, so the demand that those branch plants create for machinery and so on is offset by the *relatively* diminished demand by their parent factories for such producers' goods. Consequently, although the total American trade in industrial machinery and equipment may be approximately unchanged, part of it is transferred from domestic to foreign trade channels. The export of parts may be of considerable importance, even though in most cases it is not as large as the trade in finished goods might be. If, by the establishment of a branch factory, the parent company can reduce prices by avoiding duties, the total Canadian trade may be so much larger that the semi-fabricated portion still shipped in from the United States helps to sustain the volume of export trade. The evidence presented in Chapter V, however, seems to indicate that American branch plants are now, on the average, largely independent of the parent company in production.

It has already been explained that little can be done in the way of a statistical demonstration of the points which we have been making. However, some indication may be given of the quantities involved. Only a certain section of the exports of the United States to Canada is vulnerable to branch plant "attacks." That is, only those goods which either now are, or reasonably might be, produced by branch plants can have been in the past partially transferred from the export trade to branch plant production.

On that quest, by going carefully through the Canadian imports from the United States for the fiscal year 1932[7] it was found that, in

6. i.e., to determine what share of the export of such goods to Canada is going to American branch plants.

7. It is realized that 1932 was an extremely depressed year in the foreign trade field. It is necessary to use that year in order to be able to compare the results with the 1932 foreign investment figures used throughout this

various classes and in the aggregate, the following percentages of the total in each class were competitive with the general range of products produced by branch plants.

	Per cent
Agricultural and vegetable products, mainly food	8
Agricultural and vegetable products, other than food	4
Animal products	38
Fibres and textiles	47
Wood and paper products	53
Iron and its products	98
Non-ferrous metal products	99
Non-metallic mineral products	36
Chemicals and allied products	100
Miscellaneous products	55
Total, all imports from United States	59

It is apparent that 59 per cent of the Canadian imports from the United States consisted, in 1932, of goods which were within the conceivable range of branch plant activity. In terms of amounts, out of total imports from the United States for domestic consumption of $351,686,775, $207,780,265 consisted of that type of goods. In other words, about six tenths of the United States exports to Canada have been of a kind subject to displacement by branch plants if the conditions for such displacement are present. It is not, of course, suggested that all of the remaining exports of that kind are going to be transferred to branch factories. Many of them are no doubt heavy equipment, specialties, and so on, for the production of which the Canadian market simply does not offer a large enough volume to justify the establishment of branch plants. It has been a matter of hanging on, on an export basis, as long as tariffs and competition in Canada permit. In many cases, no doubt (although the facts cannot be ascertained), articles very similar to these exports are actually now being produced by other American companies in branch plants. For example, some American business machine producers do not have Canadian factories; others do. At least some of the exports of business machines to Canada are made by the former.

That throws some light on the question of the area of the American export trade with Canada which is capable of being superseded

volume. It is probable, however, that the relatives which are being used were not vastly changed by the effect of depression on the actual volumes.

by branch plant output. But it has nothing to do with the more important problem of the actual volume of such supersession which has already taken place. Here we can offer as evidence only a summary of the statistics presented in Chapter II.[8] In 1932 American industry in Canada had a product valued at $1,490,029,302. Of that amount $1,034,129,643 resulted from the activities of mines, railroads, merchandising companies, and other non-manufacturing enterprises which cannot be considered in any sense whatever as the displacement of what otherwise might be imports from the United States. The remaining $455,899,659 is the product of branch factories owned by or closely affiliated with American corporations—the same branch factories which were described in Chapter II. Even of that sum, however, $65,084,333 is composed of the products of lumber, pulp and newsprint companies which, because of the peculiar position of that industry in Canadian-American economy, do not seem to be truly branch-plant output. Consequently it is excluded,[9] leaving a total of $390,815,326, which may be labeled production by American branch plants in Canada of goods that might conceivably have been imported under other circumstances.

This analysis provides two totals: $207,780,265, as the exports of manufactured goods to Canada which have persisted in spite of branch plants; and $390,815,326, as branch plant output. In the absence of tariffs it is probable that as much as half of the goods giving rise to the second amount might not have been produced in Canada but rather imported from the United States or elsewhere. With the lower prices which might then have obtained, the first sum—the imports of manufactured goods from the United States—would have been larger by much more than that amount. In other words, these exports of the United States to Canada in 1932 might have been larger by more than 100 per cent if circumstances had not stimulated the growth of branch plants to the stage which they had then reached. This figure, as will be readily gathered from the foregoing analysis, is subject to a rather wide margin of error, and assumes, among

8. See Table V, p. 24. It should be explained that item 33 has been omitted in calculating the above totals, since it is almost entirely a duplication of other items.

9. Approximately the same group of products was excluded from the percentages given on the preceding page as an offset.

other things, that without this movement the Canadian economy would have had proportionate development in other directions and that Canadian purchasing power in 1932 would have been at least as great as it actually was.

All of this analysis, it must be remembered, has been concerned with branch plants and their effects. There has been no attempt to evaluate the industrialization of Canada in its larger phases. To say that in the absence of tariffs[10] and the branch plants whose establishment they have influenced, these exports of the United States to Canada would have been twice as large is not to indict the present-day development of Canadian manufacturing, which has been based at least partially on trade barriers. To raise that issue would carry us beyond the limits of this subject. To an indeterminate extent, branch plants have promoted exports from the United States to Canada. We have already referred to the shipment of parts and equipment. American-owned branch plants may very well have speeded up Canadian economic development and contributed to the increase in the national income. If so, it is probable that the resulting demand in Canada for increased quantities of capital and consumption goods was satisfied at least partially by imports from the United States. Moreover, when an American company risks enough on the Canadian market to build a branch plant, it is probable also that it will exploit that market more intensively than it would on an export basis. Consequently, the existence in Canada of as many as 900 American-owned factories may have done much to stimulate in Canada a demand for American goods, at least part of which would be satisfied by imports from the United States rather than by branch plant products.

The secondary effect of American branch plants in Canada on the export trade of each country with other countries has been considered at sufficient length in earlier chapters.[11] Even the ragged statistics which have just been presented do not have their counterpart here. It seems evident, however, that while several important American companies in Canada handle much or all of the foreign trade of the parent organization, the total diversion to Canadian branch plants of the export trade of the United States with countries other

10. And other artificial barriers to trade.
11. See pp. 202–203, 241–242.

than Canada has been relatively insignificant. When, however, American branch plants throughout the world are added to the picture, it is apparent that a considerable portion of the total American world trade in manufactured goods has been diverted to branch plants outside the United States. Especially is that true of the British Empire.

CANADIAN-AMERICAN INDUSTRY AND CANADIAN-AMERICAN TARIFFS

The existence of American-owned industry in Canada has often had an effect on tariff attitudes and controversies in the United States. American investments in Canada, particularly in industries exporting to the United States, create an influential and often well-organized group actively supporting lower tariffs on at least these types of Canadian goods. The American lumber industry is sharply divided on the tariff question, those producers without Canadian timber limits generally supporting a high tariff policy, and those with heavy Canadian investments favoring low tariff or free entry. The same has been true, though to a lesser extent, among the mineral producers. Though there have in the past been a few conspicuous cases of tariffs bringing about the migration of foreign-controlled plants to the United States (e.g., tin plate), these have never attracted enough continuous interest to influence the general trend of tariff discussions or to shape tariff policy.

There can be no question that in planning its tariff policy Canada has, throughout at least the past 35 years, been perfectly aware of the relation between the branch plant movement and tariffs. Field in 1913 could cite many examples and reproduce many quotations illustrating that fact.[12] In 1921, the *Commercial and Financial Chronicle* observed that the suggestion that Canada should take the lead in tariff reduction was coolly received, and quoted an Ottawa dispatch as follows: " 'Let well enough alone' has good material behind it for the consideration of Canadian workmen. At present there are about 650 branches of American firms manufacturing in Canada. During 1920 there were 50 American branch plants established here. . . . Nearly 500 million dollars of American money are invested in these industries."[13] And in 1931 the *Financial Post* could without exag-

12. *Op. cit.*, pp. 32 ff. See also above, pp. 200–201.
13. May 28, 1921, p. 2243.

geration print an article headlined: "Claim Tariff Brings Canada 90 New Plants; Government Points with Pride to Long List."[14] Whatever may be the effect of tariffs on branch plant development, recent Canadian governments have been convinced both that the relation is close and direct and that the more branch plants the better. Only in the last year or two have Canadian official and unofficial organizations attempted to foster manufacturing arrangements rather than branch plants in an endeavor to prevent further duplication of unneeded plant capacity.

Another result of branch factory expansion is the vested interest that those plants come to have in the tariff *status quo*. True it may be that in the beginning many of them were established reluctantly by American companies who would have much preferred to export finished articles to Canada. Once in operation on a reasonably profitable basis, however, there may be almost equal reluctance to abandon them should tariffs be lowered. It was reported that more than one of the lobbying firms at the Ottawa Conference in 1932 were American subsidiaries anxious that "Empire content" rules be stiffened and that other protection be maintained or increased to retain their Empire markets.

In general the management of American-owned plants in Canada will be found supporting a protectionist tariff policy, not only because that is part of the traditional habit of mind of manufacturers on this continent, but because if an American company has established a Canadian plant to serve the Canadian market, it is naturally anxious to retain a substantial tariff against its competitors in the United States which have not established branches. On the other hand, a number of large Canadian companies are quite aware of the dangerous competitive power of branch plants with strong backing, and are content with tariffs that leave some scope for sales by powerful American firms. In the iron and steel industry the more far-sighted producers have never supported pleas for tariffs of such a height as would almost compel the United States Steel Corporation to move into Canada on an impressive scale. It may be noted in passing that this threat has been one of the difficulties in the attempts to arrange a division of the Canadian steel market between British and Canadian producers.

14. August 8, 1931.

An examination of the list at the beginning of this chapter shows that there is no very close connection between the height of the Canadian tariff in a given industry and the significance of the American interest in it. Two of the most highly protected industries in Canada are textiles and iron and steel, yet these two industries are at or near the bottom of the table. As Canadian tariffs go, the duties on automobiles (especially the lower-priced ones, which are so largely produced in Canada) are quite moderate; those on rubber products, electrical apparatus, and all kinds of machinery are about average; and those on pharmaceutical and toilet preparations are definitely high. It is not denied that tariffs are one of the most important factors in the branch plant movement, but it is evident that the mere imposition of a high tariff will not necessarily draw in branch plants.

The recent trade agreement between the two countries has lowered many Canadian rates of duty and has done away with the arbitrary valuations heretofore levied on imports of American manufactures. But in most cases the reductions are not so great as to justify the immediate prediction that numbers of American producers will curtail branch-plant operations and return more largely to direct export to the Canadian market. Only experience under the new and more favorable tariff conditions will reveal their full effect on the branch-factory movement. Already, however, the situation previously described has emerged: American branch plants in Canada opposing tariff reductions. At hearings before the Tariff Board in Ottawa in December, 1935, the Canadian Automobile Chamber of Commerce, which includes all important American branch plants except the Ford Motor Company of Canada, Ltd., asked that the old rates of duty be restored and that the excise tax be raised from 3 to 5 per cent, on the ground that the reduced protection proposed by the trade agreement "will undermine the stability of the industry." On the other hand, while the American lumbermen as a whole have bitterly opposed any reduction in the United States tariff in the agreement with Canada, those among them who own timber rights in Canada have repeatedly urged that it be reduced.

A useful adjunct to tariff policy as a means of speeding up Canadian industrial development are the various Canadian promotional organizations in both countries which have spent time and money to induce American corporations to establish plants in Canada. The

Financial Post somewhat caustically remarked in 1927 that "Every 'Go-Get-a-Factory' campaign in Canada includes an appeal to United States manufacturers. There is hardly an American industry that has sold one pound or one yard of its product in Canada which has not been 'campaigned' by some city, bank, Chamber of Commerce, or publication in Canada to build a factory north of the Great Lakes."[15] Among the civic groups the Toronto Industrial Commission has been most active, publishing bulletins concerning Toronto's advantages, making elaborate surveys for individual American companies interested in knowing how a branch plant in that region would fit into their organization, and so on. In the United States, the Industrial Commissioners of both the Canadian National and the Canadian Pacific Railways, the trade promotion sections of several of the Canadian banks, and the Canadian Trade Commissioner in New York spend a very large portion of their time—although less now than formerly—in following up with the greatest diligence every American company which might be induced to establish a plant in Canada, or, once there, to divert the largest possible share of the export trade to that plant. The railroads, of course, are anxious that the prospective plant locate on their line; the banks, that it open an account at one of their branches. The Trade Commissioner makes tariff studies for individual American companies, advises them as to vacant factories in Canada, cost of materials, labor regulations, and so on. It seems probable that these agencies may have tipped the scale in favor of a Canadian plant for many a corporation executive who was undecided.

CANADIAN-AMERICAN INDUSTRY AND THE CANADIAN-AMERICAN BALANCE OF PAYMENTS

From the standpoint of the balance of payments of the two countries, the cross-Border investments described in this volume have had much influence. Throughout the years there have been on the debit side of the balance of payments of the United States continuous items for "investment in branch plants, railroads, mines, etc.," which have amounted to considerably more than $2,000,000,000 in 40 years[16] fluctuating from a few millions to well over $100,000,000 in

15. October 7, 1927.
16. Approximately $2,000,000,000 on account of investments still in ex-

individual years. On the credit side, of course, has been the income received from those investments, or, more accurately, the income received and remitted to the head office. In the previous chapter is all the existing information on the volume of that income and those remittances which the most careful search of records and tabulation of questionnaires yielded. The income from Canadian industry in the United States—although usually more than offset by heavy deficits due largely to the railroad investments—is probably larger than the annual new investments by Canadian companies in American subsidiaries. But how much of that income is actually remitted and how much of those remittances are offset by advances to losing subsidiaries cannot be stated on the basis of available figures. The United States has undoubtedly had a credit arising out of profits remitted from Canada, but it is altogether probable that the net movement of funds on account of American industry in Canada had been in favor of Canada since the war, due both to the heavy investments in new branch plants and to advances to subsidiaries during the depression. On the other hand, there is some likelihood that the branch plant movement in Canada is rapidly approaching a saturation point. If that is the case, any return of more prosperous business in Canada should result in a relatively large net credit from American branch organizations there which must be taken into account in any tariff arrangements between the two countries and in any calculation of exchange ratios.

It is no less important to observe, as far as possible, the effect of this industrial movement on the Canadian balance of international payments. The actual figures of estimated profits and remittances have been given in the previous chapter. The absolute amounts are large and, together with interest and dividend payments on other forms of foreign capital investment, rank second only to imports of merchandise in the items on the debit side of Canada's balance of international payments. There has been from time to time a good deal of discussion in Canada as to the forms which foreign investment should be encouraged to take. Bond issues have the advantage of leaving control in Canadian hands but the disadvantage of setting

istence in 1932, plus amounts invested since then, and plus the large but unknown amount invested prior to 1932 in enterprises which had become defunct or had passed out of American control by 1932. See pp. 19–22.

up heavy fixed charges in annual interest and principal payments. The Canadian economy is largely dependent on a few staple exports which are subject to drastic fluctuation in both volume and price. Heavy fixed charges payable abroad thus create acute problems of banking policy and monetary control whenever a slump strikes the export industries. Industrial investments of the sort we have been describing are represented almost exclusively by common stocks. When depression reduces Canadian exports, there is a partially compensating reduction in the interest and dividend item on the debit side of the balance of payments. Inflexibility of international financial relationships and alienation of control are the horns of a dilemma between which the choice, where possible, is not easy.

BRANCH COMPANIES IN THE CANADIAN ECONOMY

The impact of this vast cross-Border investment on Canadian economy is much more important than on the balance of payments. It has immeasurably speeded up both the volume and diversity of Canadian manufacturing and greatly accelerated the development of Canada's natural resources. It is impossible to measure this acceleration statistically. Without the branch-plant movement and without the large volume of American direct investments, Canadian industrialization under the stimulus of the tariff and under the general technological and cultural trends of the past sixty years would doubtless have proceeded at a substantial rate. But it is equally certain that many of the 900-odd American-owned factories would never have been established by Canadian capital and enterprise, and most of them would not have been established as early as they were. Canadian capital and initiative have actively participated in Canada's development, but in proportion to the opportunities afforded by population and resources they have been less than could be profitably employed. Many American branch plants have no doubt stepped into industries where Canadian concerns would within a reasonable time have grown up to the requirements of the market, and thus have to some extent limited the growth and expansion of purely Canadian companies. The influx of American-owned plants may also have increased the number of factories with a consequent smaller average size.

The American branch-plant movement has been responsible in

large part for the direction which Canadian industrialization has taken. It has increased the relative importance in Canada of the secondary type of manufacturing industries. Without it, a far larger proportion of Canadian industrial capital and labor would have been engaged in the primary manufacturing industries based on the Canadian environment. It has made for greatly increased diversification of industry, but whether this diversification of industry has been economically worth while, it is not our task to inquire. It has had the effect of providing a very large amount of non-seasonal employment and traffic which has helped to render less acute the problem of "peak loads," which is one of the most difficult in the Canadian economy.

Canada has also profited very greatly from having had made available to it the technical skill and research work of many large American organizations. The typical branch plant and affiliated company has at its disposal all the results of engineering skill and scientific research, as well as the managerial efficiency, developed by the parent company. Drawings, designs, patents, as well as routine analyses, tests, and advice are all available to the Canadian company as rapidly as they are developed in the United States. Canadian industry thus enjoys in large measure most of the benefits of highly organized scientific research and technological progress without having to bear the heavy overhead costs of large laboratories, testing fields, and patent departments, or the overhead costs of the process of trial and error in developing economic efficiency. It is true that many, but by no means all, of these Canadian companies are charged by the affiliated American company with certain annual payments which nominally cover the cost of these services. Occasionally these charges appear to be adequate or more than adequate, but usually they are a very small fraction of the value of the benefits received and often no charge is made at all. Independent Canadian companies may, of course, derive much immediate benefit from foreign research organizations by adopting the growing practice of contracting with large firms of engineering or scientific consultants on a service-fee basis.

In this connection a partially counterbalancing disadvantage to Canada may be noted. It is possible that these tie-ups with American or other foreign corporations with large research departments has kept back the indigenous development of industrial science in Canada. If there had been fewer branch organizations in Canada of large electrical, chemical, metallurgical and other industries, the Canadian companies might have had to develop their own research departments on a much larger scale. As it is, the opportunities for proper industrial employment for the hundreds of first-class young graduates in science of the Canadian universities and engineering schools are very limited, and a very large proportion of them have to seek employment in American industrial laboratories, where many of them have done conspicuous and brilliant work. The Canadian industrial economy doubtless could not support as elaborate research facilities as exist in larger industrial countries, but doubtless also it could afford much greater facilities than it now possesses. One result has been that industrial scientific research in Canada has become almost exclusively, but not entirely, a function of government departments (e.g., agriculture and mines), of public or semi-public research foundations, and of the large universities. In any case, the ease with which the results of foreign research are available to Canada is not an unmixed blessing.

Branch companies as competitors. Reference has already been made to the intensification of competition in Canada which accompanies the establishment of branch plants; that the number of relatively small units struggling for a share of a limited market has been substantially increased. To the Canadian manufacturer with no backing other than his own resources this competition often appears unfair. The typical branch factory many times has behind it a large and powerful American corporation which, having decided on this venture, is prepared to give it generous financial support. Doubtless if the branch is consistently unprofitable over a period of years it will be closed or sold. But having made such a commitment, the American management may keep its branch operating at a loss long after a Canadian company with similar operating results would have been forced into bankruptcy. Occasionally branch plants can buy materials and supplies through or from the parent company more cheaply than Canadian competitors. Other items in cost (e.g., patterns, designs, and research previously mentioned) may be absent or represented by nominal charges. Sometimes the parent company charges no interest on capital advances, sometimes the parent company can borrow the capital cost of a branch factory more cheaply than could a sound Canadian company of the same size as the branch plant. To the extent that such practices occur, they amount to a subsidy to production and competition in Canada. From the Canadian manufacturers' point of view they are a form of dumping which no tariff can control.

It is not to be supposed, however, that any large proportion of branch plants are in this class. As has been shown in Chapter VI, the great majority as a rule are profitable. Many are among the strong industrial units of Canada playing an important and dependable part in the Canadian economy. Most of them "play the game" loyally in trade and manufacturers' associations. Most of them quickly become "naturalized" and settle down as peaceable members of their various industrial fraternities, where their national origin soon passes unnoticed.

Branch companies in key industries. The descriptive part of this book has been chiefly concerned with a quantitative study of the American interest in Canada. It is desirable to suggest a qualitative analysis. From the point of view of importance in relation to broad economic and social control, the "key" points in the Canadian economy may be given as the export industries (wheat, pulp and paper, lumber, animal products, and base metals), the banks, the investment bankers, the railways, other forms of transportation, public utilities, the press, radio, movies, communications. The staple export trade, with the exception of pulp and paper and base metals, is almost entirely in Canadian hands. The pulp and paper industry is about one third American-controlled. Mining, other than gold, is about 38 per cent American-controlled, but this figure is as high as it is because of the classification of International Nickel as American-controlled. In the case of banks, railways, buses, airways, newspapers, and radio, American control is either entirely absent or of very minor significance. Investment banking in Canada has in the past 15 years been closely affiliated with New York, and though there is little American ownership or legal control of Canadian financial houses, there has naturally been a close working relationship. Electrical power production and distribution is 83 per cent Canadian, although the companies controlled by Americans produce a more than proportionate share of the power. In the field of communications, telegraph, cable, and wireless show no American control, but telephone service, except in the three Prairie Provinces, is almost entirely either American-controlled or under American influence. The motion-picture industry in Canada is very largely American-controlled, but in this Canada is not unique.

The whole field of manufacturing and domestic marketing from the broad point of view of economic and social control is definitely secondary to those we have been mentioning. If within this secondary group we are to assess importance, the following should probably be listed first: the electrical industries, petroleum, the metallurgical industries, automobiles, machinery, and chemicals. It will be recalled that in the case of electrical apparatus, petroleum, and automobiles, American-owned companies clearly dominate; in the machinery and engineering trades they have about 40 per cent of the business; in chemicals about 40 per cent; and in the metallurgical industries not much over 10 per cent.

Viewed from this qualitative point of view it will be seen that, however impressive vast totals may be, the American direct investments in Canada, *per se*, do not constitute economic control of Canada.

We turn now to a much more elusive phase of the subject, and one which will be fully covered in other volumes of this Canadian-American Series. A body of alien industry as large as that controlled by Americans in Canada cannot fail to have influenced both public sentiment and public policy. To what extent Canadian tastes, amusements, garb, and speech have been modified, we will leave it to the sociologist to determine. As to the extent to which it has affected community development, aroused hostility or fear of "American penetration" we may at least offer a few suggestions.

What is a Canadian company? It is inevitable that some hostility and some vague or expressed fear should have arisen under the impact of American subsidiaries on Canadian consciousness. The Canadian sees plants in every industrial city and town which he knows by their advertised trade name to be closely affiliated with American concerns. He reads in the paper from time to time about new plants being established. He notes references to the volume of American investment in Canadian industry. And, if he reads enough Canadian newspapers, he is bound now and again to see reports of speeches or to wander through editorials in which American penetration is "viewed with alarm." But the great majority of newspaper editorials that could be cited tend rather to "point with pride."

The *Financial Post* asked, a few years ago, what was to be understood by the term "a Canadian company." Editorially it gave this answer:

We invite capitalists and industrialists from other countries to come to Canada, to build plants here, to match their ability against the world in the development of our natural resources, to create jobs for our citizens (or to bring as many of their own citizens as they like to work in Canada and make their permanent residence here), to pay taxes in Canada, and add to our . . . prosperity.

Many have accepted our invitation . . . and few of us would be as well off today as we are if it were not for the admixture in our national life of a generous dosage of extra-Canadian influences.

At what points do these new . . . companies . . . cease to be foreign and become Canadian? If a store is controlled in the United States certain people urge that it be not patronized. If a dairy or bakery comes under American control, a boycott is urged by competitors. If an engineering firm had its genesis outside Canada, there are those who will label as disloyal all who gave it a contract even if 99 per cent or more of the contract price remains in Canada. There are small-minded individuals always ready to attempt to embarrass anyone dealing with a foreign-controlled insurance company, a foreign-controlled factory. . . .

. . . Any foreign company establishing a permanent branch in Canada to give good service at a fair price is a Canadian institution.

As a country with nearly two billions of dollars invested abroad, with a million native-born Canadians living outside our borders, with a national heritage larger than we can ourselves quickly and fully develop, we should be economically broadminded. Most Canadians are.[17]

A few months after that editorial appeared, the president of "a very important Canadian company, that had its origin as a branch of an American business" informed the *Financial Post* that only twice had its alien extraction been used to debar it from business and that "curiously enough one of these was a United States company contemplating the erection of a Canadian factory and the other was a United States owned company which has been here for many

17. December 25, 1930.

years." He concluded that this "invoking of nationalistic or local feeling is frequently inspired merely to eliminate competitors. . . ."[18]

The issue in local and national affairs. It is probably true that much of the consumer resistance to American companies in Canada because of their alien origin has been induced by Canadian-owned competitors. Emphasis on Canadian ownership and control is not uncommon in Canadian advertising. Some of it, however, must be the result of the "Buy Canadian Goods" campaign which is part of the Canadian commercial policy. Instances have been known when Canadian-owned companies have conducted house-to-house visitations to explain that in buying their American-controlled rival's product the housewife is letting her good money get out of the country. But while Canadian-American companies in both countries are at some pains to appear to be a normal part of the business community, they do not as a rule find hostility in either country a serious obstacle.[19]

Such hostility or opposition as American companies do meet has several bases. The most usual are those just mentioned: the preference for Simon-pure Canadian goods which may arise from several persuasive forces impinging on the consumer, in the form of local campaigns or political exhortation, and the often bitter opposition of independent concerns to their branch plant rivals. Where it is based on anything save uninteresting and dull self-interest, that latter hostility arises from the feeling that the powerful support of the parent company gives the branch plant an unfair advantage. How widespread this feeling may be we do not know. But it must inescapably be present when, for example, a Canadian paint factory, dependent on such formulae as it can develop and such advertising as it can afford, is faced by a strong American branch organization which derives its processes from the parent company and has the advantage

18. February 26, 1931.

19. Seagram's advertisement in the *New York Times,* January 24, 1935, is of interest in this connection. The text details the number of people employed in the American subsidiaries, the taxes paid to United States governments, the volume of materials used and wages paid, and so on. Although no attempt is made to deny the fact that Seagram's is a foreign concern, only the name of the American company appears on the advertisement and nowhere are the words "Canada" or "Canadian" to be found.

of the free advertising, under the same trade name, which "slops over the Border" in magazines and by radio. This technical, financial, and commercial assistance which the branch plant receives from the parent company appears to be the most reasonable cause for complaint which the Canadian business man may raise. Yet there is "nothing to be done about it." As has been said both in this chapter and many times in the Canadian press, it is that very access to the resources of the great American corporations—especially technical resources— which constitutes the most valuable contribution made by the branch plant to Canadian economy. The refutation, from the broader point of view of the country as a whole, of the argument of the independent firm is to be found in the answer of the *Financial Post* to the query "what is a Canadian company?" The matter is not one-sided, of course. In the United States the competitors of Massey-Harris, Hiram Walker, Seagram's, Fanny Farmer, Salada Tea, and, to name some non-Canadian companies, Shell Oil, American Thread, American Viscose, Gordon's Gin, might urge non-patronage of such alien concerns. Perhaps they do. But Americans and Canadians together do not seem to have been very responsive to such appeals when they are directed against companies whose sole "drain" from the country consists of a few dividends.

Occasionally the opposition to the American branch has other bases. There was the famous *Deutschland* case, in which the rumor that Canadian nickel was shipped to Germany on that submarine by the old International Nickel Company caused resentment which, though long-since forgotten, was bitter at the time. Sometimes it is felt that the "plums" in the executive positions available in branch organizations go unduly to Americans. In other cases there are special grievances. The Manitoba bus operators point out that it is virtually impossible for them to obtain franchises to operate on the American side because if they made application the American companies would be granted a five-day period within which to start operations. "This," to quote counsel for one of them, "seems iniquitous . . . because it allows American companies to invade Canada for business and prevents the Canadian companies from invading the American side with business which originates in Canada."

Fear of or opposition to American-owned companies in Canada will be found more often in barber-shops or club smoking rooms than in the public press. But even in these forums of the man in the street and the tired business man, opposition, when not particular, is only occasional. The commonest form of this fear is that American penetration may lead to American annexation. But the ghost of annexation which stalked in the reciprocity election campaign of 1911, was laid by the war and by the great expansion period which culminated in 1928–29. Occasionally it is seen by an English visitor. This is no place to discuss the annexation danger, but from almost any section of Canada newspaper editorials can be found rejecting it as in any way likely to grow from American investments in Canada.[20]

The opinion of the *Manitoba Free Press* is as typical as any. After pointing out the steady growth both of Canadian financial interest in the larger companies in Canada and of Canadian investment abroad, it concludes:

There is nothing new or startling in this tendency. Canada is only following the natural course of . . . every new country. British capital built up the railways of the world. France, Germany, Belgium, and Holland have widespread foreign financial interests. But as each new country grows in strength, ownership of its capital equipment passes into the hands of those closest to the scene of actual operation. What marks out the story as distinctive in the case of Canada has been the rapidity of the change. The tendency is one of the last ten years only. . . . By the end of another decade the ghost of foreign domination will be laid once and for all.

And almost at the same time the Ottawa *Citizen* declared that the cry of the subversive influence of "Yankee dollars" in Canada now is but the repetition of the earlier taunt of "British gold" heard in nineteenth century political campaigns in the United States. It continued:

. . . as the United States grew rich enough to get along without "British gold," so Canada every day is piling up reserves of financial strength which will make "Yankee dollars" equally inconsiderable as part of her economy.

20. See, e.g., *Financial Post* (Toronto), February 11, March 11, 1927; *Globe* (Toronto), March 23, 1927; *Gazette* (Montreal), November 19, 1927; *Citizen* (Ottawa), February 21, 1929; *Manitoba Free Press* (quoted in the *Financial Post,* January 11, 1929); *Mail and Empire* (Toronto), December 27, 1933.

Let us get ahead with business and with our national development and leave the ghostmakers to the sweetly sorrowful enjoyment of their own dolorous forebodings.

Those opinions are offered not as prophecies but as expressions of the current Canadian state of mind concerning the specter of annexation lurking in branch factory lofts.

Strangely enough, American, or for that matter any other foreign, investments in Canada have never given rise, at least in recent years, to any considered discussion in Parliament. Speeches in opposition usually come from the small Labor group; other references have chiefly been from the supporters of the government of the day taking credit for this or that new industry or factory established.

A careful search of House of Commons Debates does reveal some warning by Labor and Conservative members that American control of Canadian industrial policy may follow in the wake of American investment. The following brief extract will serve as a typical example:

I would call attention to the very rapid acquisition of our resources by Americans. Pulpwood, mining, oil, waterpower are passing under foreign control. Some day if the House will permit I should like to exhibit in this Chamber a spot map on which the American controlled industries would be marked with the Stars and Stripes. If that were done with respect to all the country there would hardly be room to place a Union Jack.[21]

On the other side may be placed the considered statement of the Prime Minister, Rt. Hon. R. B. Bennett, in June, 1931:

Fear has sometimes been expressed that these outside nations by starting industries in this country or by investing their capital in various Canadian enterprises are obtaining a menacing position in our economic life. The facts of the case reveal these fears to be entirely unfounded.[22]

The fear of American economic domination of Canada through the branch plant finds expression in the concerted efforts in recent

21. Mr. Woodsworth (Labor, Winnipeg), *House of Commons Debates,* 1928, p. 70. For other examples see *ibid.,* 1928, p. 1837; 1929, p. 49.
22. *Ibid.,* 1931, p. 2164.

years to induce British firms to open up branch plants in Canada. It is a common retort when British interests complain that Canadian buying is so largely done in the United States to ask why they have not met the American threat by the American method of investment and branch plants. Before the war, Field remarked:

It is only reasonable to infer that in the present struggle between the British and Americans for the Canadian market the relative investment of capital from either country must count for much. . . . American capital has been more particularly directed into enterprises such as are connected with the import trade of the country.[23]

And today the British are often told that they have lost much of their Canadian market because they were too conservative to adopt this new technique. The charge has only very limited justification. It is not true that British firms have entirely neglected the branch plant device. In 1932 there were about 98 *manufacturing* concerns in Canada owned or controlled in Great Britain, employing capital of $164,000,000. The number of plants is only about one eighth of the American total but the capital employed is nearly one fifth. While it may be true that British manufacturers have been slow to realize the advantages of branch plants, there are good reasons why they have not adopted this policy on the same scale as the Americans. One reason is that the Canadian tariff does not penalize British imports as heavily as American. Another is that Canada can offer almost no advantages over Great British as a base for exports. A third reason is that it is not easy to supervise a branch 3,000 or 5,000 miles away. A British director must take from three to six weeks off to look over a Canadian branch. To the American it is rarely more than an overnight journey, and he can run up for a day or two several times a month. Finally the branch plant is most effective in the large-scale production of highly standardized goods, a type of production in which Americans excel. The less standardized types of manufactures for which the British are better known lend themselves less easily to absentee management.[24]

A number of important areas in Canada either were almost entirely built up or are now dominated by American-controlled business. The

23. *Op. cit.,* p. 192.
24. See K. W. Taylor in the *Financial Post,* December 23, 1933.

obvious instances are the Windsor area opposite Detroit and the
Niagara area opposite Buffalo and Niagara Falls, New York. Other
towns have grown up around great American-controlled enterprises:
pulp and paper, as at Kapuskasing,[25] and smelting, as at Arvida.
There are other cities and towns, such as Peterborough, Ontario,
where practically all the larger industries are American-owned. In
some cases towns created by such enterprises provide interesting
examples of town planning and orderly development. In other cases
no such care has been taken. Company towns, that is, communities
dependent on a single large corporation, always present difficult
political and social problems. When this corporation is of alien
ownership or control, such problems often take on added complications. The following extracts from a speech in Parliament by Mr.
A. A. Heaps (Labor, Winnipeg) will illustrate this point:

In the past few years we have imported a vast amount of American
capital. . . . We now find company towns springing up. . . . Canadian labour men have been refused admittance to these company towns.
In other words, Canadian people are denied the right to set foot on
Canadian soil controlled by American capital. . . . [After references to
Mexico and Nicaragua] You will generally find that these investments
are followed by military occupation. . . . I do not suggest this will
happen in Canada . . . but there is no telling when we may pass laws
that may not be altogether to the liking of those to the south of us and
under such circumstances I can see us getting into a nasty squabble with
the government at Washington. . . . I would far sooner wait a little
longer for the development of our resources than see the Canadian
people become hewers of wood and drawers of water to American
capitalists.[26]

On one occasion several years ago considerable resentment was
created when a private bill was introduced into a Provincial legislature to permit non-Canadian citizens to hold important municipal
offices in a well-known company-town. The bill was hastily withdrawn, but the political irritation lasted for some time.

There is little evidence of political interference by foreign-con-

25. See Arthur Pound, "Wood, Water, and Brains," *Atlantic Monthly,*
September, 1935, p. 382, for a description of this town created by an American-owned company. See also above, p. 46.

26. *House of Commons Debates,* February 20, 1928.

trolled companies. Doubtless American-controlled companies, like most other companies, use such political pressure as they may be able to muster to further their own economic interests. Doubtless, too, like other companies, they contribute to campaign funds of one or of all political parties. But their interest is almost invariably the interest of a particular company or industry and not in any large sense a pushing of "American" interests. There is some evidence that the American-controlled motion-picture industry has at times endeavored to use political influence to obstruct quota laws in favor of British films.[27]

Pressure from foreign investment banking interests is more likely to be open and political than that from branch plants. But Canada has, hitherto at least, had more difficulties in this respect with London than with New York. Bitter pressure has been brought to bear by London financial groups on a number of occasions, notably in the long and still unsettled Grand Trunk securities disputes. But if Canada, unaccompanied by the United States, were to move along novel economic paths which involved some reinterpretation of property rights, there is little doubt but that international difficulties would arise. The "expropriation of the expropriators" could not be successfully carried out in Canada much in advance of a similar event in the United States. Or to put it in much more immediate and practical terms, a country that is dependent to a considerable extent on foreign borrowing must, if it is to borrow economically, follow social, economic, and political policies that commend themselves reasonably well to the relatively small group that controls the money market in which it borrows.

SUMMARY

The task set for this volume was the presentation of the history and present extent of Canadian-American industry. To look beyond that and prophesy the future development and fortunes of the two bodies of alien companies described in previous chapters is no easier than any other field of prophecy in the realm of economics. For the last 60 years it has always been safe to predict that, with interruptions, the cross-Border movement of industry would continually in-

27. *Investigation into an Alleged Combine in the Motion Picture Industry in Canada,* Report of the Commissioner (Ottawa, 1931), pp. 158–161.

crease. Since the end of 1932 branch company expansion has reached another plateau whose farther side is difficult to perceive. From 92 new American companies in Canada in 1932, the total dropped to 42 in 1933, to 34 in 1934, with only 15 during the first 7 months of 1935. In January, 1934, a Canadian who has been associated with branch-plant promotion for many years observed that the establishment of new plants had greatly decreased and that more United States manufacturers were seeking to make arrangements with existing Canadian firms for the production of additional lines. He expressed conviction that municipalities should discourage new branch plants where a Canadian manufacturer could take on the new line on a contract basis. In August, 1934, an American consular report from the Toronto area also noted that the movement had slowed down. Only 4 plants had been established in that region during the first six months of the year, as compared with 10 in the same period of 1933 and with 67 from May 1, 1930, to December 31, 1932. Those figures did not include scores of manufacturing arrangements. The report attributed the decline to the disappearance of the premium on the American dollar and the partially consequent revival of Canadian-American export trade. It was also suggested that the movement toward requiring a higher "Empire content" may have discouraged some companies who might otherwise have been willing to establish plants for partial manufacture.

So much for the present state of affairs. All the evidence points to the fact that the stream of new branch plants in the 4 years, 1929–32, has carried American industry in Canada close to the saturation point, and that the rate of increase in the future will be much slower. In proportion to its size, Canadian industry in the United States is much more likely to expand rapidly. Canadian corporations as a whole have not probed the possibilities of exploiting the American market from a plant "on the spot." The readiness with which the Canadian distilling and brewing companies made the venture in the past few years may be an indication that other enterprises will take advantage of any increased business activity in the United States. In the meantime there is all reasonable expectancy that the branch companies in both countries will consolidate their position, that a large number of those hastily established during the depression, under the stimulus of the Ottawa tariffs, will be withdrawn in the colder light of unfortunate experience, and that the survivors will in the future, exactly as in the past, win their share of Canadian-American business. After all, there is nothing strikingly peculiar about branch plants in countries whose relations are as friendly as those between Canada and the United States.

It has been pointed out that Americans seem scarcely aware of the existence of foreign-owned companies within the borders of the United States, but that they have been abundantly acquainted with the presence of American subsidiaries abroad. It would be difficult for American tourists to drive across the Ontario peninsula on the way from Detroit to Buffalo without observing familiar names on factory doors. Conversations with many American business men have revealed that they regard Canada not as an alien area but as a slightly peculiar northward extension of the domestic market. Several confessed that only in recent years had they begun to realize that the line between the two countries was in fact an international frontier. This familiarity has, as we have repeatedly asserted, been a powerful factor in overcoming the hesitancy that most manufacturers feel in investing in foreign properties. To a very high degree the American business man feels at home in Canada.

Some disquiet there has been among Americans over this emigration of factories; some alarm among Canadians over the alienation of control of their economic affairs. But in general the Canadian has discovered that his country can import enterprise and capital and yet find no flag behind the dollar. And the American in general has dismissed the matter as beyond his opinion, although the more observant have regretted the tariff competition which has needlessly increased the post-war migration of American plants to Canada. The railroads, stores, mines, insurance companies, banks, and the great, well-established factories which the citizens of either country have acquired in the other make major contributions to friendly economic relations; they fortify and increase the commodity trade which yet remains the backbone of international intercourse. It is only when branch plants are established in an effort to hold a market being lost through tariff increases that we must admit that nationalism has won the day.

To some extent the rate of growth of American branch plants in Canada will depend on the development of the system of Imperial preferential tariffs. If these preferences continue to increase in scope and value, if the tide of Imperial self-sufficiency flows strongly, the inducements to establish branch plants for the sake of the export market will be strengthened. But schemes of preferential tariff are an uncertain basis for permanent expansion. Canada learned a painful lesson in 1846 when, as a result of the adoption of free trade by Great Britain, large sections of Canadian industry, based on the old preferential system, were ruined. To the extent that branch plants are, or may be, dependent on tariff preferences, they run serious risk of loss if those arrangements become ineffective or are abolished.

It should also be noted that the continuance of Canada as an economic entity depends on the maintenance of east and west lines of traffic and trade. The disproportionate development of north and south traffic is a constant threat to her economic unity. The Canadian people have proved on many occasions their willingness to forego material advantages to pursue policies which they believed would ensure the continued development of a distinct Canadian economy and culture.

No estimate of the problems of the future, however, can be adequate if based solely on past trends. New elements from time to time intervene. Apart from a rather small group of specialists in this field, few people either in Canada or elsewhere are yet aware of the growing financial maturity of the Canadian economy and the extent to which Canadian industrial and investment interests abroad have already grown. Canadian investment abroad has increased rapidly in the past 20 years and in a number of recent years Canada has, on balance, been an exporter and not an importer of capital. Canadian investments of all kinds abroad now total close to $2,000,000,000. On a *per caput* basis, only two countries (Great Britain and the Netherlands) exceed Canada in importance of foreign investments.[28] If this new trend continues, and as its importance is more generally appreciated, significant changes in attitudes may follow.

Already it has had some effect on government policy. Some years ago the Canadian Government's attention was rather sharply drawn to the importance of international comity in the matter of double

28. Approximate *per caput* figures (excluding war debts) in 1930 were: Great Britain, $460; Netherlands, $315; Canada, $190; United States, $140; France, $100; Japan, $20.

taxation by the vigorous protests of certain Canadian interests in Europe against what they regarded as discriminating taxation. More recently, when the Manchurian affair was before the League of Nations, the rather peculiar position taken at first by the chief Canadian delegate was perhaps not entirely unaffected by the serious effect which the application of economic sanctions to Japan would have had on the Canadian Pacific Railway, Consolidated Smelters, and two of the largest Canadian life insurance companies. As such industrial interests and investments increase, and as their importance becomes part of the common stock of knowledge, Canadian public opinion on matters relating to international affairs will become much more articulate and will not be interested merely in tariffs and export markets. Public opinion will tend to be less suspicious of, or hostile to, foreign investment in Canada. The inferiority complex which so often appears in the Canadian attitude toward the United States will tend to pass away.

While American branch plants in Canada will doubtless continue to grow in number and in absolute size, it is probable that in the future Canada will depend less and less on capital imports for its national development. It is probable that capital imports by Canada on a large scale are entirely a thing of the past. It is not likely that Canada will in the calculable future become, from a world point of view, a significantly large exporter of capital, but, assuming the restoration of a reasonable degree of prosperity and the continuance of some approximation to an international capitalistic economy, Canadian industrial and investment interests abroad will expand considerably and will become an increasingly important factor in the Canadian economy. Perhaps the most important economic result of such a development will be an increased flexibility in the Canadian balance of international payments and hence a greater flexibility of the whole financial and monetary mechanism in Canada. And that, in the experience of the years 1929 to 1935, is a consummation devoutly to be wished.

EXCURSUS

CANADIAN CAPITAL MOVEMENTS AND THE CANADIAN BALANCE OF INTERNATIONAL PAYMENTS, 1900–1934*

BY FRANK A. KNOX

QUEEN'S UNIVERSITY

THE "direct" or industrial investments with which this book is concerned form but a part of the movement of capital across the Border between Canada and the United States. Sales of Canadian securities account for a larger movement of capital than do the direct investments. Nor has the capital which has financed Canadian development come solely from the United States. Before the war British capital was dominant in Canada. Despite the heavy investment of American capital since 1914, British capital still forms a large part of the total investment of outside capital in Canada today. But from whatever source it has come, imported capital has been the dominant influence on Canadian development since 1900. Other items of the international accounts of the country—such as the trade balance and interest payments—have fluctuated in volume in response to variations in the movement of capital. If the direct investment of American capital in Canada is to be seen in its proper perspective, its relative importance in the whole capital movement must be known and the influence of that movement on the balance of payments of Canada borne in mind.

This chapter assembles such information as is available on these topics. Tables A, B, and C indicate the total investment of British and foreign capital in Canada at the end of each year, classified according to the area from which the capital came and the type of investment to which it was applied; Table D gives the Canadian capital investment in other countries. The volume of interest and dividend payments to which

* Acknowledgements are due to Dr. Jacob Viner and the Harvard University Press for permission to publish his estimates for the years 1900–1913; to the Dominion Bureau of Statistics for the use of their most recent estimates for the years 1926–34; and especially to Mr. Herbert Marshall, Chief of the Internal Trade Branch of the Bureau, for his aid in the preparation of this Excursus.

these capital investments gave rise annually is shown in Tables E, F, and G under a similar classification. Table H summarizes Canada's balance of international payments.

These estimates were drawn from three sources. For the years 1900–1913, they come from Jacob Viner, *Canada's Balance of International Indebtedness, 1900–1913.*[1] The writer has made the calculations for the years 1913–26. For the years 1926–34, the Dominion Bureau of Statistics has very kindly permitted the use of the preliminary results of a thorough revision of their estimates of Canada's balance of international payments which is now in progress. No estimates are available for the years prior to 1900. For a detailed description of the methods of calculation by which Dr. Viner arrived at his estimates the reader is referred to his book. The methods by which the estimates have been reached for 1913–34 are described below in order to enable the critical reader to judge of the character of these estimates and the uses to which they may properly be put. To facilitate the many references which may be necessary in view of the absence of footnotes to the tables, the statement of methods has been arranged according to the three groups of tables. Under each, the methods used by each of the authorities is separately described.

Estimates of capital movements and of the other items in the international accounts are subject to a considerable margin of error; if this is kept in mind the estimates here given may be used to indicate the trend and approximate amount of change in the several items for the whole period. Because of differences in the methods of compilation used and in the range of data available, the estimates are not strictly comparable for the entire period 1900–1934. Where possible the amount of these discrepancies has been indicated by the printing of two estimates for the years 1913 and 1926—the years where the sources overlap.

ESTIMATES OF THE TOTAL BRITISH AND FOREIGN CAPITAL INVESTED IN
    CANADA, 1900–1933 (Tables A, B, C)

1900–1913. Dr. Viner has made two estimates of the annual investment of capital in Canada from other countries. By the use of his estimates of all other items in the balance of payments, he derives an estimate of the net inflow of capital necessary to balance the international accounts. For comparison with this estimate he makes a second directly from the available data as to the volume of capital imports during these years. Table A, columns I, II, and III, gives the cumulative totals

1. Cambridge, Harvard University Press, 1924.

of the annual amounts arrived at by the latter method, based on estimates for the year 1899 of $1,040,000,000 for the British investment,
$150,000,000 for the United States investment, and $10,000,000 for
that of all other countries.[2] The classifications by form of investment in
Tables B and C for the later years cannot be made from the data given
by Dr. Viner.

1913–1926. For these years estimates were made directly from the
available data. By far the larger part of the British investment in
Canada was made by the purchase of Canadian securities. Each such
security reported outstanding in 1913 in the *Stock Exchange Official
Intelligence* (London) was listed and the amount of each issue outstanding at the end of each of the years 1913–26 tabulated. This list,
expanded to include a few securities sold in London after 1913,
provided annual totals for the investment of British capital in newly
issued Canadian securities. The total British investment was found by
adding to these amounts estimates of the direct investment of British
capital in Canada and the capital employed in Canada by British insurance companies. Despite the scanty evidence available on which to base
an estimate of the direct investment, the present one is probably conservative, as the total estimate is still less than that made by Dr. Viner
by $223,800,000 (Table A, column I).[3]

The use of this method to determine the amount of the United States
investment in Canada gives much less reliable results because of two
difficulties. There is, first of all, no complete record of United States
holdings of Canadian securities. Before 1914 most issues of Canadian
securities were placed wholly in the London market; a London list of
the amount of these issues outstanding at subsequent periods may be
taken, therefore, as a fairly accurate representation of the amount of
such issues held in Great Britain. Though many Canadian issues since

2. Dr. Viner (*op. cit.,* p. 99) gives the total of Canadian securities publicly floated in Great Britain up to the end of 1899 as $989,209,497, and
securities privately sold in Great Britain and on the Continent as $60,-
000,000. Dividing the latter amount arbitrarily, $50,000,000 to Great
Britain and $10,000,000 to other countries, gives the base estimate of
$1,040,000,000 used above for Great Britain and $10,000,000 for other
countries, excepting the United States. The United States estimate used is
that given by Dr. Viner. For the annual amounts used, see *op. cit.,* pp. 126,
134, 138, and 139.

3. The direct investment was set at $250,000,000 in 1913 and was de-
creased, year by year, to $217,000,000 in 1926. Total assets in Canada of
British insurance companies, as reported annually to the Dominion Superintendent of Insurance, were taken as a rough measure of the amount of
British capital employed in Canada by these companies.

TABLE A

Total British and Foreign Capital Invested in Canada, 1900–1933
(in millions of dollars)

Year	By Great Britain I	By the United States II	By all other countries III	Total* (I+II+III) IV
1900	1,050.1	167.9	13.7	1,231.7
1901	1,065.2	186.2	17.5	1,268.9
1902	1,077.1	209.6	24.6	1,311.3
1903	1,105.9	231.7	28.3	1,365.9
1904	1,135.4	257.5	34.9	1,427.8
1905	1,211.8	289.9	38.7	1,540.4
1906	1,280.3	319.4	46.0	1,645.7
1907	1,345.5	345.4	49.8	1,740.7
1908	1,526.9	378.1	57.8	1,962.8
1909	1,739.6	414.3	62.3	2,216.2
1910	1,958.1	486.9	84.4	2,529.4
1911	2,202.5	563.1	112.2	2,877.8
1912	2,417.3	644.8	136.8	3,198.9
1913	2,793.1	779.8	172.7	3,745.6
1913	2,569.3	780.0	180.0	3,529.3
1914	2,778.5	880.7	177.7	3,836.9
1915	2,772.2	1,069.6	175.2	4,017.0
1916	2,840.3	1,306.9	175.5	4,322.7
1917	2,738.7	1,577.3	176.6	4,492.6
1918	2,729.0	1,630.0	176.6	4,535.6
1919	2,645.2	1,818.1	173.5	4,636.8
1920	2,577.3	2,128.2	164.6	4,870.1
1921	2,493.5	2,260.3	152.2	4,906.0
1922	2,463.8	2,593.0	150.2	5,207.0
1923	2,470.7	2,794.4	149.2	5,414.3
1924	2,371.6	3,094.0	150.0	5,615.6
1925	2,345.7	3,219.2	149.2	5,714.1
1926	2,354.7	3,464.5	146.3	5,965.5
1926	2,591.5	3,108.8	63.3	5,763.6
1927	2,637.8	3,338.5	63.9	6,040.2
1928	2,698.7	3,551.7	71.8	6,322.2
1929	2,773.9	3,794.4	77.3	6,645.6
1930	2,792.3	4,098.5	88.2	6,979.0
1931	2,729.4	4,056.4	84.4	6,870.2
1932	2,687.2	4,045.2	83.5	6,815.9
1933	2,731.5	3,967.4	95.2	6,794.1

* In Tables A–D the totals given are as of December 31.

TABLE B

Total British and Foreign Capital Invested in Canada, 1900–1933
(in millions of dollars)

Year	In government securities	In railway securities	In all other forms of investment	Total (I+II+III)
	I	II	III	IV
1900				1,231.7
1901				1,268.9
1902				1,311.3
1903				1,365.9
1904				1,427.8
1905				1,540.4
1906				1,645.7
1907				1,740.7
1908				1,962.8
1909				2,216.2
1910				2,529.4
1911				2,877.8
1912				3,198.9
1913				3,745.6
1913	689.8	1,299.4	1,540.1	3,529.3
1914	794.5	1,448.6	1,620.8	3,863.9
1915	945.6	1,463.4	1,608.0	4,017.0
1916	1,177.2	1,479.0	1,666.5	4,322.7
1917	1,300.8	1,463.7	1,728.1	4,492.6
1918	1,308.9	1,463.4	1,763.3	4,535.6
1919	1,283.2	1,501.9	1,851.7	4,636.8
1920	1,349.2	1,574.3	1,946.6	4,870.1
1921	1,386.2	1,460.3	2,059.5	4,906.0
1922	1,541.6	1,457.4	2,208.0	5,207.0
1923	1,606.4	1,459.5	2,348.4	5,414.3
1924	1,641.4	1,494.8	2,479.4	5,615.6
1925	1,582.8	1,519.4	2,611.9	5,714.1
1926	1,562.4	1,549.0	2,854.1	5,965.5
1926	1,436.0	1,636.1	2,691.5	5,763.6
1927	1,481.8	1,665.7	2,892.7	6,040.2
1928	1,453.4	1,700.8	3,168.0	6,322.2
1929	1,464.1	1,836.3	3,345.2	6,645.6
1930	1,622.1	1,899.2	3,457.7	6,979.0
1931	1,601.6	1,966.4	3,302.2	6,870.2
1932	1,673.5	1,956.3	3,186.1	6,815.9
1933	1,684.4	1,950.2	3,159.5	6,794.1

1914 were wholly absorbed in New York, yet a large number of issues were split between the Canadian and American markets in a proportion which was variously estimated at the time of issue and cannot now be determined with accuracy. The second difficulty lies in the fact that the direct investment of American capital in Canada is known to be large; and direct investments are even more difficult to estimate than those which arise out of the sale of securities.

The Dominion Securities Corporation and the *Monetary Times*, both of Toronto, and the United States Department of Commerce have published lists of Canadian security flotations which give for each issue the amount taken in the American and Canadian markets. All three are in substantial agreement as to the amounts of individual issues sold in New York during the years 1914–19 and the years 1923–26. For the years 1920–22 the Department of Commerce does not accept the Canadian estimates, as it apparently has done for the years 1914–19, but writes down the amounts taken in the United States by as much as 50 per cent or more in particular instances. This is especially true of issues of Canadian Provincial Government securities. But these securities were designed in every particular for the United States market. Borrowing in the United States at that time was particularly attractive because of the premium in Canada on New York funds and for other reasons. Where there is a difference as to the amount of a given issue taken in the United States, the higher estimate of the Canadian authorities has been accepted here.

Differences exist among the authorities in another respect. For any one year their lists of securities sold in the United States are by no means identical. Since there is no ground for according especial accuracy to any one of them, every security listed has been included in this compilation. Its bias is therefore to the high side, both because of the acceptance, in some years, of the higher estimates of the Canadian authorities and because of its greater inclusiveness.

The totals for the flotation of Canadian securities in the United States each year thus having been estimated, the net increase in the United States holdings was found by subtracting from the United States purchases of newly issued Canadian securities each year the amount of previously issued securities which matured or were called for redemption during the year.[4] The total United States holding of

4. In estimating this amount no attention was paid to the fact that the daily trade in such securities after issue may have altered the United States holdings considerably; the amount was set at the estimated original purchase by Americans of the security in question. There is no accurate information

Canadian securities as thus calculated makes no allowance for securities sold in the United States before 1913 and the maturities or redemptions of such securities during the years 1914–26. To fill this gap, maturities amounting to $40,000,000 have beeen spread through the years 1914–26 in accord with information made available by Dr. Paul Dickens of the United States Department of Commerce.

Uncertain as these estimates of flotations of Canadian securities in the United States are, they are much more satisfactory than those for the investment made directly in Canada by residents of the United States. The estimate here used is based on the results of a survey of the direct investments of American capital in other countries made by the United States Department of Commerce for the year 1929.[5] The Department obtained the book value in 1929 of each investment and, where possible, the date of establishment also. By assembling these dates, a table was constructed showing the number of new investments set up since 1860.[6] On the assumption that the trend in total amount of the direct investments is indicated roughly by the trend in their number, the probable amount of the direct investment at the end of each of the years 1913–26 was calculated and from these totals a figure for the annual increase found.[7]

Some idea of the validity of this procedure may be obtained by comparing the result for the year 1913—$493,400,000—with an estimate of the direct industrial investment which may be made from data given

as to the probable net result of the Canadian-American securities trade. As a consequence, all the estimates of Tables A, B, and C are in error by the amount of the net effect of this trade, not only for the United States holdings, but also for other foreign and British holdings, to which a similar procedure was applied. This matter is referred to again in the discussion of Table H, column XXVI.

5. *American Direct Investments in Foreign Countries,* Trade Information Bulletin, No. 731; see above pp. 21 ff.

6. Trade Information Bulletin No. 731, p. 42. Unfortunately the number of investments made, for which no date was obtained, was large in the case of investments in Canada. But, "It may reasonably be expected that they follow the trend of those that are known." *Ibid.,* p. 43.

7. The justification for the use of this very crude method lies in the almost complete absence of data as to the amount of these investments for earlier years. As an estimate of the annual import of American capital for direct investment, the increase in the investment during the year has an important defect. Much of this increase came, not from the import of new capital, but from the reinvestment of profits. No information is available by

by Dr. Viner. For the year 1899 he estimates the total United States investment in Canada at $150,000,000, $50,000,000 of which was in the form of security holdings and $100,000,000 in other forms.[8] By adding $516,000,000 for the increase in investments other than security holdings during the years 1900–1913,[9] a total for the year 1913 of $616,-000,000 is obtained. Subtracting $69,700,000 for the capital employed by American insurance companies in Canada in 1913[10] from $616,000,-000, there remains $546,300,000, mostly the direct investment. That this estimate is only $52,900,000 greater than that reached by the method previously described gives some ground for confidence in the reliability of the latter—as reliability goes in these matters. The amounts included in Table A, column II, as the direct investment of capital from the United States are arrived at by taking the higher estimate—$546,-300,000—as the estimate for 1913 and adding thereto the annual increases shown by the direct investment as calculated above from the Department of Commerce data. Column II includes also the estimated investment by insurance companies and the holdings of Canadian securities in the United States. For the latter a base estimate of $164,-000,000 in 1913 was used.[11]

The total investment in Canada by all other countries as given in Table A, column III, is composed of the holdings of Canadian Pacific Railway stock as reported annually by the company, and an estimated total of all other forms of investment of $140,000,000 in 1913, which is decreased annually to $120,000,000 in 1926, on the assumption that the

which the amount of the annual increase arising from this use of profits might be separated from the actual investment of new capital. Nevertheless the annual capital import, as here calculated, is not at variance with such bits of contemporary evidence as are available.

8. *Op. cit.*, p. 131.   9. *Ibid.*, p. 303.

10. The assets in Canada of "foreign" insurance companies, as reported to the Dominion Superintendent of Insurance, are taken as representative of the amount of United States capital employed by American insurance companies in Canada since the "foreign" (i.e., non-British) companies are almost entirely from the United States.

11. It was noted above that Dr. Viner estimates the United States investment in 1899 at $150,000,000, $50,000,000 of which was in securities. During the years 1900–1913, the increase in that holding was $114,000,000 (*op. cit.*, p. 303), thus making a total American holding of Canadian securities in 1913 of $164,000,000. This, together with the $616,000,000 of direct and insurance company investments, brings the United States investment in 1913 to the total of $780,000,000 given by Dr. Viner (*ibid.*, pp. 131 and 134).

interest of the investor in these countries in Canada varied approximately in accord with their holdings of Canadian Pacific Railway stock.[12]

1926–1933. Table C gives the detailed revised estimates of the Dominion Bureau of Statistics for the years 1926–33 which are summarized in Tables A and B. In estimating the British and foreign investment in Canadian securities the Bureau has followed the method used by the writer for the years 1913–26. For British holdings of Canadian securities the reports in the *Stock Exchange Official Intelligence* are the main source of information. For the takings of new issues of Canadian securities in the United States, the estimates of the Canadian and United States financial press and the United States Department of Commerce are relied upon. The net annual increases in foreign holdings of Canadian securities are calculated by deducting from the estimated total sale of new Canadian securities in foreign markets the amounts of old Canadian securities maturing or called for redemption. No allowance is made for changes in foreign holdings which may have occurred as a result of the international trade in Canadian securities previously issued abroad. The results of this revised calculation by the Dominion Bureau of Statistics give a lower total for Canadian Government securities held abroad in 1926 (Table B, column I) than that estimated by the writer because the latter includes $100,000,000 as the estimate of government securities sold in the United States before 1913 of which no details are now obtainable. Revision of the railway list has increased the total somewhat (Table B, column II).

Estimates for the remaining items were made on the basis of returns as to the total capital employed in Canadian industry, received annually through the Industrial Census, on information gleaned from the Merchandising Census, and from other sources available in the Bureau. Considering differences in method of compilation, the discrepancies between the two estimates given for the year 1926 are small (Table B, column III). Some support is thus lent to the estimates for the years 1913–1926 for which so much less information is available.

12. Dr. Viner estimated (*op. cit.,* p. 138) that the direct investment by other countries amounted to $120,000,000 in 1913. An unknown amount of securities held on the continent of Europe is included in the amount outstanding in London as reported in the *Stock Exchange Official Intelligence,* and has therefore been included in the British investment. To allow for holdings of Canadian securities in other countries not so included, $20,000,-000 has been added to the direct investment of $120,000,000, to make a total for 1913 of $140,000,000.

TABLE C

Total British and Foreign Capital Invested in Canada, 1926–1933,
Classified According to Main Types of Investment
(in millions of dollars)

Type of Investment	1926	1927	1928	1929	1930	1931	1932	1933
Government Securities:								
(Dominion, Provincial and Municipal)	1,436.0	1,481.8	1,453.5	1,464.1	1,622.1	1,601.6	1,673.5	1,684.4
Public Utilities:								
Railways	1,636.1	1,665.7	1,700.8	1,836.4	1,899.2	1,966.4	1,956.3	1,950.2
Other public utilities: (Traction, light, heat, power, telephone, etc.)	466.2	515.8	562.2	620.0	660.8	698.5	736.0	751.9
Industries:								
Wood and wood products	473.7	513.0	569.7	567.0	596.0	525.5	484.2	458.5
Mining, clay products and other structural materials	318.9	331.9	393.8	403.2	412.5	389.3	366.1	368.4
Metal industries	396.3	421.8	458.7	502.6	501.7	456.8	414.2	401.5
All other industries	451.5	483.0	516.0	546.0	521.3	495.8	460.2	459.0
Merchandising and Services	235.4	241.7	250.4	255.7	251.5	237.5	225.0	219.4
Insurance	92.7	106.0	102.1	104.5	142.6	151.6	160.5	161.6
Finance and Mortgage Corporations	181.8	204.5	237.0	266.1	291.3	269.2	262.9	264.2
Miscellaneous:								
(Agricultural lands, summer homes, prospecting, etc.)	75.0	75.0	78.0	80.0	80.0	78.0	77.0	75.0
Total	5,763.6	6,040.2	6,322.2	6,645.6	6,979.0	6,870.2	6,815.9	6,794.1

Total Canadian Capital Invested in Other Countries, 1900–1933 (Table D)

1900–1913. Dr. Viner's calculations of the amount of Canadian capital abroad are made under three headings. The first of these is the net assets of commercial banks outside of Canada, based on the monthly reports made by Canadian commercial banks to the Department of Finance. The report for December 31 each year is used to calculate the excess of assets over liabilities outside Canada, which is taken as representative of the amount of capital in use abroad by commercial banks during the year.[13] The second item is the holdings of foreign securities

13. Viner, *op. cit.*, pp. 92 f.

Total Canadian Capital Invested in Other Countries, 1900–1933
(in millions of dollars)

Year	On account of dealings with governments of other countries I	Dominion government bank balances abroad II	Commercial bank balances abroad III	British and foreign securities held by commercial banks IV	Insurance company investments V	Miscellaneous investments VI	Total (I+II+III+IV+V+VI) VII
1900			42.6	17.0		37.6	97.2
1901			64.9	21.3		39.6	125.8
1902			62.9	24.6		41.6	129.1
1903			42.2	25.6		44.6	112.4
1904			60.1	25.8		47.6	133.5
1905			72.3	26.4		50.6	149.3
1906			55.6	27.6		53.6	136.8
1907			29.4	28.0		57.6	115.0
1908			116.4	29.5		61.6	207.5
1909			142.1	33.4		65.6	241.1
1910			104.9	39.7		70.6	215.2
1911			99.8	43.3		75.6	218.7
1912			92.0	45.9		80.6	218.5
1913			104.2	47.4		85.6	237.2
1914	−24.3*	2.2	106.0	54.8	18.6	245.3	402.6
1915	−120.0*	.8	122.1	51.4	24.5	251.3	330.1
1916	−112.1*	−.4†	173.7	184.7	33.4	262.3	541.6
1917	111.7	6.5	140.7	199.1	37.3	274.3	769.6
1918	221.5	10.6	112.2	247.5	40.6	287.3	919.7
1919	211.1	6.6	111.2	263.7	41.8	307.3	941.7
1920	187.4	5.3	102.4	210.6	46.0	342.3	894.0
1921	162.8	8.3	96.3	116.5	54.1	359.7	797.7
1922	106.5	24.0	89.5	88.8	87.6	375.1	771.5
1923	40.1	8.7	93.8	110.1	121.8	408.0	782.5
1924	36.6	12.0	82.6	110.6	154.3	437.8	833.9
1925	36.4	8.1	127.1	102.4	173.7	506.3	954.0
1926	36.0	6.3	227.9	89.2	209.4	617.7	1,186.5
1926	36.1	6.3	285.4	89.2	215.7	848.4	1,481.1
1927	32.4	14.4	254.5	95.7	244.8	1,035.7	1,677.5
1928	31.1	26.7	179.5	67.4	297.0	1,203.4	1,805.1
1929	30.9	15.9	102.8	68.1	356.9	1,383.1	1,957.7
1930	30.7	28.2	64.1	94.2	451.0	1,389.6	2,057.8
1931	30.5	9.4	62.0	86.7	501.8	1,395.7	2,086.1
1932	30.5	1.2	39.4	84.8	530.1	1,395.2	2,081.2
1933	30.5	5.0	23.8	71.1	504.6	1,393.8	2,028.8

* In the years 1914–16 advances by the British Government to the Canadian Government exceeded Canadian credits to all Governments.

† Average overdraft.

by commercial banks, which are estimated to have been 60 per cent of the amount of the "Railway and other Bonds, Debentures and Stocks" reported by the banks on December 31 each year. Of the third item—holdings of foreign securities by private and institutional investors, and direct investment of Canadian capital abroad—very little is known. Dr. Viner[14] sets the total Canadian capital abroad in 1899 at $100,-000,000. Subtracting the net assets of Canadian banks abroad and the foreign security holdings in the same year[15] from this amount leaves $35,600,000 as the amount of Canadian capital invested abroad in all other forms. This amount has been used as the base estimate in Table D, column VI. The increase in miscellaneous investments abroad from 1899 to 1913 is set by Dr. Viner at $50,000,000.[16] His distribution of that amount throughout these years is used as the basis of the annual increases shown in Table D, column IV.

1914–1926. The amounts in Table D, column I, state, as nearly as it is possible to arrive at them from the public accounts and other sources, the net liability of the Governments of Great Britain and other foreign countries to the Dominion Government on account of war finance. During the years 1914–16 Canada's continued dependence on the London money market is indicated by her indebtedness to the British Government on balance. This position was suddenly altered in 1917 by the inability of the British Government to provide more dollar exchange for the purchase of war supplies in Canada and the discovery by the Canadian Government that these purchases could be financed in Canada. From 1919 on, balances due by other governments are included in the calculation.

The average balances in banks in London and New York to the credit of the Dominion Government, as given in column II, are arrived at by capitalizing the reported net interest receipts by the Dominion Government from this source, which probably gives more normal representation of their amount than would be obtained by taking the amount on deposit as reported in the public accounts for the end of the fiscal year. For the same reason the calculation of the net assets of Canadian commercial banks in foreign countries has been made each year on the basis of the average annual amount of the several items which go into this calculation, rather than on the basis of the statement for December 31.

The foreign securities held by Canadian commercial banks, as given in column III, are their actual holdings as reported to the Dominion Bu-

14. Viner, *op. cit.*, p. 92.   15. *Ibid.*, pp. 91, 93.
16. *Ibid.*, p. 94.

reau of Statistics for the years 1920–26. For the years 1920–23 they form 65.6 per cent of the average monthly holdings of "Railway, and other Bonds, Debentures and Stocks" as stated in the return made by the chartered banks. For the years 1914–19 foreign security holdings of the banks have been estimated at 65 per cent of the average monthly holdings of securities of this class during each year. The great variation in the amounts in column IV does not arise from changes in bank holdings of foreign securities, but from their purchases of Treasury bills from the British Government as part of the financing of British purchases of war materials in Canada. The amount of these bills has been estimated from information disclosed at the annual meetings of the Canadian Bankers' Association.

Insurance company investments abroad are taken as the total book value of the assets "outside Canada" of Canadian insurance companies having business abroad, as reported to the Dominion Superintendent of Insurance. As a representation of the amount of Canadian capital employed in the business of these companies in other countries this is perhaps poor. But nothing better is available for these years.

The miscellaneous investments reported in Table D, column VI, include holdings of foreign securities by private and institutional investors other than banks, and direct investments of Canadian capital in other countries. The estimates for the years 1920–26 are those made for the Dominion Bureau of Statistics by Professor K. W. Taylor. Estimates for the earlier years were made on this basis in the light of comments made at the time and since, in the financial press, as to the participation of Canadian capital in industrial ventures abroad and as to the interest of the Canadian investor in foreign securities.

1926–1933. The estimates for columns I and II are from the public accounts. Columns III and IV are based on information received directly by the Bureau from the Canadian commercial banks. The method of estimating insurance company investments abroad (column V) is the same as for the earlier years.

The Bureau's estimate of miscellaneous investments (column VI) is composed of direct investments and the holdings of foreign securities by Canadian institutional and private investors. The direct investments are estimated from a census taken in 1935 of all Canadian companies having branches abroad. The estimate of Canadian holdings of foreign securities is still admittedly very rough because of lack of information.

INTEREST AND DIVIDEND PAYMENTS DUE ON BRITISH AND FOREIGN CAPITAL INVESTED IN CANADA, 1900–1933 (Tables E and F)

1900–1913. Dr. Viner makes no estimate of the interest and dividends

Interest and Dividend Payments Due on British and Foreign
Capital Invested in Canada, 1900–1933
(in millions of dollars)

Year	On British investments I	On United States investments II	On investments by all other countries III	Total (I+II+III) IV
1900				36.0
1901				37.4
1902				39.4
1903				40.7
1904				43.0
1905				47.4
1906				51.7
1907				56.6
1908				75.9
1909				83.9
1910				92.1
1911				101.5
1912				117.5
1913				137.2
1914	128.7	39.3	10.0	178.0
1915	125.4	40.0	9.3	174.7
1916	129.9	53.8	9.6	193.3
1917	121.5	76.2	10.3	208.0
1918	121.8	85.3	10.1	217.2
1919	119.5	91.6	10.4	221.5
1920	117.3	104.2	9.9	231.4
1921	124.5	118.3	9.5	252.3
1922	121.0	120.9	8.0	249.9
1923	119.8	138.4	8.1	266.3
1924	115.0	146.1	7.8	268.9
1925	115.1	147.7	7.9	270.7
1926	114.5	163.0	7.8	285.3
1927	108.6	153.0	5.1	266.7
1928	105.1	171.0	6.7	282.8
1929	119.1	202.2	8.8	330.1
1930	120.1	226.5	9.8	356.4
1931	107.5	220.5	8.3	336.3
1932	100.2	200.2	8.7	309.1
1933	91.3	180.3	7.2	278.8

TABLE F

Interest and Dividend Payments Due on British and Foreign Capital Invested in Canada, by Type of Investment, 1900–1933
(in millions of dollars)

Year	On government securities I	On railway securities II	On all other forms of investment III	Total (I+II+III) IV
1900				36.0
1901				37.4
1902				39.4
1903				40.7
1904				43.0
1905				47.4
1906				51.7
1907				56.6
1908				75.9
1909				83.9
1910				92.1
1911				101.5
1912				117.5
1913				137.2
1914	28.8	72.5	76.7	178.0
1915	30.5	72.9	71.3	174.7
1916	40.8	74.8	77.7	193.3
1917	46.7	73.8	87.5	208.0
1918	53.0	74.2	90.0	217.2
1919	51.3	73.7	96.5	221.5
1920	53.4	73.8	104.2	231.4
1921	58.7	78.2	115.4	252.3
1922	60.7	82.2	107.0	249.9
1923	68.7	82.6	115.0	266.3
1924	70.3	80.9	117.7	268.9
1925	62.3	83.3	125.1	270.7
1926	69.6	83.3	132.4	285.3
1927	67.0	81.2	118.5	266.7
1928	67.6	85.8	129.4	282.8
1929	68.0	91.6	170.5	330.1
1930	68.8	95.9	191.7	356.4
1931	72.8	93.1	170.4	336.3
1932	72.2	70.8	166.1	309.1
1933	72.1	67.4	139.3	278.8

due on the capital invested in Canada by residents of other countries on the basis of his estimate of the amount of that investment given in Table A. He uses as his basis the estimates of capital investments in Canada which were derived from the balance of international payments.[17]

1914–1926. The issue-by-issue study of Canadian securities held in other countries by which the estimate of capital invested in Canada was arrived at, as explained above, makes possible the calculation of the interest due each year on that portion of each security held abroad. The results of that calculation are given for government and railway securities in Table F, columns I and III. The amounts in column III include not only the interest on industrial securities held abroad, which has been similarly calculated, but also the estimated dividend payments due on the capital invested directly in Canada rather than by the purchase of publicly offered Canadian securities. These dividends were estimated as a percentage of the direct capital investment, the percentages being derived from the relationship between dividend disbursements and capital employed, as shown by a sample group of companies for which balance sheets were available back to 1920 and a somewhat smaller group for which the balance sheets were available back to 1914. The estimate is but a very rough approximation, both because of this method of calculating the rate per cent of dividend payments and because of the character of the estimate of the total direct investment itself as explained above. The rates of dividend payments for the years 1920–26 were calculated by Professor K. W. Taylor for the Dominion Bureau of Statistics. Dividends on Canadian Pacific Railway stock have been calculated at the rates paid annually by the company. Earnings on the capital of United States insurance companies in Canada are calculated at the rate earned by Canadian insurance companies yearly.

1927–1933. The issue-by-issue method was followed by the Dominion Bureau of Statistics in calculating interest due on foreign holdings of Canadian securities. Dividends were calculated from detailed information in the possession of the Bureau.

INTEREST AND DIVIDEND RECEIPTS ON CANADIAN CAPITAL INVESTED IN OTHER COUNTRIES, 1900–1933 (Table G)

1900–1913. Interest and dividends received each year on Canadian

17. Cf. above, p. 297. The details of the calculation are given in Viner, *op. cit.,* p. 101. It is not possible to separate Dr. Viner's estimates either by the country to which the payment is due or the type of security on which it was paid.

Total Interest and Dividend Receipts from Canadian Capital Invested in Other Countries, 1900–1933
(in millions of dollars)

Year	By the Dominion government from British and foreign governments and from bank balances abroad I	By commercial banks on assets abroad* II	By commercial banks on their holdings of foreign securities III	By Canadian insurance companies on assets outside Canada IV	On miscellaneous Canadian investments abroad V	Total (I+II+III+IV+V) VI
1900						4.0
1901						3.9
1902						5.0
1903						5.2
1904						4.5
1905						5.3
1906						6.0
1907						5.5
1908						4.6
1909						8.3
1910						9.6
1911						8.6
1912						8.7
1913						8.7
1914	—.2	2.3	2.5	1.0	11.0	16.6
1915	—3.3	2.3	2.4	1.5	10.2	13.1
1916	—1.0	2.3	9.6	1.8	10.9	23.6
1917	.1	3.0	10.6	2.1	12.5	28.3
1918	1.0	2.7	13.5	2.5	12.7	32.4
1919	6.9	2.8	13.3	2.3	14.3	39.6
1920	13.4	3.2	11.9	2.6	15.8	46.9
1921	14.1	4.1	6.6	3.0	19.4	47.2
1922	10.7	3.6	4.4	4.8	16.5	40.0
1923	6.7	3.6	5.5	7.1	17.7	40.6
1924	4.6	3.4	5.4	8.9	18.0	40.3
1925	2.4	3.2	4.8	10.3	19.5	40.2
1926	1.8	3.9	4.1	12.2	23.2	45.2
1926	1.6		19.0	13.9	34.2	68.7
1927	1.6		17.3	15.8	46.1	80.8
1928	1.4		16.8	19.3	57.4	94.9
1929	1.3		13.3	23.1	72.9	110.6
1930	1.3		9.0	28.1	74.5	112.9
1931	1.2		6.4	28.1	65.7	101.4
1932	1.0		5.2	26.5	61.1	93.8
1933	.3		4.3	23.7	59.9	88.2

* Included in column III for the years 1926–33.

capital invested abroad are assumed by Dr. Viner to amount to 4 per cent of the total investment abroad at the end of the previous year.[18]

1914–1926. The interest received by the Dominion Government from the Governments of Great Britain and other countries and from its bank balances abroad is stated for fiscal years ending March 31 in the public accounts. These amounts have been adjusted to a calendar year basis on the assumption of an equal quarterly distribution of receipts throughout the fiscal year.

The earnings of commercial banks on their net banking assets abroad are calculated at the rate which the total net profit of all Canadian commercial banks bore to their total assets each year. The yield of the British Treasury bills which they held is calculated at a rate of $5\frac{1}{2}$ per cent, and that on their foreign bonds at the annual rate of yield of 60 high-grade United States bonds as reported by the Standard Statistics Company.

The returns received by insurance companies on capital invested abroad were calculated at the rate per cent which total earnings bore to the total assets of all insurance companies having assets outside Canada as compiled from the annual reports of the Superintendent of Insurance. The dividends received on miscellaneous Canadian investments abroad were calculated by using the rates of interest and dividends paid on all capital invested in Canadian industrial enterprises.[19]

1926–1933. Interest received by the Dominion Government from other countries is as reported in the public accounts. Earnings on Canadian bank assets abroad are assumed to have been at the same rate as the earnings reported on total assets. Interest on capital employed abroad by Canadian insurance companies is calculated at the rate of earnings on the total capital of these companies; returns on their holdings of foreign securities are computed at the rate of return earned on their holdings of all securities. The receipts on miscellaneous investments are calculated on the basis of information in the possession of the Bureau.

Canada's Balance of International Payments, 1900–1934 (Table H)

To give an adequate explanation of the methods by which the various estimates in this table have been reached is impossible within the space available. The following account is intended to give the reader a rough idea of the degree of accuracy of the estimates under the several headings of the table.

18. Viner, *op. cit.,* p. 94.   19. See comment on Table E.

TABLE H

Canada's Balance of International Payments, 1900–1934*
(in millions of dollars)

	Merchandise			Gold coin and bullion		
Year	exports I	imports II	balance III	exports IV	imports V	balance VI
1900	181.2	181.6	—.4	3.7	7.7	—4.0
1901	199.5	187.8	+11.7	5.7	4.9	+.8
1902	215.3	206.8	+8.5	.6	6.0	—5.4
1903	226.5	253.9	—27.4	.3	11.4	—11.1
1904	195.6	246.4	—50.8	2.5	10.4	—7.9
1905	221.6	262.1	—40.5	7.5	7.1	+.4
1906	252.3	309.1	—56.8	15.4	20.5	—5.1
1907	252.6	369.6	—117.0	18.7	22.9	—4.2
1908	264.0	286.8	—22.8	4.1	25.8	—21.7
1909	287.3	353.7	—66.4	1.4	8.2	—6.8
1910	294.6	436.7	—142.1	2.0	13.7	—11.7
1911	295.9	501.6	—205.7	5.7	32.6	—26.9
1912	361.9	640.2	—278.3	13.8	11.0	+2.8
1913	458.8	664.1	—205.3	12.6	30.1	—17.5
1914	425.5	512.3	—86.8			+7.7
1915	650.2	466.0	+184.2			—31.2
1916	1,109.4	780.0	+329.4			—6.8
1917	1,591.1	1,023.6	+567.5			—16.9
1918	1,239.4	930.7	+308.7			+6.0
1919	1,286.8	952.1	+334.7			+8.9
1920	1,291.8	1,342.7	—50.9			+30.4
1921	808.0	792.9	+15.1			+39.5
1922	888.1	747.5	+140.6			—50.0
1923	1,016.5	888.7	+127.8			+67.8
1924	1,061.0	793.2	+267.8			—21.3
1925	1,272.6	875.7	+396.9			—11.6
1926	1,273.8	992.5	+281.3			+30.6
1927	1,227.8	1,066.5	+161.3	64.2	31.3	+32.9
1928	1,363.3	1,220.2	+143.1	107.6	39.7	+67.9
1929	1,196.7	1,293.8	—97.1	50.6	3.7	+46.9
1930	894.4	992.1	—97.7	25.3	39.1	—13.8
1931	607.9	606.8	+1.1	70.0	2.0	+68.0
1932	496.3	416.6	+79.7	68.7	2.2	+66.5
1933	534.6	384.8	+149.8	90.3	1.2	+89.1
1934	656.8	505.5	+151.3	105.0	4.0	+101.0

* All estimates for the year 1934 are preliminary and subject to revision.

TABLE H (*Continued*)

Canada's Balance of International Payments, 1900–1934
(in millions of dollars)

	Freight			Insurance		
	receipts	payments	balance	receipts	payments	balance
Year	VII	VIII	IX	X	XI	XII
1900	3.6	9.2	−5.6	.7	+.5	+1.2
1901	4.0	9.6	−5.6	.9	.7	+.2
1902	4.3	9.9	−5.6	1.2	4.3	−3.1
1903	4.5	10.8	−6.3	1.5	3.1	−1.6
1904	3.9	11.4	−7.5	1.6	+3.2	+4.8
1905	4.5	12.6	−8.1	2.0	4.7	−2.7
1906	5.1	14.6	−9.5	2.0	4.7	−2.7
1907	5.1	15.5	−10.4	2.3	3.2	−.9
1908	5.3	14.1	−8.8	2.5	3.1	−.6
1909	5.8	15.4	−9.6	2.8	4.2	−1.4
1910	5.9	18.8	−12.9	3.0	3.9	−.9
1911	5.9	23.1	−17.2	3.3	4.9	−1.6
1912	7.3	28.5	−21.2	3.6	6.4	−2.8
1913	9.2	28.6	−19.4	4.0	6.4	−2.4
1914	41.1	80.2	−39.1	3.9	6.1	−2.2
1915	70.7	101.0	−30.3	2.0	5.7	−3.7
1916	91.7	145.5	−53.8	3.6	5.0	−1.4
1917	84.1	139.0	−54.9	6.6	8.3	−1.7
1918	83.8	144.1	−60.3	3.2	8.6	−5.4
1919	86.9	125.6	−38.7	2.9	14.8	−11.9
1920	114.4	170.1	−55.7	4.8	19.4	−14.6
1921	84.3	116.5	−32.2	4.1	10.6	−6.5
1922	78.5	94.3	−15.8	6.5	9.9	−3.4
1923	89.2	121.4	−32.2	8.1	9.9	−1.8
1924	83.0	99.1	−16.1	10.5	14.1	−3.6
1925	86.7	106.4	−19.7	15.7	18.6	−2.9
1926	95.3	112.3	−17.0	31.2	22.2	+9.0
1927	89.8	109.1	−19.3	19.2	29.5	−10.3
1928	88.3	115.4	−27.1	35.8	28.8	+7.0
1929	85.5	130.9	−45.4	32.0	24.4	+7.6
1930	68.8	100.9	−32.1	29.5	22.1	+7.4
1931	54.1	73.9	−19.8	27.5	12.1	+15.4
1932	38.9	58.9	−20.0	−14.6	+2.4	−12.2
1933	43.7	62.5	−18.8	−9.4	12.6	−22.0
1934	45.9	74.9	−29.0	..	..	−15.0

TABLE H (*Continued*)

Canada's Balance of International Payments, 1900–1934
(*in millions of dollars*)

	Tourists			Interest and dividends		
Year	receipts XIII	payments XIV	balance XV	receipts XVI	payments XVII	balance XVIII
1900	7.1	5.9	+1.2	4.0	36.0	—32.0
1901	8.0	6.4	+1.6	3.9	37.4	—33.5
1902	11.0	7.5	+3.5	5.0	39.4	—34.4
1903	10.5	7.4	+3.1	5.2	40.7	—35.5
1904	12.8	8.9	+3.9	4.5	43.0	—38.5
1905	13.3	11.4	+1.9	5.3	47.4	—42.1
1906	16.8	15.4	+1.4	6.0	51.7	—45.7
1907	16.2	15.8	+.4	5.5	56.6	—51.1
1908	19.2	18.1	+1.1	4.6	75.9	—71.3
1909	19.6	19.6	..	8.3	83.9	—75.6
1910	24.7	25.0	—.3	9.6	92.1	—82.5
1911	26.2	28.6	—2.4	8.6	101.5	—92.9
1912	29.4	33.0	—3.6	8.7	117.5	—108.8
1913	30.5	37.2	—6.7	8.7	137.2	—128.5
1914	34.8	41.8	—7.0	16.7	178.0	—161.3
1915	37.2	29.2	+8.0	13.1	174.7	—161.6
1916	45.8	29.3	+16.5	23.7	193.3	—169.6
1917	55.1	31.5	+23.6	28.3	208.0	—179.7
1918	66.8	34.7	+32.1	32.4	217.2	—184.8
1919	75.9	52.4	+23.5	39.6	221.5	—181.9
1920	91.4	62.5	+28.9	46.8	231.4	—184.6
1921	98.2	57.5	+40.7	47.3	252.3	—205.0
1922	110.5	56.8	+53.7	40.0	249.9	—209.9
1923	130.7	61.8	+68.9	40.5	266.3	—225.8
1924	149.4	68.3	+81.1	40.2	268.9	—228.7
1925	170.4	69.7	+100.7	40.2	270.7	—230.5
1926	182.2	79.1	+103.1	45.3	285.3	—240.0
1927	238.5	108.7	+129.8	80.8	266.7	—185.9
1928	275.2	107.5	+167.7	94.9	282.8	—187.9
1929	309.4	121.6	+187.8	110.7	330.1	—219.4
1930	279.2	100.4	+178.8	112.9	356.4	—243.5
1931	250.8	76.5	+174.3	101.4	336.4	—235.0
1932	212.4	57.4	+155.0	93.8	309.1	—215.3
1933	117.1	50.9	+66.2	88.3	278.8	—190.5
1934	130.0	60.9	+69.1	98.0	293.0	—195.0

TABLE H (*Continued*)

Canada's Balance of International Payments, 1900–1934
(*in millions of dollars*)

	Sundry small items			Total of all previous balances (III+VI+IX+XII+ XV+XVIII+XXI)
	receipts	payments	balance	
Year	XIX	XX	XXI	XXII
1900	10.2	7.1	+3.1	−36.5
1901	12.1	8.7	+3.4	−21.4
1902	20.9	11.9	+9.0	−27.5
1903	24.7	15.1	+9.6	−69.2
1904	23.9	18.9	+5.0	−91.0
1905	31.5	23.4	+8.1	−83.0
1906	36.7	30.0	+6.7	−111.7
1907	41.3	40.8	+.5	−182.7
1908	38.2	45.8	−7.6	−131.7
1909	46.6	46.6	....	−159.8
1910	54.2	54.6	−.4	−250.8
1911	56.7	64.7	−8.0	−354.7
1912	54.2	77.6	−23.4	−435.3
1913	51.9	86.3	−34.4	−414.2
1914	28.2	20.1	+8.1	−280.6
1915	18.3	11.3	+7.0	−27.6
1916	19.2	12.3	+6.9	+121.2
1917	20.0	18.0	+2.0	+339.9
1918	21.6	21.2	+.4	+96.7
1919	32.2	12.1	+20.1	+154.7
1920	40.7	10.0	+30.7	−215.8
1921	36.3	23.1	+13.2	−135.2
1922	31.9	16.9	+15.0	−69.8
1923	38.0	8.4	+29.6	+34.3
1924	37.8	9.4	+28.4	+107.6
1925	37.8	20.8	+17.0	+249.9
1926	41.0	22.2	+18.8	+185.8
1927	69.8	56.9	+12.9	+121.4
1928	64.7	56.0	+8.7	+179.4
1929	62.9	57.0	+5.9	−113.7
1930	49.4	54.4	−5.0	−205.9
1931	34.0	43.4	−9.4	−5.4
1932	32.6	52.8	−20.2	+33.5
1933	21.1	35.7	−14.6	+59.2
1934	18.2	24.0	−5.8	+76.6

TABLE H (*Continued*)

Canada's Balance of International Payments, 1900–1934
(*in millions of dollars*)

Year	Capital			Errors and omissions (XXII–XXV)
	imports XXIII	exports† XXIV	balance XXV	XXVI
1900	31.7	+2.9	+34.6	−1.9
1901	37.2	28.7	+8.5	−12.9
1902	42.3	3.3	+39.0	+11.5
1903	54.7	+16.7	+71.4	+2.2
1904	61.9	21.2	+40.7	−50.3
1905	112.6	15.8	+96.8	+13.8
1906	105.3	+12.5	+117.8	+6.1
1907	95.1	+21.8	+116.9	−65.8
1908	222.1	92.5	+129.6	−2.1
1909	253.4	33.6	+219.8	+60.0
1910	313.2	+25.9	+339.1	+88.3
1911	348.4	3.5	+344.9	−9.8
1912	321.1	+.2	+321.3	−114.0
1913	546.7	18.8	+527.9	+113.7
1914	349.8	16.5	+333.3	+52.7
1915	215.3	+72.5	+287.8	+260.2
1916	296.9	211.5	+85.4	+206.6
1917	168.8	228.0	−59.2	+280.7
1918	28.7	150.1	−121.4	−24.7
1919	102.9	22.0	+80.9	+235.6
1920	261.3	+47.7	+309.0	+93.2
1921	224.4	+102.6	+327.0	+191.8
1922	316.0	+26.1	+342.1	+272.3
1923	210.9	11.0	+199.9	+234.2
1924	255.7	50.7	+205.0	+312.6
1925	84.9	118.5	−33.6	+216.3
1926	247.6	230.8	+16.8	+202.6
1927	237.1	201.3	+35.8	+157.2
1928	82.3	127.7	−45.4	+134.0
1929	232.4	152.5	+79.9	−33.8
1930	341.7	100.2	+241.5	+35.6
1931	41.4	28.3	+13.1	+7.7
1932	26.2	10.9	+15.3	+48.8
1933	−21.3	+42.3	+21.0	+80.2
1934	..	..	+10.0	+86.6

† Plus signs in this column indicate that during the year there was a net decrease in Canadian investments in other countries and so an import of capital on this account, as well as on account of the transactions summarized in column I.

Commodity trade: merchandise exports, imports, and the balance of trade (Columns I, II, III). The commodity trade for the calendar year as given here differs from that which might be calculated from the monthly returns of the Customs Department because of certain adjustments. Deductions are made of some items, such as settlers' effects, which are included in the returns but involve no international payment. Additions are made for others, such as imports of merchant vessels constructed in other countries, which are not recorded by the Customs. Imports are valued at the market value of the commodity in the country of origin converted into Canadian dollars at the current rate of exchange. Since 1931 arbitrary valuations for duty purposes have distorted the statements of imports sufficiently to make an allowance necessary.

Since the gold trade has been separated from the merchandise trade in this table, gold exports and imports have been deducted from the adjusted value of the merchandise trade as given by Dr. Viner for the years 1900–1913.[20]

Gold coin and bullion trade (Columns IV, V, VI). Dr. Viner has demonstrated[21] the unreliability for the pre-war years of the Canadian Customs statistics of the trade in gold coin. The inclusion during the war of shipments of gold to and from Canada on account of the Bank of England made them completely worthless as a statement of the trade in gold coin owned by Canadians and of the trade in the gold bullion which issued from the Ottawa Branch of the Royal Mint during and since the war. A method of calculating the probable amount of unrecorded trade had therefore to be devised. The amounts here given for the years 1900–1913 are the totals of the unrecorded and recorded trade as calculated by Dr. Viner.

For the years 1914–26 the Customs returns have not been used at all. Dr. Viner's method has been applied to the calculation of the net balance of the trade in gold coin and bullion for these years. For the years 1927–33 the recorded trade has been increased by the unrecorded trade calculated by a method similar to that used by Dr. Viner. In addition, since 1931 the Canadian dollar value of gold, reported at $20.67 per ounce by the Customs, has been increased in accord with the rise in the price of gold in Canada.

Freight receipts and payments (Columns VII, VIII, IX). The receipts from exports, or the costs of imports to the Canadian economy cannot be determined exactly from the Customs returns even with the adjustments to the official figures made in this table. To the Customs

20. *Op. cit.,* pp. 32 f.   21. *Ibid.,* pp. 32 ff.

Department's valuation of exports at the "point of origin" must be added payments to Canadian railways for their transportation to the port of exit, and to Canadian ships if exports are carried by them. Imports are valued at the "fair market value in the country of origin." Their cost at the point of entry into Canada will include in addition ocean freight, if the imports are transported in non-Canadian ships, and rail freight to the Canadian Border on imports from the United States. The amount of these freight receipts and payments has been estimated by methods too detailed for description here.[22]

Insurance receipts and payments (Columns X, XI, XII). The amounts in column X are the excess of premium income over payments for losses and expenses incurred on the business of Canadian insurance companies outside Canada. Column XI is the excess of premium income over expenditures incurred on the business of British and foreign insurance companies in Canada. Since the same method was used for the whole period 1900–1933, the table is exactly comparable for this item in the balance of payments.

Tourists receipts and payments (Columns XIII, XIV, XV). Supplying the wants of people from other countries traveling in Canada has recently become an "export" of considerable importance. The estimated receipts on this account are given in column XIII. Column XIV gives the estimated expenditures by Canadians traveling abroad. In recent years the Dominion Bureau of Statistics and the United States Department of Commerce have coöperated in obtaining information from tourists as to their expenditures when abroad, classified according to their length of stay. Assuming the returns for each class of tourist to be a representative sample, an average expenditure is calculated and used in estimating total expenditures by tourists in each class reported as entering the country by the Customs.[23]

22. For the years 1900–1913 see Viner, *op. cit.*, pp. 63 ff. For the years 1926–33 see the detailed explanation of method available at the Dominion Bureau of Statistics. The methods used in making the estimates for the years 1920–26 were similar to those used by the Dominion Bureau of Statistics; for the years 1914–19 transportation statistics do not permit anything but rough estimates. The differences between Dr. Viner's estimates for 1913 and those made by the writer for 1914 arise largely from the use of different methods of computation. Either method probably gives a rough idea of the yearly change within the years to which it applies.

23. See the annual bulletin on the *Tourist Trade* issued by the Dominion Bureau of Statistics, or the annual Trade Information Bulletin on the *United States Balance of International Payments* issued by the United States Department of Commerce.

Estimates for the years since 1914 were made by the use of the estimates obtained in recent years, with such adjustments as seemed appropriate. They become increasingly unreliable therefore for the earlier years and are little more than guesses for the war years. For the method used in making the estimates for the pre-war years see Dr. Viner's volume.[24]

Interest receipts and payments (Columns XVI, XVII, XVIII). The amounts given here are the same as those set down in Tables E and F. The manner of their compilation was explained in connection with those tables.

Sundry small items (Columns XIX, XX, XXI). Under this title all the remaining items included in the balance of payments, except the capital movement, are lumped together. Dr. Viner includes here capital brought into and taken out of the country by migrants and non-commercial remittances.[25] For the years 1914–26 there is added to these the expenditures of foreign governments in Canada and of the Canadian Government abroad for consular and similar services; religious and charitable remittances; motion picture royalties. To this list the Dominion Bureau of Statistics has added for the years 1927–34 the following items: advertising expenditures in Canada and abroad; earnings of Canadians employed in the United States—mostly commuters living in Border cities.

Total of all previous balances (Column XXII). This sum of the net effect of the trade in all the items of the balance of international payments so far considered indicates the amount which remains to be settled by the movement of long- and short-term capital, or to be accounted for by errors and omissions.

Capital movement (Columns XXIII, XXIV, XXV). The long-term capital movement into Canada consists of British and foreign purchases of Canadian securities or property. The manner of estimating this foreign investment in Canada has been described above. For Dr. Viner's period, the estimates of foreign investment have been made so that the annual increase in the amounts given in Table A measures the annual net capital import. These net annual increases are given in column XXIII. During the years 1914–26 there were many reductions in the ownership of securities or property in Canada by citizens of other countries which did not involve the purchase of foreign exchange by Canadians for the making of remittances abroad. So far as possible all changes in the amount of any given security held outside Canada were

24. *Op. cit.*, pp. 83 ff.
25. Mostly money sent home by recent immigrants; see *ibid.*, pp. 41 ff.

investigated to determine whether an export of capital was involved. A separate tabulation of the capital movement was made in this manner. The calculation of the direct investment is so rough that estimated yearly net change was set down as a capital import or export, as the case might be, without any attempt at further refinements. Short-term capital movements have been included only in so far as they took the form of the sale of Canadian Treasury bills abroad.

The method followed by the Dominion Bureau of Statistics for the years 1927–34 in calculating capital imports arising from the sale of Canadian securities in other countries is the same as that used for the years 1914–26. The Bureau carries on a continuous study of the establishment of foreign branch factories and other forms of direct investment in Canada, and determines the amount of the investment as far as possible by the investigation of each case. But increases in the amount of foreign capital employed in Canadian industry, which arise from the investment of profits made in Canada are not included. Confidential returns now make it possible for the Bureau to make an estimate of the import of short-term capital. The net international trade in Canadian securities other than new flotations is not included in the calculation of capital imports.

The export of capital from Canada is calculated for the years 1900–1926 directly from the changes in the amount of the investment of Canadian capital outside Canada as given in Table D. For the years 1927–34 this method is followed for the items in columns I to IV of Table D. The capital export arising from the direct investment of capital in other countries included in column VI of Table D is derived from the current investigation of each case. The remainder of the miscellaneous Canadian investment abroad, composed of the holdings of foreign securities by Canadians, is a rough estimate only. The net increase in this amount is taken as the amount of the capital export.

Errors and omissions (Column XXVI). If the estimates of the several items of the Canadian balance of international payments made in this table were exact and if the list of items were all-inclusive, the balance on capital movement account given in column XXV would exactly offset the balances on all other accounts given in column XXII. The extent to which this does not occur is indicated in column XXVI. It indicates the errors and omissions which have been made in the estimates.

For the years 1900–1913 these errors, though considerable for some years, are for the most part offsetting. In sum, they amount to an error on the credit side of only $38,800,000. For the years 1914–26 the annual errors are large and amount to an excess credit balance of $2,534,100,000 in thirteen years, or an average of $194,900,000 per year. The errors are smaller for the years 1927–33. They amount to $429,700,000 on the credit side, which is an average annual error of $61,400,000.

The size and persistent bias of these errors since 1914 is puzzling. Many of the estimates for the items whose balances are summed up in column XXII are rough indeed. A careful reëxamination of the methods used affords no ground, however, for making such alterations as would reduce the size of the almost continuous error on the credit side shown since 1914. It is difficult to believe, moreover, that such errors as these estimates contain would not be offsetting in their effect on the balance. The only items large enough to introduce, by error, a considerable bias in the results are the estimates for the commodity trade, capital movements, and the interest and dividend payments. If the substantial accuracy of the Customs statistics be accepted, there remains to be considered only the capital movements calculation and the computation of interest payments based on it.

The estimate of capital imports through the sale of Canadian securities in other countries for the years 1914–26 which has been given here differs from other estimates most considerably during the years immediately following the war. Despite the fact that its bias is to the high side, as explained above, the errors during these years, shown in Table H, column XXVI, are no greater than in other years of the period 1914–26. The estimate of the direct investments is very rough.[26] But the whole credit resulting from the increase in the investment between 1913 and 1926 might be omitted entirely without reducing the credit bias here shown to reasonable proportions. The estimate of the investment of short-term funds is very incomplete, but it is unlikely that over a period of years this investment was conspicuously one-sided.

There is a possible source of error of considerable dimensions in the treatment of the international trade in securities. So little information is available that the estimates here made ignore the trade in Canadian securities entirely and make but the vaguest of estimates of the effects of this trade on the size of the holdings of foreign securities by Canadians from year to year. In the earliest estimates of capital movements made for the Dominion Bureau of Statistics by Professor K. W. Taylor, the net repurchase of Canadian securities by residents of Canada is set down at $123,000,000 for the years 1920–26. The allowance made in the present estimate for the net increase in Canadian holdings of Brit-

26. Cf. p. 302 and footnote 6.

ish and foreign securities amounts to $260,000,000 for the same period. If the purchase of Canadian securities be set at double the estimate made by Professor Taylor, and the present estimate of the net increase in the holdings of British and foreign securities be doubled also, the error on the credit side in Canada's international balance of payments would still exceed $2,000,000,000 for the years 1914–26. Thus even an unbelievably large increase in Canadian security holdings does not reduce the error to tolerable dimensions. Moreover the over-the-Border trade in securities has been mainly a feature of the years since the war. Yet for the years 1914–19 the error on the credit side in the present calculations amounts to $1,011,100,000. The absence of any allowance for the repurchase by Canadians of Canadian securities previously held abroad and the possibility of an inadequate allowance for the net increase in the securities of other countries held in Canada can hardly be responsible, therefore, for the major part of the errors and omissions shown in these calculations for the years 1914–26.

Nor is it likely that any large part of the error lies in the interest and dividends calculation. The balances shown in Table H, column XVIII for the years 1914–26 would have to be increased by 50 per cent to make any considerable reduction in the errors and omissions. The probability, indeed, is that these estimates are already high.

In short, the writer has no adequate explanation to offer for the size and bias of the error during the years 1914–26. It should be said, however, that its existence does not render the estimate useless. If the qualifications which its existence may entail are borne in mind, these estimates of Canada's balance may be used as indicating the direction and amount of the change in the several items with almost as much assurance as if the error were of the much smaller relative size which appears to be common in such calculations.

APPENDIX I

SECURITIES PUBLICLY OFFERED BY AMERICAN-CONTROLLED
COMPANIES IN CANADA*

(B—bond; P—preferred stock; C—common stock)

Security	Total offering	Taken in United States†	Year	Class
Sherwin Williams of Canada	1,983,700	1,200,000	1912	B
Powell River Company	4,000,000	3,500,000	1913	B
Can. Consol. Felt Co.	500,000	250,000	1910	B
Can. Consol. Felt Co.	500,000	250,000	1911	P
Can. Conn. Cotton Mills	3,000,000	2,000,000		P
Windsor Hotel	2,250,000	1,000,000		P
Aluminium, Ltd.	13,000,000	12,750,000		P
Goodyear T. and R. of Can.	4,850,000	2,850,000	1916–1917	P
Aluminium, Ltd.	20,000,000	20,000,000		B
Can. Int'l Paper Co.	25,000,000	21,345,000		B
Continental Paper Products	750,000	500,000		B
Famous Players Can. Co.	9,000,000	2,571,000		B
Firestone T. and R. Co. of Can.	1,500,000	1,500,000		B
Hind and Dauche Co. of Can., Ltd.	1,500,000	350,000		B
King Edward Hotel	3,500,000	3,500,000		B
Metropolitan Chain Prop.	3,000,000	3,000,000		B
Metropolitan Corp. of Can.	1,300,000	550,000		B
Pacific Mills, Ltd.	4,875,000	4,375,000		B
St. Regis Paper of Can., Ltd.	1,500,000	1,500,000		
Spruce Falls Power & Paper	15,000,000	12,500,000		
Canadian Westinghouse	1,226,700	1,000,000	1917	C
Imperial Oil, Ltd.	5,000,000	4,000,000	1917	C
Beaver Co., Ltd.	795,000	500,000	1918	P
Durant Motors of Can., Ltd.	1,500,000	750,000	1921	C
Can. Gen. Elec. Co., Ltd.	5,200,000	2,600,000	1925	P C
Goodyear Cotton Co. of Can.	475,000	250,000	1926	P
Kelvinator of Can.	800,000	500,000	1926	P
Can. Hydro-Elec. Corp.	12,500,000	600,000	1927	P
McKesson-Robbins, Ltd.	1,020,000	1,020,000	1927	C P
Crown Cork & Seal Co., Ltd.	1,350,000	1,312,000	1928	C
Curtiss-Reid Aircraft of Can.	1,275,000	1,000,000	1928	P
Vancouver Kraft, Ltd.	1,143,000	1,000,000	1928	B
N.S. Pulp & Paper	400,000	300,000	1927	P
Ford of Canada	3,000,000		1929	C
	152,693,400	110,323,000		

Sources: *American Direct Investments in Foreign Countries,* Trade Information Bulletin No. 731, pp. 54–55, and other data obtained from the Finance Division of the Department of Commerce, Paul Dickens, and elsewhere.

* Including those of companies which, although now controlled in Canada, were American-owned at the time these securities were issued.

† Estimates.

APPENDIX II

(Except where otherwise noted, the repatriated company is either cited
alone or else is indented beneath the new Canadian
parent organization.)

Anglin-Norcross, Ltd.
  Norcross Bros. Co., Canadian Branch, 1919
W. B. Beath & Son, Ltd., 1930, acquired Canadian interests of
  St. Paul Hydraulic Hoist Co.
  Stroughton Co.
  Perfection Body Co.
Belding-Corticelli, Ltd., 1911
Beatty Bros., Ltd., acquired business of
  Louden Machinery Co., Ltd., 1932, which withdrew from Canada
M. E. Binz Co., Ltd. (no longer a subsidiary, but still a heavy Ameri-
    can interest)
Henry Birks & Sons, acquired business of
  L. G. Balfour Co., Ltd., 1934, which withdrew from Canada
Bixel Brewing and Malting Co., Ltd., now wholly Canadian
Bowles Lunch Company, 1933
British American Refineries
  Northwest Stellarene, Ltd.
British Columbia Sugar Refining Co., acquired Canadian property of
  Sugar Factories, Ltd., 1932
Building Products, Ltd., 1925
Burlington Steel Co., Ltd.
  Canadian Metal Products Co., 1931
Canada Paper Co.
  Scutan Co. of Canada, Ltd., 1934
Canada Wire and Cable Co., Ltd.
  Standard Underground Cable Co. of Canada, Ltd., 1929 (still an
      American minority)
Canadian Atlas Steels, Ltd.
Canadian Acousticon Co., absorbed Dictograph Products Co. of
      Canada, Ltd., 1933

Sources: These cases of repatriation have been gathered from many places,
including newspapers, financial periodicals, and handbooks. Not all have
been verifiable, but it is believed the list is substantially accurate.

Canadian Bronze Co., Ltd., 1927

Canadian Car and Foundry, Ltd., 1924

Canadian Cocoa and Chocolate Co., Ltd., 1924

Canadian Gravure, Ltd., now controlled by Murray Printing Company

Canadian Motor Lamp Co., 1927

Canadian National Telegraphs
  Western Union lines in Canada, 1929

Canadian Public Service Corp., Ltd., 1931

Canadian Sumner Iron Works, Ltd.

Congoleum Co. of Canada, Ltd., 1926

Consolidated Industries, Ltd., 1928
  Hammond Co. of Canada, Ltd.

Canadian Tank Car Co., Ltd.
  Canadian Transit Co., Ltd., jointly with General American Trans-
      portation Corp.

Consolidated Paper Corp.
  St. Maurice Co.

Cosmos Imperial Mills, Ltd., 1926

Corrugated Pipe Co., Ltd.

Dodd and Struthers (now Canadian) bought Shinn Mfg. Co. of
    Canada, Ltd.

Dominion Bronze Co., Ltd., 1933 (American-owned, 1929–33)

Dominion Motors, Ltd.
  Durant Motors of Canada, Ltd., 1931

Dominion Textile Co., Ltd.
  Canadian Connecticut Cotton Mills, 1928
  Jenckes Canadian Co., 1928

Don Valley Paper Co., Ltd., acquired Canadian property of
  Rochester Paper Co. a few years ago

Eaton, Crane and Pike Co., Ltd. (100% Canadian)

Easy Washing Machine Co., Ltd., 1920 (may never have been Ameri-
    can)

English Electric Co. of Canada, Ltd.
  Canadian Crocker-Wheeler Co., Ltd., 1932

Fairchild Aircraft Co., 1934 (still a heavy American interest, but no
    longer a subsidiary)

Foundation Co. of Canada, Ltd., 1929

General Fire Proofing Co. of Canada, Ltd., 1933

Hambledon Co., Ltd., 1931

Hamilton Carhartt Manufacturer, Ltd., 1934

Hayes Wheels and Forgings, Ltd., 1922

Hydro-Electric Power Commission of Ontario, in 1930, acquired the Canadian properties of Public Utilities Consolidated Corp. (a Foshay company)

Industrial Acceptance Corp., Ltd., 1930

International Coal and Coke Co., Ltd., 1919

King Edward Hotel, 1932 (may still be heavy American bondholding interest)

Melchers Distilleries, Ltd., 1928

Mount Royal Hotel Co., Ltd., 1930

National Hosiery Mills, Ltd., 1928

National Steel Car Co., Ltd., 1927

Niles-Bement-Pond Co., 1926, sold to Canadians:
  John Bertram and Sons, Co., Ltd., Dundas, Ont.
  Pratt and Whitney Co. of Canada, Ltd. (probably still heavy American interest)

Northern Bakeries Co. of Canada, Ltd., 1927

Office Specialty Mfg. Co. (still heavy American interest)

Ontario Hydro-Electric Power Commission:
  Sandwich, Windsor and Amherstburg Ry. 1920

Packard Electric Co., Ltd.

Port Royal Pulp and Paper Co.
  Nashwaak Pulp and Paper Co., 1932

Price Brothers and Co., Ltd.
  Donnacona Paper Co., 1926; but regained by Americans in 1931

Provincial Paper Mills Co., Ltd., 1927

Puritan Chemical Co., sold Canadian plant, 1929

Quebec Maple Products, Ltd., acquired business of
  Carey Maple Sugar Co. of Canada, Ltd. (which dissolved)

Quebec, Montreal and Southern Ry., acquired by Canadian National Ry. in 1929

Quebec Pulp and Paper Corp.
  Saguenay and Chicoutimi Companies, 1929

Russell Motor Car Co., Ltd.
  Canadian Acme Screw and Gear, Ltd., 1924 (still an American minority)

Society Brand Clothes, Ltd.

Square D Company of Canada, Ltd., 1924

Steel Co. of Canada, Ltd., acquired plant of
  Phoenix Horseshoe Mfg. Co., Ltd., Montreal, 1934

Stop and Shop, Ltd.
  Montreal Piggly Wiggly Corp., Ltd., 1929
  Arnold Brothers, Ltd. (formerly A. Martin, Ltd.), 1927

Thunder Bay Paper Co., Ltd., 1929
Tobacco Products Corp. of Canada, Ltd., 1923
United Steel Corp., Ltd.
   Dodge Mfg. Co., Ltd., and Canadian Mead Morrison Co., 1932
Welch Grape Juice, sold Canadian plant, 1929
Western Steel Products, Ltd., 1928
Windsor Hotel Co., Ltd., 1927

APPENDIX III

NEWSPRINT COMPANIES IN CANADA

	Tons daily capacity	
American-Owned		
Beaver Wood Fibre Co., Ltd.	77	
Canadian International Paper Co., Ltd.	1,817 (3 mills)	
*Donnacona Paper Co., Ltd.	240	
Fort Frances Pulp and Paper Co., Ltd.	283	
Great Lakes Paper Co., Ltd.	314	
Kenora Paper Mills, Ltd.	252	
Ontario Paper Co., Ltd.	429	
Pacific Mills, Ltd.	256	
Powell River Co., Ltd.	650	
Spruce Falls Power and Paper Co., Ltd.	480	4,798
Independent		
†Abitibi Power and Paper Co., Ltd.	2,013	
Thunder Bay Paper Co., Ltd.	246	
Anglo-Canadian Pulp and Paper Mills, Ltd.	480	
‡Bathurst Power and Paper Co., Ltd.	140	
Booth, J. R., Ltd.	158	
Brompton Pulp and Paper Co., Ltd.	239	
Consolidated Paper Corp., Ltd.	1,944	
§E. B. Eddy Co., Ltd.	127	
Lake St. John Power and Paper Co., Ltd.	260	
MacLaren Company, Ltd.	240	
Mersey Paper Co., Ltd.	293	
News Pulp and Paper Co., Ltd.	37	
Price Brothers and Co., Ltd.	1,020	
St. Lawrence Paper Mills, Ltd.	460	7,657
		12,455

Source: List of companies supplied by the Newsprint Service Bureau, February 2, 1934. (The groupings are by the authors.)

* This Company was organized in 1912 by New York pulp and paper men. In 1926 it was acquired by Price Brothers, but since then it has reverted to the security holders who are largely American.

† The G. H. Mead organization, Ohio, is heavy holder of common stock in Abitibi.

‡ This company is owned by the Newsprint Bond and Share Corporation, the capital stock of which was formerly owned by six companies, but is now owned by Brompton, Price Brothers, Consolidated, and Canadian International. The last mentioned company operates it, but it is now producing very little newsprint.

§ The International company has a 49 per cent interest in this company through its associate, Canadian Hydro-Electric Corporation, Ltd.

APPENDIX IV

A. Questionnaire sent out in October, 1934, with the coöperation of the American Manufacturers Export Association, to 1,200 American corporations believed to be operating subsidiaries in Canada.

    I. Why did your Company establish subsidiaries in Canada? (Check one or more of the following, adding any needed explanation or additions.)
- a. To avoid tariffs.
- b. To obtain advantages of Empire preferential tariffs.
- c. To obtain lower transportation costs.
- d. To obtain lower wages.
- e. To obtain raw materials more cheaply.
- f. To accommodate consumer preferences in Canada.
- g. To give better after-sales servicing.
- h. Other (explain).

    II. What is the history of your expansion in Canada? (Detail will be appreciated. Use the reverse side if necessary.)

    III. What form do your Canadian organizations take (agent, branch house, subsidiary company, minority interest, etc.) and why was that form chosen?

    IV. With reference to your Canadian *operations:*
- a. What sort of contact do you maintain between head office and Canadian subsidiary?
- b. Has your Canadian subsidiary been financed partly in Canada? How? Why?
- c. What is the nature of your Canadian operations?
    1. Complete manufacture.
    2. Assembly of *parts* wholly or largely imported.
    3. Manufacture, with 25% or less imported *parts*.
    4. Manufactured by a Canadian plant on license or contract.
    5. Sales.
    6. Other arrangement (explain).

Why was that form chosen?

    d. Can you quote roughly the same f.o.b. prices from Canadian and American plants? If not, to what do you attribute the difference?

    e. Are the American and Canadian markets sufficiently different to compel production modification in the Canadian plant (as compared with the parent plant)? What type of modification?

    f. Does your wage scale in the Canadian organization differ

        1. From that in the industry in Canada? Why?

        2. From that in the American organization? Why?

    g. If your labor policy in general differs in Canada from that in the American plants, what factors account for that difference?

    h. Has your sales problem in Canada differed materially from that faced by the home office (e.g., in advertising, credit, etc.)? In what way?

    i. What portion of your foreign market (other than Canada) do you serve from the Canadian plant and why?

B. Questionnaire sent out in November, 1934, by McMaster University, Ontario, to 900 companies in Canada believed to be American-controlled.

    I. Why was your company established in Canada? (or Why did American firms affiliate with you?) (Check one or more of the following, preferably numbering in order of importance, adding any needed explanations.)

        a. To avoid tariffs.

        b. To obtain advantages of preferential tariffs abroad.

        c. Lower transportation costs.

        d. Lower wages.

        e. Cheaper raw materials.

        f. To give better after-sales servicing.

        g. To avoid exchange difficulties.

        h. To adapt product to Canadian tastes.

        i. To be able to use "made in Canada" label.

        j. Other (explain).

    II. What is the history of your Company?

        First organized—Date   Place

        Expansion and/or relocation—Date   Place

        Affiliations, mergers, etc.—Date   Company

Date of starting operations—
  a. As a sales office.
  b. As an assembly plant.
  c. With a substantial degree of manufacturing.

III. What were the principal reasons for locating your plant in its present location? (Check one or more reasons, preferably numbering in order of importance, adding any needed explanations.)
  a. Acquisition of a going concern.
  b. To be near parent company.
  c. To be near related industries (state which).
  d. To be near markets (i) domestic, (ii) foreign.
  e. Availability of factory space (i) low rentals, (ii) other reasons.
  f. Cheapness of (i) raw materials, (ii) power, (iii) fuel.
  g. Labour supply (i) skilled men, (ii) low wages, (iii) other reasons.
  h. Convenience of transportation (state which).

IV. (a) What sort of contact do you maintain with your American affiliate with respect to such matters as management, wages, prices, or other matters of general policy?
(b) Does your American affiliate supervise in detail your operations?

V. Have your operations in Canada been financed partly in Canada?
How? (common   preferred   bonds   other forms)
Why?

VI. What was the percentage of Canadian content of your product
In 1926?
   1929?
   1933?
If there was any marked change, explain.

VII. Can you quote roughly the same f.o.b. prices as are quoted in the United States by your American affiliate? If not, what is the main reason for the difference?

VIII. Is the Canadian market in your line sufficiently different from that in the United States to require production or service modification in Canada? What type of modification? (style, colour, sizes, containers, etc.)

IX. Does your wage scale differ from
    (a) that in the industry in Canada?
    (b) that in your American affiliate?

X. If your labour policy differs from that followed in your American affiliate, please explain and account for the difference.

XI. Does your sales problem differ materially from that of your affiliate in the United States (e.g., advertising, credit, etc.)?

XII. What percentage of your production was exported? (Please state principal foreign markets.)
    In 1926, 1929, 1933. If any marked change, please explain reasons.

INDEX TO COMPANIES

[Where the name of a subsidiary is almost identical with that of the parent company and occurs on the same page, it is not separately listed. Names of trademarked articles mentioned in the text have been included in this index.]

GENERAL INDEX

Abrasives companies, 75, 206, 208, 241

Advertising. *See* Operations

Agriculture, American direct investment in Canadian, 22, 24 table

Agricultural implements. *See* Iron and steel, machinery

Air lines, 135–137, 173, 266, 282

Aircraft, 87, 325

Aird, Sir John, 134

Alberta, coal deposits in, 111; gas fields in, 141, 144–145; oil fields in, 108–109

Aldred, J. E., 152

Algoma region, development of, 57 ff.

Aluminum. *See* Mining and smelting

American companies in Canada. *See* Branch companies

American Federation of Labor, 268

American Manufacturers Export Association, 25–26, 331

American penetration. *See* Penetration

Angus, 114

Animal products, 24–27 tables, 33–34, 173, 226, 260, 264, 266; output competes with imports, 271

Annexation, fear of, 287–288

Antimony mining, 7

Asbestos. *See* Mining and smelting

Assembly or manufacture in branch plants. *See* Operations

Assets, of branch companies, 25–26, 30, 32–34, 43, 47, 53, 54, 60, 65, 71, 72, 74, 77, 78, 84, 86, 88, 101, 102, 111, 131 n, 151, 158, 180; contrasted with capital employed, 25

Associated Press, 124

Australia, branch companies in, 65; branch plant exports to, 241; radio service with Canada, 133; tariffs in, 242

Automobile Chamber of Commerce, Canadian, 276

Automobile companies. *See* Iron and steel

Auxiliary branch companies, 31, 44, 46, 57, 91, 103–104, 105, 106, 111, 114–115, 141, 151, 207–208

Bache, Jules S., 93

Bacher, E. L., 209 n, 242

Backus, E. W., 44–45

Balance of payments, 277–279, 296 ff.

Bank of England, 319

Banking, investment, 16, 165 ff., 175, 249, 282, 291

Banking companies, American, in Canada, 3, 4, 11, 165–169, 215, 266, 282; Canadian, in the United States, 4, 16–17, 175, 197, 215, 249, 251, 252, 277, 306, 312–313

Belgium, branch companies in, 130

Bell, Melville, 127

Bennett, Premier R. B., 51, 201, 288

Beverages, 11, 31, 183, 205, 224–225, 243, 256, 261–262, 285

Board of Trade, British, ruling on "Empire content," 233

Bonds. *See* Portfolio investments; Securities, of branch companies

Booth, John R., 4

Border Cities, branch plants in, 221, 222

Border Cities Star, 134 n

Boston capital in Canada, early, 5, 7, 8, 139

Bow Island gas field, 144, 145

Branch companies, *American, in Canada:* in Canadian economy, 279–291; and "company towns," 289–290; competition, 275, 279, 281–282, 285–286; contrasted with European, 264, 265; effect on trade, 267–274; history and extent, chaps. i, ii; importance of in "key" industries, 282–283; industries where unimportant, 265–267; as lobbyists, 274–276, 290–291; official surveys of, 21 ff.; rate of growth of, 19–21, 253, 255, 260–261, 292; statistics of, 24–28; summarized, 264–265. *Canadian, in the United States:* extent, chap. iii, 2, 3, 17, 209, 292; financial, 175–176, 196–197, 249, 263, 277, 306, 312; insurance, 175, 196–197, 249, 251, 252, 306, 312–313; investment trusts, 175, 249, 251–252; iron and steel goods, 176, 180–183, 208, 234, 249, 250–251, 254, 286; mining, 176, 185–186, 208, 211, 249, 251, 263; miscellaneous companies, 186–187, 205, 249; motives summarized, 263–264; not new, 2, 4, 16, 17; number, 175–176; paper products, 176, 249, 250, 251; profits and losses, 248–252; railroads, 113, 116, 123, 176, 187–195, 249, 250, 251, 263, 277; utilities, 176, 195–196; value,

Niagara frontier, branch plants in, 221, 222; cheap power in, 75

Nicholls, Frederick, 72, 73

Nickel production. *See* Mining and smelting

Non-ferrous metals, American companies in Canada, 15, 24–27 tables, 28, 71–75, 129–130, 131, 173, 204, 207, 239, 242, 246, 247, 252, 256, 263, 264, 276, 283, 325; Canadian companies in the United States, 182–183, 250; output competes with imports, 271

Non-metallic minerals, American companies in Canada, 24–27 tables, 75–80, 173, 246, 248, 252, 254, 255, 259, 264, 265, 283, 325; Canadian companies in the United States, 182–183, 250; output competes with imports, 271

Norquay, Premier, 120

Norway, branch companies in, 106

Nova Scotia, mines in, 7, 112; telegraphs, 124; telephone system, 128

Number, of American companies in Canada, 19–21, 26–28; of Canadian companies in the United States, 175–176

O'Connor, 263

Ohio, Durham boats shipped from, 3

Oil. *See* Mining and smelting; Non-metallic minerals

O'Neill, George H., 169

Ontario, abrasives industry in, 75; branch companies in, 5–6, 8–9, 10, 13–14, 222, 293; branch utilities in, 147; bus lines in, 138–139; gas fields in, 140–141, 143–144; mines, 89; oil fields in, 108; pulp and paper, 36; railroads in, American, 115 ff.; telephone system, 127–130

Operations of branch companies, chap. v; acquiring a plant, 80, 83, 224–225; advertising and selling, 1, 129 n, 133, 135, 173, 185, 205, 216, 222, 242–243, 261–262, 265, 285 n, 286; assembly or manufacture, 66–67, 68, 69, 153, 202, 219, 231–236, 237–239; control, 218–219; corporate form, 218, 223; costs and prices, 36, 37, 48, 52, 207, 219, 236–239, 242; financing, 32–33, 42, 44, 45, 46, 54, 58, 59, 63–64, 65, 66, 72, 84, 91, 98–99, 120, 122 n, 127, 129, 149, 170, 182, 190, 193, 219, 224–225, 225–228, 325; liaison, policy, 229–231; license arrangements, 12, 68, 87, 225, 232, 234, 235–236, 237, 238, 254 n, 257; location, 12–14, 220–222; markets, 34, 35, 53, 56, 58, 60, 62, 64, 65,

68, 69, 77, 86, 87, 99, 100, 107, 200, 202–203, 218, 220–221, 229, 231, 234–236, 239, 241–242; "typical" branch plant, 28, 218–219, 222; wages, 37, 199, 205–207, 219, 221, 239–241. *See also* Profits and losses; Sales organizations; Securities

Opposition to branch plants, 283–289, 293

Orford nickel process, 96 n

Organization of branch companies, chaps. ii, iii. *See also* Operations

Ottawa Conference, 275

Output of branch companies, value of, 24, 24–27 tables

Pacific Coast, early American investments in, 10

Paints. *See* Chemicals

Paper and pulp, *American companies in Canada:* capital employed, 22, 23, 24; extent, 35 ff., 57, 173, 206, 210–211, 224, 226, 227, 243, 246–247, 258–259, 260, 264, 265, 272, 282, 290, 325; number of, 22; paper goods mills, 54–55; pulp mills, 52–53, 241; statistics, 24–27 tables, 28. *Canadian companies in the United States:* 175–176, 177–180, 249–250, 251, 260; importance of industry, 36; output competes with imports, 271. *See also* Newsprint

Parliament, Dominion, on branch companies, 288; embargoes pulpwood, 36; on radio broadcasting, 133 n, 134–135

Patents, 74, 128, 130, 132, 209 n, 257–258

Payments, balance of, 277–279, 296 ff.

Payne, Senator, 96, 97 n

Penetration, American, alarm at, 1, 15, 125, 134, 161; opposition to, 283–284, 288, 293

Peru, Canadian properties in, 78, 79

Peters, E. D., 97

Petroleum. *See* Mining and smelting; Non-metallic minerals

Petrolia oil field, 77

Pharmaceutical goods, 14, 28–29, 80–82, 207, 232, 276

Philadelphia capital in Canada, 58, 139

Philippines telephone system, 131 n

Phosphates, 7, 8, 9

Photographic supplies, 87, 153–154

Planing mills. *See* Lumbering; Sawmills

Plants, acquisition of, by branch companies, chaps. ii, iii, 224–225

Platinum metals, 98

Policy determination in branch plants, 229–231